EQUAL JUSTICE

EQUAL JUSTICE

Eric Rakowski

CLARENDON PRESS · OXFORD

Oxford University Press, Walton Street, Oxford OX2 6DP

Oxford   New York   Toronto
Delhi   Bombay   Calcutta   Madras   Karachi
Kuala Lumpur   Singapore   Hong Kong   Tokyo
Nairobi   Dar es Salaam   Cape Town
Melbourne   Auckland   Madrid
and associated companies in
Berlin   Ibadan

Oxford is a trade mark of Oxford University Press

Published in the United States
by Oxford University Press Inc., New York

British Library Cataloguing in Publication Data
Rakowski, Eric.
Equal justice.
1. Law. Ethical aspects
I. Title
340.112
ISBN 0–19–824079–1

Library of Congress Cataloging in Publication Data
Rakowski, Eric.
Equal justice/Eric Rakowski.
p.   cm.
Includes bibliographical references and index.

3. Social justice.   4. Law Philosophy

ISBN 0–19–824079–1

1 3 5 7 9 10 8 6 4 2

Printed in Great Britain
on acid-free paper by
Bookcraft (Bath) Ltd., Midsomer Norton, Bath

For my parents

ACKNOWLEDGEMENTS

I AM happy to acknowledge, though I cannot here begin to repay, some of the debts I accumulated in writing this book. Bill Ewald and Lisa Heinzerling commented on various drafts of Part I, forcing me to clarify my thinking and to correct missteps too numerous to count. Louis Kaplow, Steven Shavell, and Jon Schwartz helped sharpen the arguments of Part II. And Brad Hooker offered useful advice in editing Part III. I am also grateful to my D.Phil. examiners—Steven Lukes and Michael Lockwood—for their insightful comments on material that eventually found its way into this book. The John M. Olin Foundation provided welcome financial assistance in preparing Part II.

Two people deserve very special thanks. Ronald Dworkin has been a friend, mentor, and gentle critic for the past eight years. He supervised both my B.Phil. and D.Phil. dissertations, where many of the ideas in this book originate, and has always been generous with his time and advice. I believe I have learned more from him than from anyone else with whom I have worked.

My debt to Dieter Henrich is equally profound. As a college undergraduate, I initially had no intention of studying philosophy seriously, let alone making it the focus of graduate studies or a professional career. Dieter Henrich changed that. Through the force of his example as much as through conversations and lectures, he helped instill in me an earnestness and joy in philosophical thought that I hope I shall never lose. Were it not for the enthusiasm he fostered, and the encouragement he has continued to provide, this book would not merely be even more unsatisfactory than it is. There would be no book at all.

E.R.

CONTENTS

1

Introduction

"ALL hold that justice is some kind of equality," Aristotle said.[1] But what kind of equality is it? No one would deny that equals deserve equal treatment, but that formal statement leaves all the important questions unanswered. When are people properly regarded as equals, despite their myriad differences? What aspects of a person's history, character, and conduct ought to influence the distribution of social benefits and burdens? And to what extent should one or another such feature affect the allocation of goods or the infliction of harms relative to other attributes or by comparison with competing moral values?

This book attempts to answer these questions in many (though by no means all) of the larger social contexts in which they are commonly asked. In it I address two partly overlapping issues. First, what principles for apportioning scarce resources and opportunities within a political community are just, assuming that no morally licit collective projects not mandated by justice exist to which the community's members are bound to contribute? Second, how should government officials and private individuals decide whose life to preserve in situations where not everyone can be saved, either because a dearth of resources precludes the rescue of all who are endangered or because some can only be kept alive by killing others? In answering these questions, I hope to begin to explain what sort of equality justice is and what it means to treat persons as equals.

1.1. AN OVERVIEW

This book is divided into three main sections. Part I expounds and defends a theory of justice I call equality of fortune. My central thesis is that, subject to the constraints described below, no one should have less valuable resources and opportunities available to him[2] than anyone else, simply in virtue of some chance occurrence the risk of which he did not choose to incur. Differences resulting from voluntary wagers cannot ground redistributive claims, whereas inequalities stemming from ineluctable chance events call for a reshuffling of resources at the behest of the unlucky, in order to eliminate discrepancies that cannot be traced to

---

[1] *Politics* 1282 b18.
[2] Use of the masculine pronoun or possessive in place of "he or she" and its cognates, and in place of alternating masculine and feminine pronominal expressions, is of course solely for the sake of economy and felicity of expression.

individuals' choices. Because "resources" should be construed, for purposes of determining a person's entitlements, to include not only fungible material goods but also people's physical and mental capacities, those who suffer ill luck in the form of disappointing genes, a debilitating environment during their minority, disease, or unhappy accidents have a right to compensation at the expense of those who fared better, to the extent that the unlucky did not willingly assume the risk of whatever disadvantaged them and assuming that specific culprits cannot be found to make reparations. Similarly, those who are less lucky in their benefactors, including their parents, have a valid claim to part of the unearned gains of fortune's favorites. Part I's most fundamental claim is that people should ideally start life with an equally valuable bundle of resources and opportunities; once an equal division has been established, justice requires the transfer of possessions and possibilities to maintain it over time, except when people's voluntary actions, including the expenditure of time and effort and any gambles or gifts they freely make, give rise to inequalities.

This ideal of equality, however, will often prove elusive in practice. There are limits to what medical science can do to aid those who are handicapped or stricken by disease, and it would be wrong to pursue complete equality of fortune by taking from those whom nature has blessed, whether by impairing their faculties or by confiscating their earnings, if doing so would not ameliorate the plight of those who are less lucky. Even when the disadvantaged would benefit slightly from additional transfers, it seems overly zealous, in some cases positively outrageous, to demand further redistribution if recipients would derive benefits that are slight by comparison with those that contributors would be forced to forgo. Neither morality nor justice (which I take to be a subset of morality) requires considerable sacrifices of some persons for the sake of trifling gains to others, even if the ideal of equality may seem initially to point in that direction. In the case of gifts and bequests to children and relatives, moreover, a person's right to dispose of his property as he wishes, as well perhaps as collective assent to taxes that fall well short of confiscatory levies on the receipt of such property (if such assent were forthcoming), comes into conflict with the principle that unearned advantages that do not result from voluntary wagers should be fully redressed. Some compromise is necessary. Hence, I argue, justice ultimately requires something less than comprehensive equality of resources and opportunities, in addition to endorsing differences in people's holdings traceable to their free decisions to work longer, harder, or at less pleasant tasks than their fellows or to dispense with the generous (and expensive) insurance against uninvited mishap that equality of fortune mandates in the first instance.

After defending these conclusions in Chapters 2–7, I turn in Chapter 8 to consider whether transferable parts of people's bodies, such as blood and kidneys, should be viewed as resources subject to compulsory redistribution if a potential recipient is in dire need and the extraction of living tissue would not seriously detract from the donor's expected well-being. I conclude that body parts should be regarded as resources for purposes of determining a person's just entitlements, that the *post mortem* extraction of transplantable organs should be required if voluntary donations are insufficient to meet existing needs, and that forced extractions of blood, bone marrow, one cornea, or a single kidney from live donors might be permissible under certain highly restrictive conditions. Fortunately, compulsory donations by live donors would almost certainly be unnecessary if *post mortem* donations were mandatory. Indeed, if *post mortem* extractions were performed as a matter of course, if current needs remained level, and if attitudes continued unchanged, the wishes of those who objected to the medical use of their body following their death could probably be honored without rendering the supply of cadaver organs insufficient.

Part II outlines a theory of strict liability for tortious conduct. It opens with a critique of the normative foundations of wealth maximization when that goal is taken as the touchstone for laws regarding ownership and compensation for injury. Exploring the ambiguities and shortcomings of Richard Posner's prescriptions for tort law, in particular their inherent bias in favor of the wealthy, makes plain that only a theory of strict liability is, as an initial matter, consistent with the ideal of equality of fortune. Nevertheless, I argue in Chapter 10, respect for autonomy and other moral considerations renders negligence the appropriate standard of liability in three situations: (1) where the injurer acts under unforeseeable or intentional threat or compulsion, whether of natural or human origin, for which he cannot be blamed; (2) where rational persons would all choose negligence over strict liability; or (3) where the costs of implementing a rule of strict liability significantly exceed the costs of applying a negligence test and where the switch from strict liability to negligence would not result in significant uncompensated losses to any group of citizens. Chapter 11 applies these conclusions to four traditional domains of tort law.

The third part of the book is concerned with problems unique to the allocation of life-saving resources, and is largely separable from the two parts that precede it. Its concern is not with goods and services to which justice entitles people in the normal course of affairs, but with their rights to assistance or their rights not to be killed in situations where a shortage of critical resources makes it impossible to keep alive all of the members of a given group of persons. It seeks to formulate principles for choosing among lives when not everyone can be saved, and for deciding when it is proper to kill one person or animal to save another.

Part III consists of three chapters. The first deals with the moral relevance of numbers to life-saving decisions. It asks whether and when a public official or private citizen is obliged to rescue a larger group of persons threatened with death rather than a different, smaller group, simply because the two groups differ in size. I argue that, special considerations apart, both officials and ordinary citizens ought to save the greater number. My reasons for advancing this claim, however, differ substantially from those usually given in its defense, since I reject the thesis that it is objectively worse if a larger group of people die than if a smaller group with different members meets its end.

Chapter 13 tackles a complementary question. What features of people's lives (e.g. age, number of dependents, prognosis) furnish moral reasons for prolonging one life rather than another if one lacks the means to save both? Equal regard for those whose lives are at stake, I contend, requires that one abstract from all such characteristics when choosing survivors, except the potential victims' culpability for their plight and marked differences in their ages. Those choosing survivors will often be obliged to take potential survivors' future welfare into account as well, because of victims' prior assent to a policy making their expected future welfare relevant. In the vast majority of cases involving the provision of scarce life-saving drugs or medical services to responsible adults, however, these considerations will prove irrelevant, because justice requires that the availability of these goods be determined by people's own medical insurance decisions. Whether the allocation of scarce cadaver organs should be by lot, once the aforementioned factors have been taken into account, or whether people should be permitted to bid for rights to scarce organs as need arises or as part of their medical insurance contracts, remains a difficult question.

Chapter 14 rounds out this discussion of choices among lives by inquiring whether it is ever permissible to kill an innocent human being or nonhuman animal for the benefit of others. It discusses the permissibility of killing not only within a just community, but also in cases where, by slaying outsiders, such as defenseless aliens or animals, one of the community's members may advance his own interests or those of his fellow citizens. I conclude that it is always wrong to kill a cognitively normal, blameless human being against his will, unless his death is necessary to prevent grievous harm to oneself or somebody one loves for which the person saved is not responsible, or unless he is a member of a political community that has rationally and fairly adopted a policy that permits officials or private citizens to take or endanger some people's lives when seeking to prevent even greater loss of life. I further contend that animals and people whose cognitive capacities fall below those of normal adult human beings also have a right to life, the strength of which depends upon the degree to which they are conscious of themselves as subjects enduring over time.

Although it may be permissible to kill them to further the most important interests of normal human beings past infancy, the slaughter of nonhuman mammals for food and clothing, as well as for many experimental purposes, is unjustifiable under existing conditions.

A few further points of clarification might be helpful. First, the arguments that follow are entirely normative. They neither contest nor presuppose empirical work on political decisionmaking or individuals' choices in difficult straits, although application of some of the principles I defend would to some degree turn on empirical data about people's choices. Nor do I attempt to derive principles for allocating resources, assessing liability for harm, or selecting survivors from judicial decisions or government policies in the United States or elsewhere over the past half-century. Actual practice is relevant only insofar as it suggests principles for normative appraisal.

Second, in considering solutions to the problems posed above, I intend largely to ignore practical difficulties that would inevitably face any attempt to change existing attitudes and institutions in accordance with the theories I defend. No doubt inattention to second-best solutions will diminish the utility of the arguments that follow, particularly if there is no prospect of overhauling a grossly unjust system of remuneration and taxation. But even modest reform efforts need a beacon to steer by.

Third, I limit discussion almost exclusively to those duties and obligations that present citizens of a political community owe to one another. I touch only briefly on their duties to foreigners and future generations. Nor do I consider what effects the existence of neighboring states, and the possibility of emigration, might have on political obligations. Readers should imagine that the polity I discuss exists in a vacuum, its domestic relations and collective responsibilities unaffected by the circumstances of other states or people yet unborn.

Finally, as should be obvious from the foregoing summary, I shall not consider a great many matters that influence the justice of a particular distribution of resources or of a method for choosing recipients of life-sustaining treatments. I make no attempt, for example, to determine what principles ought to govern the selection, provision, and allocation of public goods the creation of which is morally permissible though not mandated by the theory of justice I develop. Other relevant topics given short shrift include the proper limits of paternalistic legislation, the nature and extent of political obligation, the bounds of just punishment, educational policy, and various questions relating to medical research. Although some of the arguments below bear on these issues, no systematic investigation of them will be essayed.

1.2. MORAL ARGUMENT

A brief discussion of methodology seems necessary in view of the considerable attention (in my opinion, excessive) this subject has received in recent years. Since there seems to me no sure or single route to normative justification and certainly no unfailing device for silencing all reasonable critics, these remarks will be largely negative and cautionary.

Philosophers perennially disagree over how principles of distributive justice may be justified. John Rawls, for example, argues that whatever rules would be chosen by self-interested, rational agents who do not envy one another and who are ignorant of their personal attributes and the technical and physical resources their society commands would necessarily be just. Hence, he believes that justification consists in showing that such persons would choose the principles advocated. Other contractarian theorists demur. Some maintain that only those principles count as just that would win assent from a society's active members if they were aware of their personal strengths and weaknesses and knew how well endowed everyone else was too. Tim Scanlon contends instead that only those principles are just that no rational person could reasonably reject as a basis for informed, unforced general agreement if he and everyone else were cognizant of his personal capacities and preferences, the skills and desires of others, and the resources his society possesses. Richard Brandt invokes a similar test (without endorsing contractarianism), claiming that a moral code is justified for a particular person if he would tend to support it were his desires and deliberation fully rational, where "tend to support" entails a reasonable belief that others would also find such a code acceptable.

In contrast, philosophers such as Roderick Firth and Richard Hare reject these approaches, and insist that justification comes from demonstrating that a suitably defined Ideal Observer would select a given set of principles. Other writers appeal to divine revelation or some allegedly privileged source of natural law. And some rely solely on their intuitive convictions to guide them in selecting principles of justice, perhaps by generalizing from the dictates of their moral sense in concrete situations.

By what criteria should these or other proposals be judged? Three desiderata that are frequently mentioned are clarity, consistency, and simplicity. These criteria for choosing among competing theories, however, provide little direction. One may only demand as much clarity and simplicity as the subject allows, and consistency can always be attained by discarding or qualifying one of a pair of incompatible prescriptions. Thus, clarity, consistency, and simplicity together form an extremely loose sieve. An indefinite number of normative theories, many of them despicable, escape their censure.

A different way to narrow the field is to appeal to the ordinary meanings of the adjectives "moral," "just," and so on and to elucidate the substantive restrictions on principles for action implicit in them. It is frequently said, for example, that a rule of conduct can only qualify as moral if it is prescriptive, if it receives pride of place among a person's reasons for action, if it is regarded as binding on all relevantly similar agents in relevantly similar circumstances, and if one could sincerely affirm it from the perspectives of all who might be affected by action in accordance with it. Unless one can accept a course of action as permissible after placing oneself imaginatively in the shoes of everyone who would profit from it or be harmed by it, such conduct should be described as immoral.

Conceptual analyses of this kind are useful to a point. One cannot hope to answer any question before one understands what is being asked, and the search for an accepted meaning of a word such as "moral" may reveal unsuspected ambiguities and nuances that provoke further reflection and perhaps significant refinements of one's outlook on some matter. The semantic requirement just stated at least serves to exclude from consideration the behavioral strategies of egoists who pursue their own advantage without being willing to approve of everyone else's acting from identical maxims. Raised to the status of principles, such strategies cannot possibly be counted moral or just, for no one would favor their universal adoption. (This is not to say, of course, that there is no reason to adopt egoistic principles. That is a separate question. It may not be rational to be moral, in whole or in part. Similarly, one might argue that morality requires everyone to pursue his self-interest above all else. I merely mean to distinguish, in a general way, between what it is moral for somebody to do and what action accords most nearly with a personal ethic that somebody is unwilling to admit that others might justifiably adopt as well.)

But even if one admits that universalizability is a legitimate limitation on moral principles, one concedes precious little. A multitude of principles are capable of being affirmed as binding on all who fall under their shadow, and in fact a wide variety of universalizable principles for allocating scarce resources have vocal partisans.

Nor can linguistic analyses carry one any further in this case. Ambitious attempts to show that conventional linguistic usage commits members of our linguistic community to a single ethical theory, such as Hare's argument that the logic of imperatives, coupled with what he deems an uncontroversial definition of "impartiality," implies that utilitarianism is the only moral theory deserving of the name,[3] invariably founder on the fact that a large number of conflicting views would indisputably be termed moral. And even if this were not so, one could quite intelligibly advocate

---

[3] *See* Hare (1981), chs. 1, 5, and 6.

changes in our linguistic practice. Since universalizability is therefore a rather trivial restriction,[4] the question remains: how is one to choose among competing moral principles, including principles of justice?

The answer commonly and correctly given is that one must consult one's moral intuitions, understood to include fairly general convictions as well as one's unreflective beliefs about the propriety of various courses of conduct in concrete circumstances. Principles one is inclined to accept prior to reflection must be tested against one another and against those judgments one is disposed to make in specific situations, while the latter are to be appraised in the light of more general convictions. By balancing one's ethical principles, once their implications have been laid bare, against one another and (often less importantly) against those judgments one feels bound to make in particular cases, pruning or uprooting those principles whose ramifications are, on reflection, unacceptable while modifying or overriding those concrete responses that clash with principles one is unwilling to abandon, one may arrive at a more coherent, more carefully considered, set of moral beliefs.

But the attainment of what Rawls calls narrow reflective equilibrium[5] among one's general and particular moral beliefs, although an essential step on the road to justification, is plainly insufficient to settle the question which moral theory is correct. As many writers have noted,[6] those principles that emerge from the process have no more claim to correctness than the pre-reflective judgments and general beliefs that entered at the start, and these may be deficient in various ways. They may, for example, be products of unreasoned prejudice, of slipshod deliberation, of misinformation, of generalization from atypical examples, or of exaggerated desires or aversions formed through childhood deprivations or educators' emphasis on perverse standards of commendation. And even if one limits the class of inputs, as Rawls does, to judgments that are not made hastily,

---

[4] This point is argued at greater length in Locke (1968) and Mackie (1977), ch. 4.

[5] *See* Rawls (1971), §§ 9, 87; Rawls (1974*a*); Rawls (1980). Useful expositions of Rawls's method may be found in Daniels (1979) and (1980).

[6] *See* Singer (1974) and Hare (1974). Joseph Raz has assembled the most comprehensive catalogue of objections to the method of narrow reflective equilibrium as a justificatory device in Raz (1982). Raz's criticisms of Rawls are predicated on the assumption that Rawls thinks the balancing process just described is adequate to justify a moral theory. This assumption, however, as Daniels has shown (*see* Daniels (1979) and (1980)), is highly questionable. Rawls appears not to rest content with the method of narrow reflective equilibrium when confined to considered moral judgments, but instead factors into the reflective process such things as theories about the role of morality in society, theories of personality and moral development, and ideals of the moral judge. Particularly in Rawls (1980), he stresses the primacy of "model-conceptions" of the person and of the well-ordered society in constructing a theory of justice. (The fundamental role such ideals can and should play in such an undertaking is further explicated and defended in Scheffler (1979) and (1982*b*).) Thus, the notion of a multi-tiered moral sense that Raz attributes to Simon Blackburn (*see* Blackburn (1971), (1980), and (1981)) arguably forms the methodological backbone of Rawls's theory as well.

under duress, or while one is emotionally disturbed, one still faces the problem of showing why all and only the remaining convictions should influence one's decision. Taken alone, the method of narrow reflective equilibrium is inadequate because it provides no rationale for rejecting some intuitions as unreliable while building an ethical theory on the remaining ones.

Its shortcomings, however, are remediable. One need only extend the list of beliefs and considerations to be worked into a coherent arrangement. Instead of weighing only pre-reflective judgments and principles, one can add to the scales (though their incommensurability probably makes the metaphor inapt) such things as: theories about moral and psychological development; views concerning the nature of personal identity; information with respect to the historical evolution of moral codes and differences among those current in different societies; opinions regarding the object or purpose of morality and the sources of moral motivation; and moral principles and ideals of a higher order, such as an ideal of the moral judge that furnishes a reason to discount evaluations made under the influence of strong emotion. By widening the scope of reflection in this way, one can surmount the bias and purblindness that may afflict simpler versions of the evaluative procedure that confine attention to pre-reflective moral intuitions.

Unhappily, the vulnerability of moral theories to objection at so many points renders their justification an exceedingly complex task. How should one choose among theories of moral evolution, or decide what the end of morality is, or assign degrees of importance to these ideals and speculations when sorting one's stock of moral intuitions?

No general reply seems possible, save the unhelpful prescription to give all arguments their due, from whatever quarter they come. There is no substitute for sober consideration of a wide range of issues and the patient sifting of opposing views, relying all the while on one's own sense of what constitutes a reasonable, coherent whole.

Nor could there be any substitute. We shall never leave Neurath's raft for firmer ground. Those who feel disheartened by this conclusion should ask what result they would have preferred. We are, after all, rational animals with nothing to rely on but our own ratiocinative powers. We cannot escape the responsibility of determining for ourselves what is right, for any putative authority, whether a voice from heaven or counsel from within, may and should be called upon to justify its edicts on matters of importance. Pronouncements acquire authority only because we adjudge them compelling. We cannot even imagine what life would be like were we bereft of the freedom to reason that this responsibility presupposes. We might, of course, wish for a simpler world, where pertinent concerns were few, explanations obvious, intuitions clear and consistent. But that world is one we will never know, and there is little point in cursing what we cannot change.

Given the immense number of considerations that inevitably impact on the construction of a moral theory, general agreement on all but the most basic rules necessary to sustain a society is apt to be very hard to obtain. Not only might people differ in the principles and intuitive judgments with which they start, and in the relative importance they assign them in case of conflict, but they might disagree about all the other ideals and theories that shape the final outcome. Their views might also diverge with regard to the role and salience of moral rules in individual and social life. And in light of profound differences in people's sentiments, upbringing, and exposure to conflicting cultural traditions and values, one can only expect that even fair-minded people will not find certain analogies equally compelling or concur on how far moral concern should reach.

But the difficulty of achieving a common outlook on normative problems comes as no revelation. Everyone who has engaged in moral argument knows that there is no certain path to consensus, short of programming everybody to think alike. One can only build as sturdy a theory as one's intelligence and insight allow and hope that one's premises and arguments are sufficiently plausible to persuade those whom one would like to convince. And since the strength of an ethical theory can only be measured relative to alternative proposals, it is essential to explain why rival views are mistaken if one's audience thinks they pose a serious challenge to one's own theory. That can be done by exposing their counterintuitive implications in certain cases, or by taking issue with the account of the nature of morality they presuppose, or by criticizing one or more of the normative or factual assumptions on which they rest. These arguments will sometimes prove long and wearisome, and in the end one's listeners may only shrug. Indeed, ad hominem attacks that take the form of tracing a rival theory's ramifications to discredit it, contrary assertions of an abstract sort about the point or character of moral principles, and the description of one's own theory's requirements in various situations, might to some people not even appear genuine arguments. From professional philosophers they expect something more solid or persuasive. But I see no alternative to these forms of argument, and thus no way to satisfy those who expect more. There is no deep level of normative philosophical discourse to which professionals have privileged access, no way to bore below the everyday appeals to principles and consequences we make routinely when engaging in moral argument. That is not to say that moral philosophical speculation is pointless. Analysis and clarification of the arguments we might make hastily, incompletely, or unsystematically should promote understanding, and understanding might in turn prompt changes in one's moral views and provide a kind of certitude that many people find satisfying. But there is no reason to believe that understanding will necessarily produce agreement. There is simply no commonly accepted benchmark for assessing the force of normative assertions or criticism, nor is one likely to be found or invented. At any rate, these convictions account for the form this book has taken. The arguments must speak for themselves.

One final note. Some readers might wonder whether the procedure for selecting a moral theory I have outlined tacitly endorses moral relativism, the view that what is right and wrong for a particular person depends upon what he or a certain group takes to be right and wrong, and is thus open to the many objections that have been brought against that doctrine. For in asking each person to weld his moral intuitions and his opinions on a vast array of subjects into as rational a whole as he can, judged by his own lights, and in claiming that moral principles can only be justified in this way, it might appear that I have committed myself to saying that right and wrong are inconstant standards that may vary from person to person.

That is not so. To recognize that a moral theory, like a scientific theory or indeed any assertion, can only be justified by demonstrating that the reasons in favor of it outweigh opposing reasons, and that each person must ultimately make up his own mind as to its correctness, is not to say that everyone will judge rightly. Sincere beliefs are not immune from error. There is nothing incoherent in the claim that one party to a dispute is wrong because he fails to appreciate the force of some argument, even though there is no way to convince him that he assigns it too little weight. Such claims are made routinely when evaluations differ.

But what does it mean to say that one person is right or his view more reasonable when two people return divergent answers to some normative question after pondering all the arguments pro and con? When scientific problems produce disagreement, such a claim often signifies the speaker's belief that the solution he thinks correct will win empirical confirmation or prove more fruitful in generating accurate predictions of observable events. But moral principles are not hypotheses concerning future occurrences. So what does it mean to endorse a moral judgment on the ground that it is correct or more reasonable than its opposite?

Proposed answers to this question have fueled an intense debate among philosophers. One would now need a short book to enter the fray properly. Since I have no intention of writing such a book here, I shall simply say, somewhat dogmatically, that it seems to me irrelevant how one answers the question, both for purposes of this book and for morals generally. Whether one describes moral argument as an attempt to cause thought and action to mirror moral reality more closely, or as a game try to render one's preferences contagious, or as yet some third thing, the practice of moral persuasion will proceed unruffled. Further refinements of the noncognitivist analysis of moral argument could hardly alter the way we marshal our reasons or try to convince, however urgent and intriguing some philosophers find the project. And arguments over the truth of moral realism seem of no practical import, though they have helped to clarify what, or rather how little, is at stake. Because the problem's outcome appears to turn on whether there are sufficient similarities between moral utterances and paradigmatic factual assertions to justify talk of a moral reality analogous to the reality of physical objects or perhaps of mathematical entities, its resolution seems to depend solely on semantic considerations and to have nothing but semantic consequences.

To ask, moreover, whether the convergence of considered opinion on a particular moral doctrine is evidence of its truth, where what is meant is that the doctrine in question corresponds to some feature of a moral universe that exists independently of people's opinions about morals but is not susceptible to direct apprehension, strikes me as utterly pointless. What could possibly constitute an answer? And what would it matter? Even if the claim that morals inhere in the world were not only intelligible but false, I fail to see why that should furnish us with a reason for abandoning our commitment to doing what we think right or just. In the end, metaethical speculation leaves everything that matters as it is. Nevertheless, those who disagree should still find the succeeding chapters of some interest, for realists, anti-realists, and agnostics almost always offer the same kinds of arguments on concrete normative problems, unless of course their anti-realism has rendered them apathetic towards the meanness and suffering around them. But those who care little about what is right and fair will surely not be reading these lines, and will therefore not be disappointed either.

1.3. SOME PRESUPPOSITIONS

Moral theories tend to burgeon. After prolonged reflection, one arrives at a position one considers sound and commits it to paper. Then the doubts creep in. Have I said enough? Any set of recommendations presupposes stances on an enormous number of complex subjects and so, fearful of an assault on one of these supports, one rushes to shore up the foundations. But these views tend to implicate still others, and the competing theories one has to rebut are legion. One therefore digs a little deeper, cuts the base a little wider. At some point, however, one must simply throw in the shovel. Although I shall try to buttress the most contentious premises on which I rely, others will have to stand unsupported. A few recurrent or pervasive assumptions that receive little defense warrant mention here.

It is not my object to persuade the amoralist to recant. Most people will find it in their self-interest to nurture what moral dispositions they have, at least up to a point, and will benefit their children by inculcating similar desires in them. But it may be that not everyone will find such efforts worthwhile. Psychopaths, for example, if left untreated, may be incapable of acting from moral motives because they lack or lacked the physiological or environmental preconditions of a sympathetic concern for others. It is, furthermore, a disputed question how far along the road to impartial benevolence self-interest can carry normal people, in part because disagreement is rife over how "self-interest" should be defined.[7] I leave these debates to others. My question is not "Is it prudent to be just?" or, more broadly, "Is it rational to be moral?", but rather "According to what principles ought a community's resources to be divided?" I therefore assume that my readers understand and attend to moral discourse, and that they acknowledge that principles of distributive justice, like all moral principles, must be acceptable from an impartial point of view. This conceptual requirement seems in fact to be more stringent in the case of principles of justice than in the case of moral rules, for while people sometimes dub the maxims by which someone lives his "personal morality," even though he would not desire or expect others to follow his example, talk of a purely personal theory of social justice borders on incoherence. One might dismiss such semantic facts as argumentatively worthless, I suppose, and aver that justice and natural right are illusions, mere veils covering the struggle for power and snares for the credulous. To those who take this swaggering line, however, I have nothing further to say.[8]

The grounds of political obligation form one of the enduring problems of

[7] An excellent discussion of the relationship between self-interest and morality can be found in Kavka (1985). *See also* Singer (1979a), ch. 10; Mackie (1977), 193–5. Gauthier (1986) explores the extent to which a theory of justice can be founded on rational self-interest alone, where people are assumed generally to be indifferent to the welfare of others.

[8] With respect to the need many philosophers apparently feel to confront the fictional amoralist, Bernard Williams perceptively says:

[I]t is a mistake . . . to think that there is some objective presumption in favor of the nonethical life, that ethical skepticism is the natural state, and that the person we have been imagining is what we all would want to be if there were no justification for the ethical life and we had discovered that there was none. The moral philosopher in search of justifications sometimes pretends that this is so, overestimating in this respect the need for a justification just as he had overestimated its effect—its effect, at least, on the practicing skeptic.

. . . When the philosopher raised the question of what we shall have to say to the skeptic or amoralist, he should rather have asked what we shall have to say about him. The justification he is looking for is in fact designed for the people who are largely within the ethical world, and the aim of the discourse is not to deal with someone who probably will not listen to it, but to reassure, strengthen, and give insight to those who will. . . . The aim is not to control the enemies of the community or its shirkers but, by giving reason to people already disposed to hear it, to help in continually creating a community held together by that same disposition. (Williams (1985), 26–7)

political philosophy, on which it might be thought that anyone advocating public tax and expenditure programs must take a position. But that supposition would be false. Principles of distributive justice, insofar as their origin is normative rather than positive, are binding even in the absence of states. The problem of political obligation, by contrast, concerns the legitimacy of applying collective sanctions against members of a political community for failure to contribute to public projects that are morally permissible though *not* morally required if no states exist. Apart from some remarks on tort liability in Part II and Chapter 14's arguments concerning the permissibility of killing by public officials, my conclusions would hold even if no existing state could legitimately make claims on all or most of its citizens for purposes other than the just redistribution of resources. I therefore say little about the thorny problem of political obligation and political disobedience.

In developing a theory of distributive justice, I take people as they are: moderately selfish, yet often altruistic if assistance would not cost them dearly; desirous of doing what they think right, but reluctant to do more than their neighbors—in short, neither saints nor cutthroats. I am not so fatuous as to believe, of course, that those whose financial position would be significantly worsened by the changes I propose in current tax laws would welcome the new legal regime, even if they thought it more just than the existing system. My contention is merely that, once in place, the rules I defend would not place excessive strains on people's goodwill or self-restraint.

Similarly, I take the world as most of us know it: a place subject to what Rawls calls "the circumstances of justice."[9] People find voluntary collaboration mutually beneficial, given the limitations on human powers, the inability of one or a few persons to dominate the rest, and the greater efficiency of production that division of labor makes possible. But people's interests often conflict, for their desires frequently outrun the supply of valuable goods. Scarcity is a fact of life. I thus assume that essential commodities are not so limited as to loose a desperate scramble for survival, in which case principles of justice could never gain a foothold, yet that resources are not so abundant as to render their allocation a matter of indifference to most people.

When interests do conflict, I shall often speak of people's *rights* to certain goods and opportunities. As usual, rights are to be understood in terms of others' conditional obligations and duties to the bearers of those rights. Whether references to moral duties may, in turn, always be translated into the idiom of rights, or whether there exist moral duties whose performance no one has a right to demand, is a question I do not

[9] Rawls (1971), § 22.

attempt to answer. Obligations refer to actions (including omissions) one ought to perform in virtue of one's voluntary assumption of that responsibility, whereas duties refer to actions one ought to perform in virtue of a personal status one did not choose to acquire. "Ought" is a primitive notion, irreducible to more basic concepts. Since terminological exactitude is unnecessary for most discussions in this book, Richard Brandt's definition of a moral right will usually serve:

We can say, roughly, that to have a moral right to something is for someone else to be morally obligated (in the objective sense) to act or refrain from acting in some way in respect to the thing to which I am said to have the right, if I want him to.[10]

For those who desire a more rigorous account, I offer the following analysis of "A has a right to X," omitting the detailed argument that would be required to justify it:

(1) A is sentient or self-conscious, or A was self-conscious at some previous time;
(2) It can be in A's interest to have X or to have had X; and
(3) EITHER
 (*a*) A is incapable of making an informed and rational choice whether to grant others permission to deprive him of X or not to provide him with X, in which case, if it is in A's interest not to be deprived of X or to have X, then, by virtue of that fact alone, others are under a prima facie duty or obligation not to deprive A of X or to provide A with X;

OR

 (*b*) A is capable of making an informed and rational choice whether to grant others permission prospectively to deprive him of X or not to provide him with X, or to authorize the past actions of others depriving him of X or omitting to provide him with X, in which case others have a prima facie duty or obligation not to deprive A of X or to supply A with X if and only if A has not granted them permission or later authorizes them so to deprive him or so to refrain from supplying him with X.[11]

[10] Brandt (1959), 436.
[11] This definition owes much to Michael Tooley's discussion of rights in Tooley (1983), 100–21. It differs from his account in three main ways. First, it makes explicit the possibility of a positive right to be provided with some good, in addition to rights to noninterference. Second, it makes clear that sentient creatures may have rights, such as a right not to be made to suffer, even if they lack self-awareness and therefore lack a right to life because continued existence cannot be said to be in *their* interest. Third, it provides for the possibility that one may infringe a person's rights by committing or omitting some action at a time when that person did not yet exist as a bearer of rights. For example, a parent's past failure to provide an ailing infant with some inexpensive medical treatment, with the consequence that the child later developed a severe, uncorrectable handicap, might be treated as a violation of the child's right to assistance, even if the child had no such right at the time treatment was withheld because it then lacked sufficient self-consciousness to be a bearer of rights that go beyond

Of course, the practical implications of this analysis will vary considerably, depending upon how "interest" is construed, how self-consciousness is characterized, and how the two are deemed to be related. But further definitions and arguments are best supplied later as needed.

Finally, a word about the concept of equality around which the argument revolves. Thomas Nagel distinguishes two types of argument for the intrinsic value of equality, which he labels "communitarian" and "individualistic."[12] The first conceives of equality as good for a society taken as a whole, that is, as "a condition of the right kind of relations among its members, and of the formation in them of healthy fraternal attitudes, desires, and sympathies."[13] Individualistic arguments, by contrast, view equality solely as a distributive principle, a standard for meting out limited resources. My concern is limited to arguments of the second sort. Even if one acknowledges that inequalities must at some point be checked if a society is to endure and furnish a safe, pleasant place to live, arguments from the disintegrative effects of large disparities in wealth cannot possibly justify strict curbs on differences among people's holdings. And even they are open to the objection that the good of society, which is of course nothing but the interests of its members heaped together, cannot take precedence over people's *rights* to various resources. I am also skeptical of the claim that the creation of some state of affairs can be good in some objective sense, even though it does not advance the personal good of any living creature. But I shall not argue these points here. Those who are attracted to objectivist accounts or what Nagel calls "communitarian" explanations of the value of equality may modify my arguments accordingly.

rights not to be made to suffer or to have one's suffering palliated, so that had the child died in infancy, no invasion of rights would ever have occurred.

Many philosophers have argued that it is improper to attribute a right to a creature if that creature is incapable of *exercising* that right, that is, deciding whether to waive or insist on the observance of that right and communicating its decision to those who might transgress the right. They would therefore object to the inclusion of clause (3)(*a*) in the foregoing definition. I see little point in responding to this objection, because the dispute lacks practical import. Those who offer the objection need not dissent from any of the substantive positions defended in this book. They could merely substitute the expression "It would be immoral to deprive X of A" for the expression "X has a right to A" in cases where clause (3)(*a*) applies. Nothing of consequence turns on the choice of language.

[12] *See* "Equality" in Nagel (1979), 108.   [13] Nagel (1979), 108.

PART I

EQUALITY OF FORTUNE

2

The Presumption in Favor of Equal Shares

EQUALITY is a protean notion. No one disputes that a just state treats its citizens as equals, without favouritism or bias, or that a just distribution of income, property, and opportunity accords equal weight to all legitimate claims. But commitment in the abstract to the moral and legal equality of persons and to the fair and equal consideration of their claims entails next to nothing in particular. People attach a variety of meanings to phrases such as "fair and equal consideration" and "treatment as equals," and thus a multitude of moral theorists can plausibly claim them as banners.[1] Benthamites, for example, hail the utilitarian calculus as the sole way to count everyone's interests once and once only. Contractarians, such as John Rawls, contend that whatever principles for regulating social intercourse would be chosen by properly motivated persons ignorant of some or all of their preferences, abilities, and convictions would be just, because the conditions under which those principles were chosen ensure their impartial selection. Libertarians, when they use the language of equality at all,[2] argue that equal consideration means respecting individuals' innate rights to personal security and the control of whatever property they have amassed through the exercise of their talents and skills or through the generosity of others.

"Equality of fortune" is another attempt to elucidate the chameleon notions of equal consideration and equal treatment as they bear on the distribution of wealth, opportunity, and income. In this chapter I lay the groundwork for the theory by arguing that, as an initial matter, justice requires that people be given equally valuable sets of resources and opportunities, rather than that the community dole out goods and opportunities so as to maximize the satisfaction of people's interests in accordance with utilitarian strictures, or so as to advance everyone's

[1] Thomas Nagel makes this point in describing theories that flow from what he thinks are the three most commonly recognized sources of moral value: utility, right, and equality. *See* "Equality" in Nagel (1979).
[2] Some libertarians go out of their way to eschew egalitarian rhetoric, perhaps fearing that it encourages the view that resources should be seen as owned or controlled by society with the aim of advancing some collective good, rather than as private possessions. *See, e.g.* Fried (1982) and (1983); Narveson (1983); Brody (1983).

ambitions the same distance. The following five chapters consider the proper responses to departures from the baseline of equal shares that inevitably occur over time, whether from people's risky activities, illness and injury, unequal effort, differences in their natural capacities, or gifts and bequests.

2.1. THE ENDS OF JUSTICE

Before turning to the question whether people's fair shares should be measured by reference to the welfare they yield or have the potential to yield or by reference to their market value in a world where everyone has equal bidding power, I should state a salient premise of my argument. Theories of distributive justice may be divided into two classes.[3] One class consists of theories that conceive of justice as a system of rules devised to benefit all who are subject to them. Although these theories differ in defining the benefits of cooperation and the proper formula for dividing those benefits, they concur in the view that principles of justice must, at a minimum, be shown to be in somebody's rational self-interest before they can be binding on him. People who have little to offer the able or intelligent by way of exchange are accordingly entitled to a relatively thin slice of the collective pie, because those who are stronger or smarter would not be willing to place them on the same footing as themselves when their contributions would be meager. Those with nothing to offer—the severely mentally retarded, people suffering from incurable, debilitating diseases, perhaps small children—can stake no claims of justice at all.

A second class of theories locates the acceptability of principles of distributive justice not in their appeal to rational individuals' narrow self-interest, but in their impartial justifiability, where that standard perforce excludes sole reference to people's self-interest, lest it subsume the first class of theories. Tim Scanlon, offering an account of morality rather than the more specific concept of justice, has labeled "contractualist" theories that propose a "system of rules for the general regulation of behaviour which no one could reasonably reject as a basis for informed, unforced general agreement."[4] To be sure, this schematic definition could encompass theories belonging to the first class if the group of persons given veto power were limited to those able to conclude mutually beneficial agreements and if reasonableness were suitably characterized. But most philosophers formulating a theory of justice who begin from a conception of morality similar to Scanlon's assume, as he does, that the set of contractors is larger than those who can harm or help us in the absence of

---

[3] Barry (1989) offers an illuminating discussion of this dichotomy.

[4] Scanlon (1982), 110. Brian Barry endorses a similar approach to the selection of principles of justice in Barry (1989), § 35.

an agreement, that it encompasses all members of a given society, or human beings generally, or all sentient beings. Likewise, they normally reject egoism as a normative theory of rationality, pointing out that common conceptions of rational or reasonable behavior do not exclude the possibility that somebody might put the interests of others before his own without acting wrongly or unreasonably.

Like Sidgwick, I see no way to prove to the satisfaction of their respective adherents that all theories belonging to one or the other class are mistaken. One can argue against a class of theories that their implications clash with certain convictions one believes one's readers are likely to hold, and I shall offer some brief arguments of that kind in sections 4.2.A, 14.3, and 14.4 in attempting to establish that morality and justice are not exclusively schemes for mutual or private advantage. It seems likely, of course, that most people will profit from acting morally or justly much of the time and that if rules of either morality or justice failed frequently to benefit those who observed them, they could not survive. But that in no way demonstrates that morality or justice cannot or does not command actions that do not fall within a class of actions or a course of conduct that tends to agents' personal advantage. There are, I shall repeatedly acknowledge, sacrifices that cannot be required for the benefit of others; but that recognition is a far cry from asserting that morality or justice can never decree that some good be forgone to forward someone else's interests.

One can also argue against an entire class of theories more abstractly, not by pointing with disapproval to their concrete ramifications, but by describing the image they present of human relations and of the moral world and then painting what one hopes one's audience will agree is a more attractive picture. In a sense, the whole of Part I constitutes such an argument. The only way to move beyond a sterile and unproductive stand-off at the level of first principles, in my view, is to set forth a theory of distributive justice in some detail, tracing the connections between substantive moral theses and moral imperatives in discrete cases. I therefore offer only the following declaratory remarks, more by way of anticipation than persuasive rebuttal, in opposition to theories that tether principles of justice to mutual advantage.[5]

[5] Yet a third form of argument, which I shall not pursue, is to show that, although certain principles of justice grounded in some notion of mutual advantage would ideally apply, they cannot be grafted onto the current distribution of wealth and income, or used to justify that distribution, because they have not been applied consistently in the past. In their place, a more egalitarian theory of distributive justice should perhaps guide the allocation of shares, at least to establish a just baseline from which to begin afresh with the favored principles of justice. After all, if midway through a game whose outcome depends partly on skill and partly on chance the players discovered that some of them had a smaller prospect of winning than the rest because the deck had been stacked against them by the person who dealt the cards and then left, surely the only equitable course would be for everyone to throw in his hand and

Underlying the claim that principles of justice must be impartially acceptable, not skewed impermissibly to the advantage of one group of persons (though some might profit more from their implementation than others), is the conviction that every person deserves equal moral consideration in virtue of his having interests, that is, a perspective from which life can go better or worse for him, and that persons who are able to reflect and choose their actions and who can respect the claims of others possess a special moral responsibility and status. All who possess this status can lay claim to shape the rules that will govern their interaction. Further, because their claims are equal, their strength, or skills, or cleverness does not lend them any leverage in the debate over mutually acceptable principles of justice or morality. They might, of course, conclude that the best set of rules attaches some desirable return to the exercise of these abilities, but they do not allow their possession or lack of certain capacities to influence the rules they select. What matters is simply their possession of interests and their capacity to choose and to temper their conduct to the choices they make; because they did not acquire them fairly and voluntarily, their natural talents or advantages are irrelevant.

Different theories belonging to the second class build strikingly different superstructures on this egalitarian foundation. Some give primacy to persons' preferences, some to their choices, others to objective conceptions of individual or social welfare or goodness. I shall discuss several rivals to equality of fortune in what remains of this chapter. What unites them is the claim—and in this section I mean only to endorse it, for, as I said, I think argument at this global level rarely persuades—that capacities or relationships or opportunities that people happen to have through no merit of their own have no relevance to the content of their just shares. To treat people as equals is to treat what is truly them, what they have remade or endorsed in themselves—their values, their preferences, their efforts, their character—as alone having moral worth, and as alone grounding

begin anew, perhaps giving an edge to those who, at the time of the discovery, had already bettered their initial positions substantially through savvy or industry, or who had experienced exceptionally good fortune. It would not do to say that, since the results of the game depend partly on luck anyway, those who are badly off might have fared even worse if everyone had been dealt a fair hand, and thus that there is no reason to start over. The stragglers would never accept this bare possibility for an accomplished fact, and those who were ahead would lack grounds for insisting that they should. Robert Nozick seems to recognize the force of this argument, for he goes so far as to say that Rawls's Difference Principle, which he thoroughly rejects as an ideal principle of distribution, might in some cases serve as a rough rule of thumb for rectifying pervasive injustices: "Although to introduce socialism as the punishment for our sins would be to go too far, past injustices might be so great as to make necessary in the short run a more extensive state in order to rectify them." Nozick (1974), 231; *see* De Gregori (1979), 21–2. While this type of argument might justify the establishment of a relatively equal distribution, it could not possibly condone all of the transfers that (I shall argue) justice requires.

claims to the resources of a world into which they, equally undeserving, were born.

2.2. WELFARE-BASED CONCEPTIONS OF EQUALITY

One prominent strand in egalitarian thought about questions of distribution identifies a person's interests as the main or exclusive basis for determining the size of people's shares. If people are genuinely equals, the simple but powerful thought runs, then what matters most to them—the sum of their desires or interests, broadly construed—deserves equal consideration in assigning rights and resources. In this section I shall discuss, somewhat cursorily, two versions of that claim: utilitarianism, which bids people maximize utility, wherever its locus happens to be; and the view that people ought to be made equal in their welfare or brought equally far along the path to their goals. The failings of both throw into relief the attraction of egalitarian theories couched in terms of opportunity or the market value of resources, as opposed to those tying duties of justice directly to the welfare people actually enjoy.

A. Utilitarianism

Utilitarianism owes what attractiveness it has as a theory of distributive justice to three characteristics: the prominent place it assigns people's welfare; its exclusion of goods other than individual well-being from moral consideration; and its apparent egalitarianism. Few are drawn to the theory because they believe utility inherently valuable, however one conceives it. What wins converts and inspires the faithful is rather that, unlike libertarian theories that allot people nothing more than a sparse set of rights to noninterference or very minimal rights to assistance, utilitarianism gives generous recognition to claims grounded in people's needs and desires. And unlike theories that pattern the distribution of income or privileges on some putative natural hierarchy, utilitarianism rejects the notion that some people deserve greater regard simply because of who they are, rather than because of what they need or want or because of what they have done. As Bentham said, "Everyone to count for one, nobody for more than one."

In what sense does utilitarianism treat people as equals? Two accounts are routinely offered. Although most utilitarians rely on one or the other rationale, the two may justify in tandem.

The first reason utilitarianism is sometimes deemed egalitarian is that it decides interpersonal conflicts by a kind of majority rule. Each person's interests or preferences, weighted according to their importance or intensity, cast the same ballot; the policy that garners the most votes prevails. What is supposed to commend this procedure is that everyone's needs or desires contribute to the final outcome in precisely the same way. Nobody's interests necessarily triumph, no one's desires are foredoomed to frustration. Of course, the will of a minority of *persons* might conquer because the preferences of its members are more puissant. But utilitarianism's defenders see nothing amiss, so long as all have an equal chance to shape collective choices. If the result is not to someone's liking, he has no ground for complaint.

Utilitarianism's appeal to equality, however, sometimes takes a different form. Instead of emphasizing the equality of desires, some utilitarians invoke the idea of a hypothetical contract between persons in a position of fair equality.[6] Advocates of this approach assume that whatever moral principles would be chosen by self-interested, risk-neutral individuals ignorant of their own desires and abilities are justified. Because such people would rationally choose whatever principles would maximize their expected welfare, the argument goes, and because utilitarianism prescribes that the total welfare of any fixed class of persons be maximized, those choosing under the conditions described would prefer utilitarianism to alternative moral codes and rival theories of distributive justice.

What is the practical upshot of these views? Unfortunately, utilitarians have been notoriously stingy with descriptions of societies that deserve the utilitarian imprimatur, whether those societies are to be composed of persons now alive or peopled with more nearly perfect citizens. Richard Brandt and Richard Hare, however, have hazarded some very rough guesses as to how resources would be allocated in a utilitarian state, assuming that its citizens were much like those of today's industrial democracies.[7]

Hare conjectures that the allocation of resources under a utilitarian regime would be "moderately egalitarian," with "gently managed egalitarian redistributions, for example by progressive taxation." He does not elaborate. Brandt claims, more specifically, that welfare-maximizing institutions would require equal real income after taxes, except for: (*a*) supplements to meet special needs, such as physical disabilities; (*b*) special benefits for the provision of certain services, to the extent necessary to provide adequate incentives to perform essential tasks and to maintain economic efficiency; and (*c*) supplements and penalties to achieve socially desirable goals, such as population control.

Both Hare and Brandt rely on the declining marginal utility of income in

---

[6] *See* Harsanyi (1982) and Hare (1974). In a related vein, Richard Brandt argues that rational persons, whether perfectly benevolent or perfectly selfish (though some qualifications are needed when Hobbesian proclivities predominate) or, like most people, something in between, would favor a welfare-maximizing moral code for a society in which they had to live. *See* Brandt (1979), esp. 214–23.

[7] *See* Brandt (1979), ch. 16; Hare (1981), 164–7; Hare (1978).

arguing that utilitarian principles entail a relatively equal distribution of income. Moreover, Brandt points to the practical impossibility of a government's obtaining information about individual utility functions to justify departures from the mean, except in the case of certain distinct classes of people, such as the handicapped. In addition, Hare (idiosyncratically) enlists envy in defense of a fairly equal distribution of income. People, he argues, inevitably envy those who have more than they do. Because envy causes bitterness and is difficult to suppress, and because its existence is desirable insofar as it buttresses a policy justifiable on independent utilitarian grounds, envy further supports reducing disparities in after-tax income.

Brandt's proposal that the ill and the handicapped receive additional income further assumes that the marginal benefit that such people derive from increased income once their afflictions have been palliated or cured is approximately the same as that which normal healthy people derive. Brandt's rationale for paying extra compensation to those who take jobs that are abnormally onerous or stressful or that require more specialized training is that inequalities of income are necessary to induce people as we know them to work well and to enter occupations that are socially beneficial. Given a free market for jobs and earned income and no mechanisms other than a tax system for equalizing income, Brandt believes that a government in possession of individuals' income–welfare curves could maximize welfare, at least in rough fashion, without obvious injustice. Neither Hare nor Brandt speaks to the questions of, among other things, capital ownership, bequests, gifts, investment, unemployment compensation, or the selection of publicly financed projects.

(i) The Problem of External Preferences

Utilitarianism has frequently been assailed even when it takes as given a class of persons whose utility is to be maximized, thereby sidestepping the objection that it yields a defeasible duty to procreate in order to increase the population of human beings (or all sentient beings) until utility attains its apex, however great the drop in people's average standard of living and however repugnant the resulting world would appear to inhabitants of our less populous planet.[8] Thus, utilitarianism has often been castigated for presupposing the possibility of interpersonal utility comparisons, when such comparisons cannot in principle be made, let alone in practice. This objection, however, seems too sweeping. Any acceptable moral theory must take personal welfare into account and compare the expected gain or loss to affected persons in evaluating possible actions. Although

---

[8] *See, e.g.* Parfit (1984), ch. 17.

occasionally one might be unsure whether one person is experiencing greater anguish or pleasure than another, one can often say confidently that some suffer more or enjoy greater happiness. Lisa's broken leg causes her more pain than Mark's stubbed toe causes him, just as Bill's long-awaited holiday is more uplifting than Sean's twentieth consecutive night of drudgery. Only if one demands extraordinarily fine comparisons between the conscious states of different persons, or of one person at different times, will utilitarianism be found deficient. But almost all defensible moral theories will fail this test too. The reasonableness, furthermore, of demanding precise comparisons is doubtful. If it is difficult to say who would benefit more from a contemplated action, then who profits most hardly seems crucial. Similarly, one's inability accurately to predict the long-term consequences of a proposed action cannot condemn utilitarianism any more than it can the vast majority of appealing moral theories.

A second timeworn objection is that utilitarianism demands too much of people because it makes few actions a matter of moral indifference and requires more saintliness than the great majority of people are willing or able to display. It is absurd, the argument goes, to ask people to put the welfare of strangers on a par with their own happiness and that of those they love, vain and misguided to demand that somebody sacrifice his own projects or pleasure whenever doing so would bring a marginally greater gain to someone else. Even to request people to strive for such goals, however unattainable perfection may be, evinces confusion over where our duty lies. While most would agree, I trust, that this argument is damning if utilitarianism in fact encourages the development of a calculative mentality and pristinely altruistic instincts, utilitarians usually maintain that the theory's implications are far less burdensome. By focusing on those dispositions and prima facie moral principles that are apt to maximize happiness in the long run, they argue, a more intuitively appealing picture emerges. Whether certain forms of indirect utilitarianism have merit in making distributive decisions on a society-wide scale is a question to which I return below.

Consider first the problem that "external" or "political" preferences present.[9] External preferences are desires concerning the assignment of goods or opportunities to people other than oneself. Examples include the wish that whites receive better health care than blacks, and that ailing adults be saved before children. No egalitarian theory of justice can heed them without sacrificing acceptability, yet utilitarianism forsakes its motivating idea and produces unattractive consequences if it excludes external preferences from its calculus.

If utilitarianism treats people as equals by giving their weighted

---

[9] *See* Dworkin (1977), 234–8; Dworkin (1985), 360–9; *see also* Hare (1981), 104.

preferences equal influence over collective choices or by maximizing their expected welfare, all things considered, then it seems that external preferences should enter the calculus along with people's personal preferences (defined as preferences for their possession of certain goods or for certain experiences, irrespective of what goods, opportunities, or experiences others enjoy), since the happiness or desire-fulfillment associated with external preferences is indistinguishable from that associated with personal preferences.[10] But if external preferences are tossed into the balance, then the theory's egalitarian veneer erodes. In that case, each person's chance of obtaining what he needs or wants will not depend exclusively on the urgency of his needs or the strength of his preferences by comparison with the competing interests of others, but also on the number of people who wish to see him favored or slighted in this competition for resources and on the intensity of their wishes. If racist sentiment runs strong, for instance, then blacks ought to be shoved towards the end of the queue for hospital beds, despite the fact that a black man's medical needs are more pressing than those of the white man who is able to leapfrog him with the help of the external preferences of the racist majority. If those suffering from muscular dystrophy enlist more desires that they be helped than others who are equally disadvantaged but who receive less attention from popular magazines and entertainment celebrities, then utilitarianism apparently decrees that their equal desert yield to the unequally weighted desires of their respective sympathizers.

Yet surely this result is a betrayal of the egalitarian commitment from which utilitarianism purportedly stems. If preferences were like votes on how a scarce public good, owned equally by all, was to be used, and if each person received one vote, then there could be no unfairness in one person's choosing, in effect, to donate his share to someone else rather than use it to advance his own ends. (Injustice would result, however, if members of a majority coalition continually traded votes for their reciprocal benefit at the expense of a downtrodden minority, even if fair procedures were employed.) But preferences are not like equal, finite shares of a limited

---

[10] The distinction between personal and external preferences might seem muddy in certain cases. For example, is the desire to own clothing of a given cut or color a personal preference or an external preference if that desire would evaporate were other people to stop following the fashion? What about the desire to own a valuable painting in part *because* it is unique and thus cannot be owned by others?

One way to handle such cases is to bifurcate the desire one seeks to classify. A desire to possess something contingent upon others' possessing or not possessing it might be divided into a (presumably weaker) desire to possess it, regardless of whether others also possess it, and a second desire that others possess or not possess it. The first desire would be a personal preference, the second an external preference. Even if one finds this solution unacceptable, however, the number of clear cases is sufficiently large to sustain the argument against utilitarianism based on the distinction between external and personal preferences, quite apart from the way in which these border disputes are resolved.

resource. Someone's preferring that he receive priority in the assignment of some good *vis-à-vis* some other person does not preclude his preferring that a friend enjoy a similar priority *vis-à-vis* that person. Therein lies the source of utilitarianism's evident unfairness.[11]

Perhaps the patient can be saved, however, by amputating this doctrinal limb. Lop off external preferences, the thought runs, count only personal preferences in the calculus of interests, and utilitarianism will be restored to the healthy, egalitarian theory it was supposed to be. Unhappily for utilitarians, implementing this strategy turns out to be a formidable task, for the limb is of elephantine proportions. And even if the surgery is performed, the prognosis is bleak: shorn of external preferences, utilitarianism still affronts our sense of justice.

Suppose one concludes that external preferences must be kept off the scales, lest they unfairly tip the balance in favor of those with more friends or admirers or accomplices. What preferences would one have to ignore? A mother's preference that her sick child be treated before a stranger's child would of course warrant no consideration, just as somebody's wish that members of a certain church, ethnic group, or political party be favored would count for naught. But the rot is far more widespread than these examples suggest. Many ostensibly personal preferences are tainted as well. The satisfaction someone receives, for instance, when he believes he has got what he deserved, and the indignation he feels when he believes an injustice has been perpetrated, would carry no weight in the formulation of social policy if these beliefs were mistaken on utilitarian assumptions, because his pains and pleasures would then flow from external preferences that cannot be counted if the injustices described above are to be avoided.[12]

---

[11] Even Hare admits the force of this argument. Although he believes that *all* preferences ought to receive their due, Hare concedes that he cannot imagine any way to include external preferences in the calculus without wrecking utilitarianism on the shoals of injustice. See Hare (1981), 104. Harsanyi would also exclude them. *See* Harsanyi (1982), 56.

The charge that utilitarianism leads to victimization in other contexts is an old one, and utilitarians have always had trouble coping with it. *See* McCloskey (1957); Smart and Williams (1973). To the extent that utilitarianism as a theory of distributive justice cannot be separated from utilitarianism as a universally applicable moral theory, the latter's weaknesses inevitably reduce utilitarianism's attractiveness as a distributive principle.

[12] Strictly speaking, the desire that goods, opportunities, and punishments be assigned according to utilitarian principles is itself an external preference. Should satisfaction and annoyance traceable to utilitarian beliefs be excluded from the calculus as well? One might think the question whether it would be self-contradictory for utilitarians to ignore them need not be resolved. Excluding preferences for distributions sanctioned by utilitarian principles, or satisfactions or dissatisfactions attendant on them, it might be said, would not affect the choice of social policies, for if an action is justified on utilitarian grounds, then a desire to see it performed cannot make it any more justified. If the leading football team kicks an extra field goal in the closing seconds, it is no more a winner. This argument fails, however, because a result that would be favored on utilitarian grounds if utilitarian convictions were not counted might not be favored if the indignation that result would arouse in utilitarians

One might further maintain that personal preferences that a nonutilitarian allowed to spring up but that would never have blossomed had he embraced utilitarianism are the illegitimate progeny of an external preference—in this case, a preference for distribution according to principles of justice that utilitarianism regards as false—and cannot be allowed to influence the allocation of resources, no matter how intense or numerous they are. To give them full weight would be to disadvantage good utilitarians who did not set their hearts on more than they deserved. Thus, someone who accepted Locke's account of justice in acquisition and who stomped off into the wilderness to erect a pine log palace for himself might have to hand over his hard-built home after years of toil to some unrelated house-hunter if that person would derive greater intrinsic satisfaction from occupying it than the builder would experience had he been a committed utilitarian from the start. The Housing Ministry would simply explain that it cannot allow people to profit from their wrongheaded convictions. Needless to say, because most people reject utilitarianism and have many intense desires that were sired by external preferences, it would be extraordinarily difficult to implement utilitarian policies that ignored such preferences. More important theoretically, the result of doing so would be an odd patchwork of happy and unhappy people that would belie utilitarianism's egalitarian pretensions.[13]

(ii) Indirect Utilitarianism

Some utilitarians are not discomfited by the preceding argument. Welfare maximization, they contend, might require that a community enshrine in its laws or engender in its citizens principles that conflict with the axiom that welfare maximization is the sole or even an important aim of individual or social action. Although these beliefs might not lead to the

because of their utilitarian beliefs, and the satisfaction the opposite result would create, were added to the balance. The question therefore remains troublesome for utilitarians, although it is unlikely in most cases to become a practical worry.

[13] A utilitarian might reply that this argument need not be met because it can be circumvented. Simply exclude from the calculus external and personal preferences attributable to the belief that some persons are not entitled to equal moral consideration, while leaving intact desires that are not antiegalitarian but that rest on counterutilitarian convictions the falsity of which is or was unrecognized.

This proposed solution is unavailing. If a large popular majority desired that Puerto Ricans or Turks or Jews live in restricted areas, not because the majority's members thought them inferior but simply because they disliked their habits or appearance, then even this more refined utilitarian would have to heed their wishes. If a miserly millionaire could not shake free from the erroneous belief that he had no duty to help those who were less fortunate, then his tax burden would have to be reduced. Such examples could be multiplied. There can be no cure unless external preferences are cut out completely. Unfortunately for utilitarians, that solution seems equally baneful.

greatest possible aggregate happiness in certain isolated instances, they assert, in the large they produce higher average welfare than any alternative set of rules and beliefs. Counterutilitarian preferences certified in this way may thus receive consideration in the joust of preferences that determines public policy or the propriety of individual conduct. In fact, according to some utilitarians, a more radical result might ensue. The theory might perform so complete a disappearing act that it becomes "self-effacing,"[14] repudiating welfare maximization as a conscious goal for both individuals and society. In any case, they contend, utilitarianism can achieve its end without ruffling most people's present moral convictions.

What form should this sleight of hand take? Two competing answers are commonly given. Both should be carefully distinguished from the more humdrum point, made by virtually all utilitarians, that welfare maximization may require the inculcation of certain desires and dispositions—as opposed to the adoption of counterutilitarian beliefs—and the acceptance of various rules of thumb that occasionally yield suboptimal results but that in the long run tend to produce the largest bounty of happiness. Indirect utilitarianism, as I use the term here, explicitly rejects welfare maximization as a goal for some or for all persons, the better to achieve it. The formation of strong attachments and the performance of actions in accordance with divers rules of thumb, by contrast, are compatible with the conscious retention of welfare maximization as an ultimate end, and are usually assumed to be ancillary to the pursuit of that goal. The criticisms that follow do not score against this more conventional view.

One form of indirect utilitarianism calls for mass deception by an enlightened minority. "Government House utilitarianism," to use Bernard Williams's label,[15] justifies deluding *hoi polloi* as to the nature of the good by claiming that, although welfare maximization is the moral ideal, most people are too stupid or intellectually too lazy to determine the right action in a particular situation. Sometimes its defenders also cite people's stubborn refusal to recognize utilitarianism's superiority to rival ethical theories as a reason for not advocating its adoption publicly. Whatever the rationale, proponents of the view that utilitarianism should remain an

---

[14] *See* Parfit (1984), §§ 9, 17.

[15] *See* Williams (1985), 108–10; Williams (1972), 110–12. Sidgwick is usually credited with the idea that utilitarianism is a working morality fit only for an elite, while the great sea of humanity must be tricked into virtue because they are insufficiently intelligent or self-disciplined or morally insightful to act on its dictates directly and reliably. *See* Sidgwick (1907), 490. Jonathan Glover lends qualified support to this view in Glover (1975), 188–9, where he tries to meet Bernard Williams's critique of this argument in Smart and Williams (1973). However, Glover does not think that most people are so dim-witted or shortsighted that they cannot take their utilitarianism straight. The only indirectness he favors is therefore limited reliance on rules of thumb and the formation of dispositions that may cause one to act suboptimally in exceptional circumstances, but that normally produce greater aggregate welfare.

esoteric morality argue that happiness can only be maximized by encouraging the bulk of humankind to believe that some other moral theory is correct. Government policies must perforce be hewn to nonutilitarian standards too, although to the extent that the elite command and are veiled from public view, they may of course act on utilitarian principles.

The problem with this patrician approach is that cognitive incompetence hardly seems sufficiently severe or prevalent to justify pushing people towards a beatitude they do not recognize. After all, the rudiments of utilitarianism, including the presumption in favor of following simple rules of thumb in most situations, are not terribly difficult to master. And deception carries costs for both the deceiver and the deceived. If intellectual indolence is genuinely a problem, then why not initiate a course of universal tutelage instead?

A more plausible explanation for a utilitarian's favoring this indirect version of the theory is the ubiquity of what he can only regard as moral blindness. But whether the infidels are wrong to huddle outside the utilitarian camp depends upon whether unabashedly utilitarian laws would be counterintuitive and whether their abstract derivation is compelling. One cannot defend utilitarianism by pointing to the intuitive inoffensiveness of nonutilitarian principles in a society pervaded by deception, for the defense must be conducted at the level of esoteric morality against intellectual sophisticates. This first form of indirect utilitarianism therefore fails to rebut the objections posed by external preferences in the preceding section, either because its assumptions are empirically false or because they beg the normative questions they seek to answer. In the next subsection, I take up the question how counterintuitive a utilitarian universe would be, and how wobbly its egalitarian foundations are.

The second form of indirect utilitarianism is a radical extension of the accepted wisdom that welfare can only be maximized if people foster certain attitudes and act, highly unusual circumstances apart, in accordance with a few simple rules that might not generate the ideal result in a given case but that tend to produce abundant satisfaction in the normal course of affairs. This second form of utilitarianism goes one step further and counsels termination of the seesaw between "intuitive" and "critical" thinking that utilitarians such as Hare commend. It holds, instead, that people will be happiest if they convince themselves that utilitarianism is false and that some rival theory of personal morality or justice is true. Occasional resort to critical thinking to keep one's behavior on course is repudiated in favor of a kind of automatic pilot. A partisan of this position would likely defend this more circuitous route by arguing that the constant slide between critical and intuitive thought itself detracts from utility and blocks the formation of powerful attachments and convictions capable of spewing forth utility at peak rates. The end remains the same, but the means are those of Pascal's wagerer, or perhaps of Huxley's Brave New World.

This second type of indirect utilitarianism presents several problems. One might be inclined to dismiss it forthwith in searching for the best theory of distributive justice, for if this view is correct, welfare maximization should *not* be the conscious end of individual or collective action, and one can turn one's gaze elsewhere. But the theory purports to be both practicable and justifiable, and should be addressed on its own terms. Certainly there is nothing inconsistent in the claim that false beliefs may increase happiness. One can readily imagine many things one would have preferred not to have known or about which one would rather have been deceived (so long as one thought one knew the truth). The question is whether the maximization of aggregate welfare should be society's ultimate goal, and whether universal delusion is the best way to achieve it.

The question of ends I defer to the following subsection. One should note, however, that in affirming the maximization of happiness as the moral desideratum, this second form of indirect utilitarianism still faces the problem of defining the ideal. If it declares that the satisfaction of external preferences ought to count in theory, even though no weight should be given to some or all of those preferences by whatever practical principles the theory endorses, then it must nevertheless explain why a moral theory should extend any consideration to desires springing from unfounded prejudice or antiegalitarian conviction. But if it excludes external preferences from the calculus, then it must say how it can do so while remaining true to the democracy-of-desire or contractarian arguments for utilitarianism sketched above. Giving equal consideration to all desires arguably cannot stop short of unfair partisanship; and people choosing moral principles from behind a heavy curtain of ignorance would not rationally forgo satisfaction of some subset of their desires, for their total happiness rests on the satisfaction or nonsatisfaction of *all* their desires.

The problem of means, however, itself appears insurmountable. In the first place, the theory presupposes the existence of a psychologically impossible state of affairs, or at least one that it would be extraordinarily difficult to maintain. As Bernard Williams has noted, even the conventional type of indirection characteristic of Hare's utilitarianism is apt to produce a kind of psychological dislocation, since utilitarianism at once counsels that one's dispositions be viewed purely instrumentally, as manipulable elements of the welfare-maximizing machine, yet also as approved checks on welfare maximization, indicators of what is personally or morally important to which one can properly defer, even though one knows that less good will thereby result.[16] Perhaps the two perspectives

---

[16] *See* Williams (1985), 107–10; Alexander (1985).

are compatible, but the price will inevitably be a guilty conscience at times, unless one abandons one's commitment to utilitarianism. The second form of indirect utilitarianism under consideration, however, goes further and commands that one believe something the truth of which one cannot convince oneself of by rational means. It is unclear whether anyone has the power to perform this feat. Hypnotism and conditioning by others do not seem to offer solutions, because if a person's ratiocinative faculties and character are left intact, he will presumably be drawn back to the truth he was trying to escape; if his character and higher-order desires are destroyed and replaced by other attitudes and preferences, he will to a greater or lesser extent have licensed his own murder—surely a high price to pay when martyrdom is not supposed to bring happiness in the next world, but pleasure in this one. Perhaps one can imagine a society whose members were so thoroughly conditioned that they subscribed almost naturally to whatever principles are sanctioned by indirect utilitarianism and could not even conceive of welfare maximization as a desirable goal. But I cannot believe that many egalitarians would welcome thought-control on so colossal a scale, even if all the victims were *equally* conditioned. In any case, indirect utilitarianism is offered as a prescription for us, here and now; imagining a different world does not render any easier the present replacement of one's beliefs by what one regards as false convictions.

Nor is it plain that the substitution of nonutilitarian for utilitarian beliefs would help. Perhaps in the very short term, in situations where happiness can be identified with pleasure, the best way to obtain it is to focus one's attention on something other than one's own satisfaction. By becoming absorbed in an activity rather than concentrating on the experience of participation, one may enhance one's pleasure and reap more desirable memories. But it seems doubtful that the paradox of hedonism has a parallel with respect to the entire set of experiences that constitutes one's conscious life. Certainly no one has offered a detailed defense of this thesis. If large interpersonal disparities in the marginal cost of welfare arise, it seems unlikely that happiness will be maximized without attending to them directly. But to the extent that a moral theory requires people to redress such disparities simply because utility can be purchased more cheaply by giving resources or comfort to one person rather than another, its indirectness dissipates, and it appears to lapse into the more conventional form of indirect utilitarianism advocated by Mill and embodied, if Sidgwick was right, in common-sense morality. This second strong version of indirect utilitarianism therefore cannot have it both ways. But it cannot have it one way either.

(iii) Utilitarian Injustice

The incompleteness or failure of the foregoing arguments for robust forms of indirect utilitarianism returns us to the vexing problem of external preferences. If my earlier arguments are correct, then utilitarianism cannot serve as an intuitively acceptable standard of justice unless external preferences are thoroughly excluded from the hedonic calculus. The arguments above exposed the difficulty of distinguishing external from personal preferences, and suggested that the results of doing so might often be intuitively unattractive. Leading contemporary utilitarians, however, have failed to appreciate just how unappealing the theory's ramifications are once external preferences are ignored and unduly general distributive rules are refined. Hare and Brandt's sketches of the utilitarian ideal bear little resemblance to the genuine article.

Consider first Hare's appeal to envy to buttress his argument that the declining marginal utility of income entails a relatively equal distribution of income.[17] If the preceding arguments are correct, this prop falls away. For envy is undeniably an external preference—a desire not for some particular good, but a desire that goods be distributed in a particular way, namely, away from someone else and towards oneself. Moreover, envy appears to warrant nothing but disapproval on utilitarian grounds, because it tends to create much petty dissatisfaction and little genuine happiness. The argument for equal incomes must therefore rest entirely on the uniformity of people's desires; I discuss below whether one can reasonably assume that such uniformity exists.

Before taking up that question, it is instructive to consider Brandt's claim that people who work in monotonous, demanding, or otherwise unpleasant occupations should be granted an income supplement.[18] Like Hare's resort to envy, Brandt's reliance on selfishness to justify his proposal is illegitimate if external preferences are disregarded. His suggested policy of remuneration could at best be licensed as a temporary concession to people's deeply entrenched counterutilitarian convictions while a better world is being built, not a permanent fixture of utopia. The incentive scheme he describes presupposes that people will act in their self-interest, toting up the rewards and costs to themselves alone in deciding what tasks to perform. But this selfish motivation is squarely at odds with the impartial benevolence of utilitarianism. For while people's desires regarding the work they do clearly bear on whether utilitarianism bids them do it, the amount of gain to themselves alone from doing that work is not the test of whether they should do the job. Grasping self-interestedness should be given no quarter by a thoroughgoing utilitarian, and its genesis should be inhibited. In an ideal world, it would be strangled as it sprouted. If that were done, however, the resulting distributive rules would be strikingly offensive.

[17] *See* Hare (1981), 165–6.
[18] *See* Brandt (1979), 319–25.

Suppose, for example, that everyone had the same utility function, including the same negative valuation of labor, the same positive valuation of leisure, and the same positive valuation of money. The only difference among people was that some were more productive than others because they possessed greater ability, skill, or perseverance. Suppose, further, that counterutilitarian preferences, such as preferences for compensation according to effort or output or the disagreeableness of one's work, warrant no consideration. In that case, the optimal utilitarian distribution of labor, leisure, and money would be one that consigned society's more productive members to lives of greater exertion, less leisure, and less money than those who labored less efficiently.[19] One cannot pretend that this outcome is just. Those who choose to work harder and longer surely deserve to keep at least some of the fruits of their additional efforts. To allot them less than the rest is to make them slaves of their less competent co-workers. But that is precisely what utilitarianism declares be done, once one sets aside external preferences and thus ignores satisfaction or anger stemming from people's acceptance of nonutilitarian theories of just compensation.

Of course, in practice such a scheme would never work. People would hide their talents and coercion would be necessary to induce those poor at dissembling but good at other things to sow that others might reap. For these reasons, utilitarians are inclined to make concessions to human selfishness, supporting incentives for training, effort, and overtime. But such concessions must be made grudgingly, rather than gladly, if external preferences merit no consideration.

The dilemma seems all but inescapable. Either one must give external preferences their due, at the cost of denying the equal moral worth of persons by giving the opponents of utilitarianism, along with the prejudiced and intolerant generally, a legitimate political voice. Or one must remove external preferences from the hedonic calculus, at the cost of what most would recognize as rank injustice. In theory, one could steer between these shoals by judiciously excluding some but not all external preferences. Such attempts, however, are bound to appear ad hoc, desperate measures to save a poisoned doctrine, and no one has yet developed a suitable sieve. Nor is it clear how distinctions among external preferences could be made without forsaking utilitarianism's two egalitarian derivations.

The injustice of ignoring external preferences is hardly limited to workers' salaries. Under an ideal utilitarian regime, such injustice would be ubiquitous. Those who were poor utility generators, whether because their desires were expensive to satisfy or relatively feeble or comparatively

---

[19] For a detailed statement of the proof, *see* Dasgupta (1982) and Roemer (1985), 163–5. *See also* Mirlees (1982).

few, would receive smaller ladles from the common pot, whereas those who turned goods into glee more readily would be rewarded with bigger bowls. Of course, utilitarian planners would in practice often lack the information necessary to dole out resources optimally. In consequence, roughly equal shares would probably be assigned, making the resulting state of affairs intuitively acceptable. This intuitive acceptability, however, by no means vindicates utilitarianism as a theory of distributive justice. Only by virtue of a dearth of information does the theory escape condemnation. The more perfectly utilitarian officials did their work, the more loathsome the system would appear.

To illustrate, take the case of severely handicapped persons. Amartya Sen maintains that, although most would say that such people deserve larger baskets of goods than do nonhandicapped persons on account of their misfortune and special needs, a utilitarian would have to give them less, because the severely handicapped are unlikely to derive as much utility from material goods as are the more favorably endowed.[20] But this result, as Sen notes, seems plainly wrong. Those born handicapped should be given extra resources to help them cope with their afflictions, as should those who later develop disabilities for which they are not to blame and against which they were unable to insure. If utilitarianism carries the implications Sen alleges, it appears gravely flawed.

Richard Brandt, however, contends that utilitarianism does not produce such unsavory results.[21] With respect to health care in general, Brandt says that its provision is justified in utilitarian terms because people are willing to pay for it; were health care a bad buy, their dollars would flow into alternative utility-producing channels. But both the relevance and the correctness of these assertions are unclear. Doubtless money is usually well spent keeping someone alive or alleviating pain, for utilitarians and nonutilitarians alike. But someone's willingness to pay for care, whether under present circumstances or in a world where incomes were equal, is not the proper standard for a utilitarian to employ in deciding how to apportion communal resources.

One difficulty is that people's choices are not always rational. People might underspend on health care or health insurance because they are unaware of the risks they face or because, as is often the case, when they are young they discount the value of later years of their lives more heavily than they do their near futures. People might spend more on health care than is rational because they miscalculate the dangers confronting them or because their anxiety at the time when they took out an insurance policy was abnormally great.

A more significant problem is that a utilitarian is not bound to let people

[20] *See* Sen (1973), 16 ff.
[21] *See* Brandt (1979), 316–19.

spend what they want to spend to keep themselves healthy or just among the living. Indeed, he is obliged to interfere with their decisions if they act solely in their self-interest. The incurably ill, for instance, cannot be permitted to buy a short reprieve at exorbitant cost, even with their "own" money, if the resources they would have purchased can be put to more profitable use. Those needing expensive services cannot be allowed to contract for them, even if they have forgone other purchases to do so, as long as other people can be expected to make better use of them in utilitarian terms. Health care's rate of exchange with utilitarianism's favored coin is to be measured from society's vantage point, not an ailing individual's perspective.

Brandt's second questionable argument concerns the handicapped in particular. Because Brandt assumes that the marginal benefit that handicapped persons derive from an incremental increase in the resources they command is roughly the same as that derived by a nonhandicapped person, he concludes that handicapped people should receive a larger quantity of resources than those who do not share their needs. But even if Brandt's assertions regarding the marginal utility of handicapped and nonhandicapped persons is generally correct, two points should be noticed.

First, Brandt compares the incremental benefit of additional resources to the handicapped once the major initial medical costs necessary to enable them to live relatively normal lives have been paid. If these costs are considerable, however, then it seems that the utilitarian would have to funnel his money into another utility generator, merely alleviating the worst miseries of a handicapped person without appreciably bettering his lot. (Perhaps this problem crops up too rarely to worry about now. But it would become pressing if very expensive mechanical aids or cures for deafness, blindness, or physical deformities became available and the question was whether to provide them to people past their prime.)

The second problem is more common. It is yet another version of the intuitive difficulty posed by people who earn a comparatively low wage but who will not benefit as much from an incremental increase in their income as will somebody who already receives a larger paycheck without doing any more work. Utilitarians would give the raise to the second person; few of us would approve. In the context of handicaps, the problem takes two forms. Some people who are despondent cannot be cheered very much by a flood of gold. If severely handicapped people fall into this category, is it just to give them less when they have so little to begin with through no fault of their own and would still benefit somewhat from the extra cash? The second form this problem takes involves handicapped persons who are not forlorn but irrepressibly happy. Removing their impediments would make life marginally easier for them, but it would not add considerably to the satisfaction they experience. Would it therefore be unobjectionable to use the money that could take Tiny Tim off crutches in order to bring a more than ephemeral glimmer to Scrooge's eyes? It is not enough for Brandt to claim that trade-offs of this kind will rarely occur and still more seldom burden public officials, given their lack of detailed information about people's moods and desires, hence that utilitarianism is not seriously damaged by the preceding criticism. The damage comes from utilitarianism's approving such trades in principle, regardless of how often they offer themselves, though the more frequently they may be made, of course, the more insupportable the theory reveals itself to be.

These objections signal a larger problem. People's capacity for enjoyment, or the intensity of their preferences, are through no merit or blame of their own not always equal. It seems unjust, however, to deprive those who are constitutionally disadvantaged of the same claim on the community's resources and opportunities that more buoyantly emotional people possess. Conversely, people *can* often affect the number and strength of their desires to a considerable degree. Yet there seems no reason in justice to channel more resources to those who manipulate their passions most skillfully or allow their desires to run unbridled. Utilitarianism errs by rewarding people both for desires they cannot help having and for desires they choose to cultivate.

These several shortcomings stem in part from utilitarianism's paying exclusive attention to the amount by which someone's welfare would be affected by marginal additions to or subtractions from his holdings, while neglecting his absolute level of well-being altogether. This is the failing Rawls seems to have chiefly in mind when he says that "utilitarianism does not take seriously the distinction between persons."[22] Utilitarianism appears to be based on a false analogy between the way in which it is rational for a prudent individual to order his life and the way it is just for a community to arrange its affairs. In concerning itself only with totals of happiness and not with its distribution, utilitarianism apparently overlooks the fact that there is no super-individual comprising a community's members who experiences the sum of their happiness, but only separate persons, some of whom enjoy more happiness, some of whom enjoy less, the one group often benefiting at the other's expense.

The first egalitarian derivation of utilitarianism described above is also based on a flawed legitimating analogy, that of a fair ballot rather than a super-organism. Majority rule may in general be a procedurally fair system of government, but whether it is *just* depends on the legislation enacted. If some people's desires are continually given short shrift because they are permanently in the minority, then injustice has occurred, notwithstanding the fairness of the ballot. In addition, the analogy to voting is weaker than

---

[22] Rawls (1971), 27.

it needs to be, for whereas all votes count equally, the intensity of people's preferences might differ, yet lie beyond their control to a significant degree. The more exact parallel is between votes and the units of desire-intensity from which preferences are constructed. But treating these ethereal units as equals and treating people as equals are by no means the same.[23]

The second egalitarian justification, which purports to ground utilitarianism's legitimacy in the fairness of the procedure by which it would be selected, likewise goes astray. One important failing is that the conception of hypothetical choice to which it appeals does not capture our intuitive notion of fairness, so far as the allocation of resources is concerned. Forcing everyone to wager blindfolded on their endowments, later luck, and the malleability of their preferences seems the antithesis rather than the embodiment of fair and equal consideration. And there is little support for the assumption that self-interested behavior alone is rational. The other failing is simply that the power of any moral justification depends on the intuitive appeal of what it endorses, and in this instance the intuitive injustice of the result manifestly outweighs whatever support the model commands.

When someone suffers an unmerited disadvantage against which he did all he could to protect himself, such as a genetically linked disease, it would be wrong to deny him compensation on the rationale that he would not derive as much delight from the additional cash as would someone who is healthy. Notwithstanding their lesser contribution to his well-being, the additional resources are his due, unless they would have almost no noticeable impact on his welfare. Moral equality entails an equal distribution of (unearned) resources, which people are free to consume, invest, or bestow on others as they choose, not merely an equal chance to compete, via one's preferences, for the means to happiness. By mischaracterizing the subjects of equality, utilitarianism loses sight of its object.

B. Egalitarian Welfarism

Utilitarianism's chief flaw is its obsession with aggregate quantities of welfare to the neglect of welfare's distribution. Egalitarian welfarism—the view that society should equalize the welfare of its members or contribute

---

[23] Derek Parfit argues that if his reductionist theory of personal identity is correct, then the case for taking persons rather than desires as the proper subjects of equality is weakened. *See* Parfit (1984), ch. 15. This claim is certainly debatable. *See, e.g.* Korsgaard (1989). Even if Parfit's argument is correct, however, it is not clear how severely the case for distributing over persons rather than units of desire-intensity is damaged. Given that the connections between the sets of preferences people have over time is generally much closer than the continuity between the preferences of different people at different times, the damage seems minimal. Only in rare cases where people's identities are radically transformed might it assume practical significance.

equally to their well-being[24]—attempts to remedy this deficiency by regarding individuals as the subject of equality, rather than treating equally the units of preference-intensity spread haphazardly over members of the relevant community. Its appeal is straightforward: personal welfare, one might argue, is what ultimately matters to people; if people matter equally, then they ought to be made (maximally) equal with respect to what they consider fundamentally important. Nevertheless, egalitarian welfarism languishes under three serious infirmities. Because these weaknesses are familiar,[25] a short summary will suffice.

The first is utilitarianism's nemesis: the problem of external preferences. Because egalitarian welfarism repudiates utilitarianism's voting analogy and its appeal to constrained hypothetical choice as justificatory devices, it can flatly refuse, without blatant inconsistency, to count external preferences when measuring people's welfare. But the same pressure exists to include them in the measurement. Why should only certain dimensions of a person's welfare be taken into account, if people are entitled to equal consideration? More pointedly, what if the most important thing, for a person's own happiness, is how well *other* people fare? It seems perverse to give someone fewer resources or less assistance just because, though his well-being matters equally, he is less selfish than his fellows. But the inclusion of external preferences, as we have seen, opens the door to manifest injustice.

Egalitarian welfarism's second shortcoming is that it cannot possibly stand alone as a theory of distributive justice; rather, it presupposes a second, more basic theory of fair shares. Egalitarian welfarism cannot conceivably require that equality be attained by reducing everyone's welfare to the level of the most agonized and despondent individual. If one asserts, however, that the theory commands levelling up, not cutting the happy down to size, one needs *another* theory of justice to specify those rights that cannot be infringed in the course of establishing as nearly equal a distribution as possible.

One might reply that egalitarian welfarism should be interpreted to require not that everybody's welfare be equalized, or made more nearly equal subject to certain constraints, but rather that resources should be

---

[24] I use the term "egalitarian welfarism" rather than the standard label "equality of welfare" because I consider, along with the view that everyone's welfare should be equalized, the view that their welfare should be increased to the same extent, even if unequal welfare results. My target is therefore broader than that of equality of welfare's critics, although many criticisms apply with equal force to both theories.

[25] Many of the points that follow are presented in greater detail, with refinements, in Dworkin (1981a). They merit repetition here, not only because part of the argument for a theory inevitably consists in demonstrating that competing theories that share one or more of its premises are on balance less attractive, but also because these observations serve as a convenient springboard for understanding and criticizing the opportunity-based theories discussed in section 2.3.

distributed so as to enhance everyone's welfare to the same degree.[26] That response, however, fails to solve the problem. For in order to advance everyone's welfare to the same extent, one must begin from some approved starting-point, and that baseline perforce presupposes some theory of justice more fundamental than egalitarian welfarism which alone enables it to acquire prescriptive force.

This dependence cannot be avoided by characterizing welfare in terms of preferences or ambitions rather than some psychic state, and not only because a person's relative success is difficult to measure. (What is halfway to becoming Secretary of State?) When considering their ambitions and preferences for purposes of either of the theory's two variants, people must be imagined as choosing and modifying their goals against the backdrop of whatever means and opportunities they reasonably expect to be available to them. Egalitarian welfarism would be a risible proposal if everyone could state a preference for the life of a maharajah. But then egalitarian welfarism must tacitly rely on another theory of justice that defines people's allotments in terms of the value of resources (including opportunities), not welfare. Given this dependence, egalitarian welfarism cannot be the main story, let alone the whole story.

Egalitarian welfarism's third weakness is equally profound. Like utilitarianism, it attaches no significance to the distinction between preferences or needs people have chosen, cultivated, or preserved, and those they have not; similarly, it ignores the distinction between the contributions people make to the community's store of resources, and the extent to which their production owes nothing to their own efforts. The first point is best illustrated by people who foster expensive tastes, that is, tastes the possession of which renders it more expensive for someone to attain a given level of welfare than it would cost were his tastes different. Egalitarian welfarism would require that the allotment of someone who cultivated expensive tastes—for flashy cars, posh restaurants, designer clothes—be increased, in order to reestablish parity of welfare, even though everyone else's stock of resources would have to fall to repair the deficit he created. By contrast, those whose predilections are more cheaply satisfied would receive smaller shares. Yet surely this would be to reward the prodigal unjustly.

A more egregious example is that of a severely handicapped person who remains happy in spite of his infirmity. Somebody who is born or becomes disabled, and who had no opportunity to protect himself physically or financially (by buying insurance), is plainly entitled to special benefits whether or not he greets life with a smile. Egalitarian welfarism, however, says just the reverse. It commands Tiny Tim to pawn his crutches to add a

---

[26] *See* Narveson (1983), 4; Frankena (1962) and (1966).

few coppers to Scrooge's purse, rather than requiring Scrooge to pay for
Tim's physiotherapy. This result is intolerable. Why should the cravings or
whims somebody has instilled or tolerated and that did or do lie within his
control qualify him for larger shares? How can greed generate a right to
gold, or envy to possession? Egalitarian welfarism seems to reverse the
relation between desires and desert: justice requires that people order their
lives, including their desires and emotions, in the knowledge of what they
are due on independent grounds. The finicky and the phlegmatic have no
valid claim to special favors.[27]

Egalitarian welfarism's unjust treatment of production mirrors its
mishandling of consumption. People's choices to labor longer or harder are
irrelevant to their material rewards, the theory declares; desires are all that
matter, regardless of whether people contribute anything to satisfying
them. The woman who slaves away at her job does not necessarily deserve
to keep even a part of what she produces, just as someone who
imprudently tries and fails may always be entitled to another shot at his
fellow workers' expense. What egalitarian welfarism ultimately fails to
recognize is that individuals are responsible agents whose tastes, whose
efforts, and whose happiness are predominantly their own concern, and
who deserve better or worse as the result of their choices. People desire,
and decide, and strive, but if egalitarian welfarism is correct, they need
never own up to the material consequences of their actions, except to the
dilute degree that members of a large insurance pool are affected by the
care they take individually. It is hard to imagine a graver affront to our
sense of justice and desert. Although we all bear the stamp of our
surroundings, our mentors, and our misfortunes, we are, exceptional

---

[27] Just as the utilitarian could argue that those who acquired expensive tastes should be
given fewer resources because they have implicitly rejected the approved goal of maximizing
utility, so too the egalitarian welfarist could argue that those who substituted more expensive
desires for desires that are cheaper to satisfy should not be entitled to a share of what
everyone else already has, for they have in effect thumbed their noses at the conception of the
good life society endorses.

While this view appears coherent, it is questionable whether its ramifications are any more
appealing than the implications it might be invoked to evade, or more welcome than the
harvest of utilitarian policies. In this view, resources would presumably have to be
apportioned as they would be if everyone had adopted those preferences that collectively
would have maximized aggregate happiness, subject to the condition that everyone's
happiness be the same. In actuality, however, no one can say what those sets of preferences
are, and even if they could, few (if any) would possess them. People would inevitably
approximate the ideal to radically different degrees, since their lives would have deviated
from their ideal paths at different times and in different measures. The result would be a
queer mosaic of happy and unhappy people, assuming that the central planners could make a
reasonable guess at the ideal distribution. So uneven a distribution of utility could only make
a mockery of the particular sort of egalitarianism the theory claims to embody. But the sole
alternative—giving *carte blanche* to those who set themselves more grandiose ambitions or
luxurious lifestyles—seems scarcely more attractive. Egalitarian welfarism is doomed to
disappoint.

circumstances apart, autonomous beings who cannot disclaim responsibility for the choices we make or the blemishes we carry. But welfare-based theories cannot acknowledge this fact without ceding priority to a non-welfare-based account of fair shares. Hence, the only serious question is which non-welfare-based theory supports and matches our convictions most faithfully.[28]

2.3. OPPORTUNITY-BASED CONCEPTIONS OF EQUALITY WITH WELFARIST ROOTS

One of the fundamental flaws in welfare-based theories is their failure to recognize that responsible individuals are the proper subject of equality for purposes of distribution. They do so either by locating the focus of equality elsewhere than in individual persons, as utilitarianism does in tying prescriptions to the outcome of a joust between preferences, or by denying the relevance (perhaps because they deny the possibility) of people's free choices to the size of their just shares. Yet, despite this decisive failing, welfare-based theories manifest a crucial insight. Material goods, occupational possibilities, and other rights and opportunities that might be apportioned are valuable primarily because they can be used to enhance the well-being of those who possess them. No theory of distributive justice that purports to extend equal consideration to all can ignore the impact of a system of allocation on the welfare of those governed by it. On the contrary, the link between, on the one side, resources, rights, and opportunities, and, on the other, their capacity for satisfying people's preferences must be at the forefront of distributive decisions. The question is how to combine this conviction with the equally important thesis that people, as responsible agents (certain exceptional cases apart), should be held accountable for their decisions insofar as they affect the resources and other welfare-enhancing rights and permissions available to others. The two opportunity-based theories discussed in this section provide related answers.[29]

---

[28] I have not discussed welfare-based theories that define welfare not in terms of the satisfaction of a person's desires or some subjective state of mind or feeling, but rather in terms of some objective ideal, according to which a person might be living well even if he denied that he was happy. Such theories currently enjoy scant popularity, not only because their definition of personal well-being is counterintuitive, but because they presuppose an illiberal and dangerous conception of the state. Without arguing the point here, I shall simply say that I share the common opinion that the state ought not to favor one conception of the good life over another, except to the limited extent that laws protecting personal security are premised on such a theory and that some relatively noninvasive paternalistic controls (if any are justifiable) rest on that basis.

[29] The proposals made in Arneson (1989) and Cohen (1989) came to my attention after the manuscript of this book had proceeded to copy-editing. Although several of their arguments might ideally have been discussed at various points throughout the next four chapters, the

A. *Equality of Opportunity for Welfare*

Richard Arneson rejects egalitarian welfarism for one of the reasons advanced above: "Individuals can arrive at different welfare levels due to choices they make for which they alone should be held responsible."[30] Suppose, he says, that two people whose tastes, abilities, and possessions are identical gamble with a sizable portion of their wealth, with one emerging rich and the other impoverished. In consequence, unless the lucky person's winnings are taken from him and given to the loser, the second person's self-interested preferences will receive much shorter shrift because he now lacks equal means to satisfy them. The fact that the two will subsequently experience different levels of welfare, however, is in Arneson's view no reason to right the resource imbalance they freely created. Similarly, if two persons could satisfy their self-interested preferences with equal effort but one concentrates on saving whales while the other vigorously pursues a hedonistic course, society has no duty to disregard their choices and equalize their personal satisfaction after the fact. Or if one of two identically situated people trades one of his preferences for another that is more expensive to fulfill but that yields no additional pleasure while the second person retains his more humble hankerings, then the diminished happiness of the first person (if resources are not rearranged) provides no reason to take from the second to add to his holdings. Because egalitarian welfarism commands just the opposite, it cannot be correct.[31]

In place of equal welfare, Arneson offers a desideratum he calls "equal opportunity for welfare."[32] Simplifying slightly, two people's opportunity for welfare is the same, in Arneson's view, when the chances they are given over the course of their lives for satisfying their ideally considered, self-

---

exigencies of late revision require consolidated treatment. Because both of their proposals begin from a critique of egalitarian welfarism, and because it seems tidiest to explain why I find existing theories wanting before describing my own proposal, I center my discussion of them here.

[30] Arneson (1989), 83.

[31] *See* Arneson (1989), 83–4.

[32] Arneson's endorsement of this aim is due as well to what he perceives as shortcomings of the goal of equality of resources. His chief complaint is that if equality of resources treats people's physical and mental powers as resources, it cannot easily avoid making talented people slaves of those who are less favorably endowed. Arneson's reason for rejecting equality of resources is, however, inadequate if the theory treats certain resources as inalienable or tempers the pursuit of certain allocative goals with a theory of rights that precludes the adoption of certain redistributive mechanisms. In fact, Arneson himself recognizes the availability of this rejoinder (*see* Arneson (1989), 92 n. 5), although he declines to say why he thinks it fails to save equality of resources (if that is his belief). I rely on such a theory of rights in Chapter 6 in arguing that enslavement of the talented would not occur. Arneson's further contention that equality of resources wrongly fails to take account of certain welfare-decreasing attributes for which a person is not responsible is discussed in text below.

interested preferences are such that, if both of those people availed themselves of the maximally satisfying opportunity presented to them at each stage in their lives, their welfare, conceived of as the fulfillment of self-interested preferences, would be identical. In practice, of course, people's welfare might not be the same. As Arneson notes, some people will fritter away their chances, or give precedence to the achievement of goals other than their personal satisfaction, or cultivate tastes that yield less enjoyment per resource unit than the tastes they displace. But so long as the same level of personal satisfaction is made available to everybody, people are treated as equal, autonomous members of a just community. Whether they seize the chances granted them is solely their own business.

Arneson's theory undeniably improves on egalitarian welfarism insofar as it makes a person's entitlements depend on his own free choices. To the extent that under Arneson's theory other people's resources and opportunities are no longer hostage to an individual's profligacy or ill-considered decisions, the resulting pattern of distribution is plainly more just. Arneson's theory, however, is open to several of the same criticisms that egalitarian welfarism is unable to meet. In addition, it raises special problems of its own.

The first difficulty is posed, yet again, by external preferences. Arneson excludes them from consideration in measuring a person's welfare and thus that person's opportunity for welfare. For a theory that accords welfare, or at any rate its possibility, pride of place, this exclusion cannot but seem odd. After all, external preferences are no less potential sources of welfare than are self-interested preferences. Some people assign them considerably more importance than they do all but their most basic self-interested preferences, and adjudge their lives successes or failures to a far greater degree according to the satisfaction or frustration of their most important external preferences than according to how well their self-interested preferences have fared. To one who declares that welfare matters preeminently (whether or not people realize it through their own effort or choices), giving external preferences no weight at all in calculating distributive shares seems an act either of apostasy or of acceptance of the unconvincing claim that personal preferences alone ought to matter to people. But sidestepping this dilemma and giving external preferences equal consideration, as the arguments above have shown, opens the gate to injustice. It would certainly be preferable to avoid the fork, as theories of equality of resources can, by making somebody's claim to distributable resources independent of whether he would use them to bolster his own welfare or to attempt to achieve some non-self-interested aim.

Abstracting from external preferences in setting distributive shares on a welfare-derived basis has another unwelcome consequence that Arneson appears to have overlooked. The self-interested preferences of people whose non-self-interested ambitions are most central to their lives are often weaker than the self-interested preferences of persons whose primary concerns revolve around their own well-being. In cases where this relation obtains, people whose lives are dominated by non-self-interested desires will need, and on Arneson's theory must be given, a more valuable stock of resources or opportunities to put them on the same potential welfare plane. In consequence, more of the community's resources and opportunities would have to be made available to those people who attached the least importance to the goal—personal preference satisfaction—on the basis of which shares were assigned. And since these people would be free to devote their resources to non-self-interested purposes, as Arneson's example of the whale-saver reveals, Arneson's theory would, to the extent preferences develop in the foregoing way, compel community members in effect to subsidize the political, environmental, religious, or other-directed personal projects of people who care most intensely about their non-self-interested preferences, however much those community members might deny the wisdom or propriety of their undertakings and resent contributing to them. In making people choose whether to satisfy non-self-interested preferences in lieu of self-directed desires, Arneson's theory would often (if the above psychological assumption regarding relative preference strength is correct) make that choice much easier for those whose self-directed desires have been pushed aside by outward-directed ambitions, by giving them more resources to divide between their two classes of aims. That consequence hardly seems just.

As Arneson's theory appears likely to bestow excessive rewards on people whose self-interested preferences are faint because they chose to develop, or became convinced that they ought to adopt, preferences not belonging to that class, it conversely appears to deny their fair share of resources to at least some people who are easily pleased. Equal opportunity for welfare seems just as bound as egalitarian welfarism to require Tiny Tim to surrender his crutches to pad Scrooge's wallet in order to equalize their opportunity for welfare. It is, for that reason, equally unacceptable as a theory of distributive justice.[33]

This criticism presupposes, of course, that somebody who remains content, even cheerful, in spite of disease, infirmity, or other ill fortune may in fact enjoy the same opportunity for welfare, defined as the sum of possibilities over the course of a lifetime for the satisfaction of self-interested preferences, as a physically and materially fortunate curmudgeon. Given the difficulties of comparing two people's opportunity for welfare on Arneson's theory, however, that supposition seems by no means secure. Equal opportunity for welfare shares with preference-

---

[33] Cohen (1989), 918, also makes this point in criticizing Arneson's theory.

satisfaction versions of egalitarian welfarism the difficulty of ascertaining when two persons would enjoy equal welfare once the impact of the satisfaction or denial of external preferences has been distinguished and deleted. That in itself is a formidable problem both of theory and of application, particularly given the often pervasive influence on a person's sense of well-being of how well projects and events turn out that are unconnected to his self-interested designs. But the problem of interpersonal comparisons is still more imposing.

Consider two ambiguities in Arneson's account. First, Arneson does not describe in detail how the huge number of welfare-opportunity cross-sections over the course of a lifetime are to be summed for purposes of comparison. Should one look only to the range of choices confronting somebody at the age of majority (or whenever people are first held accountable for their choices) and ask what his welfare would be if he unfailingly chose the maximally satisfying act at each moment over the rest of his life? Or should one repeat this estimation procedure every moment of the year, looking at the possibilities in fact open to a person each minute of his life given the choices he made earlier, and then add all these calculations together to arrive at an aggregate measure of opportunity for welfare? If the first option is the one Arneson favors, then the measurement problem not only seems impossible, even if crude approximations are used: the result of its implementation could be vastly different levels of welfare (or opportunities for welfare) later in life if some people kept to the straight and narrow whereas other people strayed from the optimal path early on and, although they later regretted their decision, could not retrace their steps. The second option, however, arguably does not hold people fully responsible for their free choices, because it requires continual recalculation of opportunities for welfare without regard to whether someone's predicament was his own fault. The second option, moreover, would not appreciably ease the task of measurement, although it seems no more unworkable (which is not to say that it is workable) than egalitarian welfarism in this regard.

The second ambiguity concerns Arneson's requirement that, in adding up the preference satisfaction expectations for each possible life history, "we take into account the preferences that people have regarding being confronted with the particular range of options given at each decision point."[34] Here, too, a familiar difficulty that one class of preference-satisfaction theories must confront, including preference-satisfaction versions of egalitarian welfarism, makes implementation seem an intractable problem. How would this requirement be implemented, for example, in the case of Parfit's Russian nobleman?[35] The young Russian knows he will

---

[34] Arneson (1989), 85.   [35] *See* Parfit (1984), 327–9.

inherit vast estates in several years. He now wants to give the land to his peasants, but he also realizes that by the time he comes into his inheritance, his moral idealism will probably have faded and he will desire to keep his land. Arneson would presumably include in his calculus of welfare opportunities the young Russian's preference that he not be allowed to choose later (by making available to him, say, the legal option of giving away now what he will come to own ten years hence). But would Arneson also include the preference of the nobleman's later self that he not have been given that choice earlier, because his opportunity for welfare would be greater at that later time were that backward-looking preference fulfilled? How are forward- and backward-looking preferences to be combined in judging overall opportunity for welfare? And how is (to take the most extreme case of preference alteration by third parties) the brainwashing problem to be handled? A person's backward-looking preferences can in some instances be changed radically so that, in duration and intensity, they outweigh his contrary forward-looking preferences. If those backward-looking preferences are to be accounted for in determining a person's opportunity for welfare, then forcible brainwashing or other involuntary conditioning might be condoned, unless Arneson adds to his theory a supplementary account of personal rights or an account of personal identity that would preclude weighing the opposed forward- and backward-looking preferences as those of the same person. Whatever course Arneson would favor, these complications, particularly if some method is employed to discount preferences according to the degree to which personal identity is attenuated or altered, would vastly increase the complexity of the necessary calculations. And when these complications are superimposed on the preceding measurement difficulties, the calculations essential to establishing a person's just allotment become mind-boggling. Try to fit together the expected possibilities open to millions of people on a variety of assumptions about what every other person will want or do, and the difficulties of even a crude sort of measurement seem insuperable.[36]

The example of Tiny Tim points to yet a further inadequacy in Arneson's current formulation of his theory. Like egalitarian welfarism, equal opportunity for welfare cannot stand alone as a comprehensive theory of justice. In some cases, equal opportunity for welfare is simply impossible, just as equality of welfare is. Some people, through no fault of their own, live short, painful lives that are beyond human power to lengthen or

---

[36] It might be possible to escape at least some of these problems if one takes the view that, so long as people could have insured on equal terms against later adversity, their opportunity for welfare was equivalent. Arneson gives no indication that he would endorse this possible resolution of some of these conceptual and measurement problems, either in the form Dworkin presents it or in the form I describe in Chapters 4 and 6.

improve. But surely it would be wrong to limit everyone else's opportunity for welfare just to make all equal, if in limiting the opportunities open to others one could not improve the prospects of those whose opportunities were naturally most restricted. Indeed, it seems wrong to require that resources be transferred to those with limited opportunities where the costs to others are very high and the marginal gains to recipients are negligible. If Arneson would for these reasons impose limits on redistribution, however, he needs to import ancillary moral principles. Equal opportunity for welfare is not a self-sufficient theory of distributive justice.[37]

One final difficulty, to which I shall return in the next subsection, concerns the types of choices for which Arneson would make people answerable insofar as those choices bear on their opportunities for welfare. As Arneson notes, there are several senses in which people might be said to be responsible for their preferences. Two are relevant. Responsibility "could mean that our present preferences, even if they have arisen through processes largely beyond our power to control, are now within our control in the sense that we could now undertake actions, at greater or lesser cost, that would change our preferences in ways that we can foresee."[38] Or people could be said to take responsibility for their preferences "in the sense of identifying with them and regarding these preferences as their own, not as alien intrusions on the self," even though they did not choose those preferences and are powerless to change them.[39] Surprisingly, Arneson does not endorse either formulation (or consider other attractive possibilities), although his theory presupposes *some* account of responsibility for preferences. He does, however, suggest that even the second formulation, which one would expect to license less redistribution than the first because it enlarges the set of preferences that justice ought to ignore, would still require (practical political and administrative considerations apart) the redistribution of resources on account of people's religious beliefs.[40] In my view, this suggestion is incorrect, and it is not borne out by Arneson's examples.

---

[37] Arneson does not address the question how unequal bequests and *inter vivos* gifts should be taxed, but his theory appears to require, unless supplemented by some constraining principle, that aggregate gratuitous transfers to an individual that exceed the mean should be shared with everyone, unless perhaps the receipt of a gift can be said to be the product of the recipient's free choice in entering into the relationship that led to the gift. Whether Arneson would qualify his commitment to equality as Chapter 7 describes is uncertain.

[38] Arneson (1989), 79–80.

[39] Arneson (1989), 80.

[40] The extent to which the following arguments are merely suggestions, rather than Arneson's considered opinions, is unclear. The waters are muddy because Arneson subsequently says that the problem of religious convictions is "tricky" and that one might contend that compensation for welfare-dampening convictions should be denied on two grounds: first, that in at least some cases a change in religious convictions brings a person "closer to the ideal of deliberative rationality" and in that way increases welfare; and second, that religious conversion should be viewed as a voluntary act. *See* Arneson (1989), 84–5. I do

Arneson offers two illustrations.[41] Consider someone "raised in a closed fundamentalist community such as the Amish who then loses his faith and moves to the city." Such a person "may feel at a loss as to how to satisfy ordinary secular preferences, so that equal treatment of this rube and city sophisticates may require extra compensation for the rube beyond resource equality." Arneson does not in fact favor extra compensation because if institutionalized it would "predictably inflict wounds on innocent parents and guardians far out of proportion to any gain that could be realized for the norm of distributive equality." But justice alone, he seems to think, would require it. As a second example, suppose "the government has accepted an obligation to subsidize the members of two native tribes who are badly off, low in welfare." The two tribes are identical, except that the religious ceremonies of the tribes require different types of cactus. If the price of one of the two cacti "rises dramatically" while the other cactus "stays cheap," then members of the first tribe, Arneson says, "might well claim" that equity requires that they receive a higher subsidy on account of the greater cost of the cactus they need; such a claim "is fully compatible with continuing to affirm and identify with one's preferences and in this sense to take personal responsibility for them."

The Amish rube Arneson describes is hard to bring into focus. Given his youth and limited experience, one might think that he would be easily pleased by comparison with his jaded neighbors, and thus qualify for a *smaller* basket of resources on Arneson's theory. Arneson must suppose instead that the Amish convert simply does not know how to enjoy himself —perhaps a perennial feeling of guilt remains as a vestige of his former faith—and that more resources than other people receive, perhaps partly in the form of psychiatric counseling, are necessary to give him the same prospect of happiness as everyone else. If this is the proper description of the rube's predicament, then Arneson has a point. Justice generally requires, I shall argue, that people be compensated for ill fortune against which they were unable to insure adequately and the risk of which they did not choose to run. If the young Amish man was handicapped psychologically by his upbringing, that is, placed at a distinct disadvantage in fulfilling his now mature preferences and realizing his considered aims relative to other people his age, then compensation (probably exclusively in the form of therapeutic services) would be due him, even if other values would prevent our providing free counseling in fact.

In this case, however, compensation would not be attributable to the

not know what it means to regard someone's new religious beliefs as "cognitively superior to the old," and thus as "closer to the ideal of deliberative rationality." But at least the second argument is readily intelligible. To what extent Arneson believes these arguments sound goes unstated.

[41] Both examples are set out in Arneson (1989), 81.

rube's religious convictions or to other commitments with which he identifies. Its justification would lie in his seeking to escape from feelings and attitudes he did not instill in himself and of which he disapproves. This is as much a handicap as physical and mental infirmities somebody did not bring on himself, and it places equal demands on others to restore an equal distribution of resources, broadly construed to include the opportunity to live untroubled by exceptionally strong, debilitating feelings of guilt induced by the actions of others from whom, for whatever reason, specific damages cannot be sought. It would be wrong to conclude from this example that people's religiously inspired expenditures invariably entitle them to reimbursement by all the rest. Contrast Arneson's case, for example, with that of the rube's father, who (we can imagine) was aware of other religions and ways of life but who remained true to his Amish heritage until late middle age, when his doubts won out. If he left the Amish community and requested an infusion of cash because he had always lived simply and had not managed to save enough money or acquire the education necessary for him to match his new neighbors' living standards, his claim would, as a matter of justice, probably be rebuffed. Unlike someone just entering his majority who bears diminished responsibility for his desires and ill-considered beliefs, he must answer for his earlier actions and omissions (unless some rule of leniency applies)[42] because he must answer for the beliefs that prompted them. He espoused those beliefs fully recognizing the life to which they would consign him. In making that commitment, he acquired no right to assistance from those who thought him misguided; in repudiating it himself, his claim grew no stronger.

The same is true of Arneson's two tribes. To the extent that his example seems to sustain the conclusion that religiously required actions influence the resources someone justly possesses because they impact on his opportunities for welfare, it does so largely, I think, because Arneson stipulates that both tribes are "badly off, low in welfare," and that the government has already undertaken to subsidize them equally (as a matter of justice or of public charity?). Under the circumstances, it might seem only fair to give members of the tribe whose religious rituals have become much more expensive (presumably through no fault of their own, such as their negligently killing all the nearby cacti) a little more money, since the government has apparently decided to maintain two ways of life at the same level; and the choice might seem especially easy because they have so little money anyway.

---

[42] I shall not take up the question whether a radical and rapid transformation of someone's values might make him a fundamentally different person who deserves the resources to make a fresh start, or whether regret for what turned out to be a catastrophically shortsighted decision might earn him some assistance.

It would certainly be too quick, however, to infer from the arguable propriety of an enhanced subsidy in these singular circumstances that all religious beliefs that carry material costs provide adequate grounds for redistribution. The problem is not just that the expenditures actually *required* of most believers by most established religions are either required *because* they entail sacrifice, which would make compensation self-defeating, or because those burdens are so minimal as not to warrant, as a practical matter, the creation of a formal program of compensation. Soaring cathedrals, elaborately inlaid mosques, gold-capped shrines are not considered necessary for salvation or spiritual health; the majority of large outlays seem rather to be acts of personal charity, praise, or thanksgiving, much more akin to saving the whales, for which Arneson would provide no public subsidy, than coping with a lame leg. Even if an expenditure is large and religiously mandated, and even if Arneson is correct in classifying religious convictions among the self-interested preferences with which (he avers) justice is alone concerned, such an expenditure does not trigger a duty on the part of others to subsidize his faith. Articles of religious faith, like other matters of conviction (e.g. a claimed duty to save the environment, protect future generations, help others beyond what justice demands, foster artistic creativity, preserve a cultural heritage) that seem more accurately described as perceived action-guiding truths than as chosen tastes or preferences, are matters for which a person must assume responsibility once he attains the age at which he can be presumed to have considered his commitments and decided to abide by them. They are not among the chance events that require a reordering of resources so that all are truly treated as equals. They instead represent aims and values people are free to pursue with the resources and opportunities to which they are entitled, as a matter of justice, on other grounds. Contrary to what Arneson appears to suggest, it would be tyrannical to force someone who has rejected for himself goals and beliefs another person has accepted intelligently and freely to advance the second person's ends through his tax payments. Insofar as Arneson's theory considers religious beliefs or other considered commitments as appropriate grounds for redistribution, it betrays an important flaw.

B. Equal Access to Advantage

Like Arneson, G. A. Cohen offers a theory that seeks to steer a middle course between equality of welfare and equality of resources as conceptions of justice, avoiding their weaknesses while preserving their strengths. Unlike Arneson, he does not believe that equal opportunity for welfare navigates that channel successfully, because like egalitarian welfarism it would offend our sense of justice by consigning people who have been shortchanged by nature to smaller shares than their fellows to the extent that, by effort or accident, they were happy in spite of the ill fortune they suffered. In place of Arneson's proposal, Cohen suggests that a just order is one that gives people "equal access to advantage."[43] According to this form of egalitarianism, the purpose of justice "is to eliminate *involuntary disadvantage*," by which Cohen means disadvantage "for which the sufferer cannot be held responsible, since it does not appropriately reflect choices that he has made or is making or would make."[44] Abstractly, Cohen's theory differs most crucially from Arneson's in two respects. First, while it defines the relevant *equilisandum* "advantage" to include welfare, either in its preference-satisfaction or its hedonic form (Cohen finds it unnecessary to choose between them for most purposes), it also, unlike Arneson's theory, includes various resources without regard to their effects on welfare. Second, it does not limit welfare to the satisfaction of *self-interested* preferences. Cohen admits that his conception of advantage is amorphous and that it suffers from an "unlovely heterogeneity."[45] In application it does have a suspiciously robust capacity to expand or contract to avoid what Cohen regards as the deficiencies or excesses of rival theories and to accommodate whatever intuitive judgments he is prepared to venture. But he says he has not yet found a conceptually neater formulation of that respect in which people should, in justice, be made equal.

As later chapters will show, I agree with Cohen's formulation of the egalitarian objective. Justice generally requires that involuntary disadvantages be eliminated; certain exceptions apart, only those inequalities in the resources and opportunities available to people that are attributable to their uncoerced decisions are just.[46] I also agree that theories that tie the size of people's shares exclusively to their welfare-producing capacity, as Arneson's theory does, fail because they would tend, for example, to reduce the compensation owed to physically handicapped people in proportion to the welfare they are able to experience in spite of their physical deficiency. And I further concur that compensation would be warranted for a physical or mental abnormality that markedly reduced somebody's pleasure or well-being through no fault of his own, even if that

---

[43] Cohen prefers to use the word "access" rather than "opportunity" because in his judgment meager personal capacity, for which amends should in justice be made, would not normally be said to deprive someone of an *opportunity* to acquire valuable things, although it would be said to deprive him of *access* to those things. *See* Cohen (1989), 916–17.

[44] Cohen (1989), 916.

[45] Cohen (1989), 921.

[46] Among the exceptions are people whose lot is poor through no fault of their own but who cannot be raised to the same level as others, or whose position can only be improved further at excessive cost. Cohen does not say to what extent redistribution should continue if the marginal gains to involuntarily disadvantaged people are small but the marginal costs to others are high.

abnormality did not reduce his earning power or his ability to acquire goods or opportunities that he desires. To use Cohen's example, if someone were able to move his arm as others do but unlike them he experienced pain whenever he did so, and if an expensive drug could allay his pain, then justice requires, other things equal, that his situation be made the same as theirs by having the others each contribute as much to the cost of the drug as he does.[47] Another example might be somebody who is born horribly ugly and who thus is deprived of many of the nonmaterial joys people typically experience, even though he is able, we may imagine, to earn an average wage. If his life could be significantly improved by plastic surgery, then he is entitled to help in paying his medical bills. Likewise, somebody who lacks a sense of smell is deprived to the extent that eating or a walk beside the wisteria after a light, warm rain is for him a poorer experience. The fact that few people's salaries depend on their noses—only a handful of people aspire to be a *sommelier*, or to spend their careers concocting perfumes—does not erase that deficit or the need to provide a material substitute insofar as that is possible. Cohen is certainly right to say that justice is not concerned solely with differences in people's resources and opportunities, without regard to their welfare. My disagreement surfaces in connection with some of Cohen's applications of the abstract standard we share.

(i) Jude and Cheap Expensive Tastes

Cohen correctly affirms that justice does not entitle people to a larger share of social wealth just because they freely cultivate expensive tastes, that is, preferences the acquisition of which makes it more expensive for somebody to enjoy the same level of welfare as he did before he acquired them. He makes an exception to this rule, however, for what he calls "cheap expensive tastes." A person has cheap expensive tastes if "he needs fewer resources to attain the same welfare level as others," which is why they are cheap, but if "he could have achieved that welfare level with fewer resources still, had he not cultivated tastes more expensive than those with which he began," which makes them expensive at the same time.[48] Consider Jude, whose "very modest desires" ballooned after reading Hemingway because he then cultivated a desire, which he could have suppressed at little cost, to watch bullfights in Spain. To achieve an average level of welfare, he now needs more resources than he formerly did,

---

[47] *See* Cohen (1989), 919. I shall not take up the exegetical question whether Cohen is correct in saying that Ronald Dworkin's theory of equality of resources would generate a different result. If Cohen is right, Dworkin's theory could be modified to provide compensation in the case of the man with the painful arm by means of the hypothetical insurance scheme described in Chapter 4.

[48] *See* Cohen (1989), 925.

though he still needs less than the mean. Cohen would give him the money to fly to Spain. Jude "still has fewer resources than others, and only the same welfare, so equality of access to advantage cannot say, on that basis, that he is overpaid." But "it seems not unreasonable to expect Jude to accept some deduction from the normal resource stipend because of his fortunate high ability to get welfare out of resources."[49]

In my view, Cohen is wrong: everybody should not have to chip in to cover Jude's plane fare. Cheap expensive tastes are no different from other expensive tastes for the purpose of determining the size of people's just shares; both should be ignored altogether. A simple example makes the point.

A community consists of two equally sized groups of people. Each group's members are identical in all pertinent respects. Because they are blind, the first group's members are unable to reach welfare level W unless they have abundant resources (construed broadly to include opportunities). The second group's members are not blind and in other respects are no worse off than members of the first group. To give everybody access to welfare level W, social resources must be divided 70/30 between the two groups, with a representative member of the first group receiving seven resource units for every three that a member of the second group receives. Jude belongs to the second group, and thus receives less than the average amount of resources ($5x$). If Jude deliberately fosters a desire to watch bulls killed slowly and painfully for no purpose other than spectators' lust for slaughter and vicarious danger, then, setting aside the question whether such desires should receive consideration (Cohen does not say how he would handle desires to rape, murder, or commit other immoral acts), Cohen would award him additional resources, so long as he needs less than the mean to keep him at welfare level W. Suppose that Jude needs an additional $1.9x$ resources to satisfy this new desire. Suppose further that every other lemming-like member of the second group also develops the same cheap expensive taste and that there are no economies of scale, so that each one of them needs an additional $1.9x$ resources. Cohen would apparently say that they are entitled to the extra resources. But look what has happened to the blind people. The extra resources needed to send the bullfight enthusiasts to Spain have come out of their allotments. The blind no longer have access to welfare level W, because their shares have been trimmed from $7x$ to $5.1x$, whereas the second group's members have seen their shares go from $3x$ to $4.9x$ to *preserve* their access to welfare level W. The result is patent injustice.

Cohen's theory goes awry because it loses sight of its objective—removing uncourted disadvantage—and instead embraces a crude version

---

[49] Cohen (1989), 925.

of equality of resources, which considers only transferable material resources in determining the size of people's shares, with the qualification that if somebody's tastes allow him to live as well as others at less cost, then he must return whatever he does not use in attaining the common level. Cohen could respond to the example in the preceding paragraph by recasting his recommendation to say that redistribution is warranted in the case of cheap expensive tastes only to the extent that everyone's access to advantage or welfare is equal after the reshuffling. In consequence, the Hemingway fans would have to settle for fewer flights to Spain, limiting their potential welfare to a lower level than they enjoyed before they nurtured their desire to attend bullfights, and the blind people would have to accept the same reduced prospect of an enjoyable existence because some of their former resources would be used to fly the Hemingway fans to Spain.

The better course, however, not just intuitively but also in terms of the guiding principle Cohen recognizes, is to deny the Hemingway fans additional resources at the expense of the blind. The reason is simply that the initial distribution of resources was presumably just, that is, it took full account of any involuntary disadvantages under which members of the two groups labored. Once that fact is acknowledged, it follows that justice requires no further redistribution on account of voluntary actions by members of either group. Indeed, this approach is much fairer than the one Cohen suggests, because it would not make it less costly for sighted people to develop a penchant for bullfights than for the blind to do so, just because blind people (on the foregoing assumptions) convert resources into welfare less efficiently through no fault of their own. Jude may fly to Spain to watch a bullfight, just as his blind friend may fly there to hear it, but each must pay his own way.

(ii) Paul and Naturally Expensive Tastes

If somebody schools himself into expensive tastes, Cohen says, then he must bear the cost of his costly preferences. But if these same tastes were forced upon him—if Louis's yen for old claret and plovers' eggs were not the residue of an affectation but the result of those foods being household fare in childhood—he cannot properly be held to answer for them and compensation is owed him, except to the extent that medical or other assistance that could cost-effectively wean him from these tastes is cheaper than compensation.[50]

These claims are unexceptionable, however unrealistic Louis's example might be. But consider Paul and Fred. Paul loves photography, which

---

[50] *See* Cohen (1989), 920, 922–3, 937.

happens to be an expensive pastime, while Fred is addicted to fishing, which costs him small change. Must Fred help equip Paul's darkroom? Cohen says he must, given two assumptions: Paul "hates fishing" and "could not have helped hating it" because "it does not suit his natural inclinations"; and Paul has a "genuinely involuntary expensive taste" for photography. It seems, however, that a third assumption is also needed: photography is the cheapest expensive taste that Paul could acquire, that is, no other activity exists that suits Paul's inclinations and that would generate welfare equally effectively. Cohen suggests that "subsidized community leisure facilities" might be warranted for people like Paul.[51]

I would be much more reluctant than Cohen to force Fred to support Paul's hobby, primarily because I find it hard to accept Cohen's assumptions. In what sense is Paul's liking for photography "genuinely involuntary"? Cohen does not say that young Paul was relevantly similar to somebody fed plovers' eggs for breakfast most mornings as a child, that he became hooked on photography as a lad under the encouraging instruction of his parents and that now, through no fault of his own, he is unhappy doing anything else. Unless Paul's case is highly unusual, he *chose* to investigate and involve himself more deeply in photography after an initially attractive exposure to it. The strength of his predilection owes more to his own decisions than to any putatively "natural inclination" he has. But if Paul engendered this interest and permitted it to become pronounced, aware of the costs that further sophistication entailed, then it seems only right that he should answer for his choice.

Perhaps Cohen assumes, as some of his language suggests, that *nothing* other than photography could or does please Paul, so that Paul will be positively miserable—and blamelessly so—if he lacks the means to pursue his hobby. If that is Cohen's assumption, then perhaps Paul does qualify for assistance. But if that is an accurate description of Paul, then Paul is an exceedingly rare person, perhaps one not to be found outside philosophy articles. Virtually everyone has a vast range of desires—some cheap to satisfy, others dear—the satisfaction of which gives them greater or lesser pleasure or welfare. People may choose to strengthen some desires or weaken others out of moral or religious conviction, affection, self-interest, or other concern, but in each case they do so in the knowledge of the possible costs, both material and experiential, of cultivating or preserving various preferences or hankerings. Those costs are a fact of life, determined by the natural availability of the objects of desire, the time and money needed to obtain, process, transport, or protect those natural

[51] Cohen (1989), 923. Cohen does not say how he would exclude from the subsidized facilities, or charge a higher price to, people for whom expensive photography is a voluntarily acquired expensive taste. Few would admit to having made choices that require their paying a surcharge when they could gain admission more cheaply by lying with no risk of detection.

resources, and the competing desires of other people. To the extent that people elect to expose themselves to, preserve, or suppress certain desires, the more or less expensive preferences they develop are beyond the bounds of justice: no correction need or should be made for them. Almost everybody would like to own expensive things or to engage in expensive activities, just as almost everybody has at least some cheap satisfactions available to him; those people who choose to indulge their more extravagant wishes necessarily choose to forgo other desirable purchases or activities. The choice is theirs to make, but it affects their bank accounts alone.

Paul's love of photography may or may not be governed by this principle. If Paul could have found normal satisfaction in other pursuits, but instead he focused all his longing and interest on photography, so that it became a driving preoccupation and nothing else held any savor, then he must learn to accept whatever frustration he feels because he is unable to afford the latest fancy equipment or travel to exotic locations to snap pictures. If he comes to regret his earlier decisions and seeks to rid himself of his passion for photography, that too is his choice, for which he would ordinarily[52] have to pay if professional counseling or care were required (admittedly a bizarre possibility in the case of photography, but perhaps not in the case of other unwanted obsessions). Only if Paul is, for whatever reason having to do with his genes or nurturing or later involuntary conditioning, constitutionally unable to lead a life as meaningful and happy as most others in any less expensive way than by engaging in photography to an extent and in a manner that is far more costly than activities in which others find pleasure and significance, is there a forceful argument of justice for compelling others to help finance Paul's passion. But then, as I said, Paul's is truly a singular case.

(iii) Berg Lovers, Monument Builders, and Intrinsic Connections between Commitments and Costs

Cohen qualifies the claim that unchosen disadvantages entitle someone to compensation in one important respect.[53] If the disadvantage is "intrinsically connected" to commitments resting on his unchosen beliefs— religion and esoteric music are Cohen's two examples of such commitments —then no compensation is required. If, for instance, someone's religious beliefs cause his welfare to diminish by inducing feelings of guilt, he is not entitled to extra resources on that account, because he would not choose (if

---

[52] A difficult question, which I leave unanswered here, is the degree to which somebody must bear the cost of what he later perceives as mistaken decisions, particularly when those decisions were costly and motivated by fundamental convictions he no longer shares.

[53] *See* Cohen (1989), 935–9.

he could) to be rid of the beliefs that give rise to those feelings. If, however, the disadvantage is "not integral to the commitment mandating" the disadvantageous preference, then satisfaction of that preference, unchosen because the beliefs from which the preference springs are by hypothesis unchosen, qualifies for subsidization. To take Cohen's two examples, if a lover of Berg's music finds it expensive to hear the music performed, and if "in a perfect world he would have chosen to have his actual musical taste, but he would also have chosen that it not be expensive,"[54] then everyone else must, as a matter of justice, contribute to his concertgoing costs. "[W]e might think it right to provide a Lincoln Center even for those who forgo an offer to be schooled out of their high-brow musical tastes," Cohen says, because their "commitment to good music" would prevent them from abandoning their taste whatever its cost, even though "they would certainly choose not to sustain the frustration that happens to accompany it [on account of its cost], and that produces a relevant disanalogy with the case of the guilty religious believer."[55] Similarly, somebody who feels impelled to erect a monument to his god has a claim to assistance from his fellow citizens, assuming that his religion does not require the building precisely because it would entail an expensive personal sacrifice. So long as he would prefer to retain the ambition without its accompanying expense, justice mandates that the disadvantage he faces—the expense of the project—be removed.[56]

Cohen's view presents a number of problems. It is not clear, for example, whether he thinks that the Berg lovers should get a concert hall if their other preferences offer them access to the same level of satisfaction as other people have available, or whether they should only get help insofar as the sum of their welfare opportunities falls short of the mean.[57] One also wonders how the aesthetically committed are to be distinguished in setting ticket prices or computing tax breaks from the large number of people who attend concerts for reasons having little to do with refined artistic values. Moreover, the problem of comparing the intensity and duration of people's preferences in determining relative disadvantage

---

[54] Cohen (1989), 927.

[55] Cohen (1989), 938.

[56] A related attempt to assimilate expensive tastes to handicaps and involuntary cravings may be found in Alexander and Schwarzschild (1987), 99–102. They, too, fail to appreciate the extent to which certain (though of course not all) desires are subject to voluntary modification over time. Indeed, as a rule it is precisely the possibility of their voluntary modification that warrants their classification as tastes rather than afflictions.

[57] Indeed, it is not clear why the Berg lovers should get a concert hall rather than something more economical—a few compact disks, for example—unless one supposes that their aesthetic commitment entails popularization. But then might not compact disks for the masses be more cost-effective? Perhaps they consider a live performance to possess some aesthetic quality that recordings lack. Even if that claim appears reasonable, however, and even if one accepts Cohen's view, one wonders whether their commitment justifies the vast increase in the amount of the subsidy.

would in these cases be extremely difficult. There are line-drawing problems too, if Cohen wishes to distinguish between actions mandated or required by a religious or other commitment and actions that are better characterized as discretionary.

By far the most important problem, however, on which I shall focus exclusively, is Cohen's special treatment of preferences that originate in what he calls commitments, by contrast with his treatment of voluntarily acquired expensive tastes. Preferences derived from commitments are preferences a person would not choose (if it were within his power to choose) to be without, despite the high cost of their satisfaction.[58] Cohen contends that even if one cannot properly be said to *choose* one's religious or other commitments, one nevertheless can be held responsible for the effects of those preferences on one's welfare insofar as those effects are intrinsically connected to beliefs that undergird one's commitment. But to the extent that onerous effects bear no intrinsic connection to the underlying beliefs, so that a person can coherently wish to be free from the effects without compromising the beliefs, they are to be treated as unchosen disadvantages for which compensation is required.

Cohen is certainly correct in saying that impediments flowing directly from a person's commitments cannot justify compelling others to give up some of what they own to boost his welfare. But why should costs that are only contingently connected with those commitments, in the sense that one could imagine their vanishing without the commitment itself evaporating, receive different treatment? Why should they not be viewed as concomitants of those commitments in the world in which we must actually live, the price a person must pay for his allegiances and which he must take into account in deciding how to order his life?

It is easy to produce examples that push one in the direction of accepting this view in preference to Cohen's. Consider the committed environmentalist who believes, rightly or wrongly, that he should devote almost all his possessions and effort to preserving the tundra and the rain forests, both because he recognizes a powerful duty to future generations and to other sentient creatures and because he thinks unbesmirched nature is somehow valuable in itself. He wishes that he could achieve these ends costlessly, but they are in fact quite expensive. Can justice really require those who think him misguided to pay for his commitment—and to pay much and repeatedly, since he would pass on virtually everything he received as soon

---

[58] *See* Cohen (1989), 927, 936–8. Presumably the decision to retain at least some of these preferences is a matter of degree. A person might well wish to retain a commitment to architectural preservation even if the protection and restoration of old buildings cost him a substantial sum of money and he experienced some frustration at not being able to do more. But he might not want to retain that commitment if the personal costs grew exorbitant because it came to dominate his life. It is unclear how Cohen would handle cases where a commitment was not wholly inflexible.

as he had it in hand—just because he would prefer that the extreme sacrifices he is making were not necessary to honor his commitment? Or consider a society consisting of two groups of people. Those in the first group want to live as comfortably as possible, whereas those in the second group believe that some deity wishes them to pass their days in contemplation. Does justice demand that members of the first group provide food and shelter for both groups, so long as the religious devotees do not consider eating or keeping dry religious transgressions? Suppose that members of the first group are convinced atheists who believe that morality permits within limits, and prudence demands, that they live as pleasurably as possible in this world because there is no other, whereas those in the second group desire to make lavish offerings to the divinity they worship because they think that the only way to secure a pleasurable life in the afterworld. The two seek the same end, but their conflicting beliefs dictate different means to that end. Why must the one group support the other? Would Cohen go beyond resource transfers to require members of the first group to desist from activities that the religious adherents consider immoral or blasphemous and that reduce their welfare when other people engage in them? If they would rather desist than pay their required contribution, and if the second group's members would also rather that they not sin, then presumably they would be paid to stop, the net result being that the commitments of one group can compel members of the other to modify their conduct significantly, but not vice versa. Or, to take another case, must we make concessions, whether material (to aid proselytizing) or behavioral, to Bible-quoting segregationists, merely because the segregationists can imagine a world that causes them less righteous indignation without ceasing to be religiously inspired racists?

Cohen's argument rests on at least two salient premises: (1) that all commitments rooted in a person's beliefs and values, and all desires contingent on those commitments, are acquired involuntarily rather than assumed freely; and (2) that all desires that are not assumed freely or that are dependent on values or beliefs that a person affirms generate a prima facie right to assistance, to the extent that failure to satisfy those desires reduces a person's access to advantageous resources or opportunities relative to others' access and to the extent that relieving a person of the cost of satisfying those desires would not be inconsistent with the commitment that generated them. Both of these premises are open to challenge.

Although the first premise is often true, it seems dubious as a universal proposition. Cohen begins by claiming that a person's religion is rarely chosen freely: "people often no more choose to acquire a particular religion than they do to speak a particular language: in most cases, both come with upbringing." Hence, "we cannot regard its convinced adherent as choosing to retain it, any more than we can regard him as choosing to retain his belief that the world is round."[59] This seems an overstatement. People who have religious faith commonly probe and reflect on its genesis and plausibility; while they may imbibe a faith when young, they need not keep that faith in the light of experience and rational scrutiny, just as, to use Cohen's analogy, people may learn new languages and even cease speaking their mother tongue altogether. And just as we can say of someone, without too much stretching, that he chooses to retain his belief that the world is round inasmuch as he refuses even to look at contrary evidence, so we can say that a believer chooses his faith by not examining it carefully.

But whatever the merits of Cohen's claim in the case of religious belief, his extension of that claim to all other commitments seems questionable. Take the Berg lovers as an example. In what sense is their commitment not chosen, in precisely the same way that a person's expensive taste for fine wine or antiques is chosen? In both cases, a person decides, generally following a pleasant initial acquaintance, to repeat and extend that type of experience, growing over time in desire and knowledge. The commitment that comes with deepened experience is a commitment that hinges on a series of choices, in just the same way that refined tastes do.

More important, in the case of both commitments and expensive tastes, desires arise and are cosseted or suppressed within a structure of beliefs about what constitutes a valuable life. Compare a partisan of esoteric classical music to a lover of fine food who believes that no preferences can be said to be more sublime or elevated or deserving than others—poetry and pushpin are on a par, so far as he can see—and who savors the gourmet's refinement of taste. Why should the one qualify for public support but not the other? Is it because the one believes that some preferences are objectively good whereas the other denies that claim (or believes that all are)? Surely that cannot be Cohen's test. Is it because the Berg lover claims that music engages his rational faculty in a way that foie gras cannot? That would be a weak claim—many aestheticians, not to mention most artists, believe that artistic communication is principally and most forcefully nonpropositional and emotive—and in any case it would scarcely separate the Berg lovers from those who find what they consider a better stimulant to reflection in the lyrics of the 10,000 Maniacs. So far as choice is concerned, I can think of nothing to distinguish a passion for classical music from a passion for travel or dancing or sports. Even if I agreed that financial support for lovers of classical music were appropriate, I would find it hard to justify subsidizing the glitterati who jet to Bayreuth while leaving Knicks fans to buy their own tickets.

---

[59] Cohen (1989), 936.

My principal quarrel, however, is with Cohen's second premise. The reason it must be rejected is not that it trivializes commitments and Cohen's exception to the compensation requirement for disadvantages attendant on commitments, although it does have that consequence, since much more often than not people wish that the ends to which they are committed could be realized costlessly rather than expensively. The reason is rather that the values and beliefs people espouse, and the objectives they pursue in light of those convictions, are constitutive elements of themselves for which they must assume responsibility. And part of assuming responsibility is accepting the costs of one's commitments, undiluted by compelled contributions from others. This conclusion follows from a simple fact that Cohen ignores: the convictions of the committed are always counterbalanced by the contrary convictions of those who do not share their commitment. The religious zealot bent on building massive monuments and initiating vast missionary projects who fails to obtain voluntary contributions sufficient to bring his endeavors to fruition finds his dreams unfulfilled because at least some others reject the cause to which he is committed. If he can truthfully be said to be disadvantaged by the desires his commitment sparks, those who reject his commitment—who have a negative, offsetting commitment—can be said to be disadvantaged if they are forced to contribute to a cause they believe does not merit the support he claims for it. Honoring commitments means, on balance, not extracting contributions from people to aid projects they would not willingly support. It means that, in general, commitments are irrelevant to the just distribution of resources and opportunities.

The examples described above of the dedicated environmentalist and the religiously resolute half of a divided society illustrate this point by making vivid the unfairness of crediting claims to promote some end based on commitments while neglecting claims *not* to promote that same end based on contrary commitments. Those examples could be multiplied. Compare, for instance, the commitments, and what Cohen would presumably classify as the compensation-deserving disadvantages that accompany them, of Nazi organizations that preach white supremacy and anti-Semitism with the competing commitments of those who oppose them. Or consider the efforts of people who attempt to stop abortions because they believe that killing a fetus is morally wrong in relation to those who attempt, out of equally firm convictions, to secure or preserve a woman's freedom to choose whether to bear a child. It would be ludicrous to compel the opposed groups to subsidize one another, and unfair to force people who do not believe that welfare-diminishing activism of either sort is warranted to support *both*.

In affirming commitments, just as in choosing to retain, cultivate, distend, or extinguish certain preferences, people decide how best to live their lives in a world where those decisions invariably come with projected costs and benefits attached. One of the shortcomings of egalitarian welfarism is precisely that it fails to recognize this truth; it decrees that people may keep or develop whatever desires they wish, be they ever so grandiose, without regard to the magnitude of the liability they would impose, and that everyone is required to help them towards their goals to the same extent that others are helped. Equal access to advantage shares this same shortcoming to a diminished extent, insofar as it gives people the freedom to pursue commitments buoyed by other people's money and perspiration, if not that same freedom to force others to cater to inflated desires that are not tied, in what Cohen thinks an appropriate way, to a set of beliefs. Neither of these wishes should be allowed to alter the size of other people's distributive shares if those wishes originate in a person's responsible choice or affirmation. Unless people's desires, whether those stemming from commitments or those based on more immediate preferences, were forced upon them by their upbringing or other manner of conditioning to which they were involuntarily subject, and unless they disapprove of those desires and wish to be rid of them, the costs of satisfying their wishes, or the frustration of leaving them unsatisfied, are of no concern to others who do not choose to make them their concern. Justice leaves those matters to private decisions, to be made against the backdrop of a just distribution of resources determined, as I shall try to show, on other grounds. The Berg lovers and the monument builder have no more right to help in satisfying their desires than oenophiles or backpackers.[60] Cohen errs in drawing the relevant line separating the chosen and the unchosen, though he rightly recognizes it as the most important divide in determining what constitutes a just distribution of resources and opportunities.

[60] That the Berg lovers and the monument builder are not entitled to subsidies does not mean that the lame pilgrim who finds it more expensive to travel to his faith's holy places cannot claim assistance as a matter of justice, notwithstanding Cohen's assumption that all three cases ought to be given parallel treatment. As I explain in Chapter 4, if the pilgrim was not responsible for his handicap, and if it did not postdate the age at which he is properly held accountable for his insurance decisions, then he is entitled to compensation sufficient to place him, so far as possible, in the same position as people with ordinary powers of locomotion. His disadvantage is relevantly similar to that of the man who experiences intense pain whenever he moves his arm. If he has no desire to move his arm, he has no right to compensation, just as a cripple lacks a right to compensation if he does not regard his infirmity as a misfortune. If neither would have bid anything for what he lacks in an auction that included personal powers, then he cannot be said to have been disadvantaged; hence, there is no deficiency to repair. But if, like Cohen's pilgrim, he rues his involuntary lack of an opportunity that almost everyone else possesses, then others owe him assistance in erasing that disadvantage.

2.4. EQUAL SHARES IN A FREE MARKET

Bearing in mind the failings but also the considerable strengths of the egalitarian proposals discussed above, what principles of distribution are just? It seems easiest to answer this question in stages, beginning with a simple case and adding complications serially. Suppose for now that every member of a group of people is equally healthy, talented, intelligent, and adult, that a finite stock of resources exists for them to divide, and that the stock of resources is not so vast relative to their number that all could realize their every wish if one or several distributions were chosen. How should they divide the resources available to them?

In everyday life, this would seem an odd question, because for all practical purposes everything worth having already has an owner whose property cannot rightfully be taken from him by a gang desirous of additional possessions. But in searching for fundamental principles of distribution, one must abstract from the regime of ownership already in place. Philosophers therefore routinely invoke some vision of a state of nature where everything is up for grabs, or call upon the more familiar images of a band of travelers shipwrecked on a desert island to which none has a prior claim, or of a group of hikers chancing on a bush of berries in the wild and having to decide how the harvest should be apportioned (on the assumption that everybody likes berries). Beginning with these artificially simple cases is useful, for they capture an important truth. Although we come into the world at different times, and somebody was always there before us, we enter in the same way, without any more right to the bounty of nature than anyone else who sees daylight for the first time. It therefore seems sensible to ask how the world should be carved up among people who are equally able but equally undeserving, before considering what difference it makes if one relaxes the assumptions of equal intelligence, talents, and health, and if one abandons a static world for one in which procreation, risk-taking, and production occur.

As these hypothetical cases frame the initial distributive question, it all but answers itself. Once welfare-based theories have been excluded from consideration, and once one acknowledges that nobody possesses any congenital or acquired advantage that would translate into superior bargaining power if such advantages were permitted by a theory of justice grounded in impartiality to influence the distribution of resources, the natural answer is that everyone should receive an equally valuable share. Nobody would settle for less, because nobody else would have a right to demand more. The presumption must therefore be that people are entitled to equally valuable shares, unless some difference between them justifies a departure from equality.

In stating that everyone would insist on receiving a share at least as large as others receive, I assume, as I said in Chapter 1, that what Rawls terms the "circumstances of justice" obtain. More specifically, I assume here and throughout that people generally desire more resources and opportunities than an equal share affords them, or at least that they would ordinarily oppose any individual or collective attempt to take part of that share from them without compensation. Thus, while it is undoubtedly true at *some* level, as Harry Frankfurt says, that what matters "from the point of view of morality is not that everyone should have *the same* but that each should have *enough*,"[61] it seems sensible to assume, in delineating generally applicable principles of distributive justice, that that level has not been reached, because in any contemporary society it is unlikely to be. Contrary to Frankfurt's suggestion,[62] it appears to me that the inequalities existing between the middle class and the wealthy in the world's richer countries *do* raise significant issues of distributive justice, even if the moral imperative of assuring that the indigent have enough to survive is obviously more pressing than correcting any injustice in the holdings of the relatively well-to-do. An egalitarian need *not* suppose, as Frankfurt asserts, "that it is morally important whether one person has less than another regardless of how much either of them has."[63] Past a certain point, everyone might be so comfortable that nobody cared about remaining inequalities, and questions of justice would become aridly academic, if they were even asked. But so long as somebody protests existing inequalities—either because he wants more resources to satisfy his own desires or because he wants more so that he can aid others who desire greater wealth—questions of justice come to the fore, and an egalitarian must confront them.

The evident appropriateness of an equal division under the circumstances described raises numerous problems of application. Some I do not tackle at all; others I leave for later chapters.

The first set of problems stems from the question: what should count as resources subject to equal division? One can imagine that a group of people dividing up resources might want to place at least some of them under collective ownership. Avenues of travel, such as roads and waterways, and scarce but essential natural resources, such as a single source of drinking water or fuel, might serve as examples. I shall not advance a theory either of public goods or of collective decisionmaking here; instead, I assume that at least some, and probably the greater part, of the resources available for division would be held privately, and confine my argument to those resources that are placed in individuals' hands.

The other principal problem growing out of the question what should count as resources is ascertaining whether certain rights that could be held

---

[61] Frankfurt (1988), 134, in "Equality as a Moral Ideal."
[62] *See* Frankfurt (1988), 146–7.
[63] Frankfurt (1988), 149.

privately should be subject to redistribution in accordance with principles of justice. Under the restrictive assumptions set forth above, the group in question need not decide, for example, whether their talents and body parts (such as kidneys and corneas) are resources to be allocated on an equal basis, since all are assumed to be equally well endowed and equally healthy. But in adapting this model to real-world problems, these questions must be addressed. I postpone discussing them to Chapters 6 and 8.

The second set of problems is clustered around the question: how are the resources subject to division to be valued? The value of ownership rights depends in part upon the uses to which they may be put. If, for example, the owner of riverfront property has the right to release toxic wastes into the water, or to divert as much of the flow as he wants to irrigate his crops, without compensating those living downstream for the resultant diminution or pollution of their supply of water, then land located upstream is apt to be worth more, other things equal, than land through which water is less likely to flow freely or clearly. Similarly, if strict controls or steep taxes are placed on the emission of sulfur oxides, then the value of coal deposits can be expected to decline relative to cleaner sources of energy. Zoning likewise affects property prices by limiting the activities that may be performed within a given area. And if property-based levies to fund permissible public works vary from region to region, so too will the cost of real estate. Thus, the question what form property and tort law should take, along with the question which tax and regulatory policies not required by principles of justice a government will pursue, must be answered prior to or at least simultaneous with the question how objects of private ownership ought initially to be assigned.

The question of the nature of collective endeavors and of regulatory standards lies beyond the bounds of this book, both because its answer would depend upon the particular preferences and circumstances of a given group of people, and because the broader questions of the ideal form of government and of the moral limits to state power are too sweeping to take up here.[64] The question what principles should inform tort and property law is the focus of Part II. Assume for now (I defend these conclusions in Chapters 10 and 11) that real or personal property may be used as its owner likes, provided he does not subject others to substantial risks of injury or invade their rights to bodily integrity and the quiet enjoyment of their possessions. Anyone who violates this rule is liable for the harm he causes, and those who cause or threaten injury may ordinarily be enjoined from

---

[64] The extent to which the state must refrain from adopting rules that advance some peoples' nonbasic interests more than others' is one large and important question from which I entirely abstract. For an overview of some relevant considerations, *see* Marneffe (1990).

pursuing a harmful or potentially dangerous course of conduct. Rights to noninterference or possession may not be expropriated by those who do not own them, upon payment of their value as determined by the state, except in rare cases where the transaction costs associated with a voluntary sale would be exceedingly large and the collective benefits of arranging a forced sale outweigh potential injustices and the loss of autonomy suffered by the involuntary seller.

Another preliminary question is how resources slated for private ownership should be characterized prior to inclusion in people's equal bundles. Should land, for example, be split into tiny plots, forcing neighboring owners to work together or, if exchange is allowed, to buy adjacent blocks? Or should land be required to have multiple owners, necessitating joint decisions on its use? Or should only plots whose size makes their independent cultivation economically sensible be made available for individual distribution?

If people are to be treated as autonomous beings whose happiness and ambitions are, from the community's standpoint, their own concern, then joint ownership of land and divisible resources should not be required, because individual control is essential to ensure the liberty of each. If ownership of a given object had to be shared, then some of its owners might never be able to attract sufficient support among the others to have their way, whereas other people might acquire disproportionate control because their desires were echoed more loudly. This would be tyranny of the majority in microcosm. People are only treated as equals whose projects deserve equal regard if they are given equally valuable shares and the power to determine how those shares are used, not just a statistically equal chance of having their wishes fulfilled by being in a local majority on a particular issue. Those who enjoy or think they will profit from cooperative ventures should be free to engage in them, subject to whatever morally permissible constraints, such as antitrust laws, the community enacts. But those who prefer to strike out on their own should not be forced to throw in their lot with others if common ownership and communal decisions occupy a small place in their conception of the good life.

Of course, if people are permitted to combine their possessions for whatever purposes they choose, those whose preferences are unpopular and who are therefore unable to find associates may be consigned to a less favorable economic position than they would hold were combinations prohibited. They are, nevertheless, in a better position than if joint ownership were required and, more important, it would be an unjustifiable abridgement of individual freedom to prevent people from acting in concert so long as they do not use their economic clout to reap monopolistic profits. Just as no one may justifiably complain if the prices of those goods he desires are high in a free market in virtue of others' sharing his desires, so too he lacks a legitimate grievance if others do not have the same beliefs or preferences and his influence over how the world goes is lessened in consequence. Individual liberty encompasses the right to compete and cooperate in this way, including the right to solicit assistance or to dissuade others from banding together, so long as any morally permissible limitations (which I leave unexplored) on collective action or market dominance are not exceeded.

Similar reasons dictate that the way in which resources and rights over them are defined prior to the initial bidding should be as sensitive as possible to individuals' desires. Subject to whatever zoning regulations political morality and the configuration of people's preferences allow, those who desire a small plot of land should be able to spend only what is necessary to outbid others for that property; they should not have to buy more than they want, just because many other people want larger plots. Likewise, those who would like to buy a slice of lake frontage should be free to forgo the purchase of rights to use lake water as a source of irrigation or as a dumping ground, even though most prospective purchasers of such property would prefer the full panoply of rights. And people who would like to become co-owners of a piece of property, or of certain valuable resources or enterprises, should be allowed to combine their purchasing power, subject, as mentioned before, to any morally permissible limits the group imposes, such as antitrust laws. Only if individuals' plans are honored by maximizing their range of choice—both at the time resources are divided and over time, since the (in principle) unlimited separability of property rights gives people more scope to reassess their projects, allegiances, and preferences and to abandon some for others—are they truly treated as persons of equal worth.[65]

Assuming that everybody is entitled to an equally valuable share of resources, and that rights to them are to be characterized as finely as people desire to maximize their freedom of belief and action, how should they be divided up?

Bundles of resources are equally valuable if each of their owners would not prefer to hold someone else's bundle; in that case, nobody could protest that he was given less than anybody else. There are several ways this state might be achieved.[66] People might be given baskets of goods that

---

[65] Ronald Dworkin calls this commitment to the maximum accommodation of individuals' desires "the principle of abstraction." He endorses it "not because costs of particular resources will be either higher or lower in more abstract auctions, nor because welfare will be overall greater or more equal, but rather because the general aim of . . . equality, which is to make distribution as sensitive as possible to the choices different people make in designing their own plans and projects, is better achieved by the flexibility abstraction provides." Dworkin (1987), 28.

[66] *See* Varian (1975), 240–2; Dworkin (1981*b*), 284–7.

were exactly the same (fractional interests in indivisible resources would have to be assigned) and left to trade among themselves. Or they might be given baskets that, though not identical, were nevertheless deemed at least as good as any other basket by their several recipients, and permitted to make whatever exchanges they thought desirable. In either case, the distribution that existed once all mutually beneficial exchanges had been completed would perforce be equal and at least as good from everyone's point of view as any other equal division, assuming that everyone knew the composition of all the bundles and the price at which each person would buy or sell all the items found in the various bundles.

The same end could also be reached by holding an auction. Each person might be handed the same large number of currency units and every item not set aside for collective ownership might be put up for bidding. Each participant could demand finer divisions or property rights than the auctioneer made initially (for the sake of convenience), so long as he was prepared to pay more for the right or newly defined resource than all other bidders. In any actual auction, of course, some limit might be necessary on personal redefinition of the objects up for bidding, in order to save time and forestall confusion; but in theory the possibility of redefinition need not be constrained. Participants could also confer and coordinate their bidding, provided that their agreements did not offend any morally required or permissibly adopted constraints—for instance, rules designed to prevent monopolization of important resources. When, after however many runs of the auction were necessary, each person had spent all his cash and no one would gain from yet another auction because no one preferred someone else's bundle of resources to his own and nobody could imagine a set of bundles that could emerge from the auction that would leave him better placed than he presently was, an equal and optimal division of the available resources would have been achieved.

One central feature of these procedures is an economic market. Because the market ensures that traders will be made as well off as they could be consistent with some initial distribution of resources, given perfect information about bid and offer prices and the absence of monopsonistic and monopolistic distortions, the market is efficiency's handmaiden. Equally significant, it poses no threat to the equality of holdings. Although trades among people whose initial shares are equal might enhance their happiness to different degrees, and although they might allow some people to increase their holdings faster than if trades were prohibited and thus to bring about greater disparities in wealth or income than would otherwise arise, no one can possibly be made worse off absolutely by market exchanges, so long as the market remains competitive. Because the market facilitates improvements in people's welfare that do not come at other people's expense—except, of course, to the extent that it allows some participants to sour competitors' voluntary gambles—it can only be regarded as beneficial, not an accomplice of evil. Trade, like other voluntary cooperative enterprises, is not an affront to justice or a violation of others' rights.

Nor is the fact that some will likely be happier with their initial allotments than others ordinarily any reason for departing from an equal distribution. If someone's tastes are relatively popular, he may benefit over time from economies of scale in the production of what he wants. Equally possibly, he may have to make do with less of what he desires than if fewer people shared his preferences. Similarly, the things someone craves might be rare or difficult to obtain, whereas others find the objects of their longing in lush profusion. None of these facts is generally relevant to the choice of a distributive result or principle. That the world, including the preferences of others, is not always as one would like is simply a fact of life. It may be an instance of divine injustice, but it is usually not the product of human iniquity. After all, people commonly have the power to alter their desires and allegiances, at least to a fairly considerable degree. Those who mope about wishing for a mandarin's mansion, or who choose to cultivate a taste for caviar, cannot blame others who are easier to please or who prize things that they think of meager value. Except in the case of involuntarily induced desires of which a person disapproves, they therefore cannot justly snatch some of their fellow citizens' cash to bring them closer to their dreams.

Of course, in the hypothetical case of an island auction, this last point seems less telling, inasmuch as those who were washed ashore unawares lacked an opportunity to shape their preferences in full cognizance of the likes and dislikes of their colleagues and of the material resources that are available to satisfy or assuage them. Some were simply more fortunate in their desires than others at the time disaster struck, even if the effects of this initial bit of bad luck would taper off to insignificance over time. But while unequal fortune of this kind might furnish a reason for some inequality in the islanders' initial shares if its influence on people's relative happiness were pronounced, it would not supply a ground for unequal allotments in an ongoing society whose members could take others' preferences and the means to meet them into account when forming their tastes and personalities. It is only right that the resources people command should reflect their cost to the community in the form of production expenses and the unallayed desires of others. Justice does not favor those who pine most ardently for luxury.[67]

---

[67] One criticism of this argument runs as follows. In an ideal world, where people's desires authentically reflected what they as autonomous agents wanted, shares assigned in the manner described would indeed be just. But in the world we inhabit, people's desires are grossly distorted by unenlightened parents and educators, mass advertising, misguided

Thus, equal consideration in dividing collectively owned resources among equally healthy and able persons means putting an equally valuable bundle of goods at everyone's disposal and allowing them to consume, invest, or gamble away their holdings as they choose, consonant with respect for the rights of others. No one's preferences, whether alone or in combination with the preferences of others, may justly constrain another person's choice of goods or the exercise of his property rights, except insofar as people are willing to pay for their privileges out of their initially equal shares. Unlike welfare-based theories, moreover, equality of fortune holds that there is no necessary connection between people's desires and the size of their just allotments (except, as I mentioned briefly and shall later argue, in the case of certain pathological desires that are best viewed as unchosen afflictions). Each person is entitled to an equally valuable stock of resources, measured by people's collective preferences in the form of market prices, whatever his tastes and ambitions happen to be. Although desires are partially constitutive of a person, they are generally also within his control and thus ultimately his own responsibility. People are free to mold their desires as they choose, given their knowledge of others' preferences, the scarcity of various goods, and the size of people's holdings determined on grounds independent of their preferences. No one deserves more market power simply because his desires are legion, his passions ardent, or his tastes more or less expensive than the norm. Whether other differences among persons—their luck in voluntary undertakings, their health, their effort, their talents, or the generosity of their relatives or friends—can justify differences in market power is the subject of the rest of Part I.

popular notions of the good life, and the very structure of the system of private production and exchange. Under these circumstances, some correction must be made for these corrupting influences to achieve a just result. Inequality in the distribution of scarce resources might therefore be justified.

Since I shall not examine justifications for paternalism in this book, and since appraisal of this argument is virtually impossible in the absence of a more precise account of the "authenticity" of desires, I shall not attempt a reply. It bears noting, however, that the view that people's preferences are radically distorted in this way might have consequences that go well beyond most calls for paternalistic intervention in individuals' decisions, which point instead to an exceptional failure on somebody's part to appreciate the risks involved in a particular activity, whether because of false or insufficient information or because of an irrational discounting of temporally distant or statistically small dangers. The pursuit of "authenticity" might easily be taken to justify coercion by relying on some notion of what is objectively good for people even though they do not desire it and would not approve of it if they were fully informed and not at all shortsighted. Given the dubiousness of the claim that some lives are objectively better than others for those who live them, whatever people's preferences might be, and a general reluctance to sanction the use of force in pursuit of an end to which most people are opposed, this line of argument would have little appeal.

3

Voluntary Choices and Emergent Inequalities

In Chapter 2, I began from the assumption that theories of distributive justice must be justifiable impartially, that they must treat all conscious bearers of interests as moral subjects with legitimate, if not in all cases equal, claims on unowned resources. I then argued that egalitarian theories of justice that define equal treatment by reference to people's welfare—whether they take the form of an egalitarianism of preferences, as in the case of utilitarianism, or the equalization of happiness or assistance towards the satisfaction of desire—are flawed in conception and counter-intuitive in application. People are treated as equals, I contended, when they are given equally valuable opportunities and unowned resources, even if those shares do not leave them equally happy or do not maximize the sum of people's happiness.

My argument ended, however, with a snapshot: the equal division of resources among equally able people at a single instant in time. In actuality, however, people's shares would not stay equal for long. One way in which initially equal holdings may cease to be equal is through luck. Fortune smiles on some people's projects but frowns on others' gambles. A few wildcat drillers find oil, most strike only sand. Lucky farmers enjoy bountiful harvests while their less fortunate competitors struggle with inclement weather and ravenous insects. Some people fall ill, go blind, break bones, or die early, whereas others lead long, trouble-free lives. Does justice require the transfer of resources after initial assignments have been made to repair emergent inequalities of these kinds?

In answering this question, I shall place considerable weight on Ronald Dworkin's distinction between "option luck" and "brute luck." Option luck he defines as "a matter of how deliberate and calculated gambles turn out—whether someone gains or loses through accepting an isolated risk he or she should have anticipated and might have declined." Brute luck, by contrast, is "a matter of how risks fall out that are not in that sense deliberate gambles."[1] The distinction is therefore between, on the one hand, risks that people must ineluctably bear or that, though they could in principle have avoided running, they had no reason beforehand to associate with an activity in which they engaged, and, on the other hand,

---

[1] Dworkin (1981b), 293.

all other risks that people knowingly run or of which they should be aware. It may in practice be difficult to say how the favorable or unfavorable outcome of a given activity should be classified, although there are paradigmatic examples of both types of luck to help one pigeonhole. Discussion of some easy and hard cases follows. The general implications of the theory of equality of fortune should be sketched in advance, however, because a single principle specifies the proper response to almost all potential sources of inequality.

Abstract for now from differences in people's intelligence and reasoning ability. My principal claim is that all inequalities in holdings arising from variations in people's option luck are morally unobjectionable, provided that no one who wanted to run the risks associated with such luck lacked an opportunity to do so. But all inequalities resulting from variable brute luck ought to be eliminated, except to the extent that a victim of bad brute luck waived or waives his right to compensation, or someone who enjoyed good brute luck is or was allowed to retain the benefits he received by those who have or would have had a claim to some part of them; and provided, further, that those who suffered bad brute luck would profit significantly at the margin from transfers designed to restore equality by comparison with the marginal cost to those providing compensation, and that any compensation paid is not excessively burdensome.

The basic rationale for adopting this principle is simple. People come into the world equally undeserving. Because no one has a greater claim to the earth or what lies on or beneath it than anyone else, all are entitled to equal shares. In actuality, of course, people enter the world at different times, and parents often desire to bestow some sizable but unequal portion of what we can assume are their just but unequal earnings on their offspring, even though children have no right to more than a certain share of their parents' wealth.[2] For now, however, suppose that all are born contemporaries and all are born adults. It is only just that each receive an equally valuable lot of resources, measured by the group's collective preferences, for people must assume responsibility for their likes and aversions and only thus can no one complain that he received less than his neighbor. And since exchange benefits those who find it advantageous without destroying equality of holdings in the foregoing sense, a market in goods may justifiably flourish as well, provided that all may trade on an equal footing and all have the same opportunity to engage in the panoply of economic activity. Inequalities stemming from people's choice of different jobs are similarly just, for except perhaps in extremely rare

---

[2] Chapter 7 considers the difficulties these facts present and the theoretical complications they necessitate.

instances, if people's endowments are similar[3] they must take credit or blame for their decisions and the unequal material rewards that trail them. Only if some avail themselves of opportunities that others lack, whether because markets fail to function perfectly or because information is not equally available to all, do those who are disadvantaged have a claim to relief.

Luck warrants parallel treatment. If an opportunity to risk one's time, energy, or resources is open to everyone, then those who seize it need not share their gains with those who are less adventurous. But neither may they demand assistance if fortune treats them roughly. As when bidding for goods at an original auction or choosing an occupation, people cannot escape responsibility for the preferences they exhibit and cannot complain if others' preferences lead them to choose goods, or types of work, or more or less risky activities that leave them more or less comfortably situated. Just as somebody cannot object to others' living more leisurely if he could have such an existence with its special joys and material costs should he so choose, so he cannot object if someone profits from a gamble he might have taken but did not. Nor can he complain if others adopt a cautious course and show him no sympathy when he tries his luck and loses. In such cases, justice demands that jackpots and empty purses fall where they may, for only in this way will it remain true that nobody prefers anyone else's bundle of resources and labor *and voluntary gambles* to his own.

But while differential option luck cannot vindicate redistributive taxation, unequal brute luck typically generates a right to recompense unless the unlucky waived their claims in advance. For the essence of the theory of equality of fortune is the imperative that people's shares be kept equal, insofar as that is humanly possible and not excessively costly, except to the extent that their voluntary actions give rise to inequalities; only by eliminating unsolicited good and bad fortune from the forces shaping people's holdings can true equality of station be attained, and the distribution of resources be made acceptable to a community of persons who regard one another as moral equals. No one should have fewer resources than his peers with which to make his way in the world or to enjoy himself therein except by choice.

Of course, past decisions may affect the amount of compensation someone deserves in virtue of his bad brute luck. To the extent that people increase their chances of contracting a certain disease through their voluntary actions, as smokers court cancer, they reduce the compensation to which they are entitled. And they may choose to waive their right to

---

[3] Chapters 5 and 6 discuss the propriety of redress for inequalities traceable to unequal effort and dissimilar capacities.

compensation—to decline what is tantamount to universal insurance coverage—if they fancy taking chances and if others agree to release them from their obligation to assist those whose brute luck is bad.[4] Independent moral principles, such as a rule exempting people from making substantial sacrifices to benefit others in some barely noticeable way, also militate against the unqualified pursuit of equality, while limitations on human ingenuity might render equality unattainable. The core idea is clear, however. Undeserved, unwagered, unchosen inequalities warrant redress. Whenever the inequitable effects of brute luck can be cancelled, they ought to be, assuming that people have not chosen to gamble on their good fortune and paternalistic legislation has not rendered their choice ineffective.

I shall elaborate and reinforce this justification for the differential treatment of brute and option luck when I consider examples of both. First, however, one sweeping objection to this entire enterprise should be dismissed. No tenable distinction between brute and option luck can be drawn, one might argue, because both kinds of chance event are equally inevitable. Far from referring to anything real or morally significant, luck is an epistemic concept, a word we attach to events that we are as yet unable to predict but that, in our fully determined universe, we might have anticipated had we possessed greater knowledge.[5] It signifies nothing more than our ignorance. But if our present ignorance of "brute" future events supplies a moral reason to mend resultant inequalities, should not our equal ignorance before the fact of future occurrences constituting option luck release us from the duty to annul whatever inequalities it causes? Both types of event are equally certain, the ensuing disparities equally real. Consistency demands that equality be maintained throughout or not at all.

The problem with this objection is that one of its assumptions fatally undermines its conclusion. It assumes that, although all events are inevitable, we can avoid certain outcomes if we so choose and that we deserve moral censure if we choose wrongly, for it assumes that it is up to us to decide whether to ensure that people's possessions remain equal, despite the fact that determinism is true. But while these assumptions are perfectly reasonable if one holds a compatibilist account of free will,[6] and

---

[4] There may be sound paternalistic reasons for not allowing people to dispense with health and accident insurance altogether. This book does not, however, explore the limits of paternalistic intervention. Nor shall I say anything about the extent to which people can be required to buy health or disability insurance to prevent them from becoming public charges, whose basic needs our sympathies would press us to meet.

[5] Quantum indeterminacy may make certain events unpredictable in principle. But unless people choose to allow some of their actions to be governed by the clicks of a Geiger counter, quantum indeterminacy is unlikely to make prediction impossible except at the subatomic level.

[6] For a careful discussion of the meanings of "avoid," "avoidable," and "inevitable" in defense of a compatibilist account of moral desert, *see* Dennett (1984), 123–30. *See also* Bennett (1980).

while common sense supports them, they can hardly be squared with the claim that we ought not to hold people responsible for their decisions to expose themselves to risks that they need not have faced or to forgo insurance against risks that they cannot help but run. If the choice of principles of distributive justice is subject to moral appraisal, then so are choices such as these. And if it is possible to avoid certain outcomes or actions but not others while in the grip of an inexorable causal process, there exists some basis for distinguishing risks that people assume voluntarily from risks they must bear willy-nilly. The foregoing objection therefore fails. If moral discourse has any sense at all, the distinction between brute and option luck is firm.

The question, then, is how familiar events giving rise to inequalities should be classified. The remainder of this chapter discusses representative cases of option luck; the next three chapters are devoted to various types of brute luck, including the unequal distribution of talents and physical abilities.

3.1. OPEN LOTTERIES

The purest example of the effects of option luck on people's holdings is the redistribution that results from a well-publicized national lottery. Participation is voluntary and open to all, so equality of opportunity obtains. People purchase tickets or refrain from buying them as they choose, cognizant of their odds of walking away a tycoon. Their preferences and some designated random event alone determine the outcome. Surely the holder of the lucky ticket has no duty to share his winnings with those who sat on the sidelines or who laid down their money and lost. Nor would they be bound to ease his sorrow had fortune proved fickle. Winners and losers elected beforehand to lead lives with a certain element of risk and must accept the consequences. Gambling poses no threat to a just distribution of goods, so long as equality of resources prevails and all have an equal chance to wager.[7]

In practice, of course, few games of chance are organized on a national scale. But insofar as the burdens on participation do not differ markedly from region to region owing to local regulation or proscription, overall equality of opportunity to gamble exists, at least in the approximate form that must suffice when principles of distributive justice are applied to the actual circumstances of social life. In a just state where a roughly equal chance to wager exists, those who benefit from fairly run betting schemes that are not prohibited on paternalistic grounds ought not to be taxed.

---

[7] Once again, I ignore the possibility that there exist persuasive reasons for imposing paternalistic constraints on gambling, though not for its complete prohibition.

Whether that conclusion holds good for our society, where opportunities to gamble differ and the distribution of resources is strikingly unjust, is another question. Assuming that a comprehensive restructuring of current holdings is a pipe dream, one might want to adapt the preceding conclusion by allowing all those whose pre-wager income or wealth is below a certain figure to buy tickets at a certain price and to retain all of their winnings, while taxing those who are financially better situated. The latter could all be taxed when they cast their bets, by charging them more for their tickets, or only those who won might be taxed on their winnings. The rationale in both cases would be that the affluent are able to risk their money more easily than they ought and that they should therefore have to contribute to a common fund an amount proportional to the injustice associated with their holdings prior to the lucky draw. The first proposal would collect that amount equally from all affluent gamblers, whereas the second would single out those whose bets paid off.

Both proposals, however, are open to objection (though probably not decisive objection). One problem is that neither taxes all persons who possess unjustly large holdings: only those who wager, or those who wager and win, would be taxed. Another problem is that the injustice associated with any person's current holdings is extremely difficult to measure. A more serious failing is that some of those who are unjustly rich and who win at games of chance would have participated to precisely the same extent had their holdings been more modest. If this counterfactual test is met—and it would in practice be impossible to determine whether it is— then it seems unjust to tax the lucky rich who fall into this group more than the lucky poor. Reliance on statistical probabilities in setting tax rates under either proposal would therefore inevitably result in numerous instances of injustice—which is not to say that the injustice of *not* correcting for unequal opportunities in rough fashion would be less.

In adapting the foregoing conclusion to our imperfect world, one might advance an even stronger argument. One might contend that *all* who win large sums should have to share them with people whose slice of the national income or national wealth is more meager than it ought ideally to be, for such a policy would move that society closer to a globally more just distribution of resources. One difficulty with this proposal, however, is that it seems arbitrary to single out lottery winners to assist redistributive plans that should have wider participation. Why not impose a steeper tax on *all* of the wealthy or high earners instead, however they came to occupy their advantageous position? That alternative would undoubtedly be more just, even if it failed to level certain peaks of wealth as effectively (although there is no reason why the tax could not be graduated to achieve identical effects in the case of lottery winners who are suddenly very rich). Of course, this alternative proposal would also be more difficult politically to enact, prompting the question whether the first proposal should be adopted if the second cannot be realized. But I shall not pursue the choice of policies in an imperfectly just state any further. My principal aim is to outline the just ideal, not to settle the best way to apply its implications piecemeal to a society unlikely to accept its full realization.

3.2. DANGEROUS ACTIVITIES

Other exemplary instances of option luck are the injuries suffered by those who engage in dangerous occupations or recreational activities. People who leap from airplanes, scale cliffs, or whirl around racetracks knowingly take their lives in their own hands and cannot expect others to foot their hospital bills or aid their dependents if fortune is uncharitable. Not everyone may have the opportunity to experience the thrills that come from perilous adventures because their nominal cost is sometimes high and there are more poor among us than a just state would allow. But while this affords a legitimate complaint to those who are unfairly denied the chance to expose themselves to fashionable dangers, the absence of equal opportunity by no means justifies an insurance subsidy for daredevils. If anything, the reverse is true, at least for those who are better off financially than they have any right to be. Those who participate in such activities might be viewed as entering a lottery whose price and potential payoffs are largely intangible, though no less real on that account.

3.3. NATURAL DISASTERS

Option luck also predominates in the case of property loss from natural disaster. To some extent, at least some minimal risk of destruction from lightning, rain, or other natural scourges is in most countries inevitable, although the magnitude of the residual risk obviously varies. If a citizen of a large and geographically diverse nation like the United States builds his home in a floodplain, or near the San Andreas fault, or in the heart of tornado country, then the risk of flood, earthquake, or crushing winds is one he chooses to bear, since those risks could be all but eliminated by living elsewhere. But not everyone possesses the same range of choice. If the inhabitants of a tiny island from which they cannot emigrate are lashed by a typhoon or have their dwellings swept away by a tidal wave, then all may be said to be victims of bad brute luck, since none of them chose to reside on that exposed bit of rock and the onslaught could not have been averted through individual or collective effort. (Even here, however, option luck might enter to some degree. For the dangers of tropical storms are well known, and no one need build on the windward rather than the leeward side of the island, using flimsy rather than stout material, on an unprotected plateau rather than beneath a sheltering ridge. Although complete safety might be impossible to obtain, the risks people face can frequently be aggravated or mitigated by the decisions they take.)

Regardless of the extent to which the threat of natural disaster is unavoidable, equality of fortune decrees the same result. As an initial matter, any losses resulting from whatever risk was a necessary concomitant to the ownership of property essential to live a moderately satisfying life in a given society would, as instances of bad brute luck, be fully compensable, assuming that assistance would not place too great a strain on the others.[8] (If an ascetic put less at risk than the baseline amount, then he would owe less compensation to others if their homes took the brunt of a storm than most of his fellow citizens owed, since by holding property whose value multiplied by its risk of destruction was less than the baseline amount, he would have reduced their probable liability to him.) All other losses, as instances of nasty option luck, would be borne solely by the owner, who might or might not have insured against such hazards.

There is no reason to stop with this initial result, however, and ample reason not to do so. With respect to brute luck below the baseline amount, what equality of fortune establishes is nothing more than a universal insurance scheme. But if a society is sufficiently advanced economically to make private insurance available, the state need not administer a single, centralized insurance program. Indeed, leaving the provision of insurance to a competitive market would almost surely lead to more efficient coverage and greater consumer satisfaction. Thus, so long as no one is denied the opportunity to purchase insurance against bad brute luck at or below the amount that justice initially requires,[9] equality of fortune applauds the privatization of insurance or, less enthusiastically, a similar diversification of plans offered by a state insurer. Whether paternalistic

---

[8] This proviso might come into play if a desperately poor island society were devastated by a volcano, earthquake, or storm, leaving survivors with inadequate resources to help any but themselves.

One might object that there is no baseline below which property losses should be deemed bad brute luck, because people could, after all, rent rather than own lodgings, furniture, means of transportation, and so on, and consume virtually all of the remaining resources they come to possess. This objection, however, is only compelling in certain circumstances. If it were in fact possible for people to rent rather than buy real property and household goods, and to place the risk of loss on the lessor instead of assuming it themselves, then the need for a baseline would evaporate, and all investment decisions of this kind would indeed fall under the banner of option luck. But one can imagine instances where this condition does not hold. Consider the case just mentioned, where a typhoon buffets an island cut off from the rest of the world and no one owns, and therefore cannot lease, substantially more property than he needs to survive. Property loss might there still be an example of bad brute luck, even if it could not be regarded as such in a large and economically advanced nation.

[9] Some extraordinarily rare misfortunes—the eruption of a volcano believed to be extinct, which destroys nearby homes and property, or a large meteorite's striking the earth with disastrous consequences—might be so unlikely as not to be covered by any insurance policy. In such cases, justice might still require collective compensation of the victims.

legislation mandating purchase of a minimum amount of insurance would be justified or wise is, of course, a separate question.

3.4. BUSINESS LOSSES

Much the same approach should be adopted with respect to entrepreneurial failures. Just as everyone needs shelter from the elements and basic supplies that might be destroyed by nature's fury, so people need to engage in productive activities if they are to survive at all commodiously, and these activities are necessarily subject to certain risks. Drought, hail, torrents, and insects may flatten crops, fish may cease to swim or domesticated animals fall sick, factories may catch fire or fresh discoveries may make products obsolete. To the extent these risks should be regarded as inevitable rather than deliberately incurred, their eventuation is a matter of bad brute luck rather than poor option luck.

Except in a subsistence economy, however, in practice no distinction between option and brute luck need be drawn and no baseline level of business risk need be established. One may simply leave insurance against business failure to the market, assuming that a brisk trade in insurance exists, as it does in advanced capitalist countries. Competition should minimize costs, and everyone could have as much or as little coverage as he desired. Society need not bear the informational and administrative costs of determining who the unfortunate are, taxing the lucky, and doling out reimbursements. Nor would universal participation, at the expense of personal autonomy, be desirable. Entrepreneurs would have to purchase their own safety nets, or risk a hard fall.

3.5. UNEMPLOYMENT

One important exception to this free-market approach might be necessary in the case of unemployment insurance. Of course, in a world where people's innate capabilities are unequal and where this affects their chances of finding work or establishing a thriving business, there are special reasons for not leaving unemployment insurance to the market. Those who stand the least chance of finding a job because of their bad brute luck in the distribution of talents would face the steepest schedule of rates, which is demonstrably unjust. I shall return to this problem in Chapter 6. But even if everyone were equally talented or if people's inherent abilities differed but insurance companies were required to offer the same rates to all, there might still be reasons for market intervention.

Those reasons have nothing to do with the injustice of a competitive insurance market, provided that insurance is available to all on identical terms and that policies provide for relief (perhaps, after a point, in exchange for some labor) as long as someone is genuinely unable to find work through no fault of his own. There is no injustice in requiring someone whose chances of being without work are very high as a result of his deliberate choice of a particular occupation to pay higher rates, unless perhaps that choice was made at an immature age, in ignorance of the realities of the marketplace and even in part of his own desires. In fact, it would be unjust to force insurance companies or a state insurer to charge everyone the same rates and thus to compel some people to subsidize others' choice of a particularly precarious line of work, just as it would be unjust to compel those who work at socially valuable tasks to support people who persist in passing their days before a television set or indulging in pursuits that profit no one but themselves. Likewise, there can be no objection to those who desire more protection against loss of a job buying additional insurance.

Nevertheless, even a suitably constrained free market in insurance might be thought unsatisfactory on two counts. First, those entering the labor market for the first time typically have the greatest need for unemployment insurance, yet they are usually also the ones least able to afford it. Second, if individual decisions completely determined the distribution of insurance coverage, some people would doubtless buy no insurance at all and, when unemployed, trust to the charity of their more fortunate or more responsible fellows. Such people might well become public charges.

Whether the first problem warrants government intervention seems doubtful. In a free insurance market, insurers should be willing to lower the rates charged to young adults if they lack the resources to pay normal rates, in exchange for a contractual commitment to pay a higher amount in the future to offset the earlier discount and to compensate them for the lost time—value of the deferred payments. Market inefficiencies might in practice generate a need for state participation, if only to act as an insurer of last resort. But there is no theoretical reason why the government should, as a matter of justice, monopolize or dominate the unemployment insurance market for young adults if they are given the allotments Chapter 7 prescribes, and certainly no reason why it should subsidize them.

The problem posed by people who shortsightedly refused to buy insurance could be solved by mandating minimum insurance purchases, either because a persuasive theory of paternalism would justify mandatory insurance—an issue on which I take no stand—or because of the crime and social strife caused by the indigent unemployed, or because of the injustice of compelling the prudent to support those who recklessly or uncaringly made no provision for their own welfare. In principle, there are therefore no obstacles to private unemployment insurance (with the aforementioned restrictions) in a world where all are equally talented.

3.6. GOOD BRUTE LUCK IN BUSINESS AND FINANCE

The fact that bad brute luck in commercial undertakings generates no redistributive rights when private insurance is available does not imply that justice is silent when *good* brute luck blesses entrepreneurial ventures or other investments. To be sure, to the extent that success crowns the implementation of a new marketing strategy or investment diversification, profits ordinarily need not be shared with struggling competitors or mere onlookers, assuming, as we have to this point, that people have the same capacity to prosper in these ways. Option luck is alone responsible. If people choose to ply the waters of commerce rather than to avail themselves of less risky alternatives, or to enter one race for riches in preference to others, then the rewards are theirs as much as the disappointments.

In actuality, of course, some livelihoods demand greater ability than others. The larger this element looms in success, and the more unequal are people's abilities, the more that brute luck explains differences in profits and the more that unusually high returns are subject to redistribution. In actuality, too, the timing of births and deaths affects success or failure to an extent that it does not influence people's opportunities to enter lotteries, and may conceivably ground some claim to reapportion the fruits of fortune. (Those claims, of course, will usually be relatively weak, since opportunities for profit almost always exist and the nature of competition is common knowledge.) But if one abstracts from these differences, important though the first may be, it seems fairly clear that most financial and commercial success, to the extent that it does not result directly from simple effort or labor or from some invention or discovery, ought to be ascribed predominantly to option luck rather than to brute luck. Although an ample amount of chance is involved in determining who emerges on top, the greater part of it consists of risks knowingly incurred, of opportunities seized, of gambles taken and hunches tested. Considerable luck is involved in introducing a new product or adopting one form of advertising rather than another, but those who enter the lists know the rules and elect to try their fortune rather than pool their efforts, rewards, and failures with some of their competitors. And while not everyone has precisely the same openings or information, what differences exist seem best attributed to diligence, perseverance, or a certain amount of randomness in the determination of success that those involved consciously accept. Manufacturers of consumer products are cognizant of the public's whims and can choose to play for high stakes in the world of fashion, or to set a more cautious course by making durable products with regard to which people's preferences are less flighty. If those who hold the lucky lottery tickets cannot justly be shorn of their winnings, then, apart from the considerations mentioned above (namely, unequal talents, inventions or discoveries that were not the outcome of some deliberate design, and such usually minor factors as date and place of birth or luck in one's friends), those who succeed in business should not be stripped of their spoils. Since approximate equality of opportunity existed and since all of the actors consciously assumed the risks inseparable from economic competition, disparities in earnings do not manifest injustice. They reflect unequal luck in a game that combines chance, effort, and innate skill. The last of these factors is, to be sure, a reason for compelling the successful to share their profits with those who are at a disadvantage on that count. But where option luck alone is involved, it would be unjust to tax the thriving.[10]

Nevertheless, the profits flowing from certain types of business ventures and some increases in the value of people's holdings must be ascribed, at least in part, to good *brute* luck. In particular, two sources of revenue— profitable discoveries and inventions—merit separate discussion. I shall take a profitable *discovery* to be the initial location of something deemed valuable at the time of its location; a profitable *invention* is an original idea that permits existing resources to be employed more usefully than was formerly possible.

A. Profitable Discoveries

Discoveries are scattered along a spectrum of brute luck. At one extreme, a girl strolling by the sea may happen on a pearl, or a landholder, clearing a plot that was thought good for nothing but farming, might strike a valuable mineral deposit. At the other extreme, a large petroleum company might find oil beneath the seabed after a careful survey, complex calculations of the likelihood of profitable drilling, and a lengthy search. Or a farmer and his pig might return with the usual sack of truffles after a morning in the woods. Between these extremes lie a host of cases. A lone

---

[10] Returns on financial investments that do not ordinarily reflect special skill on the part of investors, such as bank savings accounts and many mutual funds and shares of pooled investments, should therefore go untaxed. In fact, this rule should perhaps be extended to all financial investments, because investors can buy advice if they themselves are not financial mavens and because line-drawing might well be impracticable. This rule would have the additional advantage of eliminating the bias in favor of current consumption that typically results from an accretion-type personal income tax. *See* Andrews (1974) and (1975); Warren (1975). By allowing people's undistorted preferences alone to determine whether to defer consumption, this rule would ensure neutrality with regard to people's conceptions of a desirable life and presumably induce faster rates of economic growth.

I shall not address the question whether a tax on business combinations, such as corporations or partnerships, could be justified. My tentative view is that complete integration of personal and entity income taxes would probably be desirable from the standpoint of justice, because there seems no reason why businessmen who band together should carry a heavier tax burden than entrepreneurs who do not incorporate or form partnerships, and because such a tax appears an unjust fee for limited liability, which could always be secured by contract.

prospector might strike a thick vein of gold after a fortnight's labor, after having shouldered his pick and shovel without accurate information of the chances of success. Or a little haphazard research might reveal that a lithograph purchased long ago is exceedingly valuable. Brute luck may thus play a prominent, middling, or minor role in a fortunate discovery.

The import of its presence is plain. How much the unexpectedly wealthy must share with the rest evidently depends upon the extent to which what they discovered or the way in which the value of their property changed was a foreseeable result and motivating factor of the type of activity in which they were engaged when they discovered or purchased it. People might disagree, of course, over how that extent should be measured and hence over the way in which the percentages should be split between brute and option luck in a particular case. But the correctness of the standard seems uncontrovertible. Someone who stumbles on unowned treasure through pure serendipity merely adds to the stock of goods that ought to be divided equally, supplementing the auction that has already transpired. By contrast, a discovery preceded by a careful and deliberate quest, in full awareness of the odds of success, approaches the paradigm of good option luck. Cases that lie in between yield more or less powerful obligations to share.

The intermediate cases force hard judgments. For example, does the fact that everyone knows that the earth may contain metals and minerals that do or might in time attract high prices entail that some option luck is necessarily in play when the ground someone owns yields an unanticipated bounty? If so, how much? At what point do the probabilities of a payoff become too indefinite or the prospects of some particular mode of enrichment too paltry to give any scope at all to option luck? Persuasive argument on behalf of particular proposals is made more difficult by the fact that the concepts with which one has to work are broad and that analogies to cases in which our intuitions possess greater certainty are lacking. No doubt those who set about searching for undiscovered emeralds or oil should be guaranteed a reasonable return if their efforts are successful, at least if their search was economically sensible. But few claims are equally uncontroversial. Those who chance on valuable resources need not be granted a sizable share of their value to encourage their exploitation. Because it would often be hard, however, to distinguish cases of accidental discovery from cases with a larger component of option luck, people would take pains to make the first look like the second if the rates varied widely. The appropriateness of various tax plans would naturally depend on their efficacy and a careful consideration of the respective roles of brute and option luck in a given class of cases. In most instances of discovery and land speculation, the balance appears to tilt in favor of option luck, implying limited redistribution of the gains. But the details of redistributive policies could only be settled through careful consideration of concrete cases.

B. Profitable Inventions

Inventions invite a similar solution. By "inventions" I mean, once again, novel ways of combining or using existing resources, including what is often termed the "discovery" of therapeutic treatments or drugs. As in the case of discoveries, inventions range between two poles. At one end are those that climax a directed process of thought or attempts to solve a particular problem. At the other are novel ideas that enter a person's head unheralded, with little or no effort or reflection. Not surprisingly, the distributive principle applied to discoveries seems equally apposite here. The more time, effort, and money consumed in chasing an invention, the more probable that it should be ascribed to option luck rather than brute luck. An unexpected flash of insight without struggle or forethought (though such flashes seem rare) appears much more like manna from heaven than the lucky outcome of a lottery in which people willingly joined. Conversely, an invention that caps a long series of experiments seems more like a wager won. In the case of inventions, however, even those preceded by years of patient toil, the analogy to games of chance is less convincing than in the case of many discoveries, since differences in people's innate abilities and in unchosen aspects of their personal histories, such as their upbringing and early education, play a far more salient part in determining who builds a better computer or who develops a miracle drug than in singling out the lucky explorer or fortunate miner. But if one abstracts from such differences, as we have to this point, then the preceding distinction seems sound. The proper treatment of financial gains flowing from a particular invention should depend on the extent to which the idea came unbidden, bearing in mind that brute luck often influences when people begin the search for an invention or set out to discover something valuable, and that therefore a residual element of brute luck might be present.

As with discoveries, distinctions based on this criterion would be enormously difficult to translate into feasible policies, since those who lighted on a lucrative idea might find it in their self-interest to inaugurate sham research projects if they could lessen their tax liability by unfurling their invention at the conclusion of an apparently arduous investigation. Some injustices would therefore be inevitable by-products of workable policies. Similarly, it would be hard to distinguish in practice between those whose resources escalated in value as a result of some invention they never anticipated, such as an owner of bauxite deposits who was shocked to learn that a profitable process for transforming bauxite into aluminum had been devised, and those who purchased potentially valuable resources for speculative ends. In light of the role undeserved talents and personal characteristics assume in the generation of actual inventions, in order to forestall wasteful research conducted solely for appearances' sake, and in order to encourage the introduction of new ideas, the best course might be to treat inventions more as instances of brute luck than of option luck, and to guarantee inventors a fair return on their inventions while denying them exorbitant profits. Perhaps combining patents with an excess profits tax would do the trick.[11] Owners of resources that increased suddenly in value might also be taxed at higher rates, whether immediately or upon realization of their gains, although distinguishing between speculators and the purely fortunate might be impossible. But whatever the best practical solution to the problem, the proper framework for considering proposals seems plain in outline.

[11] The theory of equality of fortune might therefore be seen as supplying what most justifications of patent law lack: a powerful moral reason for limiting someone's right to exploit his ideas financially to the fullest extent possible. Limits on the durations of patents are usually justified by reference to the collective benefits of denying somebody exclusive rights to an idea after a period of time, together with the likelihood that someone else would have chanced on the same idea eventually. Patents themselves are ordinarily vindicated by pointing to the incentive to research and investment they provide, and thus ultimately to the public benefits they supply. What this common account lacks is an explanation of why the right to the exclusive use of an idea vests initially in the community rather than in its originator, or why, if the latter is thought to have that right, his right can be overridden by the financial interests of other people, even where their most crucial concerns are not at stake (as when a cure is found for some terrible disease). The explanation advanced above is that everyone has a right to share in another's good brute luck, which is tantamount to an addition to the stock of resources available for collective distribution, and that brute luck may enter with respect to the time when people are born and begin research, the acquaintances they make, the innate abilities they possess, the upbringing and education they receive, and whatever else influences the formation of novel ideas. Patents themselves may be justified by the degree to which option luck is present and by the need for an incentive, to which collective assent could be presumed, to seek and to introduce valuable new ideas into the stream of commerce. Similar arguments may be made with regard to copyrights.

I do not wish to claim that patents may not be justified in other ways. One might, for example, defend expropriation of the gains in excess of a fairly high rate of return that someone derives from an invention, however much option luck may seem to dominate brute luck in its genesis, on the grounds that the inventor's education, character, research opportunities, and the like are all social products and that he has an obligation to the community in virtue of all that he has received from past and present fellow citizens. Or one might attempt to justify restrictions on the amount someone may earn from certain therapeutic discoveries by appealing to the dire need of those who might benefit from treatment by comparison with his own interest in personal affluence. When the balance is so uneven, it might be said, a moral duty to muzzle greed arises. My aim is not to defend or refute these suggestions, but only to argue that the foregoing justification for patents should be added to the list of valid ones.

4

Ineluctable Risks: Illness
and Injury

OPTION luck, whether alone or in partnership with brute luck, exerts an overwhelming influence on the distribution of resources. From business to blackjack, from parachuting to mining, from decisions to insure against drought to attempts to develop a cure for AIDS, option luck affects the size of people's holdings and their ability to cope with calamity. But brute luck is often the more important arbiter of people's material and psychological well-being. Unfortunately, eliminating the inequities it breeds would frequently be a trying and sometimes an impossible task. In this chapter I take up the problems posed by bad brute luck in some of its most prominent guises—illness and injury—before turning in the next two chapters to inequalities attributable to people's differential effort and unequal capacities.

4.1. NORMAL ADULTS

Consider the position of normal adults who contract debilitating diseases or who are injured in accidents for which no one was responsible and which occurred in the course of an activity that almost everyone performs. To the extent that they did not increase the probability of their falling prey to a particular disease or being injured in some way by behaving in a manner known to worsen people's odds of experiencing such setbacks, they have unquestionably suffered bad brute luck. Acting blamelessly, they have been made less well off than their peers, not only financially, insofar as their condition diminishes their capacity for remunerative activity, but also experientially, to the extent that they have been deprived of some of the standard means and preconditions (e.g. well-functioning organs and limbs, freedom from pain and abnormally intense anxiety, a given span of years) for leading a fulfilling life. Justice therefore requires that they be made whole to the greatest extent attainable at the expense of those who have been spared similar misfortunes.

How much sacrifice can be demanded of those not crippled by bad brute luck? And what types of illnesses and accidents afford a right to compensation? These questions will have to be addressed presently, in connection with reverses suffered by minors. But they need not be answered in the case of normal adults. The ideal of equality of fortune declares, to be sure, that people are entitled to a certain quantum of compensation if their brute luck is bad and if additional material resources can substantially better their lot, and that they are liable to provide a certain level of assistance if their brute luck is comparatively good and they are able to ameliorate the plight of people who fare less well. But it does not abrogate personal autonomy. Rather, it leaves people free to settle for less compensation if they so desire and, if many others share their wish or otherwise grant them permission, to make lower compensation payments in return. Such permission would certainly be forthcoming if the relevant population were large or some individual or enterprise were willing to sell insurance against misfortune, for those who desired more protection could easily form their own insurance group and be none the worse if those who did not wish to join were not constrained to do so. Hence, justice would be equally well served by allowing a competitive insurance market to flourish, as was true of other types of bad brute luck discussed above. So long as people had an equal opportunity and the rational capacity to devote some portion of their personal holdings to measures designed to allay possible misfortunes, they could not later complain, if they neglected to look ahead, that they were treated unjustly if equality were not restored once the lightning had struck.[1]

However, one significant qualification must be made to the claim that a free market in insurance would provide just compensation, the problem of paternalism apart. The market would admirably provide for those who willingly endangered their lives or livelihoods through their choice of occupations, habits, or recreational activities. Those who smoked or ate too much would rightly have to pay more for certain types of health insurance; those who kept trim and avoided perilous workplaces would of course have to pay less. But a competitive firm would also charge higher rates to people who, because of their genes, congenital injury, or some other misfortune for which no one was to blame, were disposed to contract a certain disease or to suffer some disability that steals years of life or requires costly treatment. This result, however, would be unjust, for it would penalize people for their earlier bad brute luck. It might therefore seem necessary to insist that firms offer the same rates to all for life, health, and accident insurance, except insofar as someone voluntarily acquired an above-average susceptibility to some illness or disability or ran unusual risks. With this condition in place, the market would once again be a reliable servant of justice.

[1] I ignore, once again, the possibility that mandatory insurance purchases might be justified paternalistically when people do not fully appreciate the risks they run by not insuring, or neglect to give proper attention to the desires and feelings they will have if misfortune befalls them and they are not entitled to insurance premiums.

The fatal shortcoming of this requirement, however, is that it would unfairly place some insurance firms at a competitive disadvantage if, as might well happen, those who faced abnormally high risks due to their prior bad brute luck were not spread proportionately among insurance firms. There is no reason why participants in one or another insurance scheme should have to subsidize those who suffer bad brute luck to a greater extent than others do. Indeed, to the extent that the most alluring insurance policies attracted those forced to run unusually high risks through no fault of their own, the foregoing requirement would tend to push the most efficient insurers out of business, which would redound to the detriment of consumers generally.

There are several possible solutions to this problem, none of which is perfect.

1. First, insurers might be permitted to turn away applicants who belonged to the group of persons who were involuntarily more likely to suffer disease or injury once their proportionate quota of such persons had been met. The major difficulty this proposal poses is that of determining insurance risks and quotas in a fluid market and of monitoring firms to make sure that they heeded their obligation. Another flaw is that if insurance firms only had to take a certain number of applicants from the blameless high-risk group, and if firms did not offer equally attractive insurance policies, then some members of the high-risk group would be consigned to purchase more costly or otherwise less desirable insurance than other members of that group because the better firms would not accommodate them all. That result would be unjust. Finally, this proposal would not require everyone to contribute equally to erase the disadvantages borne by those in the high-risk group through no fault of their own; instead, it would burden nonmembers only if they chose to insure, and then probably according to the amount of insurance they purchased. Thus, this proposal would likely occasion still more injustice.

2. A second possibility would be to offer a tax credit to all members of the high-risk group equal to whatever additional amount they had to pay for insurance as a consequence of their bad brute luck. This option would eliminate the unjust treatment of disadvantaged insurance purchasers characteristic of the first proposal if the cost of the tax subsidy were apportioned equally. It would also be free from the administrative costs associated with fixing risk quotas for a large number of insurance firms and monitoring their compliance. Its chief drawback is that it would encourage insurers to raise the additional amount they charged members of the high-risk group who qualified for tax credits above the insurers' costs, and perhaps to use the proceeds from that inflated risk-premium to subsidize other insurance offerings. Moreover, members of the high-risk group would have no incentive to shop for the most cost-effective risk-premium,

since they would know that they would be reimbursed whatever amount they paid when their taxes came due.

Either or both of these failings might be corrected, albeit imperfectly. Cross-subsidization by insurers could be mitigated by government inspection of the informational and statistical bases for the risk-premiums they charged, or by government calculation of appropriate risk-premiums and corresponding limitations on tax credits. And incentives to economize could be supplied to insurance purchasers in at least three ways. First, tax credits could be given that varied in amount, depending upon the risks to which someone was involuntarily subject, and that equalled the risk-premium someone actually paid, but only up to a certain amount, thereby creating an incentive to find insurance companies whose risk-premiums did not exceed the limit. Alternatively, those who by chance fell in the high-risk group might be given a fixed tax credit set by the government, its amount dependent upon the extra risks they bore, and be allowed to select their own insurers. Unlike the first proposal, this option would allow those who found insurers who charged less than the credit to pocket the difference. They would therefore have a stronger incentive to hunt around for insurance, and insurance companies would have an incentive to compete in the risk-premiums they offered. Such a system would, however, afford members of the high-risk group a larger subsidy than they deserved, to the extent that the credit that they received exceeded the amount they actually paid for their risk-premium. Third, income tax deductions (assuming a marginal rate below 100%) could be substituted for tax credits, or credits themselves could be made partial, thus introducing an element of coinsurance and generating an incentive to buy insurance from companies whose risk-premiums were priced more reasonably than those of their competitors. The force of that incentive would vary directly with an individual's marginal tax rate in the case of deductions or with the degree to which his partial tax credit failed to cover the cost of his risk-premium. The main objection to this proposal is that it would not provide complete reimbursement to those who are blamelessly disadvantaged.

3. A third option would be for the state to subsidize insurance companies directly, rather than write checks or grant tax breaks to members of the high-risk group. This proposal would be functionally equivalent to the second, although it would be more difficult to implement if the subsidy depended upon an individual's marginal rate of income (or other) tax and if that marginal rate might vary from year to year for a given individual.

4. A fourth possibility would be for a state monopoly to provide all insurance. This alternative would eliminate the need for the state to determine the extent to which people who suffered bad brute luck in the past would have to pay a risk-premium in a free insurance market, as well

as the administrative costs contingent on paying subsidies or granting tax rebates, for it would simply make everyone's insurance rates depend on voluntary behavior alone. One of its blemishes is that it would sacrifice the efficiency and responsiveness to consumers' desires that a free market generally promotes. And like the first proposal, it would shift the burden of compensation exclusively to other insurance purchasers (which would only be a flaw if some people bought no insurance at all), and that it would presumably do so in proportion to the premiums they paid (unless the subsidy were paid for by imposing an equal charge on all insurance purchasers, although in that case the first advantage would be lost, since the state would have to measure the aggregate risk-premiums whose cost it was redistributing).

Which of these proposals would be most desirable in a certain community is an empirical question, although the first and third proposals seem plainly inferior to the second. There seems nothing more to be said at this general level about what equality of fortune demands.

4.2. MINORS AND MENTALLY INFIRM ADULTS

The multifarious cases considered above illustrate the range of situations in which brute luck may, without injustice, be transformed into option luck. This metamorphosis cannot occur, however, when people are unable to insure against adversity. Inability to insure may take two forms. A person may be physically unable to buy protection because misfortune strikes before he is born or before he possesses the wherewithal to purchase insurance. Or he may be mentally incapable of doing so, either because he is insane or mentally retarded, or because he has not yet reached the age of reason. Since the problems presented by minors and mentally impaired adults[2] seem to deserve the same treatment and since minors vastly outnumber members of the adult group, I shall frequently refer only to the rights of children. Unless otherwise noted, parallel arguments apply to the entitlements of the mentally feeble or deranged, although in some cases the claims of adults or children who belong to this class might be weaker because they lack the cognitive capacities, unified personality, and opportunity to live a rich, rewarding life that normal

---

[2] In a just state, those who came of age would always have sufficient resources at their disposal to purchase insurance, and thus the problem of what to do about unfortunate adults who lacked the means to protect themselves against disease and accident would never arise, unless of course they refused to work or did not earn enough money to buy insurance once their basic needs were met. See Chapter 7. A separate question is what treatment, if any, to give ailing persons who could have insured but did not do so, and to whom the bill should be sent. This question cannot be answered without delving into the problems posed by paternalistic legislation, and I shall not address it here.

adults possess.[3] Because the just treatment of misfortunes suffered by minors is not only an important issue in its own right but returns in another, even more significant guise when one asks whether compensation is owed to those who are at a competitive disadvantage later in life as a result of their genes or upbringing, it warrants careful exploration. After stating and criticizing several alternative nonconsequentialist approaches to this problem,[4] I expound and defend what I consider a better view.

A. Rival Rights-Based Proposals

The most starkly opposed nonconsequentialist position is that of libertarians such as Robert Nozick and Jan Narveson, and of David Gauthier. By their lights, justice has nothing whatever to say about the vicissitudes of fortune, whether luck spawns inequalities in people's material or psychological welfare during infancy, adolescence, or adulthood. Need is no title to succor, redistribution an abomination unless tied to mutually advantageous cooperation.[5] Someone who acquires property justly may keep it or bestow it on whomever he pleases; no one may take it from him without his consent. Hence, only actual contracts, and in Gauthier's case what he considers the rational division of the social surplus based on people's bargaining power, have moral force. What people would have agreed to were they older, or more sympathetic, or equally wealthy, or ignorant of their natural endowments and social position, has no bearing on their present rights and obligations. The indigent have simply to bear their afflictions stoically, no matter how wretched they are, while those born blind or seriously handicapped lack any claim to assistance. If their parents are poor or their friends few, they must pass their days begging, as in olden times. Similarly, those who are equipped with a potentially

---

[3] I discuss the moral significance of these characteristics in Chapter 14.

[4] I describe the major shortcomings of utilitarianism and egalitarian welfarism in section 2.2. Utilitarianism's chief flaw in this context is its obeisance to luck. Because it would assign resources to those who would convert them into utility most efficiently, ailing infants or children requiring expensive corrective surgery would be neglected altogether if the money necessary to treat them would buy more utility elsewhere. Even when the happiness of parents and relatives is tossed onto the scales, there is no guarantee that children will get what they need, for the cost may be very high or no one may care much about them. But no minor's right to relief from pain or some dangerous disease should depend on how emotional or devoted his parents are, nor should it turn on whether others could derive more happiness from an equally costly alternative expenditure. Justice requires not that happiness be maximized, but that people have an equal chance to lead a valuable life.

[5] *See* Nozick (1974), 183–231; Narveson (1983); Gauthier (1986), 16–18, 220. Narveson writes, for example: "I do not see . . . that the people of Indiana have even the most airily prima facie obligation to equalize their situation with that of the natives of Chad, and my intuitions concerning Olympic athletes in relation to, say, severely afflicted Mongoloids are the same." Narveson (1983), 16. Narveson thinks the same holds true within families as well: unhealthy or handicapped children deserve no more of the family's resources than their happy, healthy siblings.

disastrous array of genes cannot, these philosophers say, demand that health insurance companies offer them the same rates as everyone else, or that the government provide them with a tax break. In all of these cases, bad luck will predictably snowball, but this is just the way of the world. With respect to health and abilities, life is one vast lottery in which some hold winning tickets while others are doomed to suffer and fail. No one is to blame for this state of affairs, and no one is bound to ensure that chance evens out. Those who are snug and safe have no duty to cushion the falls of people crippled in mind, spirit, or limb, even when the latter had no chance to protect themselves against adversity. Charity may be commendable, but it cannot be coerced.

Nozick, Narveson, and Gauthier arrive at these conclusions by invoking a stylized picture of rugged souls eking out difficult lives before the formation of governments; unabashedly self-interested, they care little or nothing about people outside their family or clan. Nobody desires, they assume, and surely nobody is required, to help others who suffer from bad health or accidental injury. When these individualists establish states, they drive hard but fair bargains: they unite for mutual advantage, not to help those less able to fend for themselves. It follows that while sympathy may impel some people, particularly people as thoroughly socialized as we, to assist the unfortunate, principles of justice rooted in self-interest do not require the lucky to pay compensation.

This view invites criticism on a number of levels. Because these criticisms have been ably articulated by others, no more than a brief summary is needed. Most fundamentally, there is no good reason to embrace these writers' conceptions of rationality and justice. As Brian Barry has recently argued,[6] the search for principles of justice is best characterized as an attempt to construct a set of distributive rules that mutually respectful, fair-minded people intent on agreement could not reasonably reject. Whatever the origins of human society, the notion of impartiality most of us think principles of justice should reflect is not one of shared gain from the standpoint of self-interest narrowly conceived. Mankind's prehistory and the unreal cooperation compacts dreamed up by certain theorists have slight bearing on the selection of appropriate principles.

This conclusion is supported, in my view, by our intuitive reaction to the implications libertarian theories yield. People at the brink of death, dragged to the precipice despite every effort to remain safe and hale, seem

---

[6] *See* Barry (1989), §§30, 35, 37, 38. Barry adopts an approach sketched in Scanlon (1982). Buchanan (1990), in advocating the adoption of a "subject-centered" theory of justice and criticizing theories of justice (such as Gauthier's) that find their foundations in self-interested reciprocity, offers related arguments from intuition and notions of rational justification for rejecting these extreme rights-based views.

entitled to assistance from those who were luckier if they did not bring misery on themselves and cannot live without help. The same seems true of persons with life-threatening genetic disabilities. And it appears self-evident that a little girl suffering from polio or a collapsed lung should be given medical assistance, even if her parents cannot or will not agree to cover the costs. No one should be condemned to anguished poverty or worse as a result of chance events against which she could not defend herself. From the standpoint of politics, people's lives matter equally, and the only way to accord them equal consideration is to grant each an equal bundle of resources while ensuring that everyone has the same chance to use those goods to fashion a valuable life for himself. Each person has, after all, but one life to live. It would be tragically unfair to allow chance occurrences to ruin someone's brief stay on this earth before he has even begun to make decisions for himself. A theory of justice that always gives fortune the final word, as do libertarian theories, is a cheat. Justice is less stepmotherly than these theorists believe.[7]

Charles Fried's proposal labors under a similar mistake, for he too would make a child's rights depend on what others are willing to spend on his and other children's behalf.[8] According to Fried, all children are entitled to health care (and presumably special training or education) according to whatever provision parents generally make for their children (whether by way of insurance or direct expenditures in time of need, Fried does not say). This suggestion has the merit that everyone would have a claim to the same minimum amount of care, although parents would always be free to spend more if they wished. Its defect is that it ties entitlements to what parents would be willing to spend, not to what children themselves would spend if they were rational and could allocate as much of their fair share of resources and future earnings to insurance as they chose, or to what is

[7] At this highly general level, there may be little to do besides juxtaposing conceptions of the point and nature of morality and intuitive judgments in specific instances. More detailed criticisms of individual philosophers are of course possible. Thus, in the case of Robert Nozick's entitlement theory, one might object that even if rights, as Nozick says, "reflect the underlying Kantian principle that individuals are ends and not merely means," or that they "reflect the fact of our separate existences," Nozick (1974), 31, 33, these facts do not, as Kant himself realized, preclude compelling one person to act for the benefit of another. See Hart (1979). One might also argue that if, as Nozick elsewhere claims, rights must be respected because they are a precondition to the living of a meaningful life, then his theory implies at least minimal welfare rights. See, e.g. Scheffler (1981); Fried (1982), 97–101. Another focus of attack would be Nozick's sketchy rendering of what he calls the Lockean Proviso, in particular the origin and implications of the requirement that persons in a state of nature may only appropriate common property for their exclusive use if they leave "enough, and as good" for others. See, e.g. O'Neill (1981); Scanlon (1981); Cohen (1986), 124–30; Stick (1987a), 387–416. I find many of these criticisms compelling, and have little to add to what others have said.

[8] See Fried (1978), 127.

needed to give them an equal start in life. Fried's proposal would therefore result in at least some cases in a smaller shield for minors than justice requires, for some, perhaps many, parents would spend less of their own earnings on each of their children than each child would spend if he were rational and able to borrow against his later salary and his share of the collective inheritance. A person's right to basic health care and education ought not to be hostage to the generosity or callousness of others, even if those others are close kin.

Nor should it depend upon their conceptions of the good life. On this point Bruce Ackerman, to whose views I am largely sympathetic, goes astray.[9] According to Ackerman, people who are born genetically disadvantaged are entitled to compensation sufficient to put them on a par with their peers.[10] The chief difficulty with Ackerman's theory is not this general claim, but the way in which he construes it. On Ackerman's account, a person is entitled to compensation only from those who "genetically dominate" him, and only to the extent necessary to eliminate that domination. But, by his definition, one person genetically dominates another only so long as *everyone* conscientiously believes that his genetic endowment places him in a superior position to pursue what the person making the evaluation regards as the good life. This stiff precondition for compensation is doubly flawed.

First, the requirement of unanimous agreement is clearly too strong, and Ackerman's appeal to popular convictions arguably misguided. One of Ackerman's own examples is proof enough. If, he says, a small troop of zealots believes that the deaf, dumb, and blind are closer to God and thus no worse off overall than those whose senses function normally, then nobody (the zealots are not alone exempt) owes such terribly handicapped persons a single penny, even if the handicapped themselves regard their limitations as an unmitigated evil. That Ackerman does not think this result sufficiently disturbing to overturn his proposal is astonishing.

But would relaxing the unanimity requirement solve the problem? Suppose the deaf, dumb, and blind child found himself in the reasonable minority in a community where the zealots held sway. Could he justly be denied compensation? Plainly not. If Ackerman wished to preserve the structure of his scheme, he would surely have to limit the vote to those who held reasonable conceptions of the good, besides dropping the prerequisite of complete agreement.[11] On this approach, however, there would plainly

---

[9] See Ackerman (1980), 115–20, 129–33.

[10] Whether the same principle applies to those who are congenitally but not genetically handicapped and to minors who sustain serious, accidental injuries or who fall grievously ill through no one's negligence, Ackerman does not say. His reasoning, however, seems to extend to these cases.

[11] In discussing second-best classifications, Ackerman gives as an example universal compensation for the blind. *See* Ackerman (1980), 132–3. He neglects to say, however,

be problems specifying the constituents of "reasonableness." Moreover, once criteria of reasonableness have been laid down, it is not clear that one still needs to count heads to determine who gets what. If an objective standard exists by which the reasonableness of a theory of the good can be measured, why not use it to fix the amount of compensation straightaway by having it serve as the measure of genetic domination as well, rather than resort to a vote? Perhaps the answer Ackerman would give is that one can only dismiss a few bizarre views as unreasonable; because a great many views pass the test, the only democratic way to settle the matter is to ask the people. However, I leave the defense of this assertion to Ackerman, if he would be inclined to support it.

The second shortcoming of Ackerman's proposal is his suggestion that genetic domination should serve as the sole yardstick for assistance. Suppose that everyone were born with the same birth defect, correctable if treated in infancy. Would no one have a *right* to medical help? The objection takes less spectacular forms as well. If, for example, a child is crippled but brilliant, he may not be thought worse off than someone who is fleet but stupid. Nevertheless, if therapy could take him out of his wheelchair, would it be right to deny him treatment? Does he not have a right to demand it? Ackerman appears correct in saying that somebody who is genetically dominated by others deserves extra resources to give him the same chance of making his life satisfying. But genetic domination is not the only sufficient condition of a right to assistance. (Perhaps Ackerman does not think it is either, but then he does not discuss additional sources of entitlement.) At a minimum, minors should have a claim to whatever medical coverage it would have been rational for them to purchase given (1) their fair share of resources, (2) their average expected earnings (individualization would be impossible), (3) their statistical chance of being born handicapped, of developing some debilitating disease, or of being injured accidentally, and (4) information concerning the expense of available ways to overcome these conditions. They should then be assessed the price of that insurance when they reach adulthood. To grant them less would be tantamount to holding them responsible for not being born rich and rational, which is the height of absurdity as well as injustice.

B. Dworkin's Approach and Equality of Fortune

The minimum condition just stated resembles Dworkin's proposal for

---

whether he has jettisoned the unanimity requirement in making second-best classifications, whether he has imported some notion of reasonableness, whether he is simply assuming that everyone would view blindness as a disadvantage, or whether he is relying on some other justification.

fixing the amount of health care to which minors are entitled.[12] Dworkin contends that adult victims of bad brute luck may only claim whatever compensation is provided by any insurance policy they purchased against the particular event that laid them low, provided that insurance was available to them.[13] Similarly, he argues, minors who are unable to buy insurance should receive coverage in the amount that they would have bought had they been mentally and financially able to do so, and they should be charged accordingly when they are later in a position to pay. To give them less would be to treat them unfairly, for it would leave those who are most defenseless with no protection against injury, disease, or other disadvantages, apart from what others were willing to spare. To give them more would be to steal from the lucky, for it would burden them with a liability higher than they would have assumed and perhaps even higher than it would have been rational for them to accept. To give them not the coverage they would have chosen but rather what others consider would have been best for them in view of the odds they faced would be to abridge their autonomy unjustifiably, assuming that sound paternalistic reasons do not exist for disregarding the decisions they would have made.

Of course, the counterfactual question how much insurance people would have bought before they were born is, as Dworkin notes, at best an exceedingly difficult one to answer. At the time of the hypothetical purchase these people are not yet themselves, with a set of aversions and ambitions to guide their choice, and when they have matured, the desires and values they possess will invariably have been shaped by their disability and any special benefits or treatment they received. So at least in some

---

[12] *See* Dworkin (1981*b*), 297–9.

[13] Dworkin never says what ought to be done when someone suffers bad brute luck and insurance was *not* available or the risk in question was so slight that almost no one had the forethought to insure against it. At least three positions are possible. First, Dworkin might contend that under these circumstances equality should be restored after the fact, on the rationale that luck should not affect the relative size of holdings unless people voluntarily allow it to do so. This is the view I endorse. Dworkin might find it unacceptable, however, because it seems to entail that handicapped children should receive as much compensation as is needed to make them the equals of other children, not just what would antecedently have seemed a wise bet. The second view he might espouse holds that when insurance is unavailable, unfortunate adults are due compensation in accordance with the policies they would have bought, or would have bought if they had been prudent. This position attunes closely with Dworkin's claim that the relief *minors* deserve should be calculated in this way, in view of their inability to insure themselves. However, a third view is also consistent with that claim. Dworkin might instead maintain that no one has a right to compensation if insurance was unavailable *because people decided not to pool various risks*, rather than because people lacked the mental capacity to make rational insurance decisions. In that case, he might say, they must answer for their choices. This would be a stern doctrine in cases where some risk went widely unnoticed, but then exceptions could always be made in truly egregious situations while generally holding people answerable for not making their own risk-sharing arrangements when commercial insurance companies refused to fill the breach. It is unclear which of the latter two positions Dworkin would find more congenial.

cases, most commonly those in which the disability is severe or in which it dates from infancy, the counterfactual question used to set contributions and compensation seems in principle unanswerable.

Dworkin is not greatly troubled by this difficulty. He points out that many handicaps and infirmities have roughly the same impact on a wide spectrum of lives, so that people with diverse preferences could still be expected to buy about the same amount of insurance. And he believes that by looking at what adults spend on insurance and asking how those figures should be revised if the various disabilities were to manifest themselves sooner, an acceptable answer can be reached. At any rate, it is the best one can do. No other method of fixing costs and benefits would be more just.

I question whether that is so. Dworkin's proposal is undeniably attractive, and the measure of compensation he advocates should at least serve as a minimum. Only in that way can a theory built on the notion that people should have equal means at their command escape the embarrassing necessity of denying help to disabled persons who are proficient in other respects. In addition, Dworkin's proposal frees the rights of the handicapped and genetically disadvantaged from dependence on the moral convictions, affection, or charity of others. There are situations, however, where it too seems to lapse into injustice.

Suppose that once all of the insurance payments have been disbursed, a severely handicapped individual is still at a disadvantage *vis-à-vis* his peers because supplemental insurance would have been an ill-judged buy in the womb, given the puny odds of being born into his predicament and the marginal returns from additional monetary transfers. Assume further that additional transfers could in fact give him more of the opportunities and mobility his playmates take for granted. Should he be refused those additional benefits? Dworkin's answer is unequivocally "Yes." If he would probably have gambled on being born whole and spry, he has no claim to more assistance.

This response, however, seems to offend the fundamental principle, affirmed by Dworkin, that people ought to start life with an equal bundle of resources and that equality should be maintained over time except insofar as somebody works less hard or accepts more desirable work or has poorer option luck or finds less generous friends. If physical and mental abilities are properly regarded as resources, as Dworkin believes they are,[14] then someone who is congenitally disadvantaged ought to be given a larger stock of material goods than those born with a more enviable set of

---

[14] "People's powers are indeed resources, because they are used, together with material resources, in making something valuable out of one's life." Dworkin (1981*b*), 300. "Someone who is born with a serious handicap faces his life with what we concede to be fewer resources, just on that account, than others do." Ibid. 302. Dworkin nevertheless treats these resources differently from the way he does material resources.

capacities in order to establish or at least approach the ideal of parity. Hypothetical choices may have some bearing on *when* someone is entitled to have the resources he is owed spent on his behalf—whether, for example, some of his basic allotment should be devoted to an expensive education—but they cannot detract from this initial equality.

Of course, complete equality of resources might prove unattainable. Some people whose lives are yet worth living are so intellectually or physically restricted that it is beyond our abilities to bring them up to the level of most others, no matter how much money we lavish on them. And it would obviously be wrong to pursue equality by injuring those who are better endowed, whether through a direct assault on their physical or mental powers or by reducing the size of their holdings, if such injury would not materially improve the position of those who are singularly disadvantaged. Indeed, one can make an even stronger claim. If the marginal benefits that recipients would derive would be meager by comparison with those that contributors would be compelled to forgo, and if the burden on contributors is already heavy, then such sacrifices cannot be commanded. Morality does not require those who are more fortunate in the genetic lottery or in escaping devastating diseases or injuries while young to accept great privations for the sake of people who are less lucky if the unlucky would only benefit slightly at the margin, just as it does not require exceptional sacrifices for trifling gains in other contexts. More pragmatically, laws requiring considerable and largely unavailing transfers might encounter widespread noncompliance, and no polity could ignore such opposition. Perfect equality of resources thus may not always be achievable at an acceptable cost.

But it nevertheless remains the ideal. Justice requires that those who were unable to insure against bad brute luck be compensated until equality is reached or the burdens on the more fortunate become excessive, whether absolutely or relative to others they must shoulder. To be sure, people who were insuring against an awful outcome, particularly one whose likelihood was small, would generally make less provision for congenital disabilities and childhood accidents than the egalitarian theory of equality of fortune demands. People frequently underinsure if the risks they face are slight. And they may not protect themselves fully even if they (rationally) buy insurance up to the point where the prospective benefits, measured in terms of utility and discounted by their probability, equal the cost of the policy. Equality of fortune would therefore at times require more compensation than would Dworkin's proposal. It would never require less. For it would, at a minimum, provide assistance equal to whatever insurance coverage people would have chosen were they able to borrow against their fair and equal shares and their future earnings. Equality would be preserved, but it would be equality of a generous order, independent not only of parents' means, affection, or moral beliefs, but of people's likely bets in ignorance of their later luck.

Dworkin advances three objections to a scheme similar to this one in defending his own proposal.[15] It is salutary to see why they fail. First, he says, a theory that requires that people be made equal not only in their material possessions but in those possessions *plus* their mental and physical capacities needs some measure of a "normal" set of powers to serve as a benchmark. And he suggests, by means of a rhetorical question—"But whose powers should be taken as normal for this purpose?"—that no satisfactory measure can be found.[16] Second, he notes that in some cases no amount of monetary compensation could make someone who is badly handicapped as capable of leading a happy life as somebody born with a full complement of ordinary abilities. Third, he contends that where, as in such cases, there is no upper bound to compensation, vote-hungry politicians and their grasping constituents will tend to give the handicapped less help than they would receive if his hypothetical insurance plan were in place.

None of these points is telling. The first raises a genuine difficulty for any theory that classifies personal capacities as resources along with material goods and that mandates equal shares of both taken together. It is often hard to tote up people's talents and to determine whether two people start life on a par. But while this may be a good reason not to try to correct for minor differences, there nevertheless remain exemplary cases of disadvantage. Why should the fact that drawing the line is apt to be controversial bar the just handling of cases that clearly fall on one side or the other? In this case, moreover, controversy would almost invariably revolve around the amount rather than the need for compensation, since equality of fortune is unlikely to mandate transfer payments when Dworkin's hypothetical insurance scheme would not.

Nor does Dworkin's second claim confound the theory. It is tragic that equality at times proves elusive, but its unattainability in a given case is no reason for not proceeding beyond Dworkin's recommendation and making matters as equal as one can, provided that those spared ill fortune are not called upon to make undue sacrifices and that the victims of bad brute luck derive nonnegligible benefits from their assistance at the margin.

As for Dworkin's third point, it is unclear why, when a theory cannot set a precise limit to what someone is owed, compensation must be left "to a political compromise likely to be less generous . . . than what the hypothetical insurance market would command."[17] Dworkin is apparently

---

[15] *See* Dworkin (1981*b*), 300–1.
[16] Dworkin (1981*b*), 300.
[17] Dworkin (1981*b*), 300.

thinking of a situation where legislators accept equality as the goal but do not base compensation on his own theory, embracing, instead, a less generous measure of assistance. His speculations are thus irrelevant to the theory of equality of fortune, which could not conceivably leave the disadvantaged worse off than under Dworkin's theory. But even given his supposition, it is an utter mystery why asking for more should win one less, assuming (what Dworkin must be assuming for purposes of fair comparison) that those to whom the two requests are addressed find the rival theories equally compelling.

Dworkin's pass thus fails to wound. Other objections fare no better. It might be said, for instance, that equality of fortune is fractured by a kind of incoherence, inasmuch as it makes protection against bad brute luck contingent on adults' choices, but denies minors a similar freedom to choose. Consistency, someone might claim, requires that both cases receive identical treatment. But it would be anomalous to insist that adults share their bad brute luck fully, whether they want to do so or not. We do not in fact believe (the objection continues) that bad luck ought always to be spread around, that strangers have a duty to help others confront misfortune even when they have insured or might have insured against it, that those blessed with good health ought, for that reason alone, to pay the major part of hospitals' operating expenses. Those plagued by chronic illness, victims of sudden storms, people destined to live abbreviated lives —all deserve our sympathy, but they do not automatically qualify for assistance at our expense. If, however, one rejects the requirement of complete compensation in these cases, one ought to repudiate it in the case of infants and children as well. If actual insurance purchases form the proper standard for entitlements and liabilities, they ought always to be determinative. Of course, one cannot apply this standard without modification to those whose misfortune antedates the time when they are eligible to buy protection for themselves. Here, one must simply give them the benefit of the doubt by presuming that they would have had the good sense to buy a reasonable amount of insurance. This assumption is a perfectly natural one, and does not turn the theory into the incoherent hybrid discussed above. One can only do justice to our intuitions, including our convictions regarding the importance of consistency, the argument concludes, by recognizing that insurance purchases, hypothetical or actual, determine the amount of compensation owed to those whom fortune treats shabbily. The alternatives are incoherence and injustice.

The charge of inconsistency is, however, mistaken. Equality of fortune does not have one standard of compensation for minors, another for adults. In both cases, the theory requires that disparities stemming from unequal brute luck be removed, so far as this is possible without making inordinate demands on those who pass through life relatively unscathed.

Deferential to the value of autonomy, however, it allows responsible adults, paternalistic constraints aside, to settle for less protection if they desire and if others are willing to release them from their obligations in return. Because exchanges of this kind would certainly occur if the relevant population were large and its economy fairly advanced, equality of fortune would yield the same result as Dworkin's theory in the case of adults: a competitive insurance market, subject to the requirement that no one be forced to pay higher rates because he suffered bad brute luck in the form of accidents, illness, or unwelcome genes. But the starting-point in the case of adults and minors is the same—complete elimination of the effects of bad brute luck, with the qualifications mentioned—and the divergent treatment of adults and minors in the end stems from the fact that adults may responsibly waive the protection to which they are entitled whereas minors lack that capacity for autonomous decision.

Indeed, if incoherence is present anywhere, it infects the view that relies on hypothetical insurance purchases to specify the compensation due disabled children. For that view holds, without explanation, that although the physical and mental powers that nature dispenses unequally and alters to varying degrees constitute resources for purposes of determining a just distribution, since they are means for achieving people's ends, people need not be made equal with respect to those resources as they must with respect to the material goods that fortune scatters among a given population before an equal division of the lot is effected.

Dworkin's defenders might attempt to vindicate the special status of personal powers in the following way. Powers and material objects are equally resources, they might admit. But since respect for autonomy is a sufficient reason for granting departures from equality in the case of adults, it should provide an equally forceful justification for departures from equality in the case of minors. Of course, infants and children cannot be consulted until they have matured. But by modifying their entitlements in conformity with the choices they would probably have made, one can at least approximate the ideal of total autonomy within the bounds of equality. Certainly it brings one closer to that ideal than does insistence on a more thoroughgoing sharing of brute luck than almost anyone would voluntarily have accepted.

This objection is a powerful one. In the end, however, it seems to me uncompelling. If autonomy were a weightier value here than equality of condition, the uppermost concern if we are to treat people as equals, then maybe the imperfect form it takes in this hypothetical insurance scheme would be sufficient to override the claims of equality. But the principle calling for complete equality of resources and rights seems instead to deserve pride of place. One reason for thinking it the preeminent goal is the nature of the alleged autonomy invoked by proponents of the hypothetical insurance plan. It is one thing to allow responsible agents to gamble with their health and material well-being, cognizant of the odds they face and the costs they are likely to sustain. It is quite another to presume that someone would have gambled were he given an opportunity to do so and to treat him in accordance with what one thinks he would have done even though he did not actually make such a decision. This presumption is particularly dubious when his future happiness would be substantially lessened if it were made and others would only be marginally benefited if it were not. Should not those who are shortchanged by fortune be given the benefit of the doubt?

The question acquires added sharpness when one recalls that those whose autonomy is ostensibly being respected do not yet exist, in at least one crucial respect, at the time the hypothetical choice would have to be made, since they do not yet possess the desires, the reflective abilities, and the stable personality necessary for free choice. And the preferences, particularly the aversion to risk, they come to have as they grow older will invariably be affected not only by the brute luck they enjoy, but by the compensation they are paid or the liabilities they are assessed to correct for differences in that luck. Hence, the appeal to autonomy in this context is rather specious, because whatever assumptions are made will, to the extent that their practical consequences affect later development, be evidentially self-fulfilling, in the sense that emergent preferences will tend to confirm whatever assumptions are embedded in compensation programs.

And even if the policies in place exert little influence on the genesis of people's preferences, those preferences will undoubtedly reflect the good or bad fortune of those who acquire them, and thus provide an unreliable guide to how someone would have chosen were he ignorant of the luck he was destined to enjoy. This unreliability, moreover, is not merely a contingent fact for which one might make allowances. It is inherent in the question posed, for someone cannot come to hold a relatively constant set of likes and aversions if he has not lived, and he cannot live without being lucky or unlucky. The autonomous subject is therefore a fiction under these circumstances. It is not as though one were asking how a friend, with whose habits and desires one was familiar, would decide under certain conditions. One is asking, instead, how someone not a person would decide, and that question, to the extent that it is intelligible, hardly seems capable of furnishing a reason sufficiently powerful to override the demands of equality.

These objections might be thought equally damaging to the theory of equality of fortune, since it, too, relies on assumptions about how much insurance people would have bought if a very large number of minors fall victims to what we, judging from contemporary experience, would deem exceptionally bad brute luck, and since it seems also to need assumptions about what goods and services, including education, people would have purchased by drawing on their future earnings and inheritance in determining what people are owed, even though preferences are profoundly influenced by the nature and quantity of the resources whose nature and quantity they are supposed to specify.

In reply, two points bear notice. First, my claim is not that appeals to what people would have spent under certain conditions are useless in view of the difficulties mentioned, but only that these difficulties supply a reason for not giving them precedence over equality of resources *plus* endowments when the two conflict. Sometimes there may be no alternative to such appeals, as in the case of educational programs. Second, although I have hitherto asked, as Dworkin does, what people *would have chosen* in some cases, there is no determinate answer to that question. These cases require an independent account of how adults should *choose for* minors— an account I cannot supply here.

There is still another apparent difficulty with basing entitlements on people's hypothetical choices, as Dworkin does, when their personalities are inchoate, although this one seems surmountable. If people had to choose among a set of principles for the distribution of resources in ignorance of their actual desires and brute luck, one might ask, would they stop with some form of insurance against gross misfortune? Might they not also choose to exploit members of small, unpopular minorities, given the small odds that they would turn out to be the unlucky ones? Or would they subscribe to a utilitarian scheme of distribution, since they might thereby maximize their expected happiness? The notion of choice from behind some type of veil of ignorance seems in tension with the concept of equality that the above theories attempt to elaborate. Once one starts down that track, there seems no way of stopping short of undesirable policies.

Fortunately, the slope is neither as steep nor as slippery as it may initially appear. Recall that Dworkin's purpose in referring to hypothetical choices is to mimic as nearly as possible the autonomous decisions of adults concerning compensation for bad brute luck. Adults know how their desires, capacities, and attributes compare with those of others, hence a sizable number could not be expected to agree to utilitarian social codes or the unusually cruel treatment of members of certain groups. It is only appropriate to stipulate that those making hypothetical choices regarding insurance against bad brute luck possess the same information about themselves. But given this information, those who would stand to lose were utilitarianism or some other oppressive plan adopted could hardly be expected to assent to their own detriment. Nor could their objection be ignored if they were but a minority, since Dworkin rightly takes for granted that everyone is entitled to an equally valuable bundle of resources and that they may only be given less if they agree to accept a smaller share in return for some other actual or possible benefit. Finally, to those who point out that many adults gladly join in games of chance, so that if the average adult's behavior rightly serves as a model for hypothetical choices, one should imagine those mythical beings who are selecting insurance policies playing a lottery of sorts as well, there is a simple reply. The aim of resorting to hypothetical choices is to give autonomy the widest possible scope. The autonomy that those choices represent, however, is no substitute for people's actual, responsible choices. It is merely a second-best approximation when actual choice is impossible. But because it is only second-best, because people's aversion to risk differs widely, because wagers of this kind are not self-evidently rational, and because it is unnecessary to make assumptions about people's fondness for gratuitous risk-taking inasmuch as they can later bet to their heart's content when they become adults, it would be wrong to assume that those picking an insurance policy would also buy lottery tickets. Equality and actual autonomy should be compromised as little as possible. Fortunately for those who feel drawn to both theories, only in exceptional instances would the implications of Dworkin's view and equality of fortune diverge and those instances might in practice prove unidentifiable, given the difficulty of distinguishing between compensation according to hypothetical insurance decisions by idealized minors and full compensation subject to the qualifications that marginal gains be significant and that absolute costs not be excessive.

5

Occupational Preferences, Effort, and Desert

LUCK in voluntary undertakings and luck in physical well-being are two important causes of differences over time in the resources and opportunities people have to consume, exploit, invest, or give away. An even more important factor in most people's lives, to the extent that it can be separated from the acquisitive risk-taking discussed in Chapter 3, is the work they do. A person's occupational performance reflects not only his preferences for one type of work over another, but also the effort and perseverance he brings to bear and the abilities and aptitudes given him by nature or engendered or shaped by his parents and environment. This chapter and the next consider the extent to which justice requires correction for inequalities originating in these ways.

5.1. PREFERENCES FOR JOBS AND LEISURE AND UNEQUAL EFFORT

That one large source of inequality—people's divergent preferences regarding various types of productive activity—cannot ordinarily justify compensation if people's abilities are equal admits of little argument. Preferences for different kinds of labor are, from the standpoint of justice, indistinguishable from preferences for different goods when unowned resources are divided, or from preferences for a greater or lesser degree of risk in one's habits, leisure activities, or business ventures. A theory of justice that treats people as equal, autonomous decisionmakers must, in general, take them as responsible for their tastes and predilections. If some people agree to perform tasks for which others are willing to pay handsomely, but which are considered less desirable than many alternative forms of labor and therefore must be better rewarded in order to attract enough workers, then they are entitled to pocket the premium their labor commands. Because everyone is assumed to have the same abilities, whatever differences in holdings accrue can be traced only to differences in their preferences, and they alone must assume credit or blame for their desires.

Abstracting once again from differences in people's strength, intelligence, and other useful abilities, the same is true of inequalities in resources flowing from people's decisions to work longer or harder than their fellow workers. More industrious workers, who toil extra hours or who exhibit greater concentration because they attach more value than do their comrades to certain material possessions or the activities they make possible relative to the onerousness of the labor necessary to obtain them, are entitled to the additional resources their perspiration makes possible. Their decisions to trade off work for leisure or slack for hard work at the rate they do are just like their earlier choices between different lots of resources and rights in the initial auction, or between different goods in the marketplace. Laziness or an aversion to a certain type of work cannot furnish title to the rewards of another's exertions any more than a hankering for the rare and costly can supply a right to extra cash at an auction of unowned rights and resources or afterwards. Equality can only be preserved perdurably by allowing equally talented persons to reap what they sow. Just as an equal initial division was defined so that no one preferred anyone else's bundle of resources and rights to his own, so no one would prefer anyone else's bundle of resources and rights *and labor* to his own bundle at some later time if equally gifted people kept what they produced.

This result is neither hard nor unreasonable. A person's mature preferences are not often imposed from without, his own wishes to the contrary. Their inception, to be sure, may be explained by reference to the environmental and pedagogical influences to which he was exposed and to his native constitution, just as other elements of a person's character may be traced to factors beyond his control. We all come into the world naked and blank, apart from our genetic predispositions, and can hardly choose the persons we are to be before we acquire some desires to guide our choices and the ability to make those choices effective. But the fact that people do not create themselves *ex nihilo* does not absolve them from responsibility for their actions and character once their reason, experience, and capabilities cross a certain threshold. Except in extreme cases, a person's desires, values, and behavior lie sufficiently within his control, in the long term if not immediately, to justify holding him accountable for his decisions. At any given time we may not be entirely happy with our evolving creation (only the smug are), but to the extent that we are ashamed or discontented, we ourselves are usually primarily to blame. This seems especially true of a person's capacity for extended or concentrated work if he is free from physical infirmities, if not with respect to the development of various skills or intellectual abilities. No one should be required to contribute to another person's upkeep because the second allowed himself to become someone unable or unwilling to keep his nose to the grindstone with equal determination.

Equality is not forfeited, moreover, by permitting those who accept unpopular jobs or who work more sedulously than the norm to pocket their additional earnings. For to the extent that labor markets function well, no one is deprived of the chance to have the extra resources they acquired in exchange for the alternative or added work they did. Nor does justice demand that those who follow unremunerative callings out of deeply held convictions rather than more casual or easily relinquished preferences— the priest who would not forsake his mission at any price, the artist struggling in obscurity against the aesthetic sense of his age, the daughter who selflessly devotes much of her life to her parents and siblings—be given greater rewards, partly at the expense of people who fail to share their beliefs or zeal, than the market (including voluntary donations) would confer. However worthy some of us might deem a particular cause, and however admirable we might think its proponents, justice does not favor any creed, or aspiration, or lifestyle in allocating material goods or opportunities. Even if it would be misleading to say that people *choose* at least certain careers or endeavors—those pursuits seem rather thrust upon them, perhaps inescapable from their perspective—they nevertheless endorse the convictions that steer and motivate their efforts; they do not view them as curses they are unfortunately unable to shed, as afflictions they would rather sunder from their highest-order preferences and values. So long as they do not sincerely disapprove of the course they are following and genuinely desire to be rid of the ambitions that consign them to poverty, they have no right to assistance in fulfilling or discarding their aims.

Some people, of course, will derive more satisfaction from their work than others will, just as some people will take more joy in a fixed quantity of wealth than will those whose favorite things are more costly or whose material ambitions are more grandiose. But that difference in satisfaction provides no reason to depart from an equal distribution. For insofar as people choose to retain their aversion to certain forms of work, continue to tolerate their expensive tastes, or remain loyal to their monetarily unprofitable convictions, they choose the lesser material means that attend those preferences and beliefs.[1]

---

[1] G. A. Cohen dissents from this conclusion. If the desires of other people are such that they are willing to pay well for work that Adrian enjoys doing but will not spend a dime for the services that Claude would like to provide, then in Cohen's view Claude has a right to redress. *See* Cohen (1989), 932–3. This view, as Cohen rightly notes, is consistent with his treatment of divergent leisure preferences, and I would reject it for the same reason (and with the same qualification) that I would repudiate his approach to decisions regarding consumption. See above, section 2.3.B(ii). The desires of other people for goods and work, the natural availability of resources, and present technology are all background facts, in the awareness of which people must generally decide (assuming, as the present discussion does, that they are equally able) how to arrange their lives, how to use their allotted resources, and how to go about replenishing or increasing them. Those who are unhappy with the likes and aversions they allowed themselves to retain or acquire because those desires are costly to satisfy or, with respect to occupational preference, yield lower wages than they would like should alter them or berate themselves, not press others for assistance under a putative claim

It is important, however, not to overstate the extent to which fortitude, concentration, perseverance, and whatever other attributes comprise the more amorphous quality of effort are characteristics within a person's control. The abilities with which people are born do differ, and these differences frequently affect people's initial successes, which in turn often influence the amount of satisfaction they take in accomplishment and their consequent desire—and over time their capacity—to strive and succeed. In addition, some are better conditioned to the demands of certain occupations, or to the roomier set of rigors the overcoming of which we ascribe to effort, than are those deprived of similar training at home, in school, or elsewhere through no fault of their own. This second set of differences is especially glaring in contemporary American society— consider the disadvantages under which poor children from ghetto communities are raised and their understandable lack of motivation—but differences of this kind would exist as well, albeit to an appreciably lesser extent, in a society where resources were distributed as justice requires. Although a lack of drive or concentration can often be ascribed to a slovenly or easygoing disposition somebody allowed himself to develop and now regrets, it appears that sometimes people simply cannot work as hard as they would like, for in spite of their best attempts their attention lapses, distractions prevail, or their determination evaporates. To the extent that a person's capacity for prolonged or unswerving exertion may be stunted by a comparative dearth of natural ability, or to the extent that determination and focused endeavor are the products of a disciplined upbringing or of ambitions and a global optimism that owe more to the influence of parents, social environment, schooling, and restricted occupational opportunity than to choices for which individuals can claim credit, differences in effort should be classified with differences in endowments as instances of bad brute luck. Inequalities in material possessions or opportunities arising from these differences should to that degree be handled in the manner described in the next chapter.

It is worth pausing to clarify this position, for it rests on at least two contestable premises. The first is that a person's ability to make an effort is at least partly a capacity from which he can abstract, rather than entirely a

---

of right. Justice does not require that everyone be given the chance to experience a given level of welfare no matter what preferences that person develops. As we have seen, that is one of the major flaws of egalitarian welfarism. Consider Adrian and Claude again, and suppose that Claude is only happy penning poems; the problem is that everybody else thinks his work doggerel, and no one will pay to read them. Would Cohen seriously propose that everybody else be taxed so that Claude might be paid the average wage, provided only that he spends a full eight hours each day scribbling puerile rhymes? So long as Claude freely acquired his vocational predilection knowing the market for the services he intended to provide—and there are few cases one can imagine in which he could be said to have had it forced on him—it is no fault of others, and certainly not one for which they must pay, that he lives a pauper.

dimension of an individual's self from which he cannot step back, and that people in fact differ in this capacity. It is hard to know whether this claim is empirical, although not subject to anything approaching conclusive confirmation or disproof, or whether it should be regarded as definitional (assuming the disjunction is genuine). It is always possible to explain visible differences in people's industry and determination by postulating that they possess equal capacity for effort but that their preferences regarding its exercise are not identical. As George Sher has noted, however, "[w]hile persons who exert different amounts of effort always *can* be viewed as drawing differently upon similar effort-making abilities, this suggestion may seem implausible when the difference in their efforts is pronounced, systematic, and obviously disadvantageous to the less industrious."[2] If, for example, two seemingly equally talented people display markedly different tendencies to stick to a task and to overcome impediments in carrying it to completion, not just in the classroom but on the playing field and in a variety of personally significant pursuits as well, and if both seem on questioning to attach similar importance to success in these activities, then a difference in willpower or effort-making capacity seems the best explanation of their unequal accomplishments. The most persuasive account of the differences Sher describes seems to be that people's capacity to strive varies, and that they can generally decry or approve, at least in reflective, inactive moments, the extent to which they are able to flex this mental muscle.

The second assumption informing this approach is that people ordinarily can distance themselves from their capacity to concentrate and persevere, and can strengthen or weaken this capacity over time in sufficient measure to hold them responsible for their comparative prowess in this regard. Of course, self-mastery of this kind is sometimes absent. People can be so thoroughly conditioned to fail, or so dispirited or beaten down by circumstance and experience, that they are unable, at least persistently and without assistance, to achieve the self-reflection essential to discipline and develop their power of exertion. In certain extreme instances, one should perhaps even characterize other people's efforts to instill self-control in such a person as guided by personal or moral ends of the agent other than the promotion of the individual's autonomous choices, since that person is unable to gain the critical perspective on his own desires and capacities necessary to choose freely. But while the assumption of long-term self-control may not always be fulfilled, it seems reasonable in a sufficiently large preponderance of cases to treat differences in people's efforts, entwined as they often are with people's desires and ideals of character (some people, for example, enjoy a gentler pace and little mind the quiet

[2] Sher (1987), 29.

poverty that sometimes attends it), as an inadequate ground for redistribution.

5.2. A RAWLSIAN CHALLENGE

Although it may prove difficult to disentangle people's preferences for
work over leisure and their decisions to work longer or harder from the
effects of natural endowments and other factors over which they lack
substantial control—not only theoretically but above all operationally—
the distinction nevertheless seems vital and defensible. Before considering
redistributive policies that might give effect to this distinction in connection
with Chapter 6's discussion of measures for redressing differences in
natural endowments, it seems necessary to defend this distinction against a
broadside attack that appears implicit in John Rawls's theory of justice.

Rawls denies knowledge of their convictions about desert to persons in
the original position not only because possession of that information would
preclude agreement, or simply transmute the debate over distributive
principles into a dispute over the contours of the original position or the
proper characterization of persons in it. He does so also because, in his
view, those convictions are at worst social accidents, at best the
conclusions, rather than the limits, of an argument from fairness.

Rawls's attack on notions of desert that are prior to the original position
starts from a weaker claim: "it seems to be one of the fixed points of our
considered judgments that no one deserves his place in the distribution of
native endowments, any more than one deserves one's initial starting place
in society."[3] To this uncontroversial assertion, which even libertarians such
as Nozick accept, Rawls conjoins what he labels "the principle of redress."
"This is the principle that undeserved inequalities call for redress; and
since inequalities of birth and natural endowments are undeserved, these
inequalities are to be somehow compensated for."[4] Needless to say,
Rawls's second premise is less ingenuous than the first. Nozick and others
argue that just because no one deserves the talents, parents, and social
advantages that are his at birth does not mean that he is not *entitled* to
retain whatever benefits flow from them, without sharing his good fortune
with those who are less lucky. Nevertheless, I think Rawls correct in
contending that the undeserved inequalities of birth may (though not
always) warrant redress. As he notes, the outcome of the natural and social
lotteries "is arbitrary from a moral perspective. There is no more reason to
permit the distribution of income and wealth to be settled by the
distribution of natural assets than by historical and social fortune."[5] Where

---

[3] Rawls (1971), 104. References to *A Theory of Justice* will hereafter be abbreviated "*TJ*."
[4] *TJ* 100.
[5] *TJ* 74.

all desire some good and no one possesses a superior claim to it, the only just course is to divide it or its fruits equally, assuming that division is possible. Hence, natural abilities, as Rawls says, should for some purposes be regarded as a "common" or "collective" asset, and though talents cannot be culled from infant minds and limbs and reapportioned, all should "share in the benefits of this distribution whatever it turns out to be."[6] Similarly, one person's good luck in his parents or mentors is no reason to leave his resultant advantage undisturbed when it is both possible and morally desirable—as is usually the case with respect to unequal brute luck in children's health—to ensure a more even distribution of resources than would prevail were such chance inequalities allowed to reproduce themselves unimpeded and enlarged in people's material circumstances.

Rawls does not apply the principle of redress, however, solely to inequalities of birth.[7] He further relies on it to banish all moral convictions from the minds of his hypothetical contractors. Moral desert sets no bounds to the choice of distributive principles, Rawls appears to contend, because the principle of redress applies to *all* material inequalities that arise between people, or at least to all inequalities resulting from effort rather than voluntary wagers. Indeed, the notion of moral desert, Rawls might be construed as saying, is incoherent. Not only do people not deserve their natural capacities or the social stimuli that shape their development because they have not chosen or created them, but they also bear no responsibility for their diligence or their decision to work overtime, since these choices also reflect the chance influences of nature, parents, and teachers. Hence, people do not deserve any part of what they achieve by virtue of their efforts or character, and the only intelligible notion of desert is that of a right secured by fulfilling some institutional requirement:

Thus it is true that as persons and groups take part in just arrangements, they acquire claims on one another defined by the publicly recognized rules. . . . But what they are entitled to is not proportional to nor dependent upon their intrinsic worth. The principles of justice that regulate the basic structure and specify the duties and obligations of individuals do not mention moral desert, and there is no tendency for distributive shares to correspond to it.[8]

---

[6] *TJ* 101, 179.

[7] It is unclear whether Rawls would endorse an extension of this principle of compensation to the effects of bad brute luck (though not poor option luck) later in life. Rawls never discusses the duties owed to those who fall prey to disease or unanticipated disaster, nor does he elaborate the Difference Principle's implications with respect to gamblers' winnings. The most one can say with certainty is that he never repudiates the view that inequalities traceable to brute luck and option luck should be treated differently.

[8] *TJ* 311. Rawls makes similar claims at various points in *A Theory of Justice*:
Even the willingness to make an effort, to try, and so to be deserving in the ordinary sense is itself dependent upon happy family and social circumstances. (*TJ* 74)

Rawls's argument from the effects of undeserved advantages and the principle of redress to the exclusion of convictions about desert in its non-institutional sense from the minds of the original position's contractors is, however, far from unassailable.[9] As Nozick points out, "It needn't be that the foundations underlying desert are themselves deserved, *all the way down*."[10] In fact, it is hard to imagine how the foundations could possibly go all the way down, since the regress would apparently be infinite. Moreover, if Rawls believes that moral desert attaches to a decision only if nothing that entered into the decision depended on or was influenced by a person's abilities or environment, and if he thinks the apparently limitless regress can be stopped, then the concept of desert that emerges seems almost unintelligible. It is hard to imagine, if this is Rawls's view, what he believes the preconditions are for genuine responsibility, for the notion of an uncaused material cause freely choosing among courses of action according to a system of values the chooser was in no way caused to adopt borders on incoherence. Without rehearsing the hoary debate over universal causation and moral accountability, it seems clear that the truth of physical or psychological determinism, or the fact that *some* of what enables a person to prosper or causes him to fail comes to him unearned and unbidden, seems no reason to abandon the commonsense view regarding desert. In simplified form, this view distinguishes two relevant aspects of a person: the self, which includes desires, values, and character traits of which a person approves; and the physical and mental powers that fill its quiver. A person's voluntary actions, including those that contributed to the formation of his productive powers, constitute legitimate foundations of desert, whereas traits for which people are not responsible,

> The assertion that a man deserves the superior character that enables him to make the effort to cultivate his abilities is equally problematic; for his character depends in large part upon fortunate family and social circumstances for which he can claim no credit. The notion of desert seems not to apply to these cases. (*TJ* 104)

> [I]t seems clear that the effort a person is willing to make is influenced by his natural abilities and skills and the alternatives open to him. The better endowed are more likely, other things equal, to strive conscientiously, and there seems to be no way to discount for their greater good fortune. The idea of rewarding desert is impracticable. (*TJ* 312)

[9] Admittedly, the passages quoted in text and in the preceding footnote could be read, and perhaps should charitably be read, as advancing the weaker claim that, while some people deserve more than others because people's willingness to try is not reducible to social circumstance and other environmental factors even though it is "dependent" upon them, nevertheless sorting out the effects of genuine desert-creating effort from the effects of undeserved inequalities is in practice hopeless; any institutional attempt to reward desert is "impracticable." Of course, this reading is also problematic, for if it is correct, one wonders why Rawls says that the notion of desert "seems not to apply" to cases where superior character is shaped by family and social circumstance, not merely that the notion of desert is, for practical reasons, difficult to apply. But this exegetical dispute would not repay added attention. My apologies to Rawls if, in seeking to rebut a possible objection to my view, I have improperly attributed that objection to him.

[10] Nozick (1974), 225; *see also* Dennett (1984), ch. 4, and works cited therein.

such as their innate capacities and unwanted or ungovernable obsessions, cannot provide moral title to rewards or a moral basis for sanctions. This distinction may be, and often has been, justified by appealing to two convictions: our belief in our personal efficacy and autonomy, that is, our introspective awareness that certain things are within our control whereas other things are not; and our belief, implicit in almost all practices that involve praise and blame, that moral judgments are properly made regarding those actions we can control, and that we deserve benefits or punishments, approval or resentment, because of what we have voluntarily done or neglected to do. Acknowledging that determinism is true at some level, or that much of what makes us the people we are cannot be laid to our credit, cannot extinguish these convictions, nor do I think it can or should alter our views about what people merit.[11]

To be sure, no one deserves to be born the person he is as he makes his self-conscious debut on the stage of life, with proclivities formed primarily by genes and environment. Moral desert is bound up with action or inaction on the basis of self-approved desires, and one can hardly act responsibly before one possesses the experience essential to an adequate understanding of the world and oneself. That is why the criminal law treats juvenile offenders differently from adult lawbreakers, and why much less stringent standards of moral appraisal apply to children, when any do. As most people mature, however, they develop the capacity to reflect on their actions and personality, and to shape, within limits, their conduct and characters as they will. Over time, that is to say, they become moral agents, capable of deserving things not just in an institutional sense (conformity with social rules) but also in a normative sense (conformity with a moral law not necessarily dependent on social conventions).

Of course, the choices someone makes will be profoundly affected by his upbringing and initial complement of talents, and if determinism is true this link can be traced completely, at least in principle. But this link, if it exists, seems unable to excuse a person for his deeds except in certain extreme cases, as when his ratiocinative powers are impaired or he is unable to master abnormally strong desires and disapproves of what he has done. Nor does this presumed connection seem capable of stealing a person's responsibility for decisions regarding a job and the amount of time and care he lavishes on his work, thus making those decisions irrelevant to the just allocation of resources, although it might in some instances lessen their impact (at least in the short run) insofar as those decisions are dictated by a person's abilities rather than his considered preferences. The legitimacy of our commonsense notions of voluntariness, responsibility,

[11] For fuller discussion of this point, *see* Strawson (1962); Bennett (1980); Wolf (1981); Sher (1987), ch. 2.

and desert, and prevailing views of the relations between them, do not seem significantly undermined by the fact that people do not merit all of their capacities or choose all of the values and desires that make them what they are.

Indeed, despite Rawls's dismissive references to moral desert in defending his methodology and thus the Difference Principle, he himself appears to invoke the concept in his discussion of retributive justice.[12] "The purpose of the criminal law," he declares, "is to uphold basic natural duties, . . . and punishments are to serve this end. They are not simply a scheme of taxes and burdens designed to put a price on certain forms of conduct and in this way to guide men's conduct for mutual advantage."[13] Someone who transgresses the criminal law, Rawls says, manifests a "bad character"; because he is responsible for that character, he deserves the punishment meted out to him. But if a person is responsible for those aspects of his character that lead him to invade others' rights, why is he not responsible for more estimable dimensions of his character as well? Why can one only morally deserve what one does not want?

Rawls never says. He asserts several times that principles of distributive justice ought not to be viewed as the converse of the criminal law, but he offers no argument to that end. He merely repeats Hart's observation that we do not generally view criminal penalties as nothing more than especially stiff taxes,[14] which of course proves nothing. No doubt most people believe that taxes can be raised at will to serve the general good, at least within a certain range, whereas criminal penalties cannot be made more severe without limit just because the public would benefit from rougher measures. Taxes are generally viewed as tools to advance the general welfare, in accordance with the collective will, while criminal sanctions are commonly viewed as attempts to mirror some standard of natural justice. But this observation does not entail that natural canons of justice set no bounds to tax and expenditure policy. Beyond a certain point taxation may itself be criminal. And just as a wide range of policies may be just, provided that line is not overstepped, so may a wide range of criminal penalties be just, so long as someone is not punished more than he deserves.

The parallel, moreover, is intuitively compelling. If a law were passed requiring all less able persons who worked longer and harder than their better-endowed counterparts and who therefore received higher gross salaries to pay much higher taxes, so that their salaries after tax were no higher than those of their more talented but lazier colleagues, almost everyone would protest that such a tax is unjust because it deprives people

[12] As G. A. Cohen points out, Rawls's discussion of distributive justice apparently relies on it as well. In holding people responsible for their expensive tastes because those preferences generally lie within their control, Rawls seems to attribute to people the qualities he elsewhere assumes they lack. *See* Cohen (1989), 913–16.

[13] *TJ* 314–15.

[14] Hart (1961), 39.

of what they naturally deserve. The fact that we do not ordinarily view criminals as taxpayers or taxes as criminal is therefore no argument against the possibility of a noninstitutional notion of desert or of a natural standard of distribution. And if criminals are responsible for their bad characters and deserve punishment for their reprehensible conduct, then why should one not conclude that diligent people are responsible for their greater effort and that they deserve to keep the fruits of their decision to labor rather than loaf? For his part, Rawls offers no reason to think that conclusion mistaken.

Two courses are therefore open to Rawls if he is unwilling to accept the view defended above. He could, first of all, concede that the possible existence of noninstitutional principles of desert in distribution follows from the acceptance of criminal moral responsibility, yet contend that this possibility is in fact an empty one: as it happens, there are no distributive principles corresponding to acknowledged retributive principles. The problem with this argumentative gambit is that the assertion is implausible that desert in distribution is but a phantom possibility. One way to give it the lie is to construct an intuitively appealing theory premised on the reality of distributive desert. That is the aim of this book, but a single counterexample is enough to make the point. If one of two equally advantaged persons works harder and more productively than the other, and if they are not engaged in a search or an experimental endeavor where both recognize and accept that luck may be a decisive factor, then it seems evident that the first deserves more remuneration than the second. Yet if the position I have attributed to Rawls were right, the first person would lack a moral claim to higher wages. One might assume that in a society whose economy was regulated by the Difference Principle the harder worker would have a legal right to more resources, because in general one must pay people higher sums to induce them to labor more and thus to improve the situation of the least advantaged class. But it seems merely to be a fortuitous circumstance, given Rawls's assumptions, if the harder worker does have such a right. If all those who worked harder happened to like their work, so that it was unnecessary to give them a higher or even an equal salary to coax them to produce more primary goods for others to enjoy, then it is difficult to see why a premium should come their way where the Difference Principle holds sway (although Rawls seem to take for granted that equal pay would attend equal work). But this result seems the reverse of just. Someone may choose to forgo the income to which he is morally entitled, but he does not deserve it the less for his refusal to accept it. The claim that there are no natural standards of desert in distribution, and that the Difference Principle accords with our strongest intuitions in this regard, is unpersuasive.[15]

---

[15] The variant of the Difference Principle discussed by Thomas Nagel in "Equality" is even more intuitively offensive. *See* Nagel (1979), 106–27. Nagel describes a view he calls

The second course open to Rawls is to retract his claim that wrongdoers are responsible for their misdeeds and morally deserve punishment, taking the courageous line that responsibility and desert are worthless notions save in their institutional senses. The main difficulty with this maneuver is that it substitutes two implausible assertions for one. Not only does it offer no reply to the conventional wisdom concerning responsibility, merit, and blame, or to the formidable challenge posed by the intuitive appeal of contrary principles of distributive desert. It doubles this failing by making identical claims about the undeserved character of criminal sanctions, as though there could be no moral argument against executing shoplifters if this were the most efficacious penalty and thus a prudent choice in the original position.

Denying the reality of distributive desert in its noninstitutional sense also has implications Rawls overlooks. If no one is responsible for his character or conduct in the sense that Rawls and Kant seemingly think moral desert requires, then in the most just of possible worlds (if only it were realizable) everyone should apparently receive an equal stock of primary goods, no matter how they filled their days, for all are equally undeserving. In fact, equal welfare seems the moral desideratum, for if people are not responsible for their characters, their actions, their environments, and their good or bad fortune, then they cannot be responsible for the values and preferences that make their lives unequally happy. People's autonomy and rationality, which Rawls elsewhere so celebrates, seem morally irrelevant epiphenomena. In practice, it seems reasonable to depart from a rule of strict equality and to permit improvements in one person's stock of primary goods if they do not come at the expense of a less advantaged person. But it is hard to imagine how Rawls can extract the view he favors from these premises.

For the Difference Principle does not seem to imply, as Rawls apparently assumes, that all who do the same work should receive the same wage that the last economically employable worker is willing to accept in return for his services. Even if one grants that departures from equal wages are justified to the extent that the least advantaged class benefits and that

"egalitarianism," according to which justice requires that everyone's most basic needs be satisfied before anyone's less pressing needs are met, then that the next tier of needs be satisfied before anyone's claims at a higher level are fulfilled, and so on up the ladder. Admittedly the view has some appeal if one assumes that all who are subject to this regime work with equal diligence and on socially beneficial tasks, the only differences between them being that some are luckier, or more talented, or born into better families. But if the more pressing needs of some go unmet because of their own insouciance or imprudence, then those who have acted more responsibly hardly seem bound to forgo less pressing satisfactions in order to elevate the station of their carefree or careless neighbors. The principle Nagel describes gains what attractiveness it has from the fact that its prescriptions coincide in certain cases with those of more defensible principles. When their prescriptions diverge, however, it is clearly Nagel's principle that must be abandoned.

no one should have to work past the point where the material compensation he receives just balances the marginal disutility of his labor, it does not follow that people should receive equal pay for equal work. On the contrary, if departures from the ideal of equality are only justified to the extent that they are necessary to prompt people to work for the benefit of those born with less or those who are unlucky later in life through no fault of their own, then it is immoral to pay someone more than the sum for which he would be willing to work, provided that the sum exceeds the minimum wage. If the standard salary for physicians in a perfect labor market were three times that of the average member of the least advantaged class, and if someone were willing to work as a doctor for that basic wage, then he appears to have no moral right, under Rawls's theory, to triple that amount. To the extent that Rawls would allow him to keep the extra money, he seems to contravene his most fundamental distributive principle.

Rawls's argument for excluding views about moral desert from the original position seems therefore to fail on two fronts. Rawls offers no persuasive reason for thinking that moral desert in matters of distribution, let alone with respect to retributive justice, is an incoherent notion. And he is unable to demonstrate that the Difference Principle accords with widespread, and seemingly correct, intuitive convictions about distributive desert—a test Rawls must recognize as legitimate in view of his endorsement of reflective equilibrium as the argumentative objective. The idea, furthermore, that principles of justice can best be derived by appealing to the outcome of a prudent wager by suitably straitjacketed people is itself somewhat bizarre, and appears to offer scant attraction once Rawls's argument against moral desert in distribution has been rebutted. Whether taken to imply the Difference Principle, a variant of utilitarianism couched in terms of primary goods, or some welfarist view, Rawls's refusal to accept effort and productivity as legitimate sources of material entitlement fails to treat those of like talent and diligence equally.

6

Unequal Endowments

Thus far I have assumed that people possess roughly the same mental and physical capacities to obtain the material and nonmaterial preconditions of an enjoyable life. In fact, however, people's mental and physical powers vary markedly as a result of their genes and upbringing, allowing some to augment their initial stock of resources and rights more quickly or painlessly than less fortunate individuals who display equal or greater diligence. Differences in traits and talents, moreover, may significantly affect the quality of people's lives, irrespective of their impact on earning power. The question is whether justice requires compensation of those whose powers are deficient without their being to blame.

The answer can only be that it does. Many of the skills and much of the social prowess that people acquire can be attributed to their own choices and may therefore be grouped with effort and option luck as sources of inequalities in holdings and happiness that cannot ground redistributive claims. But to the extent that personal powers take the form of handicaps or their obverse, they are properly viewed as instances of worse or better brute luck and thus as furnishing a moral reason for removing or reducing inequalities to which they give rise. To admit this point is not to deny the tight interplay between people's abilities and their desires, values, and character. People's capacities powerfully influence the personalities they come to have and hence the decisions they make with respect to their private and public lives. They even affect the worth they attach to those capacities. But although the dependence of personality on native endowments makes ranking people's collections of talents and abilities relative to one another problematic, almost all human beings can step back reflectively from their own contingent capacities to a considerable degree and evaluate their usefulness in meeting the ends they seek. Native endowments are resources, even if they are also more than that, and rightly affect the transferable material goods people may hold in a community that regards its members as equals.

What effect should they have? I consider three answers to this question. I begin by describing an approach I do not endorse, namely, a hypothetical insurance scheme, similar to that examined with regard to handicaps in section 4.2.B, for the related problem of differential talents. I then criticize Dworkin's variation on this plan. Although the practical implications of the hypothetical insurance approach I describe and Dworkin's own proposal are apt to be the same because several averaging assumptions must be made to render Dworkin's suggestion workable, without those assumptions his approach would, I maintain, lead to inequitable results. Finally, I attempt to adapt equality of fortune's method of handling bad brute luck in the case of ill or injured minors to the problem of unequal endowments. In practice, all three proposals would produce similar results, but the paths to those recommendations move over different terrain.

6.1. THE HYPOTHETICAL INSURANCE APPROACH

What would justice require if hypothetical insurance purchases afforded the proper standard for adjusting people's holdings in light of personal characteristics they did not choose and which they never willingly assumed the risk of having? Because the terms of compensation for bad congenital brute luck are fixed, on this approach, by asking how much insurance rational people would have bought against suffering various disabilities, and because the absence of certain capacities may equally be viewed as disabilities relative to those who have them, the correct method for determining the just level of liabilities and benefits arising from differences in abilities, one would think, is to ask the following question. How much insurance, with what provisions for payment, would a rational person buy if he had the same quantity of resources as everyone else and could insure against the possibility of his lacking certain talents (musical or artistic ability), powers (intelligence, prolonged concentration), aptitudes (the physical preconditions for athletic excellence or heavy work), and desirable physical characteristics (beauty, average height), cognizant of the statistical distribution of these qualities throughout the relevant population and of the difference their absence ordinarily makes to someone's life, but ignorant of his own endowments?

On the assumption that those buying insurance are ignorant of their own ambitions and tastes, but that they must decide on coverage knowing only the statistical frequency of various abilities and of particular preferences and plans throughout a given population, the answer to this question seems fairly clear, especially when the question how much insurance they would buy against other types of bad brute luck is answered concurrently. People would insure heavily against severe handicaps and debilitating childhood diseases and injuries that have serious long-term effects, since these are likely to decrease their chances of earning a decent wage, to make the establishment of certain desirable personal relationships more difficult, and to bring high bills for medical treatment and special services in their train. They would also insure, somewhat less heavily, against lacking abilities such as normal intelligence and good motor control, on the proviso that these did in fact enhance the difficulty of their making their way in the world, securing the material preconditions of a contented life, and experiencing a variety of pleasures, such as those that attend the solution of complex problems or the crafting of beautiful artifacts, that come free of charge to those who have such abilities and for which substitutes are available to someone with additional money to spend. They would insure, moreover, against not having parents who supplied them with the affection, encouragement, and educational resources they needed to develop their innate potential and to acquire the convictions and discipline necessary to make their lives successful and happy.[1] Finally, people would insure against poor luck in their search for employment once they had completed their training or education. Because, however, the success of attempts to find a fulfilling job with a good salary depends at least as much on option luck as on brute luck—the preparation one undertakes, the sedulousness with which one trains, and the perseverance with which one looks for employment all reflect personal choices for which even adolescents and young adults can largely be held responsible—and because it would be unfair to reward someone who is able to work or to work at a more lucrative job than he has, but who refuses to do so, initial unemployment insurance and insurance against not finding a suitable job would be of limited duration and provide relatively meager benefits. (Insurance against later unemployment could be left to the market, as explained in section 3.5, provided that insurance companies were forbidden to discriminate against victims of bad brute luck or one of the tax or subsidy schemes outlined above were adopted to shield the unlucky.)

Beyond that point, however, it is doubtful that people would buy insurance. They would not insure against lacking what is, by general admission, an outstanding collection of natural endowments, because insurance against not having exceptional talents would be a bad risk. The fact that few possess those qualities means that most people who bought insurance would receive a very small return on what would surely be hefty premiums, while those rare souls who were born with enviable powers would be liable to pay a very large sum, possibly forcing them to work at the most profitable employment they could find to pay their debts to the insurance company, even if they abhorred the work they had to do to make ends meet. In fact, the payoff for the majority who bought such policies would probably be still lower than these cursory reflections indicate,

[1] Insurance of this kind would be less essential, of course, if parents' failure to supply a minimum amount of support and direction were legally actionable or if the state required parents to meet certain standards in child-rearing, providing assistance itself for children whose parents or guardians failed to fulfill their obligations. Because both of these options would be preferable from the child's perspective to handing him a larger stock of resources when he was fully grown and when he could only reeducate himself and remodel his personality with great difficulty (if at all), one must imagine those making hypothetical choices to insist on these policies, and thus on their becoming law in a just state.

because insurance companies would likely introduce some measure of coinsurance and put the burden on claimants of proving that they occupy one place on the scale of actualized abilities rather than a somewhat higher station owing to nature's unkindness rather than to their personal failure to develop their natural aptitudes, thereby reducing a claimant's chances of collection. Hence, insurance would be purchased against falling noticeably below the wide band of normal powers—the further below, the higher the dividends, assuming that money would still be able to buy pleasure or relief from pain or tedium—but none would be purchased against not ending up at a particular point above that band. Nor is it likely that insurance would be purchased against falling in one region of the band rather than another, both because this type of protection would not be an attractive bet, given the costs and fairly small expected returns, and because the difficulty of proving that someone's natural endowments (as opposed to his developed skills and abilities, which reflect minor differences in brute luck but more importantly his own decisions and preferences over time) placed him in one category rather than another would mean that such fine-grained insurance would probably be unavailable or, for administrative reasons, prohibitively expensive.

What form would the premiums of these insurance policies take? It is tempting to say that everyone who did not qualify for benefits would be required to pay an equal share of the total amount of money disbursed, since each was initially given an equal quantity of rights and resources and since by hypothesis each would have chosen the same policy. But a second look evokes doubt. Hypothetical insurance purchasers, one might argue, would make a person's contributions depend upon how much he earned, on the suppositions that the marginal utility of additions to someone's stock of resources declines as the quantity of resources increases, making a graduated system of contributions less painful collectively than one which required equal shares from all, and that the higher someone's income, the less he is likely to dislike work. The steepness of the resulting pattern of tax rates would depend upon the degree to which most people valued marginal increases in income at different levels of income, the likely distribution of incomes, and some average measure of people's aversion to risk. The chief difficulty faced by this way of imagining hypothetical insurance purchases is stopping the slide into utilitarianism. If the scale of insurance rates is up for choice along with the purchase of insurance itself, why would those making the choice not adopt a utilitarian principle of compensation? The answer must be that those selecting rates and policies would reject utilitarianism and other welfarist theories for the reasons stated in section 2.2, and would seek to preserve their freedom to choose their goals and values by adopting rules of payment and compensation that do not make shares depend upon a person's desires or preferences in any given case, but that generally result in greater average happiness than a rule billing everyone equally.[2]

Whether or not this argument for assessing contributions in proportion to income is compelling, the system proposed does not seem discriminating enough. If the rate of tax were based on income irrespective of its source, then clear instances of injustice would result. If, for example, two people are equally talented and one works at some socially beneficial task while the other goes swimming, then it seems that the first should not have to share any of his extra earnings with the second or assume a larger share of their joint obligation to others who are less fortunate. (If his extra labor alters their relative positions at all, it appears that the first person should have to pay *less*, not more, inasmuch as he gives rise to a larger consumer surplus through his productive labor and thus marginally improves the lot of others more than does the aquatic aficionado.) Likewise, if one person has more riches than another because he recently won a lucrative lottery while the second lost or refrained from betting, then it seems unjust to require him to pay more compensation, since their unequal holdings stem from as clear an instance of differential option luck as one can imagine.

How might the tax plan be amended to accommodate these criticisms? Consider the following suggestion. Eliminate the proposed tax on additions to someone's stock of resources brought about by paradigmatic cases of good option luck. Tax those who enjoy considerable financially advantageous brute luck at rates that rise with their returns on investment.[3] Tax all people whose brute luck or sets of natural endowments are roughly the same, using their pre-tax income as a measure, at equal rates. Finally, have those rates vary directly with the total amount they earn for working a specified number of hours or fewer per week, so as not to tax those who earn more simply because they voluntarily work longer than the norm and to avoid enslaving people by forcing those who choose to work less than the specified number of hours to work longer, as would happen if a person's tax were a function of how much he could earn per hour rather than of his total earnings. (Tax might be imposed on income from work in excess of the specified number of hours, but perhaps at a lower rate. Whether or not a lower rate would be appropriate, the chosen rate would presumably be tied to the amount the taxpayer earned over the first thirty-five hours (or whatever figure was selected as the threshold amount). Some averaging function would be needed in the case of people who labored longer, else everyone would claim that those earlier hours were their least remunerative.)

---

[2] A similar argument could be made, of course, on behalf of tying the rates of insurance against minors' bad brute luck to adults' income, instead of charging every adult the same amount for the protection he enjoyed as a child.

[3] See the discussion of inventions and discoveries in section 3.6.

Would this system of taxation harbor residual injustices? Lamentably, the answer is "Yes." Those who earn more per hour are not always better endowed or the recipients of better brute luck in their parents, their education, their peers, and the opportunities that were available to them. Taxing everyone's earnings at the same progressive rates would therefore inevitably be unjust to some.[4] Moreover, this proposal would not tax two equally talented and fortunate people the same amount if one worked shorter hours than the other and one or both worked less than the threshold number of hours, even though they valued their talents equally. (The same is true if both worked more than the threshold number of hours, if one worked longer than the other, and if income for work in excess of the threshold number of hours continued to be taxed.) And it might be thought unfair because it leaves out of account those non-income-producing powers and the non-income-producing component of income-producing powers that people value, meaning that some people will receive more resources (to the extent that powers are regarded as resources) than others without having to compensate the less lucky.

But these injustices, the plan's defender might reasonably say, are either inevitable, or required by the protection of competing values, or illusory. Thus, the first—taxing two people the same because their incomes are identical, even though their brute luck differs—could not be eliminated by any workable tax-and-expenditure system, or perhaps even by any theoretically possible system, given the difficulty of separating the effects of brute luck, natural endowments, and personal preferences on someone's earnings or fully developed skills and abilities. The second—not taxing two equally able people the same total amount if they do not both work full-time—might be seen as necessary to avoid coercing people to work, as well as a concession to the difficulty of ascertaining how much someone values the income-producing capacities with which he was born. And the third alleged injustice—leaving out of account non-income-producing powers—does not seem genuine, because those who lacked certain endowments that in whole or in part are valued for reasons other than the income they produce and that are important to leading a moderately fulfilling life (e.g. eyesight, minimal intelligence) would receive compensation while those selecting insurance plans probably would not choose to impose higher tax rates on those whose complement of non-income-producing powers exceeds the minimum level. They would not do so because those powers do not, by definition, increase their ability to compensate those who are less fortunate, because forced labor is undesirable, and because non-income-producing powers are difficult to rank relative to one another.

---

[4] A proponent of the hypothetical insurance approach who believes that the attenuated autonomy involved in the choice of rates takes precedence over equality of resources might not regard this consequence as an injustice.

No doubt the system sketched above admits of refinements, and disagreements would arise over the proper level of benefits, particularly in the case of payments to those holding jobs but unable to obtain more profitable employment for which they are qualified and of which they are desirous. But these broad conclusions appear correct if equality of fortune is rejected and if the hypothetical insurance solution to the problem of compensating persons with congenital disabilities is stretched to cover the case of other natural endowments.

6.2. DWORKIN'S PROPOSAL

Although Dworkin favors reliance on hypothetical insurance decisions to determine the scope of redistribution, he rejects the preceding argument because, he claims, it is vitiated by two untenable assumptions. The first problem with basing contributions and compensation on whatever insurance people would buy against lacking certain natural endowments if they knew only their statistical chance of suffering these misfortunes is epistemological. Because a person's natural endowments, his luck over time, his choices, and his effort are closely intertwined, it is impossible, Dworkin contends, to determine how much natural *potential*, that is, how much *capacity*, for the development of various skills or qualities exists in a given population and how much potential any member of that population possesses. Hence, there is no way to obtain the statistical information necessary for hypothetical insurance purchasers to make their choices. Nor is it possible to prove, except in a few cases (and then only in a very rough way), that someone lacks a particular endowment and is therefore entitled to compensation. In the case of handicaps and debilitating diseases, this problem is much less formidable, and thus the hypothetical insurance approach to setting the proper level of compensation is workable. But with regard to natural capacities, unavoidable ignorance prevents justice from being realized in this way.

The second problem with this proposal, Dworkin says, is that it is impossible to say how much a particular person would value some natural capacity or trait and thus how much insurance he would have purchased against not having it before he was born, hence before he had any traits at all. The difficulty presented by the close interdependence of endowments and preferences returns in a new form. Since the preferences and values a person develops are significantly influenced by his natural abilities, one cannot tell how much one or another ability would be worth to him when he had none of them, or rather no preferences shaped by them. For then not only would there be no ground for informed choice: there would be no self left to do the choosing. This problem would not be unmanageable if almost everyone valued various traits and capacities to roughly the same degree. For if they did, one could proceed as in the case of insurance against severe handicaps, which everyone can be presumed to want to approximately the same extent, and assume that everyone would buy an average amount of insurance against lacking the endowments in question. But people do not in fact prize different capacities and talents equally, rendering the problem insoluble as posed. Dworkin concludes that an alternative approach to devising a just system for mitigating the effects of unequal natural endowments must be sought.[5]

Before examining Dworkin's own proposal, it is worth noting that both of these objections seem overstated. Disentangling the effects of chance, choice, actions, and aptitudes on the formation of somebody's skills and the creation of his opportunities for enlarging his stock of resources is indeed a hopeless project. But the scheme set out above does not presuppose the possibility of accurate dissection. By lumping together the contingent influences of brute luck in all its guises, including a person's parents and his physical and mental powers, by supposing that people would only insure against debilitating handicaps, against the absence of a minimal complement of talents and traits that prevents them from finding employment above a certain rank, and against unemployment or employment at a job below the level at which they could and would like to work, and by keying taxes (premiums) to actual earnings rather than people's earning potential, the plan just outlined obviates the need for fine discrimination between those aspects of someone's situation and person for which he is responsible and those for which he deserves neither credit nor blame. And if people would only insure against deficiencies that are particularly costly, either because they are expensive to treat or because they prevent people from finding employment or earning a modest salary, while forgoing insurance against lacking discrete natural endowments, such as musical or artistic ability, because only the former would be good bets for hypothetical insurance purchasers, then Dworkin's second objection is irrelevant. The fact that people cherish particular abilities differently would not necessarily affect their insurance decisions, for it would be unwise to insure against coming into the world without one or another specific aptitude or trait or without having one to a certain degree, given the statistical distribution of attributes and of preferences with regard to those attributes. People would only insure against especially undesirable eventualities, and with respect to these their choice of coverage would not vary greatly—at least no more greatly than their decisions concerning appropriate insurance against handicaps, which Dworkin does not think so considerable as to invalidate all attempts to base transfer payments on them. The above solution therefore seems both a feasible and a consistent

[5] *See* Dworkin (1981*b*), 316.

elaboration of the hypothetical insurance approach to providing victims of bad brute luck with just compensation.

Spurning this proposal, Dworkin defends a very similar plan, but he comes to it by a less direct route. Desirable natural endowments, he says, are usefully viewed as resources. At first blush, it might therefore seem that they should be treated like all other resources gavelled at an original auction. If they were, people would be charged the price their physical and mental powers would have fetched had they been put up for bidding, with those who are better endowed receiving fewer material resources than those whom nature treated less generously, in order to bring about equality of resources overall. But it would be unfair in at least some instances to require people to pay the auction price of the powers they happen to possess, since they did not choose, and may not even want, the strengths and aptitudes they have. If redistribution were patterned on the hypothetical auction prices of people's powers, then those who possessed extremely desirable qualities would have to labor at one of the most lucrative occupations open to them in order to pay for their talents, even if they detested the well-paid jobs from which they had to choose and would rather have been born with a different collection of abilities. Yet surely it is wrong to condemn someone to a life of involuntary servitude just because he came into the world with capacities that many other people covet. The state may not charge people the value of their talents *to others* in order to finance compensation, irrespective of the value they themselves place on those talents. Moreover, this proposal seems to imply that those who suffer from disabilities or from a dearth of powers should receive compensation equal to the negative auction price of their disabilities or lack of abilities, that is, equal to what they would accept, in the way of material resources, to put up with those disabilities, or perhaps what others would be willing to pay to avoid having them. But this formula yields no determinate answer, since some fates are so horrible that people would give all they had to escape them or so awful that nobody would accept any amount to live with them. Perhaps one could argue that all of the material goods up for auction should go to one or a few of the most miserable persons, while the rest lived on the fringe of subsistence. But this suggestion has little appeal.

Even if this proposal must be rejected, however, some correction for unequal talents must be made if equality of resources is to be achieved. Yet what plan will serve? One cannot circumvent the foregoing objections by requiring people to pay not the auction price of their powers but the price *they* would have paid, up to but not over the auction price, and shuffling material goods around on that basis to restore equality. For once again the problem of dreadful handicaps obtrudes itself, and in any case this proposal founders on the two objections noted above, namely, that one cannot determine how much a given individual would have bid for his capacities before he had any at all, and that one cannot discover what someone's natural endowments are for the purpose of levying the tax, given the tight interconnections between volition, environment, and natural endowments in the development of a person's traits and abilities. If the hypothetical insurance approach described in section 6.1 is also unsatisfactory, then what is left?

Dworkin suggests the following:

[L]et us suppose, not that people are wholly ignorant of what talents they have, but rather that for some other reason they do not have any sound basis for predicting their economic rent—what income the talents they do have can produce. Or even whether the economic situation will be such that these talents will find any employment at all. There are, of course, many different ways of imagining such a state of affairs, and it does not much matter, for present purposes, which we select. So let us fall back on our immigrants once again. Suppose that, before the initial auction [at which each person receives an equal share of resources] has begun, information about the tastes, ambitions, talents, and attitudes toward risk of each of the immigrants, as well as information about the raw materials and technology available, is delivered to a computer. It then predicts not only the results of the auction but also the projected income structure—the number of people earning each level of income—that will follow the auction once production and trade begin, on the assumption that there will be no income tax.

Now the computer is asked a further hypothetical question. Assume each immigrant knows the projected income structure but is ignorant of the computer's data base, except for its information about himself, and is therefore radically uncertain what income level his own talents would permit him to occupy. He supposes, in fact, that he has the same chance as anyone else of occupying any particular level of income in the economy, though he takes the number projected for that level into account. Assume that there is no monopoly in insurance, and that insurance firms offer policies of the following sort. Insurance is provided against failing to have an opportunity to earn whatever level of income, within the projected structure, the policy holder names, in which case the insurance company will pay the policy holder the difference between that coverage level and the income he does in fact have an opportunity to earn. Premiums will vary with the level of coverage chosen, must be the same for everyone at any particular coverage level, and will be paid, not out of the policy holder's initial stock of resources . . . but rather from future earnings after the auction at fixed periods. How much of such insurance would the immigrants, on average, buy, at what specified level of income coverage, and at what cost?[6]

Unlike the question posed above concerning the amount people would have bid for the powers with which they were born, this counterfactual question about insurance purchases, Dworkin believes, admits of an answer. People would, in general, buy insurance against not having the

---

[6] Dworkin (1981*b*), 316–17 (footnote omitted).

talents or opportunity to earn some moderate wage—to earn at, say, the thirtieth percentile of income on the scale projected by the computer—but would balk at insuring against not being able to earn at some much higher level. The reason is that the former is a smart bet in terms of welfare while the latter is not. Because almost everyone (certainly more than 70% of the population) would be able to earn a moderate wage and thus would not qualify for compensation, and because the level of earnings insured against would be comparatively low, the cost of the policy would be small while the cost of not insuring and losing one's bet—no income at all—would be quite large. Assuming that people are not risk-neutral over the whole of their utility curves and that the marginal value of income declines as total income increases, insurance of this sort would be a good bargain: the expected welfare-cost of insuring would be less than that of not insuring. Conversely, insurance against not being able to earn a very high wage would be a bad bargain, Dworkin argues, because it would amount to choosing a large chance of a very small addition to one's income over a small chance of losing a very great deal. For the cost of the policy would be exceedingly high yet the average payoff quite low, given the odds against a particular individual's having what it takes to be a top earner, and those who did have the capacity to earn high incomes would have to work strenuously at jobs that paid large salaries to fulfill their insurance contracts, even if they hated the work. Gambles of this sort, Dworkin maintains, are irrational or at any rate unpopular. So on average people would guard against not being able to earn a decent wage, but not invest in more expensive precautions.

If the state acted as the sole insurance agent, a tax-and-expenditure plan would result in which income taxes took the place of insurance premiums and government grants served as dividends. Ideally, taxes and benefits would be tailored to individuals' responses to the counterfactual questions they would have to answer for the computer to make its calculations, Dworkin says, but in practice one would have to take the mean level of insurance and treat everyone alike. Assuming that Dworkin is correct, it might seem, at first glance, that everyone who was unable to earn at the assumed coverage level would receive the difference between that level and what he could earn, while all the rest would pay the same amount of tax to finance those payments. But appearances mislead. Dworkin notes that insurance firms would presumably offer premiums that amounted to an increasing percentage of the policy-holder's income, in place of a flat-rate premium. Because graduated rates would be more attractive to prospective buyers, given the declining marginal utility of money, a progressive income tax would result. Insurance companies would also resort to coinsurance to reduce people's incentive to hide their talents if they were capable of earning at just about the coverage level, so those who were unable to earn the average amount would receive a bit less by way of compensation than the difference between that amount and the salary they were able to earn. Finally, insurance companies would protect themselves against false claims and hold down the cost of their policies by placing the burden of proof on those demanding benefits. This requirement would have the additional desirable effect of freeing governments from the need to collect a mountain of information about each citizen, with possibly significant invasions of privacy, in order to discover his earning potential. Thus, Dworkin concludes, equality of resources can be achieved and maintained over time through a refined, graduated income tax.

This conclusion differs only slightly from the system of transfers derived in section 6.1. And those few modifications that would make the two coincide are not only consistent with Dworkin's reasoning, but seem either to be natural extensions of it or to be required by other aspects of his theory. Thus, his proposal to tax income irrespective of its source offends against the principle that differences in holdings resulting entirely from differences in option luck give rise to no redistributive claims. But it could easily be altered, as suggested above, to exempt certain forms of income, such as bingo bonanzas, from taxation. Dworkin's proposal also rides roughshod over the distinction between differences in earnings due to unequal endowments, opportunities, and brute luck, and differences due to choice, unjustly assimilating the latter to the former by tacitly assuming that differences among salaries are all of the former sort. But this shortcoming can to some extent be repaired without reliance on coercion by not taxing, or taxing at lower rates, those who elect to work longer than a specified period of time on what they earn during those extra hours on the job, and perhaps by allowing certain tax-free bonuses to workers who are more productive in virtue of their greater effort or diligence. Lastly, Dworkin's "underemployment" insurance, combining unemployment insurance with insurance against not having as desirable a job as one is qualified to hold, would furnish fairly high benefits of apparently unlimited duration, which would obviously be unjust if it compelled the great majority of workers to support those without a job through their own choice rather than a straitened market. It might be amended, however, to limit the period over which all but certain disabled or incapacitated people could qualify for benefits, or at least for full benefits, on the assumption that they are responsible agents capable of retraining, reeducating, or relocating themselves if their jobs are not to their liking or if they cannot find jobs at all. Dworkin might also leave unemployment insurance to the market. Paternalistic legislation could perhaps be justified that required people to purchase a minimum amount of insurance, at least if they lacked a certain sum of capital to fall back on.

If these modifications were adopted, Dworkin's proposal would yield prescriptions almost identical to those set forth in section 6.1. All that would separate the two proposals is an extra step in Dworkin's reasoning which, he claims, would ideally allow a more just, personalized solution to the problem of determining the compensation someone is due or the tax he should pay. In attempting to extend the hypothetical insurance approach to the absence of particular abilities, I asked how much insurance people would generally buy against lacking particular endowments and against other forms of bad brute luck as juveniles, knowing only the statistical incidence of those endowments and incapacities, their likely effects, and the means available for alleviating misfortunes if they are painful or dangerous. And I argued that people would only insure against debilitating deficiencies, initial underemployment, and manifest incapacity to earn above a certain wage. By contrast, Dworkin imagines that each person knows what endowments he has, what his attitude towards risk is, and what the income structure of his society is, and asks him how much insurance he would buy against not being able to earn a given wage if he did not know how likely he was to find employment at or above that wage. It appears, however, that this extra step to individualize results is not only unnecessary, since Dworkin himself settles for contributions and compensation based on an *average* person's preferences as the only practicable plan. This extra step is also objectionable, for it either relies on information that is unobtainable or, by using a surrogate for the unavailable data, allows injustice to seep into the system.

Recall the computer program that figures prominently in Dworkin's recommendation. In order for the computer to predict the outcome of the initial auction and draw a map of the resulting economy, listing the number of people at various occupations prior to the imposition of any tax, it needs to have, as part of its data base, a record of people's "talents." By "talents" Dworkin cannot mean people's natural endowments as distinct from their developed capacities and skills, for then he would succumb to his own objection that it is impossible to determine somebody's native abilities. He would also be setting the computer a hopeless and pointless task, since the structure of any actual economy will be determined primarily by people's mature preferences and acquired skills, not by their innate aptitudes and capacities. "Talents" must therefore refer here to whatever skills and abilities a person has at the time the computer makes its determination, regardless of how he acquired them.[7]

This proposal, however, is troublesome in several respects. For one thing, it means that the amount of tax someone pays will be based in part on the effort he expended and the choices he made in sharpening his

---

[7] This conclusion represents an inference, since Dworkin often uses the ambiguous word "talents" to denote native endowments. *See* Dworkin (1981*b*), 312–14.

natural gifts, and that the benefits for which a person qualifies will depend on his own stubbornness or misguided choices in training or education as well as on whether nature was miserly when meting out his talents. Yet, according to the ideal of justice Dworkin defends, two people should not receive different initial stocks of resources or have to transfer any additional goods they acquire simply because they like different things, cherish different ideals, or pursue different aims. Nor should one be assigned greater liabilities because he works harder or longer on the assembly line or in shaping his incipient abilities than do most others. Moreover, those who are incompetent at some activity they enjoy, and who are therefore unable to support themselves at the occupation they would prefer to make their calling, should not receive compensation if they cannot find employment of the kind they most like and who sulk rather than turn what talents they have to more profitable use. By making the tax someone is liable to pay or the benefits he is eligible to receive depend on what he has made of himself rather than solely on what nature has helped to make him, Dworkin's plan unjustly penalizes the assiduous and ambitious while unfairly indulging those who persist in trying trades for which they are not fitted.

Of course, to some extent injustice of this kind is inevitable, if that portion of a person's developed talents that is properly ascribed to good genes and parents cannot be traced. But it can be mitigated by limiting the duration of benefits to the unemployed and to those whose jobs are not as challenging or as lucrative as they would like and by coinsurance. Insofar as Dworkin accepts these measures, he admits that his computer program does not specify correctly how much compensation someone is due at a particular time, for someone who refuses to cultivate talents that could win him work always deserves to be on the dole on that static model, even if he is capable of getting off it. However, if the means test were based on capacity to earn, including the capacity to earn that someone would have if he underwent some course of training or study, rather than on the skills someone had at a given time, and if the threshold capacity were low, then this objection would largely evaporate, because the amount of injustice, insofar as it is avoidable, would be small.

A second failing is much more serious. The acceptability of Dworkin's proposal depends on people's not having the slightest idea what income their developed capacities would enable them to earn in the computer's ideal economy. If they possessed this information, each could express a preference for an insurance plan that was to his personal advantage but that would not benefit most other people. The consequence would be that those who were untalented would be due large benefits, those who were luckier would owe little compensation, expenditures would greatly exceed receipts, and the system would go bust. For example, those who knew that they had an excellent chance of finding a high-salaried job might tell the computer that they would only buy insurance against not being able to earn a minimal amount, and from an insurance company, moreover, that did not charge much higher premiums proportionately to those who in fact had enviable earnings.[8] Those who only had a slight chance of taking the business world by storm might, conversely, declare their preference for an insurance plan that guaranteed people a high minimum income, taxed middle-income earners (a class to which they might some day ascend) only moderately, but imposed a hefty tax on those who earned stratospheric salaries. Needless to say, if both had their way, the state would run large deficits and the resulting pattern of taxes and benefits would be manifestly unjust. But there is no way to guarantee that expenditures would equal receipts and that a just outcome would emerge, given Dworkin's assumption that no monopoly in insurance exists and that those asked what coverage they would purchase could choose from among the range of plans that would be on offer in a free market, *unless* people did *not* know what their chances were of falling into one or another income group. It is therefore essential to the success of Dworkin's proposal that those filling out questionnaires for the computer be ignorant, or pretend that they are ignorant, of their likelihood of earning a particular wage.

A further condition for the fairness and fiscal solvency of Dworkin's plan is that attitudes towards risk-taking and preferences for material resources be evenly distributed throughout the population.[9]

Unfortunately, neither condition would necessarily be fulfilled in any actual society. And if people acted in their narrow self-interest, neither condition would be fulfilled. In any ongoing economy, people inevitably know where they stand in the hierarchy of earnings or earning potentials.

---

[8] In a competitive insurance market, insurance companies would offer a range of policies pairing income and rate of tax on compensation, since the marginal utility of money differs between people at different levels of income, since people's aversions to risk differ at various income levels, and since insurance companies could earn the same profits on many different types of coverage. For reasons he declines to state, however, Dworkin would not allow people to choose from a host of possible policies, even though he imagines that "there is no monopoly in insurance." Dworkin (1981*b*), 317. Instead, he stipulates that premiums "must be the same for everyone at any particular coverage level." *Ibid*. Dworkin also neglects to say how progressive the rates would be on the monopoly plan he alone considers. Perhaps he would favor a popular or average set of rates from among the plans that a competitive insurance market would offer, as he does in choosing the point at which wage-earners are transformed from beneficiaries into taxpayers.

[9] To state this condition more precisely, it is necessary that, as people's actual incomes (or their potential to earn, if the principle is cast in those terms) rise, people do not tend to be more willing to risk not being able to earn a decent wage or tend to conceive of a decent wage as lower in absolute terms or tend to want to dispense with progressive rates than do those with lower actual incomes (potentials to earn), or, if they tend to be more willing to do any of these things but less willing to do others, that on balance they do not tend to prefer insurance plans that are more in their own financial interests than they are in the interests of poorer people (people with lower earning potentials).

They would therefore have an incentive and an opportunity to lie about their attitudes and preferences in supplying information to the computer, in order to pay less tax or receive higher benefits than their actual preferences and attitudes warranted. They would also have an incentive to develop preferences and attitudes that would lessen their tax burden or increase the compensation for which they might qualify.

Even if one assumes, as Dworkin apparently does, that people would provide the computer with an honest account of their attitudes and preferences, or that some reliable method of expunging the expected element of prevarication from their responses exists, the second condition —an even distribution of preferences for material resources and of aversions to risk—would still not be met. Because a person's preferences and talents, in the sense of developed skills, do not ossify the moment he reaches adulthood but evolve as he ages, because people continually enter and leave the labor force, and because changes in technology and popular tastes that affect the market value of someone's skills occur constantly, surveys would have to be taken at regular intervals and the computer program rerun frequently. Every person, knowing the way in which taxes and benefits are allocated, would therefore have ample opportunity and incentive to prune or plant preferences and attitudes towards risk that are to his advantage. Indeed, even if people's preferences never altered once they put adolescence behind them, the problem would not vanish but only be pushed back a step (though probably thereby lessened), for parents would then have an incentive and an opportunity to instill preferences in their children that would be most likely to conduce to their financial success when they became adults, given their gifts and inclinations. If people were successful at shaping their preferences or their children's preferences in this way, or if by chance those who in fact had high incomes or the potential to obtain them would not favor insurance plans that would have them pay as much as those who could not find work whose pay exceeds a certain threshold would be entitled to under the plans they favored, then the system Dworkin proposes would not be financially self-sustaining unless the poor were given less or the wealthy taxed more than Dworkin thinks they deserve to be. The problem, therefore, is that if his system is the correct embodiment of justice, then justice is an unattainable ideal under certain not unusual conditions.[10]

A third flaw in Dworkin's individualized system for determining a

[10] Lack of veracity would pose a problem for the hypothetical insurance approach outlined in the previous section too. That problem, however, would be less serious than in the case of Dworkin's proposal, because the first approach does not attempt to individualize benefits and burdens and because any averaging function that was used to establish levels of contribution and compensation would tend to play one set of self-interested responses (those of the rich) against another (those earning low salaries), arriving at a compromise that should approximate the appropriate schedule of rewards and payments.

person's benefits or liabilities is that even if the preceding objection proved irrelevant in a particular case, the resulting pattern of transfers could well be intuitively unsatisfactory. If a person's taxes were a function of his aversion to risk, as would be the case on Dworkin's plan, then two equally talented people engaged in the same work and earning identical salaries could owe vastly different amounts. If one were shy of gambles and advocated sharply progressive rates while the other loved taking chances and preferred that everyone who owed taxes be taxed at a flat rate, or if one would simply have purchased considerably more insurance than the other at the same set of rates, and if both happened to fall in an upper-income bracket, then the first would be required to hand over a substantially larger portion of his income by way of tax than the second. Yet surely this smacks of injustice, not only because two equally talented and equally hard-working people owe different amounts, producing horizontal inequity, but also because the second fortunate person would be able to retain almost all the benefits of his genetic and environmental brute luck. Similar disparities in treatment could be found among identically situated people at the lower end of the income scale and at any point in between if Dworkin's proposal were implemented. Intuitively, this seems a good reason for adopting the rival hypothetical insurance approach.

In reply, Dworkin might say that the system would for administrative reasons have to base liabilities and benefits on an average person's preferences, and that if averages were used, these inequities would not occur. This rejoinder, however, misses the point. The question is not whether, given the practical problems involved in implementing Dworkin's plan, some crude approximation yields intuitively acceptable results, but whether the ideal specifies accurately what justice requires. This question still deserves a negative answer.[11]

---

[11] Dworkin appeals at several points to the practical necessity of making simplifying assumptions in attempting to excuse intuitively unsatisfactory features of his individualized approach. He notes, for example, that if two people would have purchased identical insurance policies against not being able to earn at the sixtieth income percentile, if their preferences for work and leisure were identical, and if their talents were the same except that one of the two was exceedingly photogenic and could therefore earn above the sixtieth percentile, even though she had no interest in a career as an actress or model, whereas the other could only earn at the fiftieth percentile, then the first would be enslaved by her natural beauty and have no choice but to labor at a job she detested in order to pay her premiums, while the second would live much more happily. Dworkin attempts to justify this anomalous result by saying that the first person merely had worse option luck, and that it was imprudent to insure against lacking the skill necessary to earn at such a high percentile of income. *See* Dworkin (1981*b*), 323. But sensing that his readers might not find this justification persuasive, since the two did enjoy identical brute luck (to the extent that they wished to achieve certain aims) and would have been taxed equally in an ideal world, he mentions that "this unfairness, if it is unfairness, would disappear in any plausible translation of the hypothetical insurance market into an actual tax scheme." *Ibid.* Similarly, Dworkin notes that at least some of those who would have insured against not being able to earn a lofty income might find it impossible to prove their

Alternatively, Dworkin might take issue with this third objection by decrying the apparent injustice as illusory. There is nothing unjust, he might say, in demanding higher tax payments from one of two equally talented people who earn the same income but who have different attitudes towards risk. If the two bought identical houses and one purchased more insurance than the other against a fire that never occurred, then the first would be left with less spare money, just as the more risk-averse fellow with the higher income taxes would have less disposable income. In both cases, a person's attitude towards risk, in conjunction with his later luck, determines what portion of his initial equal bundle of material resource he retains. But while one *can* view the disparity in their income taxes in this way, one might well wonder whether this is the *best* way to view it. After all, two equally talented people in a world where everyone had the same talents would owe the same amount in taxes, and if distributive principles should attempt to mirror the just patterns of holdings in that idealized society, then it seems that the two should be taxed equally in this case. Moreover, even if reliance on hypothetical insurance purchases were proper, it seems that one ought to regard a person's good or bad fortune in his abilities as having occurred at birth, and base taxes on some *averaging* assumption about how much people would have insured if they were ignorant of their endowments, as was done in the case of bad congenital brute luck and as the proposal in section 6.1 recommends. So both the intuitive propriety and the theoretical correctness of Dworkin's individualized proposal are subject to doubt.

Finally, Dworkin's ideal solution is open to the criticism that it makes a person's benefits or taxes turn on his potential to earn rather than on his actual earnings, yet earning potential, by Dworkin's own admission, is not discoverable, since choice and chance are too closely intertwined in the formation of someone's character and talents.

Dworkin is aware of this difficulty.[12] In attempting to mitigate its seriousness, he points out that insurance firms could introduce coinsurance and put the burden of proving that they are unable to earn a certain amount on policy-holders, and contends that both should be adopted because they are in the mutual interests of insurance purchasers and the firms with which they deal. He further contends that while it would indeed be difficult for someone to discharge the burden of proving that he could not possibly earn at a certain high level even if he undertook an extensive course of training and worked at his job doggedly for another twenty years,

inability if the burden were placed on them, as he suggests it should. But he dismisses this problem because the *average* coverage level, which would have to serve for all in any actual tax-and-expenditure system, would likely be low. See ibid. 326. In neither case does the impracticability of Dworkin's ideal lessen its theoretical inadequacy.

[12] *See* Dworkin (1981*b*), 324–6.

it should be possible for someone to demonstrate his inability to earn at the low average level of coverage that Dworkin believes would be chosen.

However, these measures only solve part of the problem—and much the smaller part at that. The computer needs to estimate what someone is capable of earning when assigning liabilities as well as benefits. The question is: how is it to make these estimates, and how is someone to defend himself against unfairly high taxes if he believes that his potential has been overrated? If the aforementioned distinction cannot be made, there appears no adequate answer.

Of course, this might furnish a good reason for basing taxes on actual earnings rather than on potential earnings, as a second-best solution that gives rise to acceptable injustices. And there might, as Dworkin says, be independent reasons for this expedient as well, such as the intrusiveness, excessive administrative costs, and coercion that would probably attend an individualized system of transfers. In fact, these independent reasons seem sufficiently compelling on their own to prompt abandonment of the proposal to key rates to earning potentials. If Dworkin defers to them, then this fourth objection is no more damaging to his plan than it is to that sketched in section 6.1, whose decision to make actual earnings rather than possible earnings decisive for tax purposes is motivated by the same considerations. But if Dworkin defers to them, then his theory seems not to improve upon the first proposal, while it labors under the additional disadvantage of lacking a convincing reply to the second and third criticisms above. Whether either proposal is superior to equality of fortune is the question to which I now turn.

6.3. EQUALITY OF FORTUNE

Equality of fortune maintains that people should have equally valuable resources and opportunities at their disposal, except to the extent that their voluntary actions, including any gambles they freely take, give rise to inequalities. Differences in holdings stemming from differential brute luck ought therefore to be erased, so long as restoring equality does not place inordinate strain on the more fortunate and so long as recipients continue to receive significant benefits at the margin from goods given them. Because natural endowments are nontransferable resources, and because their presence or absence is a matter of brute luck, unequal abilities should apparently be dealt with in the same way as congenital disabilities and accidental childhood injuries. Resources should be taken from those whose complement of powers is above average and given to those whose abilities fall short. Because people might not value their capacities as highly as others would if they were able to bid for them at an auction that included natural abilities, the value of a person's abilities, and the appropriateness of transfers, should not be determined solely by reference to the prices that various powers would fetch in an original auction that included abilities as well as natural resources. Rather, the total amount each person would have paid for a set of abilities must be determined, thus making the hypothetical auction price of a particular ability a maximum but not a minimum. The difference between that amount and the total amount that somebody would have paid for the abilities that in fact came his way must then be calculated. To the extent that the difference for each person is greater or less than the average difference, he is entitled to receive, or obliged to make, transfer payments to cause the actual distribution of resources to approximate more closely the ideal of an equal distribution.[13]

Unfortunately, this solution is open to a powerful objection. Except in the case of obvious disabilities, one cannot say whether someone lacks certain natural endowments, since his developed capacities are the complex products of his choices, his opportunities, and the influence of other people as well as of his native abilities and aptitudes. Those who excel manifestly had the capacity to do so, but it is often impossible to determine whether one person was born with abilities that dwarf those of most other people or had an opportunity to realize them. Many abilities are latent rather than apparent, and those that are in evidence may not have found their fullest possible expression. Any answer to the question what someone could do *if* he earnestly tried is conjectural, even if given by the person himself.

How can equality be achieved if the extent of inequality is unknown, indeed unknowable? As with hypothetical insurance schemes, equality of fortune or any similar theory of justice would apparently find it necessary, once obvious disabilities had been compensated, to abstract from inequalities in non-income-producing powers, because no reliable measurement of their value or of someone's possession of them is possible, because differences are apt not to be so considerable as to cause much complaint, and because their effects on the quality of someone's life—as reflected, for example, in the friends he comes to have—are more likely to turn on his choices and option luck than on the constitution of those powers themselves. Unlike hypothetical insurance schemes, equality of fortune would then ask, I think, not what insurance people would buy against an inability to obtain various amounts of money for their services, but how production and distribution should be arranged so as to mimic as closely as possible the economic system that would exist if people's endowments were in fact equal.

This project is not necessarily quixotic. To be sure, one cannot possibly

---

[13] I ignore complications caused by the fact that people's preferences for various capacities are interdependent: how much somebody would pay for some power could well depend on whether he was able to obtain certain complementary capacities.

devise a system of taxes and transfers that would leave everyone with exactly the resources they would have had if talents were equal, since imagining such a world involves arbitrarily stipulating which set of talents everyone would have had in equal measure and then speculating about what those people would have desired and what they would have produced if they had exploited those talents to different degrees. And the inhabitants of that world, having different capacities and presumably different ambitions from ours, would not be us. But one can ask, more generally, how wages would be determined and products distributed in a world where talents were equal, and see whether a similar system of remuneration and allocation could be established in a society where natural endowments differ.

If resources and opportunities were distributed equally at some point in time, if differences in people's brute luck were insignificant, and if everyone had the same native capacities and upbringing, then whatever pattern of production and earnings resulted would be just. The availability of goods and services would be determined by the sum of people's preferences with respect to both consumption and work, and a person's income would depend on four factors: (1) his option luck, not only in business ventures and private gambles but also, no less important, his decisions concerning the acquisition of skills and knowledge and the pursuit of one form of employment rather than another; (2) collective preferences for various products and services, which define the sphere within which he could make a living; (3) the scarcity of factors of production; and (4) his own preferences, along with those of other people, with respect to performing different kinds of productive labor at different rates of pay. Abstracting from non-wage factors that influence rates of pay, such as geographic location, and from market imperfections or monopolization, everyone performing a certain job with the same diligence would receive the same wage. Moreover, apart from entrepreneurial income that involved some element of brute luck, wages would go untaxed. Differences in earnings would be a direct function of differences in the length of time someone worked, differences in effort and resultant productivity, differential willingness to accept various jobs or to undergo special training, and luck in finding a particular job.

This idealized economy offers the following moral. Justice requires that people's real salaries not exceed the amount necessary to keep them from transferring to another job were they in a perfect labor market where all were capable of working at the full range of jobs, unless that amount is less than would be accepted by the last economically employable worker performing the same job, in which case they would be entitled to the amount required to keep that worker on the job. In a world where endowments were as unequally distributed as in our own but in which resources were distributed equally and the same opportunities were available to all, the conditions for a just *pattern* of wages, that is, the size of salaries relative to one another, appear approximately to be fulfilled for those jobs for which the overwhelming majority of people have the necessary abilities—say, those jobs that collectively constitute the bottom half of the income scale, to take a very rough estimate. In our world, the pattern is distorted in various ways by market imperfections, inequalities of opportunity and education,[14] discrimination along sexual, racial, ethnic, and other lines, and an unjust distribution of wealth, and these distortions would have to be taken into account in drawing implications from this model. Some jobs within this range, moreover, command low wages not because everyone can do them, but because few are willing to pay to have them done (professional cellists who are not star soloists would be an example). But assume, for purposes of this outline, that these complications do not exist. People who hold jobs over the lower half of the income scale are paid whatever amount is necessary to attract the last economically employable person who is willing to take one. The pattern of wages is therefore to that extent just, although the absolute amounts paid to these workers are almost certainly too low, compared with what they would be in a world where these workers shared the talents of presently more affluent persons, since in that second world some of the workers now earning at or below the mean would almost certainly take jobs that are now restricted to more talented persons, while the latter would probably not move in equal numbers to jobs presently occupied by less talented workers, given the greater challenge and interest of the jobs they currently hold. Hence, if those workers who presently labor with less lucrative natural endowments were better endowed, the absolute level of their present wages would rise, probably without greatly affecting the prevailing pattern, while the actual wages of more talented persons would in most cases fall once equilibrium was established.

But suppose that the pattern of remuneration throughout the bottom half of the income scale in this ideal economy were approximately just. The wages of two classes of workers would then have to be determined: people whose natural endowments were so meager that they could not find a job

---

[14] I set aside the difficult question how education should be organized and financed in a just state. Its resolution requires inquiries into: the extent that parents should be able to determine the content, including the religious or ideological cast, of their children's instruction; whether and subject to what conditions private schools should be permitted to exist, and the degree to which their costs should be underwritten by the state; whether children's education should be paid for by the community generally, through taxes imposed on all, whether the parents of those receiving instruction should pay all or most of the bill, or whether the costs should be charged to the children themselves once they mature; and the total amount of resources that should be devoted to education at various levels, from elementary and secondary education to technical training and graduate study. These matters deserve a book of their own.

or could only find one at an extremely low wage; and those whose special talents allowed them to earn a higher salary than the majority of persons in a free market.

The mentally and physically handicapped would first be assisted according to the principles for compensating victims of bad brute luck set out in Chapter 4. Once compensation had been paid in the form of special training programs, medical treatment, and cash, the question would arise whether members of these groups were at a noticeable disadvantage in competing for jobs that paid a fairly good wage. If they were not, then nothing more need be done for them in the name of justice. If they were, and if, in consequence, they were unable to find work or to rise above some minimal station, then they would qualify for further assistance. The benefits they would be due would vary from case to case, but it seems clear that they ought not to live much worse, materially speaking, than someone working in a job whose difficulty is such that almost everyone could perform it if he applied himself. Indeed, no one should receive much less than that amount except by choice or temporary ill luck in finding a job, and no one would if the labor market were truly competitive. Those who receive less in an actual imperfect labor market, but who would gladly work at more demanding, better-paid jobs if they could find them, should receive compensation bringing their total of wages plus compensation closer to the wages of the average worker. (Complete equality might be unwise, because it would remove all incentive to search for better jobs, and because claimants' veracity might be doubtful and difficult to assess.)

What about those who are more talented? Recall that in a world where talents were equal, salaries would also be equal, except when someone worked longer or with greater concentration and effort than his colleagues, or at a job which was generally considered more dangerous or onerous than most and so had to offer higher wages to attract workers. Impressionistic evidence suggests that jobs that require special talents or traits, such as a high degree of intelligence, imagination, or determination, would not be less appealing to people who had the talents to perform them than intellectually much less demanding jobs, even if both carried the same salaries. The intuitive plausibility of theories of motivation that include something like what Rawls calls the "Aristotelian Principle,"[15] which holds that human beings enjoy the exercise of their realized capacities to the extent that they have developed those capacities and in proportion to the complexity of the tasks they perform, further supports that conclusion. If it is correct, however, then there is good reason to believe that allowing especially talented people to keep all of the money they can earn in a free market is not only unjust in a great many cases where their salaries exceed

---

[15] *See* Rawls (1971), §65.

the norm, since people would not be able to garner them in a world where talents were more equally distributed. It is also unnecessary to coax them to labor at those socially beneficial, because economically supportable, tasks.

This does not imply that nominal salaries presently in excess of an average manual worker's wage should be reduced, either directly through caps on income or indirectly through taxes, to the level they would most likely attain in a world where everyone could perform the jobs in question. There are at least two problems with that idea. First, any guess as to what salaries would be in such a world must, for reasons already stated, be highly conjectural and only tangentially relevant to the problem of specifying disposable income in a world where talents are vastly unequal. Second, setting salaries at that level, if it could be ascertained, might be wrong if by offering somewhat higher salaries, in our world of unequal talents, one could achieve a Pareto-superior outcome.

In searching for a better proposal, it is salutary to recall one's desired ends. Those goods should be produced and those services provided that people most wish to purchase, as measured by their willingness to pay for them. Furthermore, they should be produced and provided without forcing anyone to work at a wage he would not freely accept; slavery is anathema. Yet it is also desirable to minimize the extent to which people profit from their possession of natural capacities that others lack. In addition, the principle of equal pay for equal work should if possible be honored, both because it is intuitively just and because those who did the same work would receive the same wage in a society where all had equal natural talents and markets functioned smoothly. Finally, possible Pareto improvements should not be sacrificed, so long as we can do so without committing grave injustice.

How can these various ends be fulfilled simultaneously? Suppose that everyone were asked what the minimum salary is that he would accept to perform any job that currently carries a salary in excess of the mean wage, assuming that he is in fact capable of performing that job. Suppose, further, that everyone were asked how much he would be willing to pay, in various systems of relative prices and at various possible salaries, for the numerous goods and services that might be made available if talented people applied themselves to their production or provision. Now suppose that the answers to all of these questions were fed into a computer that was programmed to assign talented people to jobs at salaries equal to or in excess of those they indicated that they would accept for the work to which they were assigned, subject to two constraints. First, everyone assigned to the same type of job must be paid the same salary. Second, people are to be assigned to positions so as simultaneously to maximize the value of what they produce or provide, measured in terms of what people stated they would be willing to pay for those goods and services, and to minimize the total amount spent on their salaries and other factors of production. When these two goals pull in opposite directions, the computer would trade one against the other in accordance with some predetermined function deemed the fairest compromise between the two objectives.[16]

Would this plan for determining real salaries achieve its desired results, ignoring temporarily the administrative problems that would attend its implementation? It seems that it would. No one would be forced to work for less than he was freely willing to accept. Each person performing the same job would be paid not the amount necessary to keep him at that job, but the amount that would be necessary to retain the last economically employable person capable of performing that job, thereby guaranteeing that all who did the same work would receive the same income, as would be the case in a world where talents were equal and markets perfect. In addition, the need to ascertain what salaries services would command if talents were equal would vanish, and no Pareto improvements would be sacrificed (unless perhaps an upper bound were placed on salaries). Finally, the economy would produce those goods that people most wanted and were able to purchase, which is what one would expect in an ideal world where people started life with equal endowments and markets were frictionless.

Equality of fortune therefore seems to entail the following principle of remuneration. Each worker performing a job which a great many people are capable of doing should, if not handicapped or otherwise disadvantaged, receive the free market wage insofar as markets operate without distortions. Each worker holding a job by dint of his special talents, however, is to be paid an amount equal to whatever salary is necessary to attract the last economically employable person doing the same work, that last person's identity being determined not by the market, as at present, but by a computer assigning specially talented persons to jobs in accordance with their preferences for work at various rates of pay so as to maximize public benefit, measured by the sum of people's willingness to pay for possible goods and services.[17]

The resulting salaries of talented people would, on this system, often top

---

[16] I leave this function unspecified, since the weights to be assigned to these competing objectives would likely vary between communities, and because I conclude that this entire approach is unworkable.

[17] Dick (1975) offers a somewhat similar though very vague proposal that calls for net compensation according to the principle of "equalizing differences in pay." He proposes a free labor market with taxes designed to remove the element of economic rent in the salaries of people who, on account of their enviable endowments, are able to bid up their wages higher than they could if all possessed the same powers. Somewhat surprisingly, Gauthier also favors taxing away the element of "factor rent" in people's salaries, that is, that portion of their salaries that is unnecessary to induce them to labor at their job and that they are able to obtain only because they possess some rare talent. *See* Gauthier (1986), 272–7.

the average worker's salary, although in some cases they might be less, if enough talented people expressed a readiness to work for lower wages at particular jobs. Their salaries might at times exceed the salaries they would be able to earn if talents were equal. But these deviations from the actual salaries of less talented workers and the salaries they themselves would be paid in a world where natural capacities were distributed less arbitrarily would be justified by the gains to those who earned less, which would lead them to prefer the system to one which depressed the salaries of talented people still further but as a result produced less of what they wanted, by the principle of equal pay for equal work, and by the conviction that it is wrong to force people to work for less than they would voluntarily accept.

If this proposal were implemented, workers with rare gifts as well as those without would still not take equal satisfaction in their work, for temperaments vary, conceptions of the good life differ, people make mistakes in acquiring skills or developing specialties, two persons might not be equally lucky in finding employment of the type they desire, the resources and technology that exist at a given time constrain the choice of jobs, and people's preferences, both for work and for goods and services, restrict the range of available occupations. But inequality of satisfaction is no reason to fault the plan, because these differences in people's joy in their work would obtain even if everyone had the same natural capacities.

The foregoing proposal, however, remains incomplete. Assuming that the real salaries of talented people should be specified by the foregoing formula, what should their gross salaries be? And how should goods and services be allocated?

At first glance, the most attractive option would probably be to allow a competitive market in talented labor to flourish, which would seem to ensure that labor went where people were most willing to pay for it, making product and factor prices an accurate reflection of people's economic desires. One could then tax all talented people, the thought runs, on an individualized basis in accordance with the information they supplied to the computer, so as to realize the just pattern of salaries. The money so collected would then be distributed equally among the populace. The alternative, it seems, is to have the computer set salaries and assign jobs, which would be administratively cumbersome and which would impair the efficient functioning of labor and product markets, as people sought to change jobs or abodes and as new products or services were developed.

This initially attractive suggestion is flawed, however. It depends on the truth of two related assumptions: first, that a competitive labor market could continue to exist if, whatever talented persons' gross salaries were, they knew that their net salaries would equal the amount set by the computer; and second, that the jobs talented people held in a competitive labor market without a redistributive tax on incomes would be the same jobs that they would hold, though at a lesser salary, if the system of remuneration described above were realized. Both assumptions are false. Beginning with the second assumption, if the salaries set by the computer prevailed throughout the relevant section of the economy, then the incentives for talented people to move from one position to another would differ from those that actually exist, since the relative size of salaries would doubtless shift, especially in view of the constraint that the rent people earned as a result of their possession of scarce abilities be minimized while ministering to consumers' desires insofar as that is practicable. But if this contention is correct, then the second assumption must be wrong: imposition of the redistributive regime on an economy free of income taxes *would* result in many people's changing jobs.

The first assumption must be similarly misguided. For the inauguration of the computer-based economy would not only alter the real and relative salaries of talented people: it would spell the end of a labor *market* as well. One objective of the computer program would be to minimize the component of people's salaries traceable to the paucity of their natural powers in the general population, and that objective could only be achieved by assigning people to positions, rather than by relying on the free market's price mechanism. Hence, the closest approximation to a just system of remuneration would involve the assignment, by some type of central planning agency, of talented people to jobs whose salaries exceed the mean.

The major shortcoming of this plan, of course, is that it would probably be impossible to implement. And even if it were feasible, the cost of realizing it, counting both administrative expenses and inefficiencies in assignment and distribution, would likely be staggering. Neither veracity nor compliance would be easy to obtain. The computer would, after all, require a great deal of information to make job assignments properly, including estimates of people's preferences for a wide range of goods and services at different prices and income levels and sincere statements by talented workers concerning the work they would be willing to do at various salaries. It would also require many people to settle for lower salaries than they could earn if they were free to make their own arrangements with customers or employers. The temptation for talented individuals to manipulate their responses to their personal advantage might often prove irresistible. And it seems quite likely, given people as we know them, that many employers and exceptionally able workers would attempt to circumvent the computer's edicts through black market transactions or under-the-table payments of one kind or another. In addition, the computer's program would have to be run frequently to take account of changes in people's preferences and skills, to correct for the entry or exit of persons from the labor pool, and to provide for the development of new products, and the constant reallocation of capital and workers would add considerably to the chaos and inefficiency.

Nor do these difficulties seem eliminable. Deliberate misinformation and the inefficient allocation of productive resources could only be avoided effectively by means of a market, and a market economy is incompatible with the computer-centered scheme described above. Of course, one could attempt to approximate the computer's results by enacting an income tax which varied from occupation to occupation, hoping to capture most of the economic rent not attributable solely to people's preferences for one type of work over another that would otherwise flow into the pockets of privileged workers. But ascertaining the size of these unjust rewards would be difficult, because the problem of inaccurate information would persist. The best that could be done, it seems—a frustrating conclusion to this lengthy discussion—would be to impose a graduated income tax, subject to the qualifications described above concerning overtime pay, the exclusion of lottery winnings, and so forth.[18] Whether the rates of tax on higher incomes that equality of fortune implies would exceed those of either of the hypothetical insurance schemes is an open question. The answer depends on whether the taxes that would cause disposable income to approximate most closely the computer's salaries would on average exceed those that people in upper income brackets would impose on themselves if faced with the hypothetical choices to which those schemes key tax rates. My guess is that the tax rates mandated by equality of fortune would be at least as high as and probably higher than under the other two theories discussed in this section, because the efficiency losses that would set bounds to these rates would also set bounds to the hypothetical insurance plans, and because before that point was reached the pursuit of equal discounted earnings over time, except as corrected for the inordinate length or undesirability of certain types of work, would almost surely yield higher rates than would be chosen by someone betting on his talents when ignorant of his earning power unless he were *very* risk-averse.

As in the case of brute luck, equality of resources therefore issues prescriptions that resemble those of theories that make entitlements depend on people's presumed insurance purchases, though as before it appears to provide slightly more compensation for the naturally unfortunate. Which interpretation of the ideal of equality one prefers will depend, once again, on which set of implications one finds intuitively more congenial and on what sort of equality one believes justice to require in a world where fortune plays favorites. Dworkin and others claim that equal opportunity to insure against bad brute luck, given an equal distribution of resources, is all that justice demands, and that when equality of

[18] See above, pp. 124–5.

opportunity does not exist, those who lacked it should be treated as they probably would have been had they had a chance to insure. However, in light of the attenuated notion of autonomy on which this approach relies, and in view of the central importance of equality of result in establishing entitlements, equality of fortune maintains instead that all hold equally valuable bundles of resources to whatever extent is practicable and morally unobjectionable, and that parity be preserved after chance has spread her charms unless someone voluntarily waives his right to full compensation.

In the end, it may be of little consequence which theory supplies the most compelling account of distributive justice. Equality of fortune and hypothetical insurance approaches stem from similar ideals, and in practice would differ only slightly. The implementation of any of these theories might additionally reduce disparities between the talented and the inept so much that people were untroubled by the differences that remained. In that case, there would be little impetus for moving further in the direction of a more equal distribution of resources.

7

Gifts, Bequests, and Intergenerational Obligations

DISCUSSIONS of distributive justice are often confined to the obligations adults owe to their contemporaries. In the desert island scenarios that commonly figure in these discussions, the hapless travelers swim ashore with little more than the shirts clinging to their backs, and none gives birth, raises a family, makes gifts to friends, or dies while stranded on the island. But these hypothetical circumstances are highly artificial. People do not begin life at the height of their powers, marooned with a handful of others on an uninhabited atoll, where no one has a prior claim to the goats and the guavas. They are, as it happens, born into families (if they are lucky)[1] of various sizes, most often in societies where all of the material resources were apportioned before their arrival. Some of their parents are rich, some poor. Some will be generous, others niggardly. The same is true of their friends. Left untouched, gifts and bequests can create large disparities in people's holdings, especially when their effects are compounded over time. Forbidding them altogether would be as undesirable as it would be ineffectual. And a cap on donations would constitute an unwarranted limitation on a person's control over his possessions. The question this chapter confronts is what measures, if any, justice requires to repair inequalities produced by gratuitous transfers of wealth or the unrecompensed provision of services.

Oddly enough, this problem has received scant attention. Libertarians often boast an easy answer, because their theories usually accord owners of property an almost unqualified right to dispose of their land and chattels as

---

[1] In some communities, this requires considerable luck indeed. According to the 1980 United States census, for example, over 60% of all black babies born in 1979 in large East Coast cities, such as New York and Washington, D.C., were born out of wedlock. The vast majority of those children are raised in low-income, single-parent households. Those who contend, as do many libertarians, that people are not entitled to a certain quantity of resources when they enter the world or as they grow, but rather must make do with what their parents and others choose to give them, would condemn large numbers of unfortunate children to poverty, wretched educations, and lives of petty crime or menial work (unless assistance was provided through public or private programs motivated by charity rather than considerations of justice). Even if some libertarians would reject this implication with respect to the United States today, on the ground that the current distribution of wealth and opportunity reflects past iniquity, they would have to admit the possibility of its replication once redress had been made for past wrongs in accordance with some principle of rectification. It is hard to view these consequences as just.

they see fit and because libertarians frequently choose happy, well-to-do nuclear families as their models. But the plight of orphans and neglected children, not to mention the circle of poverty to which many people might (as at present) be condemned in a libertarian world, should give one pause. Utilitarians are even more reticent about inheritance and gift taxes than they are about industrial organization and economic systems. For them, rules governing bequests and gifts should embody whatever mix of incentives would maximize utility, given extant social, political, and economic institutions and the preferences and attitudes that people have (or would have in a more perfect world with different institutions), taking into account their cultural, religious, and moral traditions and beliefs. Because the choice of these rules depends on empirical information that is often unavailable or on the design of utopian institutions that utilitarians never manage to describe in detail, utilitarian writers have largely neglected this topic. To their credit, John Rawls and David Gauthier recognize the large and recurrent problems posed by intergenerational obligations, but their discussions of these issues appear hasty and confused. Philosophically, this is largely uncharted territory. Although I cannot provide a complete map of what turns out to be trickier terrain than appearances might suggest, it would be irresponsible not to set out a few signposts.

7.1. THE BASIC STIPEND

An acceptable account of people's obligations to give and share must start with the acknowledgement that everyone born into a society is entitled, at a minimum, to the same quantity of resources that all who participated in the original division of the community's goods and land received.[2] The fact that someone is a latecomer through no fault of his own should not reduce the size of his fair share of social resources.

Indeed, some people believe that membership in a later generation *increases* the size of a person's entitlement, barring a general calamity, such as a war or prolonged economic depression, or some personal disaster which prevented his elders from bequeathing more than they received either when resources were first divided or from their parents by right. Those who hold this view commonly claim that people have a duty to save for future generations and to leave them with more than they themselves

---

[2] An exception to this principle seems warranted in at least some cases where the community has experienced economic devastation in the interim, whether as a result of internal strife, external aggression, or natural disaster. In these cases, later generations would ordinarily be obliged to share an earlier generation's bad brute luck. Later generations might have a morally compelling complaint, however, if they were handed smaller shares as a result of some person or group's negligently, recklessly, or intentionally wasteful or wrongful conduct.

inherited. Why this should be so, however, is puzzling. Members of future generations are, after all, the equals of their predecessors from a moral point of view, no more and no less. Temporal differences seem ethically irrelevant.

Nevertheless, two leading political philosophers—Rawls and Gauthier —sanction this view. Their arguments on behalf of it are in my judgment unconvincing. As Brian Barry points out,[3] Rawls's argument that members of one generation are obliged to increase the next generation's stock of knowledge and capital in accordance with what he calls the "just savings principle"[4] actually consists of several separate strands of argument, none of which has much strength. Rawls's stipulation that persons in the original position would be motivated to care for members of the next two generations seems somewhat ad hoc, and he never explains why caring for people entails leaving them *better* off than members of the current generation, or why caring ceases to mandate sacrifices once a stage which is "not one of great abundance" is reached.[5] Nor does Rawls explain why, if that motivation is present, a rule of justice is needed to ensure that appropriate investments are made. He also does not satisfactorily reconcile this savings requirement with the Difference Principle, which would ordinarily preclude a requirement that members of the earlier, poorer generations sacrifice for later, wealthier ones. In addition, Rawls's attempt to view savings as part of an ongoing cooperative enterprise, in which later generations are obliged to participate insofar as they benefited from their predecessors' contributions, founders on the simple fact that no cooperation is possible with either the distant future or those who lived in the past. And nothing Rawls says explains why we are obliged not to behave in ways that would harm people born more than two generations into the future. (I take up this last issue in sections 14.3 and 14.4, where I set out the view that our moral duties extend to all who will ever live, whether or not we might gain from cooperating with them.)

Although Gauthier notes that relations among persons belonging to nonoverlapping generations might seem to fall outside the scope of justice as defined by his contractarian approach, he concludes that in fact justice requires one generation to invest for the benefit of its successors in conformity with the principle of "minimax relative concession" for dividing the surplus that social cooperation generates.[6] It is unclear, however, why each person should obtain the same *relative* share of the social surplus, whenever he lives, when the result is that members of earlier generations receive much smaller *absolute* shares. That hardly seems a wise bargain for Gauthier's rational founding contractors to make. It is also an odd bargain

---

[3] *See* Barry (1989), 189–203.   [5] Rawls (1971), 290.
[4] Rawls (1971), § 44.   [6] *See* Gauthier (1986), 298–305.

to imagine them making, since, as Gauthier himself recognizes, they cannot stand to gain anything from the actions of future persons for whose enhanced welfare they would be required to abandon some of their own ambitions. And it remains something of a mystery why new people are automatically made parties to the social contract, entitling them to a share of earlier generations' resources, when a foreigner who comes upon an established society is not, in Gauthier's view, entitled to part of what that society's members have accumulated; he must, instead, take the then-existing status quo as a starting-point for bargaining, and must offer tangible benefits if he is to induce members of that society to part with their resources voluntarily.[7]

Even if the view that later generations are entitled to increasingly large shares is rejected, however, the principle that somebody's absence from the initial distribution of resources ought not to lessen the size of his share holds considerable appeal. At first glance, this principle might be thought to yield the following corollaries. (1) If a society's population remained constant over time, with the number of births balancing the number of deaths, then each member of a later generation could claim as his minimum due the same amount of resources that each member of an earlier generation received from his predecessors or in the original auction. Everyone would be obliged to contribute to a central fund, whether during his lifetime or upon his death, an amount at least equal to that which he initially received as his due (rather than by way of gift), and the fund would provide each new member of society with his just allotment when he came of age. If the population stayed level, the fund would be self-sustaining. (2) If, however, a society's population fell from one generation to the next instead of remaining constant, then it might seem that each member of the earlier generation would owe the later generation, taken as a group, less than he initially received as a matter of justice (i.e. excluding gifts and inherited property in excess of that amount), but not so much less that each member of the later generation started off no better than each member of the earlier generation had, for that would unfairly benefit the earlier generation's members. Justice requires, one might suppose, that the two generations split the difference: each of the first generation's members would have to pass on an amount that differed from the higher sum he initially received by as much as the sum that each of the second generation's members received exceeded the sum that the first generation's members initially received. Or, since that formula fails to take account of the interests of members of the third and later generations, perhaps part of the difference that the first two generations would otherwise split should be set aside and invested for later generations. (3) Finally, if the population

---

[7] *See* Gauthier (1986), 282–98.

were increasing, then it appears that members of each successive generation would have to settle for smaller shares than their forebears received, since it seems unfair to require someone to hand over more, or much more, than he was given. (One might, however, demand that each person relinquish a fraction of the amount he initially received before his death, as the population swells, in order to give each newborn the same stock of resources to work with during his lifetime as his predecessors had. Indeed, if there were reason to expect the population to grow, perhaps members of the earlier generation ought not to divide up all the available resources if this approach is correct, but rather should put some aside, in trust, in order to ensure that everyone, no matter when he is born, starts with the same amount. This proposal would not gratuitously deprive members of the earlier generation of the use of certain goods without benefiting their successors if the resources set aside were made available for a fee to whoever wished to use them.)

These principles are certainly consistent with the unexamined assumption of some philosophers, such as Rawls and Gauthier,[8] that generations as groups have obligations to future generations as groups. But though these conclusions might appear to follow from the premise that no one should receive a smaller stock of resources than those present when the world was split into shares (unless perhaps the population has grown in the interim), the inference is specious. If new people just appeared in the world from time to time, like fresh boatloads of unwitting settlers, and did not owe their birth to the actions of present members of society, then the foregoing principles would in fact come into play. But babies are not brought by storks whose whims are beyond our control. Specific individuals are responsible for their existence. It is therefore unjust to declare, as the above principles do, that because two people decide to have a child, or through carelessness find themselves with one, *everyone* is required to share their resources with the new arrival, and to the same extent as its parents. With what right can two people force all the rest, through deliberate behavior rather than bad brute luck, to settle for less than their fair shares after resources have been divided justly? If the cultivation of expensive tastes, or silly gambles, or any other intentional action cannot give rise to redistributive claims, how can procreation?

One might try to argue that because additional persons will in time benefit people other than their parents, everyone ought to contribute to the stock of resources to which those additional persons are entitled; it would be unjust to allow them to profit without paying the price. But externalities of this sort rarely seem significant, and in any event parents and siblings are apt to be by far the major beneficiaries. It is highly

---

[8] *See* Rawls (1971), 284–93; Gauthier (1986), 302–5.

questionable, furthermore, whether one person may compel another to pay for a benefit the latter did not request. If A landscapes B's yard while B is away on holiday and then demands that B pay him for his trouble, even though B never agreed to pay, then A has no legal right to payment. Nor does he appear to have a moral claim. This line of argument thus offers little promise. At best, it may generate a light duty to contribute to the support of someone else's children in cases where positive externalities are noticeable.

What does this conclusion entail? It implies that the obligation to provide each person born after the original auction or its modern analogue[9] with a bundle of resources equal in value to that which each of the auction's participants received falls wholly or almost entirely on those responsible for his existence.[10] Under present social conditions, this obligation is almost always incurred by a child's natural parents,[11] unless a foster parent or other benefactor voluntarily assumes it; if it became possible to produce babies in laboratories, then it would pass to whoever

---

[9] How the initial distribution of resources could and should be replicated or approximated in countries where the distribution of wealth is currently very unequal and almost certainly unjust is a question I shall not try to answer here. Confiscation of all holdings above the shares to which people are entitled and their redistribution among those who have less through no fault of their own might be possible in theory but in fact prove too disruptive personally and economically. Less sudden and sweeping measures to correct the maldistribution of wealth and income might be more desirable. But precisely what compromise should be struck, and how much popular opposition could morally be suppressed through the exercise of state power, are questions whose answers will vary with time and place. Problems would also beset immediate enforcement of the requirement that parents pass on resources equal to the basic stipend when their children reach majority if some people had minor children and lacked warning or opportunity to save before the new requirement took effect, even if private or state loans were made available.

[10] This obligation does not extend beyond the provision of a basic bundle of resources, and thus does not obligate only a person's parents to compensate him for whatever bad brute luck he later suffers. Those who are present at the original auction are morally bound to share in one another's brute luck unless they agree on some modification of that duty, even though they are not responsible for one another's existence. New additions to the pool are in this respect not relevantly different from those already there. Nor should their inclusion matter to most people born before them, since one would expect the new arrivals' good and bad brute luck to even out if the group is large, resulting in no net effect on current claims to compensation.

[11] I say "almost always," because in exceptional circumstances a child's parents may not be responsible for its existence, or answerable in equal measure. For example, if a woman became pregnant because a contraceptive device failed even though she used it properly, and if she refused to have an abortion performed, then the responsibility for supplying her child with the resources it is due may fall to her and the father, or it may fall to the manufacturer of the contraceptive device, or it may be shared among them, depending upon the claims made by the manufacturer at the time of sale, upon established rules of liability, and upon the significance for liability of the woman's decision not to abort the fetus. Or if a child is conceived through rape and the mother will not consent to an abortion, then the responsibility for seeing that it receives its fair share of resources seems not to rest equally with its two natural parents, but appears to fall wholly upon the father. Other instances of differential responsibility might arise through prior agreements between the parents.

was responsible for bringing another life into being. To create a person for whom one cannot provide in this manner violates his right to a minimum amount of property, and is thus morally impermissible.

What should be done when parents or other responsible parties cannot or will not give their offspring their due is a question I shall not explore. Those who took their obligations seriously would insure against not being able to give their children their basic stipend because of premature death, disability, or unemployment. But whether insurance ought to be mandatory, at least for people who have neglected their duty with respect to one or more children, or whether offenders should be incarcerated or penalized financially, are issues whose answers will depend upon the gravity of the problem in a particular society, the effectiveness of various countermeasures, the importance one ascribes a child's right to his basic stipend or other people's right not to have to furnish it because of the parents' neglect, and the legitimate limits of paternalistic legislation, all of which lie outside this inquiry. Likewise, the problems of what form the resources parents must give their children should take (how much and what kind of education? food? shelter?), and how these required transfers should be coordinated with expenses which one can safely presume that children would, if rational and far-sighted, want to incur in the form of loans made against their future earnings, are matters that vary with societies and their technological and economic resources. It would not be especially profitable to consider them in the abstract. Finally, I shall not attempt to say what protection children should enjoy against abusive or negligent parents, though it is clear that some should be provided. (Should children, for example, be taken away from their parents and raised in foster homes or institutions if their parents are guilty of certain infractions? Which ones? Should prospective parents have to pass tests in order to obtain a license to raise children before they are allowed to give birth to any, or allowed to keep those that they have?[12]) These issues deserve a longer, more careful treatment than I can manage here. It suffices to repeat that in a just society spared economic calamity for which it is not morally blameworthy, children would receive goods and services at least equal in value to the resources each of the society's original members carried away with him when resources were first divided, and that these stipends would be supplied by those who called them into existence.

7.2. THE DIVISION OF INTESTATE PROPERTY

The amount of resources that someone born into an ongoing society may permissibly receive is not limited to this minimum entitlement. Because a

[12] This may sound flippant, but some writers take the idea of licenses seriously. *See, e.g.* LaFollette (1980).

person's right to dispose of his property may not be curtailed (except perhaps for paternalistic controls and measures designed to ascertain intent, e.g. competency and witness requirements for wills), people will often acquire property by gift in excess of their basic share, given the love that parents often bear their children, the generosity people sometimes manifest towards friends or an anonymous posterity, and people's tendency to consume less than they acquire, if only because prudence dictates that provision be made for the morrow and eventually people die before the morrow arrives.[13] Someone may come to own an amount in excess of his basic stipend without winning or earning it in two ways: through the death of somebody who left no directions for the division of his estate or whose intentions regarding its disposition cannot be inferred or presumed; or through bequests and gifts.

The first of these cases is likely to be of marginal importance. When someone dies intestate and there is no reason to think that he intended his property to pass to certain identifiable individuals or groups, the just way to allocate his belongings, once outstanding debts have been paid, is clear. Because no one has a stronger claim to what he left behind than anyone else, his estate is properly regarded as an addition to the pool of resources available for general distribution, and should be divided equally among all those alive at the time of his death. Since children would have as much right to this property as adults, they would receive shares of equal size. The circle of beneficiaries should include all who are alive at the time of the distribution, along with babies in the womb who are later born alive, rather than just those who have attained majority by that time. A child's receipt of his share of the estate would not reduce by a commensurate amount his parents' obligation to supply him with what to that point was deemed a basic bundle of resources, since the fact that they and all other adults received equivalent shares means that the basic stipend has, in effect, been raised by the amount of each individual's share of the estate. It ought, moreover, to remain at that new, higher level for all future generations, since each person conceived subsequent to the division of the estate has a right to the same amount of resources that his contemporaries received in what one might call the updated auction.

The reason for defining the class of beneficiaries expansively is one of fairness. If already conceived children were not included, their parents would owe them, in addition to what would have been their basic stipend, an amount that exceeded what would have been their share of the intestate's estate had they been included in the division. For parents' receipt of a share of that estate would oblige them to provide each of their

---

[13] Sometimes the opposite happens, of course. In the absence of mandatory old-age health insurance, many elderly people would probably exhaust their resources on nursing and hospital care before they died.

children with a stipend enhanced by the amount they received, and that amount would obviously be greater if the estate were split evenly among adults rather than the larger class of adults plus minors. Parents and prospective parents would therefore oppose this proposal unless a two-parent family only had or was destined to have but one child and the number of minor children in the population alive at the time of the division exceeded the number of adults then alive,[14] for except in that extra-ordinarily unlikely situation, the sum of parents' new obligations would exceed their slice of the estate if the estate were divided among parents alone. That result seems unfair, because it would increase parents' obligations to their children *after* the children had been conceived, even though parents had decided to have children in the expectation that they would owe them a certain amount. Of course, virtually all adults who do not have children would fare better if the intestate's estate were divided exclusively among adults, and children would do better too in terms of the shares they were owed (although parents might simply reduce their voluntary gifts by an offsetting amount). It might thus seem arbitrary which group one should favor, and in any case the matter is of little importance, given the small sums that are involved on account of the fact that few people are likely to leave their accumulated wealth to society at large, or can reasonably be thought to have wanted to do so. Because there is no unfairness in distributing intestate property to children as well as adults and no reason to limit distribution to adults other than non-parents' desire for larger shares, however, whereas there is arguably some unfairness (though insurance would be possible) in choosing the smaller set of beneficiaries and something odd in not counting children as persons, I would weakly favor including children as well as parents among the distributees.

The conclusion that the class of beneficiaries should be defined broadly cannot be sidestepped by claiming that the property of those who die intestate should go exclusively to those who have not yet come of age and received their basic entitlement from their parents or guardians so as to reduce the latter's liabilities, or to all parents in proportion to the number

---

[14] Let x equal the value of the intestate estate, a the number of adults in the population, and c the number of minor children in the population. A two-parent family with two children would never do better if the class of beneficiaries were restricted to adults, because the money they received together ($2x/a$) they would have to pass along to their children, each of whom would be entitled to an additional stipend of x/a. In contrast, if the class of beneficiaries included children, two parents would together retain $2x/(a + c)$, which is certainly better than nothing. A two-parent family with only one child might come out ahead if the smaller class were used, because in that case they would together keep $2x/a - x/a = x/a$, and that amount could conceivably exceed what they would keep if the class were bigger, namely, $2x/(a + c)$. However, x/a only exceeds $2x/(a + c)$ if c is greater than a, and it is extremely unlikely that the number of minor children in any population would exceed the number of adults.

of children they had. Both of these suggestions fail because they would
deprive those who are not parents, or who decided to have small families
rather than large ones, of their equal right to property left to no one in
particular. Hence, the estates of all persons dying intestate and without
presumed beneficiaries should be divided equally among those living, or
conceived and destined to live, at the time of the owner's death, and the
basic allotment of resources, as determined by the updated auction, should
continue at a higher level for all subsequent generations.

7.3. DIRECTED GIFTS AND BEQUESTS

Few people, however, are likely to want their property to pass equally to
everybody who survives them. In almost all cases where someone dies
intestate, we assume that he would have wanted his estate distributed
among his family or relatives rather than paid into the public treasury, even
when the kin who benefit are remote. And most people designate the
objects of their bounty through lifetime transfers or wills. The most
common sources of unearned goods in excess of a person's basic
entitlement are therefore gifts and bequests. What has justice to say with
respect to their legitimacy?

The first point to note is that if the foregoing theory is correct, no
constraints may be placed on the way someone spends his original stock of
capital, his income, and any other goods he has received from others, once
he has discharged the obligations of assistance that justice imposes on him
and contributed his share to those morally permissible collective projects
he is bound to support, provided that he does not use his money to injure
others or otherwise encroach illicitly upon their freedom. It is his decision
whether to become a gourmand, to support the arts, or to leave his
children a sizable legacy. If someone elects to eat his way through his
earnings, or to go to bed hungry in order to acquire fame through
philanthropy, then no one can gainsay his choice.

But it does not follow from a person's freedom to keep or confer that
those who benefit from his largess may pocket all that he bestows on them.
A countervailing principle comes into play, which restricts the receipt of
benefits even if it does not limit their dispensation. Whether beneficiaries
may keep what they have been given depends, as an initial matter, on the
extent to which they have been favored by good brute luck. In most cases,
as in the case of finding a job that suits one's ambitions, elements of both
brute and option luck are interwoven. How much the recipient of a gift or
bequest must share his good fortune with others therefore turns in part on
the degree to which his acquisition of benefactors and their generosity
towards him is a matter of unsolicited chance rather than of his intentional
actions, the intentional actions of others, and others' preferences, and on

the degree to which people are required to divide the fungible benefits of this form of good brute luck with those who are less fortunate.

Most generalizations with respect to the role of brute luck in gift-giving are honeycombed with exceptions, but one might be sufficiently solid and important to incorporate in public policies governing redistributive taxation. The material gains in excess of the basic entitlement that people receive from their parents generally depend more on brute luck than do the friends or spouse someone has and the financial benefits he receives in consequence. To the extent that this relationship holds, there exists a good reason for treating gifts and bequests to children more like one would pure cases of good brute luck than for treating transfers between friends or spouses in this manner. Net transfers from parents or grandparents to members of younger generations would then be taxed more heavily than property that one spouse gives, or upon his or her death leaves, to the other. They would also be taxed more heavily than transfers from younger to older generations if, as seems true, parents earn the assistance of their children more frequently than children deserve their parents' help.

It is, however, difficult to say how nearly any of these classes of gifts approaches or departs from archetypal instances of good brute luck, or whether exceptions to the rule are so common as to render its enforcement unjust or, if those exceptions generate a right to relief, administratively unworkable. So far as gifts from parents to children are concerned, the approximation to cases of unadulterated good brute luck generally seems quite close. Children do not choose their parents. And although rebellious offspring may forfeit their parents' love, to the extent that they enjoy it and profit materially from it they do so largely because, in a society based on the nuclear family, they were through no merit of their own better placed to win their parents' affection than were other people. They also do so because parents often become attached to their progeny through the activities of procreation and child-rearing, for which attachment children are in no wise responsible, and because many parents feel, whether or not mistakenly, that they have a moral duty to provide generously for their children and to leave them the bulk of their property when they die. If these observations are correct, and if exceptions are not too numerous at whatever level formed the threshold for redistributive transfers (a question one cannot well address in the abstract), then gifts from parents to children ought to be regarded largely as instances of good brute luck from the children's perspective and treated accordingly. Nevertheless, the counter-vailing principle that if someone chooses to spend his money on another person rather than on himself, he need not be munificent towards the world at large, must be given its due, as explained in section 7.4. So too must an opposing argument from collective consent, which I also discuss below.

Transfers between friends and spouses are more problematic. If everyone were equipped with and used one of Ackerman's transmitter-shields,[15] which allowed him to beam messages costlessly to his fellow citizens and to receive from them those signals he chose, then the formation of friendships and any gifts that flowed from them might be attributed in fair measure to option luck, since everyone could send word of his preferences and qualities to whomever he wished, listen or not listen to what others said about themselves, and take whatever initiatives he liked to contact all those with whom he might want to enter into more intimate relationships. Even in this science-fiction world, however, brute luck would play a salient role in the genesis of pairings and the depth of attachments. Close friendships are usually bound up with shared experiences. Those experiences depend on physical proximity and thus are invariably influenced by where and when someone happened to be born and to live at a particular time. Moreover, to which of the many messages someone chose to listen and respond, and the order in which he followed them up, would to a great extent be a chance affair, since the number of close friends one can have is limited and since the wording of one's own messages, one's selection of recipients, and one's choice of a program for winnowing incoming signals would all be infected by arbitrariness and uncertainty. And in a world like ours, with only the crudest forerunners of the transmitter-shield at our disposal—the newspaper advertisement, dating services, and various styles of dress and address—brute luck plays a much more commanding part, unless one assumes that a fair cross-section of potential friends exists throughout one's society.

Brute luck may therefore dominate in the case of interspousal gifts or gifts between friends as well as in the case of gifts from parents to children, particularly given its sizable part in bringing people together. Despite brute luck's force, however, the contributory effects of option luck ought not to be overlooked. One can, after all, discover the identities of the rich and open-handed, and make whatever overtures one thinks appropriate, even if some are, by chance, more enviably situated than others to curry favor.[16] Large gifts between adults, furthermore, are rarely made capriciously, but almost always follow a lengthy association in which the beneficiary sacrificed his personal projects to some degree for the donor. Gifts are seldom entirely gratuitous. If someone is not prepared to give what it takes to receive, then it is hardly a matter of luck that no one leaves bales of banknotes on his doorstep. Staunch friendships and marriage are voluntary associations that ordinarily require patience, affection, and self-renunciation if they are to endure. When they flourish, the credit rarely belongs to

[15] *See* Ackerman (1980), § 40.

[16] Given a just distribution of resources, the possibility of forming such associations would be significantly greater (though it might still be small) than it now is.

Providence, and therefore the right that others might have to part of the assistance that friends lend one another, financial or otherwise, is often attenuated.

The upshot of these ruminations is that although thick threads of brute luck are inevitably intertwined with settled preferences and deliberate choice in the cords that bind spouses and friends, their role in bringing and holding people together and in prompting transfers of wealth is in most cases probably less decisive—though it might on average still be quite considerable—than in the case of gifts and bequests from parents to children. If so, the degree to which beneficiaries must share their good fortune with others is therefore smaller too. And the people with whom they must share it are arguably also fewer in number. The fact that children cannot help but have parents whom they lacked an opportunity to select and who rarely assist their children in proportion to what they adjudge their merit relative to other potential beneficiaries provides a good reason for requiring that good brute luck in one's parents be shared to the same extent with all other persons, not just with other people who are under age at the time one is born or receives one's gift. In contrast, because people can influence to some degree the friends they have, those people who shun close personal relationships seem to have less title[17] to the benefits that accrue to those who are fortunate in their friends. But while it would be feasible to tax transfers between friends at lower rates than gifts from parents to children or between close blood relatives, it would be practically impossible to divide proceeds from the former tax unequally among those who received less valuable gifts, according to the relative importance of option luck in determining the total amount that they received. And it would probably be impossible to distinguish among donors according to the prominence of brute luck in the origin and continuation of a relationship leading to a gift or bequest. Perhaps the best one could do is make benefits inversely proportional to the total value of whatever someone was given over an extended period of time, although this plan would only constitute a very rough simulacrum of the just result.

Finer distinctions might be introduced within the aforementioned classes. One might want to tax cumulatively large net transfers from one person, or from all donors combined, to another person at higher rates than one taxes smaller gifts, on the rationale that recipients of extremely valuable (aggregate) gifts enjoy considerably more good brute luck than the norm, given the slim odds of being born to wealthy and generous

---

[17] Often they will still have some title to those benefits, even if less than others do. For many times a person's disposition to make friends or seek intimacy is profoundly influenced by childhood experiences for which he is not accountable, and his chances of success may be affected by characteristics of body and manner that he did not wholly choose.

parents or of acquiring friends who possess those attributes.[18] One might also want to treat gifts between spouses or constant companions differently from gifts to other friends, except in cases where gifts to the latter serve primarily as rewards for exceptional services, since the former often involve proportionately more desert and therefore entitle recipients to a larger share of whatever material benefits they obtain. Finally, some means would have to be devised to prevent parents from escaping the hefty gift tax by making presents to friends' children in return for corresponding gifts to their children.

7.4. TWO COUNTERVAILING CONSIDERATIONS

Precisely how high the rates of tax should be in the cases just described is an extremely difficult question. Two distinct arguments must be considered in determining whether the degree to which brute luck featured in a particular gratuitous transfer should alone set the rate of tax.[19] First, there is the balancing argument to which I alluded above. People should be free to use their property for the good of others rather than themselves if they so choose, and to select the objects of their generosity without being obliged to act similarly towards everyone else. Yet, good brute luck should be shared with those less lucky. Whether the right to control the use and benefits of one's justly acquired property should be given any weight at all when it pulls in the opposite direction from the principle calling for the

---

[18] If this policy were enacted, it would be difficult for one family to amass much greater wealth over the course of several generations than do other families, given an initial equal distribution of resources (though much would turn on how progressive and how high gift and inheritance taxes were). This result seems intuitively desirable. But even though huge disparities in wealth would rarely occur, the question arises what should be done if one industrious, miserly, and extraordinarily lucky generation followed upon another, each passing on at least some of its accumulated wealth to its successors until, after several centuries, inheritances within that family far exceeded those of nearly all other families.

One response would be to establish almost confiscatory marginal tax rates on cumulative receipts of a certain magnitude, thereby preventing this situation from ever arising, albeit at the cost of severe disincentives to save past a given point and thus almost certainly of lessened investment and economic growth. Another would be to strike the balance between redistribution and productivity at some spot further down the line, allowing such disparities to arise, if they ever do, rather than sacrifice the collective benefits that flow from incentives to husband one's resources for the sake of one's posterity. As I note below, which solution one favors will depend on one's judgment as to the relative importance of redressing inequalities in brute luck and of allowing people to do what they please with resources they acquired justly, as well as on the likely effects of a particular policy in a given society.

[19] Determining the degree to which brute luck rather than option luck lies behind a gratuitous transfer is, as the preceding section shows, itself a difficult undertaking. Even if brute luck generally plays a larger role in the case of gifts from parents to children than in the case of gifts between friends, it may well dominate in both cases. I offer no guess as to their average percentage contributions. Nor is it clear whether the injustice that would attend a failure to accommodate, for administrative reasons, what would otherwise be exceptions to the rule is so great as to scuttle attempts to establish different rates along the lines discussed.

redress of differences in brute luck and, if so, how much impact that right should have, is a hard moral question which people will answer differently. In my view, it does deserve considerable weight, but it is difficult to quantify the relative force of these competing principles in the abstract.

The second argument for not allowing tax rates on gifts and bequests to depend exclusively upon the degree to which a transfer was the product of brute luck is grounded in a prediction concerning collective assent to a modification of that rule. People would not allow brute luck alone to be decisive, the argument runs, because the world that would result from that tax system would be inferior to one in which taxes on gifts and bequests were lower. Consider the likely effects of making brute luck sovereign when assessing taxes on gratuitous transfers. With respect to at least some transfers, very stiff rates would result. But the stiffer the tax on transfers of wealth, the more frequently people would attempt to evade it, the more difficult it would be to administer fairly, and the more potential donors would tend to consume rather than save. Parents might give less to their children and siblings might leave less for their near relations if a larger chunk of those gifts were taken by the government for redistribution— although it is unclear whether this disincentive effect would be pronoun- ced, or even whether the opposite effect might be induced. Family farms or businesses might have to be liquidated to meet tax liabilities when parents passed them on to their children. Investment and economic growth could well decrease over the long run. Perhaps more important, such a rule might promote an undesirable kind of social atomism, undermining the love and sense of shared enterprise that characterizes many families and some friendships. In view of these predicted consequences, the argument concludes, collective assent to a modification of the rule basing tax rates on brute luck alone could be presumed.

This argument seems quite forceful, although its power would diminish insofar as taxes on gifts and bequests were determined not solely by the degree to which brute luck was present, but by that fact in conjunction with the countervailing principle that people should be free to confer their material resources on others rather than use those resources themselves if they are so inclined. But to what extent collective assent could be presumed to a modification of what would otherwise be the prevailing rates of tax it is impossible to say. Its answer would plainly depend upon whether majoritarian, supermajoritarian, or unanimous approval were required. It would also turn on dispositions and attitudes that differ appreciably among cultures, and it might be shaped as well by the degree to which a community's distribution of wealth and income was in other respects just. The question therefore seems not to admit of any clear answer in the abstract.

7.5. THE BASIC STIPEND OVER TIME

In section 7.1, I argued that parents generally have an obligation to confer on each of their children a bundle of resources equal in value to that which they or their ancestors received when collectively held resources were first divided. In section 7.2, I further contended that a person's receipt of an equal share of the assets of someone who died intestate and whose intentions regarding the *post mortem* disposition of his property were unknown and cannot properly be presumed augments the size of the basic stipend that the recipient owes to any children he conceives after that date, and that those children in turn owe that augmented amount to their offspring. Intestate property distributed equally to all constitutes an addition to the pool of resources available for general distribution and thus to the bundles of resources to which people can claim title, just as valuable minerals discovered subsequent to the initial distribution increase the size of everyone's basic share.

Do taxes collected on gifts and bequests constitute a like addition to the community's resources? At first glance it might seem intuitively appealing to conclude that they do. If taxes on gratuitous transfers were so treated, then everyone (including the taxpayer) would be entitled to an equal share of the proceeds of good brute luck collected through those taxes, and amounts so apportioned would increase the basic stipend accordingly. One could then expect the basic stipend to rise steadily over time—faster in times of economic expansion, assuming gifts and bequests burgeoned, slower in lean times. Later generations would thus benefit, in what might appear an intuitively appropriate way, from improvements in the community's material well-being. And they would do so substantially, though not entirely, as a matter of right rather than generosity, thereby tempering whatever disparities arise. At the same time, parents would apparently not be burdened unduly, for they would only be asked to pass along as large a stipend as they had received prior to the time they conceived a child, and they would not even have to transfer this sum if their holdings were significantly depleted by some general misfortune for which they could not be blamed and against which they could not be expected to have insured.

I do not believe, however, that these conclusions can be sustained. Consider other transfers mandated by equality of fortune to correct for differential brute luck. Redistributive measures designed to compensate for differences in people's talents, for example, cannot be thought to add to the basic stipend, for they serve to offset current, ongoing inequalities in resources. Such measures do not pretend to allocate equally new additions to the stock of resources to be shared by all. Instead, they are defined by reference to disparities in the brute luck of people then living, and are designed to erase those differences so far as technology and morality allow.

Nor do the premiums people pay to insure against disease or unforeseeable accidents, which take the place of compensation they would otherwise owe to members of the community who suffered bad brute luck, subtract from the basic stipend they are obliged to confer on their children. These payments, too, have as their purpose the correction of present inequalities in people's fortunes, although to the extent that insurance is made voluntary, option luck largely displaces brute luck in determining the streams of payments and receipts.

Redistributive tax proceeds culled from good brute luck in the gratuitous transfers people receive seem indistinguishable from these other redistributive measures in crucial respects. Those who enjoy good brute luck of this kind do so only by virtue of the fact that other people are less fortunate, since good and bad are relational concepts and the payments justice requires of them are calculated to help right this imbalance. Unlike the division of new discoveries or the sharing of intestate property, to neither of which anybody has a privileged claim and which therefore have the same effect on everyone's entitlements, the purpose of these redistributive payments is to go some distance toward evening out existing *differences* in the brute luck that people experience. They do not add to the sum of collectively owned and thus equally divisible resources, and so do not increase the amount parents are obliged to pass along to their children.

On reflection, this result is intuitively sound. Suppose that a large sum of money changed hands in a given year through unmerited *inter vivos* gifts and bequests. It hardly makes sense to say that parents' obligations to their children depend solely on how greatly people's unearned receipts of gifts vary, so that (1) if everybody received the same amount in gifts as a matter of good brute luck, the basic stipend would remain stable, but (2) if half the population was showered with presents and the other half neglected, everybody's obligation to provide their children with a fixed bundle of resources would increase. If all the differences among beneficiaries in the second case were eliminated entirely through redistributive taxes, the two cases would yield identical consequences, so far as people's current holdings were concerned. Parents would no more be able to provide for their children in the second case than in the first. Yet the approach outlined above would mandate larger intrafamily payments. To enhance parents' burdens in the second case but not the first, because fluctuations in the unmerited receipt of gifts were large rather than trifling, would be the reverse of just.

Nor should one be dismayed by the fact that the basic stipend would probably not rise briskly over time if this account of the implications of equality of fortune is correct. For children—and not only children—would still fare very well. If a community grew more prosperous, so that gifts and inheritances increased, then those whose parents gave them no more than the required minimum would benefit richly from redistributive taxation. They would not fall markedly behind those whose brute luck in their parents or friends was considerably better. Indeed, it is the alternative approach I first sketched that could have dispiriting consequences. For if the basic stipend increased swiftly because disparities in the receipt of gifts were large, then parents would not be able to partake of the good luck they never enjoyed directly but only obtained through redistributive payments (at least until after they had paid their children the required stipend), for they would have to save that entire amount to convey to their offspring— despite the fact that they would not have been saddled with an equally demanding obligation had people's desires to please their friends and children been more uniform. And having more than two children would soon become prohibitively costly, not merely for one generation of parents but for all parents into the limitless future. An acceptable theory of justice could not have these consequences. Equality of fortune does not.

Needless to say, the preceding remarks do little more than outline the implications of justice with regard to gifts between members of an otherwise just community. A complete discussion would have to specify how present arrangements should be altered to approximate an initial equal division of resources, or how the theory should be modified to cope with the status quo if drastic changes in current holdings lie outside the realm of possibility. It would also require more detailed examination of possible tax plans, the disincentives they would create in a society like our own, their likely effects on familial relationships and friendships, and prevailing attitudes towards tax rates lower than are necessary to eliminate disparities in brute luck. Attention would have to be paid as well to financial instruments that might be introduced to facilitate parents' mandatory contributions to their children[20] and to effect the collection and distribution of tax revenues. These issues would repay careful study.

---

[20] Might the state, for example, guarantee children their shares when they become adults, allowing parents to repay later in life whatever assistance the state provided at that time?

8

Justice and the Transfer of
Body Parts

MOST philosophers assume that the goods available for distribution in accordance with a theory of justice are limited to tangible items outside the domain of a person's body that can be transferred without physically injuring either the recipient or the transferor. Because this supposition is nearly universal and rarely questioned, the preceding discussion of equality of fortune made but fleeting reference to principles that assign people rights to others' time and energies, let alone their organs. Yet part of this supposition deserves further scrutiny. One may be able to dismiss theories that accord people equal shares of one another's labor or time, or that require them to pay in taxes the difference between what their innate capacities would cost in a hypothetical auction where all had equal bidding power and what an average set of capacities would cost, on the ground that these schemes would prove unworkable or would unjustly burden those who valued their talents or productive capacities less than did those who would have bid most for them in a hypothetical auction.[1] But the claim that some people who are handicapped or facing death from disease are entitled to parts of others' bodies in order to remove their disabilities or save their lives when the donor would not be similarly injured or endangered is more difficult to rebut. Why, for example, should someone born blind have a right only to material compensation that cannot substitute for sight, rather than to an eye from somebody who has two that function well? Or why does treating people as equals only entail that someone suffering from a terminal kidney ailment be given some chance of receiving dialysis treatment or a voluntarily donated organ, rather than a kidney from somebody who has two and who can live with one? Any complete theory of justice, particularly one committed to the equal worth of persons and their right to an equal stock of resources, must answer these questions, however bizarre they might sound on first hearing.

This chapter examines the more important responses that have been or might be offered to them. It opens with a defense of nonvoluntary *post mortem* transplants and the mandatory transfer of organs from live donors

---

[1] A fuller discussion of such theories may be found in Nozick (1974), ch. 9; Varian (1975); and Dworkin (1981b), 311–12.

(under certain restrictive conditions) for the benefit of responsible adults who elected to join a mandatory transfer scheme and for the benefit of children, in cases where the benefits would be large and the sacrifices demanded of donors not excessive. It then answers critics of nonvoluntary transplants, arguing that none of their objections is compelling on close inspection. I conclude that compulsory renal or corneal transplants, as well as forced blood donations, are justifiable to redress significant inequalities if cadaver organs are unavailable and if potential recipients never waived their right to receive an organ in exchange for a lessened risk of having to donate one of their own. Fortunately, if cadaver organs were collected routinely, notwithstanding the wishes of decedents or their survivors, nonvoluntary extractions of organs from live donors would almost always be unnecessary.

8.1. THE ARGUMENT FOR COMPULSORY ORGAN TRANSFERS

Is it ever morally permissible to transfer organs or blood from one person to another against the donor's will? The argument for thinking such transplants not only morally licit but at times even morally required is straightforward. Justice demands that people be made equal in the resources they hold and that the resulting distribution not be Pareto-inferior to any other equal division. Human tissue is properly regarded as a resource, for it is something that a person needs to accomplish his ends, no different in this respect from the nutrients necessary to sustain life or the intelligence essential to prudent or productive action. It is true, of course, that unlike material resources, human tissue cannot be taken from a living person without physical invasion, sometimes quite substantial in extent. That crucial difference might ground a compelling argument, based on an asserted right to bodily integrity, for forbidding all forced transfers. Arguments along this line will have to be addressed later. But the initial characterization of tissue as a resource, along with land and personal capacities, seems reasonable, given its utility and, unlike talents, its potential transferability. If this characterization is correct, then if someone lacks blood, bone marrow, or an organ essential to his survival or the enjoyment of a normal existence through no fault of his own when people who are otherwise similarly situated could supply his need without suffering an equally serious privation, equality of resources fails to obtain. It follows that transfers of tissue are permissible to rectify natural imbalances so far as possible, assuming that parity cannot be approached to the same degree at smaller cost through the provision of medical services or mechanical devices that serve the same purpose as living tissue or through other types of compensation. If all conceivable resources were included in the imaginary auction that represents the benchmark for an initial equal distribution, then this policy would apparently emerge in the course of the bidding. No one would have to accept the darkened, sometimes despairing life of a blind person or rest content with a foreshortened, painful existence if transplants could bring release from these fates, and few would elect to do so.

This initial statement of the argument, however, is too simple. As with other kinds of bad brute luck, a distinction must be drawn between people who are able to decide responsibly whether or not to insure against organ failure by participating in an organ transfer scheme and those who, because of age or infirmity, lack the capacity to do so. It is also necessary to distinguish among potential recipients on the basis of their probable prognoses if a transplant were performed. Finally, one must separate compulsory extractions from live donors from the mandatory *post mortem* harvesting of transplantable organs.

Consider first the distinction between nonvoluntary extractions from dead and living donors. It seems obvious that organs should only be taken forcibly from the living if the supply of cadaver organs fails to satisfy the needs of disease and accident victims. Removing organs from a corpse involves no pain or possible injury to the donor (except perhaps some irrational anxiety before the donor's death with regard to the later disposition of his body),[2] whereas the removal of a kidney, bone marrow, or a cornea from a living person invariably does. But what justification can be offered for mandatory donations absolutely, not just for the preferability of *post mortem* extractions to nonvoluntary extractions from live donors?

Equality of fortune maintains that organs, like native capacities, are resources. If their nonlethal transfer were feasible at low cost, their natural distribution would apparently be altered at the time of the original allocation of resources (or its contemporary analogue) to effect as equal an aggregate distribution as was humanly attainable, taking into account the distribution of other resources as well. But organ transplants, though not impossible (unlike transfers of cognitive capacities or physical prowess), are often inconvenient and risky for both donors and recipients. They are also expensive.[3] These drawbacks might not bar the compulsory redistribution

---

[2] According to a Gallup report prepared for the National Kidney Foundation in February 1983, one in five respondents gave as a "very important" reason for not wanting his kidneys removed after his death "I don't like the idea of somebody cutting me up after I die." This objection may only betray inadequate reflection or a misunderstanding of the cosmetic consequences of organ removal. Bodily decay is, of course, inevitable. And the extraction of corneas or internal organs does not ordinarily preclude an open casket funeral.

[3] The average costs of various transplants (not including lost wages) performed in the United States in 1985 were as follows, according to one source: heart $57,000–110,000; kidney $22,000–30,000; liver $135,000–238,000; pancreas $30,000–40,000; cornea $4,000–7,000. "Vital Facts About Organ Transplants," 69 *Consumers' Research* 29 (May 1986). Another source offers slightly lower figures: heart $60,000; heart and lungs $81,000; kidney $20,000; liver $85,000; pancreas $23,000; bone marrow $71,000. *The Economist*, June 8, 1985, p. 78.

of organs if cadaver organs were unavailable. They provide a compelling reason, however, for transferring cadaver organs in preference to organs taken from live donors to achieve the results that equality of fortune demands. Rational persons could be expected to support a policy of compulsory cadaver donation, given the disparity between the cost to the unwilling donor and the gains to potential recipients. Or, at the very least, it seems highly unlikely that they would oppose such a policy with anything approaching unanimity, and the burden of justifying, by reference to collective consent, a modification of the rule that equality of fortune yields is on those who would change the rule. It is certainly not asking overmuch of someone (or his relatives) to relinquish his organs when he can no longer use them and to live with the knowledge that through his death he may become a greater benefactor than his will indicates. As John Harris puts the case:

Is the squeamishness, sentimentality or ignorance of relatives of the dead a sufficiently important value to warrant protection at the cost of hundreds of lives annually? . . . If the state can order *post mortem* examination of the dead on the slightest pretexts, where for example there is the vaguest suspicion as to the cause of death, how much more important and useful it would be to be able to order *post mortem* transplantation! If the ability to use cadaver organs for transplants were automatic there is no doubt that many hundreds, perhaps even many thousands of lives could be saved annually at the same "social cost" that we already (willingly?) pay for judicial certainty as to the cause of death.[4]

Justifying nonvoluntary *post mortem* harvesting is therefore unproblematic. Harvesting of this sort should also suffice to meet the current shortfall in donated organs. The number of potentially transplantable cadaver organs presently far exceeds demand, at least in medically advanced nations where ailing patients can be sustained by artificial organs temporarily, where recovered cadaver organs can be kept viable long enough to permit their shipment and insertion,[5] and where large data banks enable medical authorities to locate and prepare suitable recipients swiftly.[6]

[4] Harris (1983), 228–9. Harris also advocates killing irreversibly comatose people if necessary to obtain organs for transplants. *See* Harris (1980), 87–8. I defer discussion of proposals to kill one person in order to obtain an organ or organs to save or improve the life of one or more others until Chapter 14. Those proposals do not seem to raise problems of distributive justice proper, since what is at issue is not the allocation of resources among persons belonging to a group whose membership is not contingent on the allocation, but a choice between the lives of persons not all of whom can be kept from death.

[5] At present, kidneys are ordinarily viable for between 24 and 72 hours. Hearts, livers, and lungs can usually be used within the first day after death. Corneas can be transplanted or grafted for up to four or five days if preserved promptly.

[6] John Harris (1983) cites a 1975 report by the British Transplantation Society in the *British Medical Journal* which states that, whereas 2,000 Britons needed kidney transplants each year during the early 1970s, only 450 transplants were performed annually. At the same time, however, 6,000 people, many of whom were young or middle-aged and thus ideal donors,

In view of the superabundance of transplantable cadaver organs, certain moral complications need not concern us. If, for example, there were a dearth of livers, then suicide, the excessive consumption of alcohol, or other behavior that would foreseeably result in the destruction of a transplantable liver might be thought immoral and perhaps even rightly forbidden, since equality of fortune regards people with healthy organs as trustees of those organs who are only allowed to benefit from their exclusive possession of them because they cannot be shared and because death or grave disability would probably result from their transfer. Given the plethora of suitable livers that would exist were *post mortem* extractions routine, however, no such restrictions on personal conduct would be necessary or warranted (if indeed they would ever be justifiable).

Besides removing one moral impediment to self-destructive conduct, the excess supply of cadaver organs that would come into being were *post mortem* extractions routine might allow exceptions to be made for those who strenuously objected to the removal of one or more of their organs following death. Certainly if organs were in short supply, any irrational resistance a prospective *post mortem* donor or his kin might feel towards the extraction of a viable liver or kidney should be disregarded. The existing policy, which in most jurisdictions requires prior consent by the deceased or the assent of his next of kin upon his death before a needed

were killed each year in automobile accidents, and a large proportion of their organs could have been transplanted despite the fatal injuries they suffered. Many other potentially suitable *post mortem* donors died from other causes. Since each of these people would probably have been able to provide two kidneys for transplantation, simply seizing all cadaver organs for transplantation would apparently solve the problem in a single stroke. In the case of eyes, mandatory *post mortem* removal of the cornea and lens would unquestionably eliminate the need for live donors, because the blood supply to the cornea and lens is low, because corneas can be preserved for several days after death, and because it is unnecessary to match the tissue types of donors and recipients.

United States statistics tell a similar story. In 1983, approximately 72,000 Americans depended on dialysis treatment to sustain life, according to the Health Care Financing Administration. (The reason the per capita figure is so much higher than the British figure of ten years earlier is that Medicare coverage was extended to cover dialysis expenses beginning in 1973. Supplementary programs in many states ensure that complete renal care is available to everyone who needs it. Comparable programs did not exist in Britain in the early 1970s, nor do they exist today.) Of the 72,000 Americans on dialysis, perhaps 20,000 could have benefited from transplants, although only 6,000 transplants (using both live and deceased donors) were performed in 1983. It is estimated that around 20,000 Americans—1 in 12,000— die each year in circumstances allowing their organs to be harvested for transplants, yet in 1982 organs were collected from fewer than 2,200 of them. *See* Lee (1986), 366; Hansmann (1989), 66–7.

Accident victims could also supply people waiting for other organs. Although only 87 pancreas transplants were performed in 1984, it has been estimated that up to 5,000 people could benefit from transplants. "Vital Facts About Organ Transplants," 69 *Consumers' Research* 29 (May 1986). Similarly, only 308 liver transplants were performed in 1984, even though the number of estimated beneficiaries may be as high as 5,000. *Ibid.* The corresponding numbers for heart transplants are 346 and 15,000. *Ibid.*

organ may be removed, is therefore indefensible, given current shortages.[7] But modifications that displease only a small minority without jeopardizing the welfare of potential recipients are preferable to those that outrage a substantial portion of the populace. Hence it may be enough, as some suggest,[8] to make *post mortem* extractions automatic except when the deceased explicitly forbade *post mortem* appropriation of his organs before he died or his next of kin protest.[9] By shifting the burden of consent or objection in this way, a sufficient number of transplantable organs might be obtained, given current views on the desirability of *post mortem* donations,[10] without offending those who preferred not to help.[11] Potential

[7] The rule in most jurisdictions in the United States is that *post mortem* extractions may be performed only if the decedent consented prior to his death—say, by signing a donor card— or, in the absence of prior consent by the decedent, if his next of kin grant permission. In practice, however, the consent of the decedent's kin is a prerequisite to extraction even if the decedent signed a donor card, because doctors and hospital officials are generally unwilling to act contrary to the wishes of surviving relatives, partly out of fear of liability or bad publicity. *See* Lee (1986), 379; Task Force on Organ Transplantation, *Organ Transplantation: Issues and Recommendations*, Washington, D.C.: DHHS (1986), 29. Over two-thirds of the states now require doctors to ask the next of kin after a suitable organ donor has died whether they are willing to donate his organs for transplantation. Since 1986, the federal government has imposed this requirement on hospitals receiving funds under Medicare or Medicaid. Omnibus Budget Reconciliation Act of 1986, Pub. L. No. 99-509, § 9318, 100 Stat. 2009. Required consent laws have thus far had only a slight impact, increasing organ donation by a mere 10–20%. *See* Childress (1989), 94.

[8] *See, e.g.* Muyskens (1978).

[9] At least fifteen states have embraced this policy with respect to the removal of corneas for transplantation, but only when state law requires that an autopsy be performed on the decedent. These state laws typically authorize the coroner or medical examiner to remove corneal tissue from a decedent so long as he is unaware of any objection by the decedent prior to his death or by his next of kin. *See, e.g.* CAL. GOV'T CODE § 27491.47 (West 1989); FLA. STAT. ANN. § 732.9185 (West 1989); GA. CODE ANN. § 31-23-6(b)(1) (1985 & Supp. 1987); MICH. COMP. LAWS § 333.10201–10205 (1980 & Supp. 1987); N.Y. PUB. HEALTH LAW § 4222 (McKinney 1988). Such laws have hitherto withstood legal attack. *See, e.g. State v. Powell*, 497 So. 2d 1188 (Fla. 1986); *Georgia Lions Eye Bank, Inc. v. Lavant*, 255 Ga. 60, 335 S.E.2d 127 (1985); *Tillman v. Detroit Receiving Hosp.*, 138 Mich. App. 683, 360 N.W.2d 275 (1984). These laws have been responsible for sizable increases in the number of corneal transplants performed in states that have adopted them. For example, the number of corneal transplants in Georgia grew from 25 in 1978 to over 1,000 in 1984; Florida witnessed an increase from 500 in 1978 to over 3,000 in 1984. *See* Childress (1989), 98. However, state legislatures have thus far declined to extend such laws to the removal of other organs, even though the transplantation of other organs would often bring larger benefits—such as life itself—than the granting of sight to the blind. Legislatures have also refused to authorize state officials or physicians to remove organs from deceased persons in situations other than mandatory autopsies. Although there does not appear to be any significant opposition to "presumed consent" laws dealing with corneal transplants, a survey taken in 1985 revealed that 86.5% of the respondents believed that doctors should not have the power to appropriate organs in the absence of a signed donor card and without consulting the decedent's next of kin. Manninen and Evans (1985), 3113.

[10] According to a Gallup report of February 1983, 72% of those aware of organ transplants said that they were very likely to give permission to have the kidneys of a loved one donated after his death, and half said that they were very likely to donate their own child's kidneys if the child died accidentally. Curiously, only 24% said that they were very likely to want their own kidneys donated after their death—a low response which, like the low percentage of the

donors' unwillingness to make the effort to obtain and sign donor cards, the impossibility of contacting next of kin shortly after someone's death to acquire permission to extract an organ, the reluctance of doctors to ask permission, disregard of a decedent's express desire to donate if his next of kin object after his death, and the often unreflective responses of relatives when asked to grant permission should not cost as many lives as they do.

Finally, if enough cadaver organs were available to supply all who needed one and if survival and rejection rates were not appreciably below those of transplants from living donors,[12] then there would be no reason to forbid voluntary donations to recipients chosen by the donor or to ban the sale of transferable tissue by living donors. Those who relinquished their blood or organs voluntarily, whether gratuitously or in return for payment, would not be depriving other potential recipients of resources to which they had an equal or greater right, and so could not be condemned or constrained on that ground. Gratuitous donations would presumably be highly uncommon, however, if cadaver organs were in ample supply, confined almost exclusively to cases (if there are any) where an exact tissue match would produce a significantly higher survival rate; and sales would probably be limited to medical researchers.[13]

population that has signed donor cards, might stem from a fear that those who agree to donate their organs will receive inferior medical treatment if their lives are in danger, because attending physicians will be overly eager to extract their organs. In a 1987 Gallup poll, 82% of the respondents said that they might donate the organs of a loved one, while only 61% said that they would permit extraction if the donor was their child. *N.Y. Times*, May 3, 1987, § 1, p. 28.

[11] Despite the large increase in *post mortem* corneal transplants under such laws, some are skeptical about their efficacy with regard to internal organs. Hansmann (1989), 61, notes that "presumed consent" laws in Europe have not produced notably higher donation rates than now exist in the United States.

[12] The difference is in fact inconsiderable. *See* Lee (1986), 383 n. 123. Cadaver corneas are no more prone to rejection than corneas taken from live donors, whereas the five-year survival rate for cadaver kidney recipients is approximately 85%, compared with a survival rate of slightly over 90% if the kidney was donated by a living relative. Comparisons are only meaningful in these two cases, since all other potential transfers (excepting partial pancreas and liver transplants) either involve the death of the donor or are impracticable, as in the case of *post mortem* bone marrow transplants. The current difference in survival rates between recipients of cadaver kidneys and recipients of kidneys from living donors cannot ground a convincing objection that cadaver organs should not be used in place of compulsory extractions from living people, because the present difference in survival rates is primarily attributable to differences in rejection rates and a shortage of organs that often precludes a second transplant when one fails. If cadaver organs were harvested routinely, no shortage would exist and the difference would take the form only of marginal additions to cost, anxiety, pain, and inconvenience brought about by a slightly higher chance of having to undergo a second operation. This difference is not sufficient to reject cadaver transplants as a strategy of first resort in lieu of compulsory extractions from living donors.

[13] A somewhat different question arises in connection with researchers' use of tissue removed for therapeutic purposes—for example, the use of a spleen to develop profitable cell lines after it had been removed from a patient as part of a standard cancer treatment. See *Moore v. Regents of the Univ. of Cal.*, 51 Cal. 3d 120, 271 Cal. Rptr. 146 (1990). It would seem that such tissue should be treated the same as cadaver organs once severed from the

This argument assumes, of course, that buying and selling blood or organs is not immoral and that it is in any case preferable to nonvoluntary transfers. Not everyone shares the first of these assumptions.[14] Charles Fried, for example, castigates those who sell their blood or organs for the same reason that he denounces prostitutes:

> [W]hen a man sells his body he does not sell what is his, he sells himself. What is disturbing, therefore, about selling human tissue is that the seller treats his body as a foreign object. . . . The shame of selling one's body is just that one splits apart an entity one knows should not be so split.[15]

I argue below that Fried's principal contention is false. The link between expendable parts of someone's body and morally significant aspects of personal identity is *not* especially tight; Fried's conclusion that giving up an organ "splits apart an entity one knows should not be so split" is therefore much exaggerated. Perhaps significantly, Fried later seems to retract this claim in a footnote: "My conclusion is that it is personally bad (in a just society), though not in any sense wrong, to sell blood. It is certainly wrong to compel its donation. It is certainly good to give it freely: I have an excess and others badly need it."[16] What Fried means when he calls the selling of blood "personally bad . . . though not in any sense wrong," I shall not attempt to divine. I merely note that if selling a part of one's body entails splitting an entity that should not be split, then so does donating it. One cannot proscribe selling on this ground without prohibiting donation as well.

In questioning the propriety of selling human tissue, Fried has an unlikely ally in Peter Singer.[17] Unfortunately, Singer's position is no less

patient, making it potentially valuable collective property which the community may dispose of as it deems wise. The patient whose tissue was extracted would not be compensated as a matter of justice (as opposed to any reward scheme deemed administratively desirable). Some public body would presumably have to decide which researchers would receive the tissue, whether by way of subsidy or sale. (The California Supreme Court, lacking legislative authority and forced to decide in *Moore* a case framed in terms of traditional causes of action in tort law, held that the patient lacked a property interest in his spleen that his physician might wrongfully appropriate; the court did say, however, that Moore could sue for his physician's alleged failure to inform him of the uses to which the physician intended to put Moore's spleen prior to seeking his consent to operate. It remains unclear what redress might be available under California law for the latter tort.)

[14] Indeed, federal law in the United States has, since 1984, rendered it "unlawful for any person to knowingly acquire, receive, or otherwise transfer any human organ for valuable consideration for use in human transplantation if the transfer affects interstate commerce." National Organ Transplant Act, Pub. L. No. 98-507, title III, § 301, 98 Stat. 2346 (1984) (codified at 42 U.S.C. § 274e (Supp. III 1985)). This prohibition was extended to the sale of fetal tissue by the Health Omnibus Programs Extension Act of 1988, Pub. L. No. 100-607, § 407, 102 Stat. 3116. Federal law does not ban the gratuitous donation of organs, nor does it forbid the sale of blood, semen, or hair. Most states also ban the sale of human tissue, apart from blood.

[15] Fried (1978), 142.

[16] Fried (1978), 143 note.

[17] *See* Singer (1979c).

ambivalent than Fried's. He argues against more stalwart champions of the market that it is not self-evident that people have a right to sell blood or organs, because sales might affect the way donations are perceived. But Singer neglects to say whether he believes that people do have such a right after all the arguments have been heard. Singer's hesitancy to declare himself may be of no consequence, however, since the sole argument he offers against allowing the sale of blood is woefully weak:

If blood is a commodity with a price, to give blood means merely to save someone money. Blood has a cash value of a certain number of dollars, and the importance of the gift will vary with the wealth of the recipient. If blood cannot be bought, however, the gift's value depends upon the need of the recipient. Often, it will be worth life itself.[18]

The chief flaw in this argument, of course, is that it proves far too much. It provides a reason for barring the sale of *anything*, since allowing something to be traded perforce makes its value as a gift depend upon the wealth rather than the need of the recipient. Even if one arbitrarily confined the argument's scope to life-saving resources, it would have no force, for it would still supply as strong a reason for prohibiting the sale of food, medicine, and doctors' services as for prohibiting the sale of human tissue, and no one disputes people's right to buy and sell wheat or penicillin. Outlawing the sale of some life-preserving resource in order to raise its value as a gift, moreover, scarcely seems justifiable if somebody dies who would otherwise have lived because no one made him a present of what he needed.

I therefore see no reason to qualify or abandon the assumption that the sale of human tissue is morally permissible. To be sure, in a society characterized by a grossly unjust distribution of property the state *might* be justified in blocking such sales in order to prevent exploitation of desperately indigent people, though this issue is an extremely difficult one. As Hansmann points out, the increased risk of death to a 35-year-old from giving up a single kidney (and assuming—which the theory under consideration does *not*—that the donor lacks a right to a transplant if his single kidney fails) is about the same as that associated with driving a car 16 miles every workday—a risk we ordinarily allow people to run in return for higher wages.[19] In addition, the poor are disproportionately represented among those needing transplants, and their poverty need not bar them from receiving transplant organs if they purchase catastrophic health insurance or, as at present in the United States, the federal government picks up most of the tab. On the other hand, the decision to sell an organ, unlike the decision to accept most forms of employment, is irreversible once the operation has been performed. And organs, unlike blood, are not

---

[18] Singer (1979c), 77.   [19] Hansmann (1989), 72.

renewable (the liver provides a limited exception, permitting transplants of part of an organ in some cases), though *another* person's kidney or cornea could be purchased for a replacement transplant if sales were allowed. The problem of regretted donation could be mitigated by mandating a minimum waiting period, and exploitation could be reduced by setting a minimum price, though this might in turn put more pressure on members of indigent families to sell their organs to improve the family's finances. In a just state, of course, this objection would be substantially weaker.

For reasons of public safety rather than individual morality, government officials might also wish to spend public money to encourage donations rather than buy whatever blood is needed, since the commercialization of blood donations might increase the percentage of donors carrying hepatitis, AIDS, and other blood-borne diseases, assuming that inexpensive screening techniques are unavailable, to the extent that monetary payment creates an incentive for donors to conceal their knowledge that they do or might carry those diseases.[20] The same is true of organ sales. But neither this caveat nor the preceding objection supports the claim that the purchase or sale of human tissue is inherently immoral in a just society. And slippery-slope arguments—e.g. by treating human tissue as a commodity, people's respect for human life will be undermined and the slaughter of the socially unproductive will ensue—carry scant conviction.

In light of the achievements of medical science in the advanced industrial democracies, particularly new techniques for preserving organs for transplants and recent improvements in immunosuppressants, such as cyclosporine, this chapter could well end here. Cadaver organs taken from people who did not object might well fulfill existing needs, and even if there remained a shortfall, it could certainly be made good by extracting some organs from people who objected to their removal before their death or whose relatives wished to keep their bodies intact after they died. But it is nevertheless instructive to ask whether and when mandatory transfers from living donors would be just, both because the need for donated organs might outstrip the supply of cadaver organs in certain emergencies and because pursuit of an answer teaches something about the moral limits of force.

Suppose, then, that equality of fortune represents the ideal of justice. As a general rule, any emergent inequalities traceable to differential brute luck ought to be eliminated, unless someone antecedently agreed to accept less compensation than he would be due should misfortune overtake him in return for reduced liabilities if others are the victims, and unless compensation would be unduly burdensome at the margin in view of the

---

[20] The risk to recipients rather than moral revulsion is the principal reason for the shift from purchasing blood or blood products to a system of almost exclusively altruistic donations in the United States. *See* Childress (1989), 100.

cost to those providing assistance and the good it would realize. Hence, it appears that those who lose their vision or find their life imperiled by diseases or accidents for which they are not responsible are entitled to blood or certain of its components, bone marrow, one kidney from somebody who has two healthy kidneys, or one cornea from someone who has vision in both eyes, provided that five conditions are met. (The same analysis applies to much rarer partial pancreas and liver transplants.) First, there must be a chronic shortage of these tissues or organs once voluntary donations, purchased supplies, and cadaver organs have been taken into account. Second, the expected benefits to recipients must be substantially greater than those promised by artificial organs or other forms of treatment. Third, the transfer of blood or an organ must not be likely to result in the death of the donor or disabilities as debilitating as those that afflicted the recipient prior to the transfer. Fourth, the benefits to the recipient must be significant; small improvements would not warrant the imposition of substantial risks or sacrifices on donors. Fifth, prospective recipients must not have relinquished their entitlement to such relief.

In addition, mandatory transfer schemes would only be just if they limited unconditional rights to transplants to people who did not flirt with disaster by engaging in risky behavior. The rights of those who did run abnormal risks should be an inverse function of the unusual perilousness of whatever actions led to their blindness, serious kidney ailment, or other deficiency that could be cured by bone marrow, kidney, or corneal transplants, or by the transfer of blood or blood components. To assign everyone who was in need an equal right to a transplant, regardless of what caused his plight, would be grossly unfair, for it would enable people who took bigger chances with their vision or health to foist part of the additional risk on those who were more cautious. It would also be contrary to the self-interest of most participants in the scheme, since if replacements were always available, people's incentives to protect themselves against loss of vision, renal disease, or other maladies would be lowered. Reduced incentives might in turn lead to a higher incidence of those misfortunes, and thus of transplants, than if the schemes were never introduced or if qualifications were built into them, though the extent to which these consequences ensued would also depend on the strength of ancillary incentives, such as the desire to avoid pain and the risk of unsuccessful, possibly harmful surgery.[21] Hence, only those who were born blind, those

---

[21] Similar points are made by Trammell and Wren (1977) and Singer (1977b). Singer also notes that, to the extent that organ transfer schemes enhanced the life expectancy of those with bad genes and the concomitant probability of their having offspring, they would decrease the average quality of life of future generations and further pollute the gene pool. It is unclear, however, what he thinks follows from this fact, apart from the desirability of genetic engineering to remove deficiencies or to lower someone's predisposition to contract a fatal kidney disease or go blind. Singer apparently does not believe that people born with the

who lost the use of their kidneys or eyes or who experienced blood-related disorders through disease, accident, or intentional injury before they were responsible for their actions, and those whose misfortunes were unconnected to recognizably dangerous behavior should qualify automatically as recipients of transferred organs. Others would ideally have their chances of receiving a new cornea, kidney, bone marrow or blood discounted or withdrawn, depending on the circumstances that led to their need.

However, the second part of this solution might be thought troublesome in two respects. While there is little problem identifying victims who are under age or suffering from diseases whose incidence cannot be correlated with actions they typically perform, it might be difficult or impossible to collect the information necessary to discount fairly someone's chances of receiving a transplant if his need arose through an accident or a disease whose frequency was known to be a function of certain kinds of behavior in which the victim had or may have engaged. In addition, denying someone sight or freedom from painful dependence on a dialysis machine because snake eyes came up on a computer's random number generator might strike some people as grotesquely cruel.

Whether this second worry is legitimate seems doubtful. The procedure just described is undoubtedly fair, and the charge of cruelty seems misplaced, inasmuch as victims whose chances of receiving a transplant depended upon the whirl of a wheel would not be subjected to such treatment arbitrarily or unexpectedly; rather, they would have brought it on themselves by doing things they realized would lessen their odds of receiving a transplant if they needed one. But the question of its validity need not detain us, for the usual solution to problems of measurement and segregation eliminates the second difficulty as well.

When the assignment of a good depends upon the recipient's maintenance of a standard of behavior about which the acquisition of precise information is impossible or prohibitively expensive, the most sensible course is often to define a class of actions that disqualify an agent from receiving the reward and to place the burden of proving that he did not perform any of them on whoever wishes to receive the good. In certain cases, of course, the only evidence that an individual might offer is his own affirmation. If such cases arose frequently and if dishonesty were common —and there would certainly be a strong incentive to lie if sincerity meant the denial of an eye or a kidney—then it might be necessary to rule out

genetic disadvantages he has in mind or a better-than-average chance of acquiring serious disabilities later in life should be prohibited from having children. But if they are not to be denied the same right to procreate that other people possess, then it also seems that they ought not to be deprived of the more important right (to those facing death) to a life-saving transplant that other people are assumed *arguendo* to have. Singer's point therefore seems irrelevant to this discussion.

transplants in those cases. Much would turn on the relevant facts. Needless to say, any system that divides actions into the permitted and the proscribed when desert varies along a continuum and when the information necessary to assign a particular action to one of the two categories is sometimes sparse inevitably risks committing injustices. But sometimes there is no better alternative. Since it is hardly conceivable that anyone would risk his eyesight lightly even if a mandatory transfer scheme were operative, both because he would only qualify for at most one cornea if he were blinded and because injuries to the eye are apt to be painful, disfiguring, and produced in ways that often cause additional and sometimes more serious impairment, a rule that denied transplants from living donors only to those who intentionally blinded themselves or who performed patently reckless actions (such as welding without goggles) would probably be fair and acceptable to all. As for renal failure, most kidney disease is congenital, genetic, or viral in origin, particularly if diabetes is properly classified under these headings. However, to the extent that someone's troubles may be ascribed to alcohol abuse or hypertension he neglected to have treated, it may be appropriate to grant him no more than access to dialysis facilities and a chance of receiving a cadaver organ in time.

One further problem attending the selection of recipients under a compulsory transfer scheme is that a high proportion of those who do go blind are very elderly. Would people in advanced old age who lost their vision qualify for transplants, even if that entailed taking corneas from much younger people? Under the theory of equality of fortune, they would not. The theory's desideratum is the equalization of brute luck over the course of a lifetime; removing an eye from someone young in order to help someone who has already enjoyed a lifetime of stereoscopic vision would generally accomplish just the opposite. Perhaps more important, recall that equality of fortune permits people to enter into voluntary arrangements altering the pattern of liabilities and benefits that justice initially prescribes. Since it would be in everyone's antecedent interest to exempt those who were not well past their prime from sacrificing an eye to aid someone whose life had all but run its course, one could expect unanimous approval of that policy by people in their youth, and it is not unduly harsh to hold them to their commitments when they grow old.[22] Whether mandatory transfers would occur within the class of elderly persons

---

[22] A similar argument could be made to deny transplants involving involuntary donors to adults whose prognoses were poor or whose expected quality of life would likely remain very low even if a transplant were performed successfully. See sections 13.2 and 13.3. In the latter case, the marginal ratio of costs and benefits would also militate against the compulsory transfer of organs from living donors.

would depend upon the availability of cadaver corneas, the risks involved, the prospects of success, and the preferences of the aged.[23]

How would donors be chosen if someone were in need, if the preceding conditions had been met, and if he requested a transplant? The fairest method would be to select one randomly from among the set of suitable donors who had not expressed a considered desire, and who had been allowed, to withdraw from the scheme.

The more difficult question is when withdrawal should be permitted or presumed. Its answer depends upon whether equality of fortune or a theory that bases compensation solely on hypothetical insurance purchases provides a more persuasive account of the requirements of justice. As with compensation for handicaps, the implications of these theories do not vary appreciably.

According to equality of fortune, minors deserve medical assistance equal to the greater of two amounts: (*a*) that which is necessary to put them on a par with their peers or to make them more nearly equal in their physical abilities or the suffering they have to endure, subject to the constraint that such measures not place inordinate burdens on others or require large sacrifices for trifling gains at the margin; and (*b*) that which they would receive under whatever insurance plan or ancillary treatment plan it would have been rational for them to purchase. Theories that make compensation depend on hypothetical insurance purchases would limit relief to the second amount. Under both approaches, compulsory transplants would therefore be morally imperative if the risks and suffering to which donors were subject were less dreadful than the plight of someone denied a transplant, assuming that the invasion of any rights to bodily integrity that donors possess, any anxiety potential donors might experience, and the costs of such transplants did not outweigh their net benefits and the greater peace of mind of potential recipients. If the alternative to a transplant were death, blindness, or life on a dialysis machine (at least until a live donor or cadaver organ turned up) and if the odds of obtaining donated organs were slim, then participation in organ transplant schemes would probably be prudent.[24] Even if the benefits promised by such schemes failed to offset the expected costs to participants, equality of fortune might, unlike the hypothetical insurance approach, nevertheless

---

[23] *See also* below, pp. 181–2, where I argue that equality of fortune does *not* endorse compulsory organ transplants for adults anyway, but sanctions only voluntary arrangements.

[24] If adults overwhelmingly chose not to join voluntary organ transfer schemes, as they would be free to do under either theory, one might argue, by extrapolating from that result, that it would be irrational for children to join one. Whether this empirically based conception of rationality should be utilized here, perhaps modified to take account of presumed differences in children's and adults' anxieties and attitudes towards risk, turns on one's general definition of rational choice. I leave that large topic unexplored. See section 13.3 for discussion of a related problem in selecting transplant recipients.

require them if the costs were not excessive and if the medical peril imposed on donors selected at random were not so considerable as to render compulsory donations unjust.[25]

The way in which the two theories would handle transplants to and from adults is identical, although their reasons differ slightly. Equality of fortune would endorse the preconditions for the forcible enlistment of living donors described in the preceding pages, mandating random selection if those preconditions were met. But as with other types of insurance against bad brute luck, it would permit people capable of responsible decision to waive their right to assistance. Prudent persons would relinquish this right *vis-à-vis* another individual only if that other person made an identical waiver. Hence, theoretically, a complex pattern of entitlements could emerge, with a given individual finding himself in the pool of potential donors to some (who in turn would be among his potential donors) but not to others.

The administration of so complicated a system, however, would be costly and difficult. It would also be unnecessary. For if organ transfer schemes were popular, they could be made entirely voluntary, subject to the requirement that participation be open to all on an equal basis, so as not to place victims of genetic or congenital bad brute luck at a disadvantage. Those who wished to assure themselves of a transplant should they need one could sign up for a transfer plan tailored to their degree of risk-aversion. A plurality of plans would be possible and even desirable, enabling people to choose with some precision the levels and types of risk to which they exposed themselves. As in the case of other types of insurance against bad brute luck, people would prefer this system of voluntary participation to one involving mandatory membership coupled with complex arrangements for waivers of rights and releases from liability, since it would offer a wider range of choice and be cheaper to run than the universal compulsory scheme without subjecting participants to greater insecurity. Voluntary organ transfer schemes would therefore

---

[25] Other matters would have to be settled if the compulsory transfer of body parts between minors became an established practice. Would parents or friends of the chosen donor, for example, be allowed to offer the prospective recipient, through his parents, cash or services in lieu of an eye or a kidney? Would they be allowed to offer similar goods to other suitable donors to induce them to take the chosen child's place? Could the wealthy band together in their own insurance schemes to pay poor parents to allow their children to provide the bulk of the donations? Would these proposals be just if people had unequal means with which to buy proxies and if parents of prospective recipients demanded different amounts to waive their rights?

I am inclined to think that all four questions should be answered negatively, provided that the distribution of wealth and income is just, because even well-intentioned parents should not be permitted to deny their child something as important to its future development and happiness as a transplant organ. My inclination is to return the opposite verdict with respect to adults who joined voluntary transfer schemes and who did not wish to contribute when their number came up. But I make no attempt to defend these conclusions here.

supplant a single mandatory plan if a fairly large number of people desired them.

But what if voluntary transfer schemes proved unpopular, not because they were imprudent wagers or placed inordinate demands on those called upon to relinquish a kidney or a cornea, but because those facing the greatest natural risks signed up first and others were reluctant to join, or because the vast majority of people had some irrational aversion to such schemes or would be prone to so much anxiety if they knew they might have to donate an organ that it would not be worth their while to join? In this case, if no one were interested in participating, paternalistic measures requiring participation would not only appear heavy-handed, but they would never come up for serious consideration, since those in power would, by hypothesis, lack any enthusiasm for implementing them. If a small number of people desired coverage (two would do, if they had the same tissue type and both had a pair of healthy kidneys or working eyes), they would constitute an insurance group of their own, and could make the necessary contractual arrangements. Only if someone desired to subscribe to a transfer plan but was unable to find a suitable donor/recipient who shared his interest (perhaps because he was more likely to need a transplant than most people) would a problem of justice arise. And here the evident impracticability of establishing a system of choosing and coercing a donor should the would-be participant be in need and the social and personal cost of subjecting almost everyone to some risk of donation whenever someone else was accidentally blinded or contracted a grave renal disease without hope of obtaining an eye or a kidney elsewhere would take precedence over the minor injustice that failure to create it would betoken.[26] Equality of fortune supports voluntary organ transfer schemes for adults, or none at all.

Hypothetical insurance theories would reach exactly the same result. Entitlements would only depend on people's choices from behind a thin veil of ignorance if they were unable to choose responsibly the risks they were to run, and in the case of normal adults the prerequisite of responsible choice is clearly fulfilled. Voluntary organ transfer schemes that did not discriminate against people with genetic or congenital propensities to contract certain eye or kidney diseases would therefore be just. As for the rare individual who desired the protection such schemes afforded but who could not obtain it because others irrationally refused to sign consent forms, the excessive cost of catering to his idiosyncratic desire would pardon the small injustice of denying him his wish. That anyone would complain is doubtful, especially if priority were granted in the allocation of cadaver organs by way of recompense.

[26] Perhaps the lone person who wanted to participate in a rational transfer scheme could be placed first in line for a cadaver organ if he ever needed a transplant, though that would create a powerful incentive to lie about what one would have done but could not do.

8.2. ARGUMENTS AGAINST INVOLUNTARY ORGAN REMOVAL

If the arguments of the preceding section are correct, justice may require the compulsory donation of a cornea, bone marrow, or a kidney in certain cases where minors were blinded or fell victim to serious diseases treatable through bone marrow or kidney transplants. These situations would seldom, if ever, arise if cadaver organs were made available for transplantation as a matter of course, but they could conceivably occur.

No doubt many would balk at this prescription. The thought of forcing someone to surrender an eye or a kidney even though he did not agree to do so beforehand if someone else found himself in need would probably spark considerable indignation. Of course, popular resistance might be traceable to the novelty of this recommendation, the fact that most people's dispositions have been schooled by laws and moral instruction founded on mistaken theories of justice and morality, and the instinctive repugnance many feel toward deliberate injury, even if performed in order to bring great gains to others. The question, however, is whether our initial unwillingness to accept the conclusions that equality of fortune seems to entail can be vindicated by showing that those conclusions are incorrect. I shall argue that they should be accepted on reflection, though I expect some readers to be persuaded by one or more of the objections I consider. To the extent that those objections are not inconsistent with the bedrock principles of equality of fortune—and most, perhaps all, of them are not— those who think them convincing but who accept the development of the theory in earlier chapters would embrace a slightly different conception of equality of fortune from mine. As I noted in Chapter 1, moral disagreements of this kind, insofar as they stem from conflicting moral intuitions, may not be eliminable.

One objection to mandatory organ transfer schemes has been offered by Charles Fried and, with qualifications, by Ronald Dworkin. Both recognize that an egalitarian theory of distributive justice presupposes a distinction between persons, on the one hand, and, on the other, goods allocable to them on a basis of moral equality. And both argue that in practice that distinction should be drawn so that body parts are treated as elements of a person rather than as resources whose distribution is governed by principles of justice.

Fried's argument appeals to the alleged irrationality of organ transfer schemes from the perspective of someone deciding whether or not to join one at the risk of having to surrender some part of his body to help another participant in the scheme. Fried writes:

[A]ll rational persons would find that their liability to contribute to such equalizing schemes would be so deadly an assault upon their personal integrity that the benefits that might accrue from such schemes, should they happen to be at the less fortunate end of the initial natural distribution, would not be sufficient to make this assault upon their integrity seem worthwhile.

. . . [T]he argument must be that certain attributes—for instance one's bodily organs . . . —are so closely related to a conception of one's self, that to make them available for trading-off in a scheme of morality would be, as it were, to gain the world and lose one's own soul. Less metaphorically, a rational person in an initial position would feel that to purchase benefits at the risk of having to make a contribution of these most intimate attributes is to purchase benefits at the risk of having to become another person and thus to commit a form of suicide.[27]

Fried's claim, however, seems enormously exaggerated. Although the loss of a cornea or a kidney might force someone to alter his habits, rarely would it transform him so completely that one would be inclined to speak of him as an entirely different person; the removal of bone marrow or blood would have an even less significant impact. One might speak of the creation of a new person if a professional athlete or an avid outdoorsman were compelled to abandon those pursuits around which he had built his life, but the appropriateness of that description is always a matter of degree, and in the case of most people it seems obvious that the changes effected by the compulsory donation of an organ or a cornea would not be so profound as to justify talk of the death of one person and the creation of another. Fundamental changes in someone's most important values and desires might make it natural to refer to him as a new person if they occurred rapidly enough, as when somebody undergoes a sudden religious conversion or thorough brainwashing. For we conceive of personal identity, in its morally relevant sense, largely in terms of identity of personality, the principal components of which are a person's dominant ends and his moral convictions. But rarely, if ever, does the loss of an organ cause such a metamorphosis, especially when young children are the donors and they have no firm personality to lose. Nobody regards those who lose an eye or the use of a kidney through accident or disease as giving up the ghost, and those who donate their organs to save someone from death or despair are not classified as suicides. Since Fried himself commends donations of this kind,[28] one can only conclude that he does not take his rhetoric seriously.

But perhaps Fried's conclusion can be sustained without recourse to hyperbole. In a cryptic passage, Dworkin appears to argue that even if it would be absurd to speak of compulsory blood donations as murder, there can be little doubt that the loss of an eye or a kidney may have acute repercussions on the way a person sees himself and leads his life. Although losses of this kind need not bring about a complete change of identity,

---

[27] Fried (1970), 205; *see also* Fried (1978), 140–3.   [28] *See* Fried (1978), 143.

sometimes they will, and at other times they will markedly alter a person's character and bring about a partial change. The problem, Dworkin seems to say, is that politicians and others attempting to achieve equality of resources are fallible. They might therefore err in their assignment of a part of somebody's anatomy to the category of resources rather than of personality, and thus demand from him what he cannot give without ceasing to be himself. Rather than risk such deplorable consequences, Dworkin appears to argue, it might be better not to allow any compulsory transplants at all. In his own words:

[T]he idea of equality depends on, and so cannot furnish, instructions about where precisely to draw the line between the person and his circumstances. We need to explore the concept of a person more carefully for these instructions, and two politicians both committed to equality of resources may draw it differently. Would it be outrageous to require blood donations according to some fair lottery? Kidney donations? Eye donations? We might well wish to resist this chain of questions by adopting a prophylactic line that comes close to making the body inviolate, that is, making body parts not part of social resources at all. We might justify this by appealing to the importance of protecting the person, and the danger in adopting any line less bright. That kind of impulse contributes, I think, to our repugnance in contemplating even minor maiming as a punishment, even when a convicted criminal would prefer losing, say, a finger to a long jail sentence.[29]

Dworkin's argument is open to at least three objections. First, one might concede that allowing officials to determine when body parts are distributable resources and when they are not creates the possibility of error and injustice. But one might nonetheless maintain that the gains from pushing beyond the prophylactic line Dworkin proposes far outweigh the risks it entails, just as the benefits of having a criminal justice system that punishes suspected offenders who have been tried and found guilty outbalances the danger of imprisoning innocent people. The cost of not venturing beyond the line Dworkin seeks to draw, after all, is to be reckoned in the *lives* of people who have unjustly been left to die or *years* without vision endured by those wrongly denied a chance to see. Moreover, the peril of passing beyond the just rather than the prophylactic line will presumably be reduced if officials are cognizant of their fallibility and the seriousness of their decisions. Can one conscientiously play safe to the degree Dworkin advocates?

Second, it seems doubtful that the risk of overstepping the bounds of justice is worrisome in this instance, because any conceivable transfer of organs that did not involve the death of the donor would very seldom, if ever, change his personality so profoundly that the forced donation of

[29] Dworkin (1983*a*), 39.

some part of his body would be akin to unjust incarceration or murder.[30] This is particularly true when the involuntary donors are young children whose personalities are still fluid. Certainly a temporary loss of blood or the loss of some bone marrow could not have this consequence. And the two most radical transfers that would not require killing the donor—renal and corneal transplants—would not entail this consequence either, except perhaps in rare cases. Those who lose their vision in one eye or the services of one of their kidneys are not normally viewed as different persons on that account, nor are those who donate an eye or a kidney voluntarily. But if the worst case is not greatly to be feared, because it is practically impossible to go too far, then empowering officials to decide when body parts should be transferred should not pose much danger of murder, assuming that a radical transformation of someone's personality should indeed be so regarded. Hence, there appears no need for a bright line making the body inviolate.

Third, one might question Dworkin's explanation of our unwillingness to contemplate penalties that maim or disfigure lawbreakers. Is it plausible to claim that our revulsion at such penalties, even on a small scale, stems from the realization that permanent physical damage can transform someone's conception of himself, coupled with the fear that once on that road we will find it difficult to keep from racing to particularly grisly extremes? Is that explanation plausible when the punishments we do administer are also likely—indeed, that is their purpose—to alter felons' personalities in important ways, and are in perhaps most cases no more rehabilitative than permanent physical scars? A more compelling explanation, I believe, would refer to our conviction that a lawbreaker ought not to be stigmatized for life, so that even after he has served his time he is penalized in more subtle ways by those who recognize him as a former criminal. It would also derive from our instinctive aversion to any type of physical deformity and our concomitant reluctance purposely to consign anyone to such a fate. If this alternative explanation is correct, however, then the reasons Dworkin cites for a prophylactic line find no echo in our reasons for preferring to imprison rather than maim criminals.[31]

[30] Perhaps Dworkin would say that the limits justice imposes lie well short of the point where someone's personality is radically transformed. If so, his argument relies on a more fundamental premise, that compulsory removal of a cornea or a kidney entails a greater invasion of a person's right to bodily integrity than justice permits. I consider that argument below.

[31] Dworkin's reference to a case where a convicted criminal would prefer losing a finger to sitting in jail for several years is particularly puzzling. If one supposes (as one must, for purposes of comparison) that the prison sentence in question represents an optimal mix of deterrence, crime prevention, retribution, and whatever other ends incarceration is supposed to serve, then it is perplexing why Dworkin assumes that we would initially be inclined to grant the criminal his wish. By hypothesis, doing so would at least partly undermine the objectives his incarceration would further. The presumption should therefore be *against* granting him punishment that he considers less fearsome than incarceration and that would return him to the streets, perhaps to commit yet more crimes.

This is not to say that the latter reasons cannot be invoked in arguing against compulsory transplants. Transfers of this kind would not brand a person as a lifelong pariah—they should instead have the opposite effect, or elicit sympathy—but at least in the case of corneal transplants they would permanently deform the donor, to the extent that glass or blind eyes do. Moreover, our reluctance to maim or torture criminals (and perhaps this is part of Dworkin's point) seems in part due to our abhorrence of the infliction of acute anguish and perhaps permanent physical injury on somebody over his desperate protests, when at any moment we might release him from the ordeal. Placing someone under lock and key, by contrast, does not typically produce the same intense distress in the jailor or terror in the prisoner. Perhaps the similar reaction we could well experience in pinning someone to a table, strapping him down, and cutting away some part of his body could contribute to an argument against the transfer of organs under duress.

It is unclear, however, how much our feelings in the two cases would parallel one another and how relevant they are to the morality of the actions under consideration. No doubt part of what makes torture and maiming so loathsome is their almost universal pointlessness. Even when they are not gratuitous, the same results can often be obtained by less painful means. But if it were necessary to torture a terrorist to save the lives of many innocent people, many of us would probably suppress what revulsion we still felt (it would likely be diminished under the circumstances anyway) and do what was necessary to rescue the blameless from harm. Perhaps forcing someone to relinquish some part of his body so that another person may live should, and in time would, be seen in a similar light. To be sure, the person selected as a donor would be guilty of no crime. But if justice requires that such transfers be made, his resistance might be seen as more like that of an evasive taxpayer than of the intended victim of senseless violence. And even if we found that our emotional response to forced transfers of body parts did not differ significantly from our response to maiming criminals, we would still have to ask how much store we should set by that response if we were convinced that what we were doing was right. The fact that a doctor and his patient both shrink from the sight of blood is a poor reason for cancelling a life-saving operation. Perhaps in time, once compulsory transfers were established practices, attempts to flee the scalpel would be infrequent, greeted by others with scorn rather than sympathy. Perhaps our present reactions stem from what are generally laudable dispositions that give the wrong verdict in this particular case, together with a failure to realize what justice demands. Maybe they would alter once we perceived our duty more clearly. It is difficult to predict changes in attitude or to assess the moral importance of dispositions that are deeply ingrained. It does seem proper, however, to discount emotional responses and reactive judgments if they clash with what, on reflection, we consider morally imperative.

But if our visceral reaction to taking organs from unwilling donors is one of intense revulsion, can it really be our moral duty to perform such operations? Can we regard our emotional responses as the inevitable product of a commendable set of dispositions (e.g. a desire not to cause others to suffer) which it would be a mistake to uproot but which at times we must simply ignore in doing what morality demands?

Some philosophers think not. Thomas Nagel, for example, says of our inhibition from causing pain to innocent children that "we cannot come to *regard* it as a mere inhibition which it is good to have," for that, he believes, would be to falsify the phenomenology of our moral conflict when we are placed in a position where we can only spare some people substantial harm by hurting others to a lesser degree.[32] "The dilemma must be due to some special reason against *doing* such a thing. Otherwise it would be *obvious* that you should choose the lesser evil, and twist the child's arm [in order to obtain the use of a car to speed badly injured friends to a hospital]."[33] Only if we accept the existence of "agent-relative" reasons that give rise to "deontological constraints" on action, Nagel argues, can we adequately account for our deliberations in situations of this kind. If there are such reasons, however, and if the reason that figures in Nagel's example of torturing a child to help injured friends is among them, then it seems that a case might be made against compulsory organ transplants as well as against making children suffer.

Two replies seem warranted. The first is that the charge of falsifying the phenomenology of decision seems more properly directed at Nagel than at his opponents. Nagel claims that "the phenomenological fact that has to be accounted for is that we seem to apprehend in each individual case an extremely powerful agent-relative *reason* not to torture a child," which "presents itself as the apprehension of a *truth*, not just as a psychological inhibition."[34] But, at least when I look inward, introspection reveals this claim to be specious. When I shrink from hurting others, I do so not because I think that there is a strong agent-relative reason for not making them suffer—namely, that it is especially bad *for me* to be the agent of evil —but because I realize that they wish to avoid suffering and because I believe that this constitutes a forceful *agent-neutral* reason for not harming others if no one else will thereby be spared a greater harm. The truth I seem to apprehend is an agent-neutral truth. And my reluctance to harm in order to help *does* appear on reflection to stem from an inhibition which, though natural, has been strengthened through training because my mentors, and later I myself, regarded it as a good disposition to have. (I would not call it "just" an inhibition, as Nagel does, since having the right

[32] Nagel (1980), 129.   [33] Nagel (1980), 126.   [34] Nagel (1980), 129.

dispositions seems to me a matter of supreme moral importance. In a sense, they are the stuff of which we, and morality, are made.)

Nagel's explanation of the origin of the dilemma he describes seems, furthermore, to be erroneous. The reason why it is not obvious that one ought to twist the child's arm to get the car keys is not, I think, that one spies a special reason against doing such a thing. Rather, the explanation is that, although one recognizes that hurting the child is by far the lesser evil and to that extent *clearly* imperative if there is no better alternative, it is not evident that there is no other way to achieve the good at which one is aiming without doing even this much harm. Once one is sure that no superior course exists, the necessity of twisting the child's arm to save several friends from serious injury or possible death follows forthwith, one's inhibitions notwithstanding.

Whether or not this account of the phenomenology of decision is more accurate than Nagel's portrait, a second point deserves mention. Even if Nagel is right in affirming the existence of agent-relative reasons against harming people, there can be no doubt, as he himself concedes, that powerful agent-neutral reasons exist for worsening their lot in order to prevent much greater harm to others. It is therefore admittedly a matter of judgment, on Nagel's theory, whether the claims of justice and the awful fate that a few unfortunate people would face if no transplants were performed are weightier than whatever agent-relative reasons there are to refrain from dealing others a much less terrible blow. If transplants carry few risks, if the other conditions listed above have been met, and if certain mandatory transplant schemes are required by justice, then the disparity between the potential losses to donors and the expected gains to recipients would probably vindicate the schemes, even if Nagel's theory were correct.

A somewhat different argument—and to my mind the most forceful objection to compulsory tissue transplants—rests on the counterintuitive-ness and impracticality of requiring large sacrifices of one person to help people towards whom he has no special regard or affection, especially when most others are not called upon to make similar sacrifices and he receives no reciprocal benefits, apart from the assurance of help if he later finds himself similarly in need. Justice, it can be argued, simply cannot demand that someone part with something as valuable to him as an eye or a kidney, even if his not doing so means the blindness or death of somebody else. The problem is not just that this prescription offends our moral intuitions, in particular widespread views about people's right to maintain the inviolability of their bodies. In a world of the sort we inhabit, where impartial benevolence is a rare and fragile flower outside the happiest of families and a few small circles of friends, people will invariably act according to their perception of self-interest in matters of importance to them. To be sure, they may occasionally be willing to forgo their own immediate advantage to help strangers, particularly when such sacrifices occur frequently and form part of an established pattern of conduct from which each of the participants can expect to gain more over time than he surrenders. And even when a reciprocal exchange of benefits is unlikely to occur, pity, sympathy, or fraternal feeling will often impel people to help others in need or to renounce some small gain so that others may profit more. But, the objection runs, one cannot expect the bulk of humankind to chain themselves to a set of principles as exacting as those that would maximize their antecedent self-interest behind a veil of ignorance when those principles call for large, unrequited sacrifices. One can insist that they be "minimally decent Samaritans,"[35] but no more. Any acceptable, practicable moral code, one might claim, must include what Samuel Scheffler calls "agent-centered prerogatives,"[36] which allow individuals to attach greater importance to their own welfare and undertakings than to the concerns of others in deciding what to do. Contrary to what utilitarianism might appear to imply, they cannot be regarded as machines whose job is ever to effect the optimal state of affairs from an impersonal consequentialist perspective.[37] A morality that demanded that much of

[35] The phrase is Judith Jarvis Thomson's. Brian Barry endorses a view of the kind I describe here in his review of Fried's *Right and Wrong. See* Barry (1979).

[36] Scheffler (1982*a*).

[37] Although the question what duties individuals in affluent nations have to alleviate the suffering and to improve the living standards of the destitute in other lands falls outside the scope of my inquiry, it is worth mentioning that sentiments of the sort just expressed seem to underlie the popular and appealing view that if citizens of wealthy countries have a moral duty to help the poor abroad, that duty cannot be too taxing; so long as someone does his (nonutilitarian) share, he can sleep with a clear conscience, even if the fact that others have not done their part means that many people will starve whom he could still help.

Consequentialists often assail this view. They insist that the distinction between acts and omissions is morally irrelevant, and sometimes go on to argue that not giving additional assistance, with the result that more people die than would otherwise perish, is as bad as strangling those extra people with one's own hands in order to keep the resources one might have given to save them. *See, e.g.* Glover (1977), 104–6.

John Harris makes this argument by way of analogy. Suppose you were one of five excellent swimmers collecting sea shells on a remote beach when a boat capsized, spilling one hundred helpless children into the surf. Suppose, further, that the other four swimmers were unwilling to break off their search to rescue the drowning toddlers. You would not be blameless, Harris says, if you decided to call it a day after hauling in your twenty. It is your duty to pull children from the sea until your strength gives out or nothing more can be done. The fact that there are four indifferent bystanders is morally irrelevant, Harris contends: you are bound to act just as you would had you been alone on the beach when disaster struck. *See* Harris (1980), 143–55.

From the standpoint of someone defending the conception of morality outlined in the text, however, these objections at best beg the question. They presuppose the correctness of a notion of morality we simply do not share, and on reflection are unwilling to adopt. One can admit that it is tragic that people die when one might have saved them. One can concede, furthermore, that the moral obtuseness of others increases one's duty to help. But one need not also grant that someone does wrong if he does not surrender his last penny or last ounce of strength to keep others alive. No one could be expected to agree to or comply with so demanding a moral code. Harris's argument by analogy fails completely because the parallel

people would surely founder, sooner rather than later, on the fact that altruism is, as Broad said, almost invariably "self-referential," a powerful force where the welfare of those whom one loves deeply is concerned, but a force whose pull falls off precipitously as one moves outside the family to the spheres formed by one's neighbors, one's countrymen, or human beings generally. To ask someone to surrender an eye or a kidney to help a brother or a friend may not be unreasonable; to ask him to do the same for a stranger is apt to sound ridiculous.

All of these points can be admitted, however, without conceding that the liabilities justice imposes on people cannot be other than innocuous, or that the state may not require more of its citizens in the pursuit of equality than it would be reasonable to expect them to surrender without prodding. Equality of fortune, as we have seen, plainly asks more of people (for example, by way of compensating the congenitally handicapped or those who are unlucky in childhood) than they would give if not compelled, and the use of force and the threat of force are justified if necessary to achieve that end. To be sure, there are limits to how far the state may go. Even if it can rightly hold people to a higher standard of conduct than they would display if coercion were absent, it cannot force some people to devote their lives entirely to the service of others, making them slaves of the naturally less fortunate; nor can it ordinarily take the life of one person in the absence of his prior consent in order to keep several other persons alive.[38] The question is therefore whether compulsory organ transplants, in those few cases where justice seems to require them, lie within or without those limits. The question is indeed difficult, at least where the donation of an organ rather than blood is involved. The surrender of a kidney or a cornea entails a considerable sacrifice, even if it does not typically work a fundamental change in someone's personality. Nevertheless, if the risk of death from the removal of a kidney were small (as it is), if all donors were

---

is flawed at precisely the point where it must be sound if he is to persuade. Certainly the existence of four idle swimmers does not release one from the duty to save as many children as one can: one ought to act as one would if they were miles away. The same is true of one's duty regarding those starving in faraway lands, at least to a substantial extent: if others do not do their share, one ought to provide as much assistance, or almost as much, as one would if others who could in fact help were unable to do so or never existed. To this extent the analogy holds. But it does not follow from the fact that one ought to abandon the search for sea shells and spend the whole afternoon, if need be, pulling frightened children from the waves that one ought to abandon all the things that matter in one's life (with the exception of saving lives) and spend the whole of one's years doing nothing but altruistic deeds. The vast difference in the arduousness of the two courses of action crucially affects their obligatoriness. Suppose boatloads of children overturned every day, that you and others could rescue them if everyone contributed one day a month, but that each of the others was only willing to spend half a day each year manning the rowboats. Unfortunate though it is that many souls will perish as a consequence, would it really be reprehensible of you to decide that, after a point, your life comes first?

[38] See below, section 14.2.

guaranteed a replacement if their one remaining kidney failed, if corneal transplants were not grossly disfiguring (and they are not), if cadaver organs were unavailable, and if mandatory transfers saved innocent people from blindness or death while effecting a more equal distribution of resources, then I am inclined to think that the state may perform the transplants on minors if the conditions set forth above are met. But there is no incontestable or precise way to balance these competing considerations against one another, and it seems likely that people will disagree over the weights they give those arguments and the conclusions they reach.

A somewhat different argument for the conclusion that justice cannot demand such large sacrifices of people was suggested by Ronald Dworkin in conversation. One might distinguish, he said, two ways of conceiving the equal shares that justice requires. If one regards equality as a *goal*, then any transfer of an organ from someone who has two to somebody who has none might be seen as an increase in equality and *unarguably* justifiable according to a theory that construes justice as equality of resources, assuming that the transfer is beneficial to the recipient and not fatal to the donor. If, however, one regards equality as a *right*, then one would have to say that everyone has a right to 1.995 functioning eyes or kidneys (the total number of functioning organs in the relevant population divided by the number of people) and weigh the violation of someone's right involved in removing one of his kidneys or corneas against the advance towards someone else's right to 1.995 eyes or kidneys brought about by giving him one when he has none. And where rights of this kind are in conflict, it is not *obvious*, Dworkin said, that mandatory transfers can be justified. Indeed, Dworkin himself thought them unjustifiable.

Dworkin's suggestion, however, is perplexing. For it is unclear how weights should be assigned to violations and partial vindications of rights if those weights are not assigned according to the contribution towards or detraction from equality as a goal that each violation or vindication makes, taking into account the value of both to the persons concerned. Dworkin evidently relied on some other method for measuring the relative importance of the alleged rights at war here, but he did not shed more light on the intuitive balancing process at work.

The result he reaches, moreover, is questionable. After all, one eye or kidney is not merely half as good as two. It is not like taking $1 from someone who was given $20,002 to hand to someone who was given $20,000 when both had a right to $20,001.99. If the transfer of an organ meant release from blindness or life itself to one person, and if it meant reduced peripheral vision or a slightly greater risk of death from renal failure to the other, then the gains and losses would not be of the same order. Suppose that the only way to keep alive someone who was denied his fair share of material resources was to give him one-fourth of somebody else's fair share, with the consequence that the second person lived slightly less well but was by no means significantly disadvantaged in the pursuit of his principal goals. Would Dworkin really insist that the first person be left to die if the second had a hard heart? I think not. But if this violation of someone's rights is justified, why can there be no justification for the analogous case of compulsory organ transfers? What if somebody would in fact trade one kidney for the one-fourth share that would otherwise be taken from him?

Some might protest that, although it may be permissible to require sacrifices of the magnitude that organ donation would entail if a great many people were forced to make them, the sacrifices under consideration would certainly be rare, and would thus constitute instances of intolerable victimization. If all were called upon to make the same contribution, one might claim, that would be fine. But to single out a few individuals to bear the entire burden is unfair and therefore unacceptable.

This argument is spurious. It appears to rely on a principle of fairness which, though valid within a certain domain, is inapplicable to cases of this kind. Certainly it is wrong, other things equal, to demand exceptional sacrifices of one person if the same result could be attained by requiring equal smaller sacrifices from him and from others who are similarly situated. But in this case other things are not equal. If cadaver organs failed to stem the need, the only alternatives to not transplanting a few organs from donors chosen at random would be either to allow a few other people to be victimized by nature in even more egregious fashion, at the cost of still greater injustice, or needlessly to impose risks or suffering on non-donors equal to that which donors experience, just to keep everyone on a par. Since neither alternative is preferable to the recommended course, the objection fails.

The final criticism of compulsory organ transfer schemes implicit in the foregoing objection is practical. Compulsory transfer schemes might well be difficult to administer, open the possibility of abuse by the responsible authorities, and incorporate invidious distinctions between supposedly equal citizens. If the schemes were instituted, for example, all children would have to be examined by a physician, potential kidney donors tissue-typed, and their names and addresses kept on file. Some parents might refuse to allow their children to undergo the required examination, making it necessary to threaten, and perhaps to use, force to secure compliance. When a donor was needed, one would have to be chosen randomly from among those who were suitable. Abuse by the authorities could become a problem, since bribes would doubtless be offered to spare some selected donors. Some sort of regulatory commission would therefore be necessary to ensure that donors were chosen fairly. Once a donor had been picked, parents of those whose numbers were called or adults selected in accordance with a voluntary scheme might attempt to conceal their children or hide themselves. They might also assault those who attempted to take them into custody. Once a prospective donor had been apprehended, he might fight desperately to escape; if friends or relatives frequently attempted to help, then extensive security precautions might be necessary in hospitals where such operations were performed. Finally, the possible need to grant exemptions from donation could well provoke bitter disputes. Many people might think that a head of state or perhaps some other senior government official should not be forced to undergo a dangerous operation which, even if things went smoothly, would incapacitate him for some time, restrict his movements, and maybe even reduce his competence thereafter. But a similar argument could be made on behalf of surgeons, or soldiers in wartime, or pregnant women, or for that matter anyone who would have to change occupations or dramatically alter his lifestyle. Certainly it would be best to minimize exceptions, but once some have been made, it is difficult to hold the line against others. And no matter what policy was chosen, resentment would fester.

It is impossible to say a priori, however, whether these potential problems would pose major obstacles to the implementation of the transfer schemes. One reason for thinking that they would not prove overly troublesome is that the administrative chores they would necessitate, such as registration, preliminary examination, fair selection, and the granting of exemptions, are shared by systems of selective military service, where they have not proved insuperable. Since the number of compulsory transplants would be quite small—a tiny fraction of the number called up for military duty in many North American and West European nations each year—and since the risk of serious injury would be trifling by comparison with that which conscripts are asked to run in wartime, the problems of administration and compliance should be even less formidable. Resistance by those whose numbers were chosen would, of course, probably be more determined, because someone whisked away to the hospital would know that, should he reach his destination, he would not return intact; a young man sent off to war, in contrast, could hope to return unscathed, however unrealistic that hope might in fact be. But if the penalties for resistance and interference with the program were severe, there seems no reason to think that this difficulty could not be overcome as well. In a just society, it might even be minimal, if citizens generally accepted the moral propriety of the prescriptions defended above. Needless to say, any attempt to carry out coercive transplants in our own society would probably encounter stout opposition, at least at first; it would, furthermore, surely be criticized as undemocratic and perhaps excessively expensive. But that is not a decisive objection to the permissibility, in more nearly ideal circumstances, of compulsory organ transfers, even though it might justify temporary or even permanent restrictions on their performance. It is, from the perspective of one who credits the preceding arguments, merely one incarnation of the familiar problem of convincing a society's defenders of the status quo's fundamental injustice.

PART II
CORRECTIVE JUSTICE

9

The Problem of Liability Rules: The Failings of Wealth Maximization as a Normative Ideal

PEOPLE's wealth and happiness may be diminished as much by the actions of others as by natural chance and their personal choices. Often the frustration of another person's aims is unquestionably permissible, an ineluctable concomitant of freedom of association or a market economy. Competitions for jobs, friends, or scarce consumer goods offer familiar examples. Other types of interference, however, seem improper, or at least of doubtful propriety. Toxic fumes from a chemical plant may choke neighboring homeowners. Drunk drivers may stray from their lanes, running down pedestrians or swerving into oncoming traffic. Excavation efforts may damage adjacent buildings, or jostled shoppers slip and suffer injury. This Part seeks to determine when nonmarket harms of these kinds, caused (in the colloquial sense of the word) by the conduct of someone other than the victim, warrant redress.

Debate over the desirability of alternative rules of tort liability typically proceeds on the assumption that a just distribution of resources prevails and that the relevant question is what scheme of legal obligations to superimpose on that structure. Despite its popularity, this approach is misguided. The principles and circumstances under which one person is obliged to compensate an injured party cannot in fact be properly determined once a theory of fair shares has been constructed and goods and opportunities assigned accordingly. The former project's completion is rather a precondition of a just allocation of resources, for the values that people attach to material goods depend upon the uses to which they can be put and the potential liabilities their owner incurs. Resources cannot be divided justly without knowing the rights and risks their possession and use entail. Theories of tort and property law are therefore integral parts of a theory of distributive justice, not extraneous additions. In formulating liability and property rules, the question is what principles cohere most tightly with the claim that each person is initially entitled to an equally valuable bundle of resources and that later differences in luck and earnings will generate the distributive consequences detailed in Part I, and what modifications to those principles reasonable persons would consent to make.

Strict liability and negligence have long provided tort law's dominant competing paradigms. Each of these theories has found supporters along the entire spectrum of moral views, from firm deontologists to thorough-going consequentialists. Current law, however, does not consistently embrace either standard. More important, neither strict liability nor negligence, at least in their pristine forms, seems to accord fully with popular intuitions about what rules are desirable. If an oil tanker spills its cargo, sullying beaches and devastating the local tourist industry, it seems wrong to excuse the tanker's owners from compensating victims merely because they took every cost-effective precaution. But it seems equally wrong to hold someone liable for all the harm he causes when trying to help another person in apparent distress, however skillfully he furnishes assistance, or to make a passerby pay the hospital bills of somebody who fell when he unintentionally brushed against her on a crowded, icy street. Both strict liability and negligence, in the sophisticated forms in which they have been defended, are therefore encrusted with qualifications and exceptions.

Over the last two decades, advocates of the economic analysis of law have attempted to accommodate our moral intuitions in a simpler way, by explaining the bulk of extant tort law in terms of the single criterion of wealth maximization. They have claimed, moreover, that the moral bases and practical implications of wealth maximization should appeal to deontologists and consequentialists alike.

This chapter explores this purported shortcut to a coherent, appealing theory of tort law by examining the most influential account of the normative foundations of wealth maximization, that of Richard Posner. This chapter's focus on wealth maximization seems particularly apposite because of the attraction such a theory would surely hold, at first blush, for people carving up a collectively held stock of property into equal pieces and therefore eager to expand the common cake as much as possible. By probing the shortcomings of wealth maximization, I shall try to show how its dictates must be modified to produce more just outcomes in certain recurrent situations and to isolate those facts that should guide the choice between stricter and looser standards of liability. Chapter 10 summarizes those lessons. Chapter 11 then applies them in sketching liability rules to govern such traditional concerns of tort law as intentional injury, nuisances, abnormally dangerous activities, and collisions. Discussion is confined to the appropriateness of compensation for nonmarket injury; possible penal sanctions are not considered, nor are property rights treated systematically.

The theory I propose presumptively favors strict liability for harm caused by an agent when he willfully or unintentionally transgresses rules protecting personal or property rights or governing the use of public goods, such as roads and waterways. Negligence, however, becomes the appropriate standard of liability in three situations: (1) where the injurer acts under unforeseeable or intentional compulsion or duress, whether of natural or human origin, for which he cannot be blamed; (2) where rational persons would all prefer negligence to strict liability; or (3) where the costs of implementing a system of strict liability substantially exceed those of predicating liability on lack of reasonable care and where substituting a negligence test would not result in significant uncompensated losses to any group of citizens.

9.1. SPECIFYING THE PRECONDITIONS FOR APPLYING THE WEALTH MAXIMIZATION CRITERION

In *The Economics of Justice*, Richard Posner argues that laws generally, and tort law in particular, should be fashioned to maximize social wealth.[1] Guido Calabresi makes a similar claim with respect to accident law: legislation should strive to minimize the aggregate nominal value of injuries suffered, precautionary measures (including forgone opportunities), insurance costs, litigation expenses, and the time and worry devoted to accident-related transactions by actual and potential injurers and victims, provided the rather elastic bounds set by a community's sense of justice are not overstepped.[2] A host of other writers approaching legal issues from an economic perspective follow suit, taking wealth maximization as the sole or dominant end of rational legislation.[3] In view of the prominence of this approach today, it seems wise to expose its ambiguities and moral undesirability before formulating a more defensible guide to lawmaking.

In Posner's lexicon, a person's wealth is the minimum amount of money that he would accept in exchange for all the goods he owns, the services from which he benefits, and the natural and social advantages he enjoys, so long as he acquired these desiderata in accordance with "ethically proper

---

[1] The most comprehensive statement of Posner's position is contained in chapters 3 and 4 of *The Economics of Justice*. References to that work will hereinafter be abbreviated "*EJ*." Posner has recently qualified his endorsement of wealth maximization, however, acknowledging that it needs supplementing by some other theory to specify an initial distribution of rights and resources, and that it should perhaps be tempered by independent moral principles because its unmodified implications are in certain cases counterintuitive. *See* Posner (1990), ch. 12. Although Posner's advocacy of wealth maximization as a normative ideal is now less sweeping and less confident, it remains useful to survey the shortcomings of wealth maximization taken as a comprehensive principle of justice, in order to forestall a repetition of Posner's early errors and to guide the construction of a more defensible account of justice.

[2] *See* Calabresi (1970), esp. chs. 3, 15, and 16.

[3] *See, e.g.*, Polinsky (1983); Shavell (1980).

principles" of distributive justice.[4] A person's wealth includes not only those goods, rights, or services that he could sell on an established market, but also those objects of value, such as friendship or free time, that could conceivably be monetized.

The ideal of wealth maximization declares that a given right—whether to property, services, personal freedom, or whatever—should come to be held by the person or group of persons that is willing to pay the most money (or money equivalent, such as material goods or labor-time) for it. What someone would be willing to pay for a right is equal to the minimum amount he would accept in exchange for it if he already possesses it justly, or the maximum amount that he would spend for the right if it is not yet his. Although that ideal, I shall argue, is incoherent and ethically objectionable unless qualified in numerous ways, its application plainly presupposes a background set of entitlements capable of specifying people's offer and asking prices for a given good, which in turn determine that good's optimal assignment. The remainder of this section criticizes Posner's account of the origin and nature of the pre-existing entitlements upon which the imperative of wealth maximization should be brought to bear; section 9.2 attacks the application of that imperative to a prima facie just distribution of entitlements.

Wealth maximization, as Posner describes it in *The Economics of Justice*, is a master principle of distributive justice. It not only mandates the conversion of any existing allocation of rights to the most just distribution possible:[5] it also specifies the proper initial distribution of entitlements,

---

[4] *See EJ* 60–5.

[5] In a second preface added to *The Economics of Justice* in 1983, Posner qualifies his endorsement of the ethic of wealth maximization because of "the rather bizarre results that its unflinching application could produce." He considers the example of a wealthy man of normal height who wishes to increase his stature and who purchases the entire supply of a scarce growth hormone, thereby depriving an indigent dwarf of his only chance to stand shoulder to shoulder with his fellow citizens. Posner's verdict: "one recoils from the implications of allowing the market to control [the hormone's] allocation completely." Posner refrains, however, from offering a principled restriction on applying the norm of wealth maximization. And his tentative concession threatens to destroy the entire superstructure he has erected. Suppose that under a wealth-maximizing regime the wealthy are able, over time, to control virtually the entire supply of decent housing, superior education, and desirable jobs. Would not that result be at least equally "bizarre" and even more unacceptable? One suspects that Posner would not find it so, but one looks in vain for some indication of how he would distinguish that case from the one that disturbs him. He may believe that poverty and the attendant lack of access to education and employment are nearly always, or frequently, the fault of the poor. But not only is that belief plainly wrong to at least a substantial degree in all contemporary industrial societies: it cannot explain why the dwarf's lot warrants special solicitude. He may not be answerable for his height, but who is to blame for his penury?

In *The Problems of Jurisprudence*, Posner returns to this example. Without saying whether he believes that the distribution of a scarce growth hormone should be left to the market, Posner says that "what seems impossible to maintain convincingly in the present ethical climate is that the wealthy parent [of a child of normal height] has the *right* to the hormone by virtue of being willing to pay the supplier more than the poor parent [of a dwarf] can." Posner

that is, it dictates how resources to which no one has a morally superior claim should be divided. Wealth maximization thus declares an optimal starting point and ensures the preservation of that ideal over time. Setting aside, for the moment, the contours and coherence of its maintenance function, how can the principle of wealth maximization determine people's initial shares? And, if it can, is the result intuitively acceptable?

The difficulty of the first question is evident. The assignment of a right according to parties' relative willingness to pay for it presupposes that at least one of the contenders possesses the wherewithal to outbid his rivals; the principle of wealth maximization requires that people have certain rights before it can specify how their rights should be altered. Hence, the theory is perforce incomplete: the initial distribution of entitlements must be specified by some more fundamental theory of distributive justice.[6] Posner, however, refused to bow to logic in *The Economics of Justice*, perhaps because he feared that by endorsing principles of distribution other than wealth maximization, he would open himself to the objection that they should take precedence over wealth maximization in contexts other than the initial assignment of rights. Instead, he attempted to conjure basic personal and property rights out of the wealth maximization ideal itself.[7]

Posner's argument opens with an empirical claim. No matter how property rights are initially assigned, he contends, after several generations of economic activity both aggregate social wealth and the market and shadow[8] prices of desired goods will be much the same. This is so even if all such rights originally belong to a single person. But if some distribution of a certain amount of wealth will inevitably arise, says Posner, then rights should initially be assigned to effect this result as quickly as possible. And the way to achieve this end, he asserts, is to give everyone a property right in his own person, allowing him to determine how his body and labor are to be employed, and to split land allotments into the smallest economically efficient units. Thus, the ideal of wealth maximization can generate a just

---

(1990), 380. He thus seems to say that wealth maximization *might* not furnish the sole source of distributive principles, without himself taking a stand on this critical issue. *See also* Posner (1985), 96. More generally, since writing *The Economics of Justice*, Posner has concluded that the various objections raised against the theory he there advanced "are sufficiently troublesome to make me regard wealth maximization as an incomplete guide to social decision-making." Posner (1985), 101. He has so far neglected to state, however, precisely what modifications he would support.

[6] This point has not been lost on previous critics. *See, e.g.* Dworkin (1985), 251–5; Bebchuk (1980), 684–8; Kronman (1980), 240–2.

[7] *See EJ* 111–12. Posner has recently recanted, conceding that "wealth maximization is inherently incomplete as a guide to social action" because it cannot specify fully the initial distribution of material resources and rights. Posner (1990), 375, 378.

[8] A good's shadow price is the amount that it would command *if* there were a market on which it were traded.

initial allocation of entitlements, as well as furnish the means for its preservation.

Unfortunately for Posner's position in *The Economics of Justice*, nothing can be made from a vacuum. A string of indefensible claims could only persuade someone who was already convinced on other grounds. The first problem is that the empirical assumption from which Posner starts—that the same state of affairs will result, no matter what the original configuration of personal and property rights—is implausible. In fact, Posner himself seems to reject it, both explicitly and implicitly. He rejects it explicitly when he argues that monopolies are inefficient because they impede the maximization of wealth.[9] If a monopoly prevents society from reaching an economically optimal state, then it must bring about a state of affairs that would not otherwise have come into being. But if society's resources are initially assigned to a single person, thereby creating the largest monopoly imaginable, the same states of affairs will not unfold over time as when resources are distributed in such a way as to preclude monopolistic production. So Posner's postulate of economic fatalism appears, by his own admission, to be false.

More generally, Posner rejects that postulate implicitly by assuming, in advocating adoption of wealth-maximizing policies, that such policies make a difference. If a society were bound to end up at the same place, no matter how resources were spread about and what policies were followed, then there would apparently be no reason to seek the maximization of wealth rather than some other objective.[10] So it seems that either fatalism or wealth maximization must go.

Posner might reply, I suppose, that this is a false dilemma. The destination cannot vary, he might say, but some roads are swifter than others; a policy of wealth maximization makes a difference not in the terminus but in the time of arrival.

This rejoinder, however, cannot be reconciled with Posner's observations about the inefficiency monopoly breeds, unless one makes the unwarranted assertion that all monopolies are short-lived and sterile. It further affronts common sense and experience. Economic organization matters: compare the two Germanies after 1945. So does the distribution of wealth: nothing like the antebellum South would ever have existed had blacks and whites obtained equal freeholds in 1800 (and had blacks been equally well educated and freed from legal discrimination). Affluence not

---

[9] See *EJ* 72, 91–2.

[10] If there is a reason, then it must be traceable to some normative principle other than wealth maximization and therefore potentially in conflict with it. Posner is understandably reluctant to surrender the purity of his system by acknowledging such a principle, for doing so would invite challenge along the entire gamut of distributive questions. Posner's confession of incompleteness in the second preface to *The Economics of Justice* and in *The Problems of Jurisprudence* raises precisely this problem. See above, p. 202 n.5.

only affects how long and hard people work and what occupations they pursue, it influences their reproductive decisions and innovativeness as well. The claim that all roads eventually pass through the same valley is insupportable.

One reason that Posner reached his surprising conclusion in *The Economics of Justice* is that he then believed that if one person were initially assigned the right to another's labor, making the second person a slave of the first, the second would almost always end up purchasing his freedom; and once somebody has a right to his own labor, he seemed to think, material resources proportional to his skill and energy will just as surely come his way. But neither belief is well founded, and the second begs, or at least dispenses all too briskly with, one of the central questions of distributive justice.

Posner's claim that those who started out slaves when resources were initially assigned would almost invariably secure their freedom, no matter how resources were allocated, is merely wishful thinking. Not only does his assertion seem to imply that innumerable slaveholders in countless societies over the sweep of history acted irrationally by not allowing their human chattel to earn their liberty—an implication that negates his contention that economic rationality is not uniquely an attribute of modern capitalist societies, but is evident even in primitive forms of social organization[11]—but it fails to stand even the simplest test.

Consider Dworkin's example of Agatha and Sir George.[12] Agatha is able to write spellbinding detective stories, for which the public pays handsomely. She prefers, however, to spend much of her time on interior design, at which she earns a pittance. Suppose that Sir George owns Agatha's labor, making her his slave. As an economically rational slaveowner, Dworkin argues, Sir George would apply to Agatha whatever mix of rewards and sanctions would maximize his return. Agatha could never buy her freedom, because to gain release she would have to pay Sir George an amount equal to what he would glean from her work under a system of optimal incentives, and if she did that she would be forced to lead exactly the same life that she led under Sir George's enlightened despotism —or worse, if lenders required high interest payments—to keep Sir George or her other creditors at bay. If she gained her freedom, it would be freedom in name only. By contrast, if Agatha held the right to her own labor, she would spend most days furnishing homes, write a detective story when her bank balance dropped, and never surrender the right to do as she pleased. Hence, Dworkin concludes, wealth maximization does not yield a

[11] *See EJ* chs. 6 and 7.
[12] *See* Dworkin (1985), 254–5, and Dworkin (1983*b*), 295–6; *see also* Bebchuk (1980), 687–8; Kronman (1980), 240–2; Baker (1980), 951–3.

determinate initial assignment of labor rights; who eventually owns the right to Agatha's labor depends on who was given it at the start.

Posner's reply in *The Economics of Justice* is transparently flawed. He says that Dworkin's argument "ignores the fact that if Agatha were free she almost certainly *could*—not would—write more detective stories than she would write if she were a slave," because she would have a greater incentive to keep her nose to the grindstone if she pocketed the profits.[13] So, Posner assumes, Agatha could produce stories, if free, worth $1.2 million in the same amount of time that it would take her to write $1 million worth of stories as a slave, and could therefore buy her freedom for $1 million and still have one-sixth of her time left over for other pursuits. The initial assignment of the right to Agatha's labor, he concludes, does not determine who would come to hold it.

But this result hardly follows. First of all, the sense in which Posner uses "could" is obscure: what prevents Agatha from working as intensely when enslaved as when free, other than her *decision* not to do so? The impediment, if there is one, seems not to be incapacity but lack of will. Second, Posner's assumption that Agatha would purchase her freedom *if* she would have marginally more time for herself by doing so (which, as we have seen, is false if Sir George is a rational slaveowner) would not always hold even granted Posner's presuppositions. As Dworkin notes,[14] Agatha would have to forfeit her financial security for a slight increase in the control she exercises over her life, and many people would doubtless consider this an unattractive trade. Third, to the extent that Agatha's productivity would be affected by the actuality or the prospect of liberation, it is hard to imagine the paper freedom she would have if Sir George originally owned her labor and sold it to her at its net present value making any difference at all. She would, as Dworkin points out, remain the slave, formalities apart, of either Sir George or some moneylender. Fourth, freedom would only matter to Agatha if it allowed her more time for less taxing projects than spinning tales. But then Posner's counter-example cannot parry Dworkin's objection. For if the opportunity to do other things enhanced Agatha's productivity, then Sir George would make such opportunities available to her. He would, if rational, offer her the same inducements that freedom waved before her. Posner's example only carries force if one assumes what Dworkin quite reasonably does not, namely, that Sir George is *not* an enlightened, economically rational master. Fifth, Posner manages to lend some credibility to his example by stipulating that Sir George views Agatha as a productive asset. But once this arbitrary stipulation is removed, Agatha's hopes of gaining release

---

[13] *EJ* 110 (emphasis in original).
[14] *See* Dworkin (1985), 255.

rapidly fade. If Sir George regards her not only as a pulp mill but also as a sexual plaything,[15] or if he simply takes delight in the feeling of domination that slaveholding fosters,[16] then he might demand more to part with Agatha than she could ever earn on her own. The initial assignment of the right to her labor would be decisive. Finally, it must have occurred to everyone who has followed this crazed debate that a theory that makes so fundamental a right as that to personal freedom turn on whether someone could and would buy it back if it fell into somebody else's hands— something that even Posner admits people might not be able to do, although he mistakenly believes that such cases would be exceptions, not the rule[17]—is profoundly misguided. Any acceptable theory of justice must account for and accommodate people's right to order their lives in an intuitively appealing way—for example, by taking it as axiomatic or by tying it to some more fundamental notion of equality. The ideal of wealth maximization barely tries.[18]

This parade of imperfections signals a larger problem. Even if the initial assignment of the right to someone's labor were determinate in a world where rights to all other goods were already allocated (which it is not), its initial assignment can hardly determine who will own it if other entitlements have not been apportioned. Somebody initially assigned a large stock of resources would always be able to secure the right to his own labor, whether or not he started with it; somebody absolutely destitute, who had little earning potential but who was desired as a slave for consumption purposes by someone sitting atop a hill of silver, would never know freedom.

Posner's claim that making people the owners of their own labor rights will speed society to the only possible equilibrium is therefore doubly unfounded. First, who eventually owns a person's labor rights is not independent of who first owned them, even if each right is viewed in isolation against a completely determined background of entitlements. Moreover, who owns them *will* almost certainly affect future production, contrary to Posner's fatalistic assumption: Agatha will arrange furniture if free and write mysteries if not. Second, indeterminacy of ownership is unavoidable, by Posner's own admission,[19] if other rights have not been assigned. So even if Posner were right about Agatha, he would need some

---

[15] *See* Bebchuk (1980), 688.

[16] *See* Baker (1980), 952.

[17] *See EJ* 71, 102.

[18] Posner now appears to recognize the force of this last objection. *See* Posner (1990), 379–80. Unfortunately, he declines to reveal his own views, saying merely, by way of social observation, that convictions regarding the fundamental, non-economic character of certain personal rights are "too deeply entrenched in our society at present for wealth maximization to be given a free rein." *Ibid.* at 380.

[19] *See EJ* 111.

formula, derivable from the ideal of wealth maximization itself, for distributing rights other than the right to a single person's labor. He offers none.

The problem is more acute than Posner realizes. If one imagines people bidding for rights and resources at some global auction, then one must concede that the *order* in which labor rights are assigned will inevitably influence the final pattern of ownership, quite apart from how other resources are initially parcelled out. Those who acquire a right to their own labor early will have more wealth with which to bid for slaves later. Again, some principle is needed to specify the order of assignment, and wealth maximization is unable to supply it.

This difficulty cannot be removed by Posner's suggestion[20] that people should be thought of as able to borrow against their future incomes in bidding for rights at the moment when they are initially assigned. For the amount that people will later be capable of earning is in turn a function of how entitlements, including labor rights, are first distributed. To appeal to future income to determine initial shares, when future income depends on initial shares, is to turn an embarrassingly tight circle. Because these criticisms could be repeated with respect to all objects of value other than labor rights, the problem of indeterminacy is of truly colossal proportions.

These criticisms cascade to a common result. Posner's premise of economic fatalism cannot be sustained. The distribution of entitlements with which a society starts affects, often profoundly, the distribution that prevails several generations hence, not merely whether destiny runs or crawls. What is perhaps most curious about Posner's argument is that he thinks the latter matters. If a certain economic result is inevitable, his minor premise runs, then the sooner society achieves it, the better. But why? He cannot justify this proposition by reference to individual rights, or invoke some goal independent of wealth maximization (such as an increase in aggregate utility), for that would introduce a second distributive principle alongside wealth maximization which in some instances might prescribe a different result and compel him to adduce some reason—which might be impossible—for invariably giving the latter precedence. The "main point," Posner says, is to abide within a moral universe defined by the principle of wealth maximization alone, so that "[a] just distribution of wealth need not be posited."[21] But speed is not a value that wealth maximization alone can beget, unless the constellation of desires and dollars is such that people are willing to pay for it. But whether people would pay depends upon both the initial allocation of entitlements, which is in issue here, and the fated future (who would hurry economic depression?). So whence this urge to telescope history?

[20] *See EJ* 71–2.   [21] *EJ* 81.

Posner's answer is puzzling. The reason for creating at the start a pattern of rights that is bound to arise anyway, Posner declares, is that doing so minimizes transaction or agency costs.[22] Speed is a byproduct, not an independent aim. This rationale, however, contains a covert appeal to values such as consent or increased aggregate welfare, along with optimistic empirical assumptions about the direction of economic development. Posner's explanation therefore merely suppresses the tension between those at least potentially rival values and his favored ideal; it does not eliminate it. Posner's explanation seems particularly strained inasmuch as his favored conception of wealth maximization does not generally approve compulsory reassignments of rights, of the sort he defends in this hypothetical case, when transaction costs do not block wealth-maximizing exchanges but only render them more expensive.[23] If compensation is normally required for the surrender of a right in cases where the surrender is almost certain to occur if wealth would be maximized in that way, then why not here?

Perhaps the answer lies in Posner's attachment to a particular result and his determination to reach it however he may. Posner favors (or at one time seemed to favor) a social order in which the compulsory redistribution of wealth is limited to transfers that reduce the net costs of crime or that find favor with the majority's altruistic sentiments,[24] a society in which the nonproductive, even those born handicapped, have no claim to public support,[25] and in which the moral propriety of untaxed inheritance is taken for granted.[26] He apparently wants, moreover, to vindicate something like the status quo in what seems a neutral, automatic way—an idle hope, since *any* distributive principle, be it wealth maximization or utilitarianism, itself wants normative justification—and to advocate the immediate adoption of wealth-maximizing legal rules without approving some radical realignment of existing property rights in order to cleanse them of accumulated inequities.

As we have seen, however, Posner's purported derivation of an initial assignment of resources from the ideal of wealth maximization itself cannot withstand scrutiny. Indeed, any attempt to justify a distribution of resources by arguing that all developmental paths lead to the same terminus faces a seemingly insuperable epistemological problem, for how can one know that the social order one seeks to ground constitutes the

---

[22] *See EJ* 112; Posner (1985), 93–4.

[23] The difficulties that attend wealth maximization's alleged endorsement of market exchanges when transaction costs are low are canvassed in section 9.2.

[24] *See EJ* 80–1. Posner now seems less sure about the position he advanced in *The Economics of Justice*, although he remains reticent about the degree of his ambivalence. *See* Posner (1985), 101; Posner (1990), 381.

[25] *See EJ* 76, 100.

[26] *See EJ* 82.

point of convergence rather than a queer twist along one of many meandering roads to the fated destination? An advocate of wealth maximization must make recourse to some independent principle of distributive justice, at least to mark the point of departure. The question then becomes whether wealth maximization, applied within a just order, is a commendable ideal.

9.2. THE PRESUMPTION IN FAVOR OF MARKET EXCHANGES

Wealth maximization results when material goods, opportunities, the benefits of services—anything somebody values—are held by those willing to pay the most money for them. According to Posner, the value of a good whose possible reassignment is being considered is, in the case of the present owner, his asking price, that is, the smallest sum he would accept in return for it, and, in the case of all other persons, their offer prices, that is, the most money they would part with to acquire it. The ideal of wealth maximization declares that if the present owner's asking price for a good is less than at least one other person's offer price, then the good should be transferred to the person whose offer price is highest, in whatever manner would minimize transaction costs. Whether the person with the largest offer price actually pays the present owner for the good if his offer price trumps the owner's asking price is irrelevant. What matters is that resources flow to their most valued uses. Usually, Posner contends, compensation should be required when a good changes hands and transaction costs are low, for the consummation of a voluntary exchange is the best evidence that the shift in ownership maximizes wealth (assuming no negative externalities) by improving both parties' lots, and because the costs to the government and affected parties of ascertaining interested persons' unexpressed valuations of a given good, of transferring it, and of litigating the correctness of the government's estimates (if legal challenges were allowed) would likely be substantial. But in principle transfers may be compelled even when transaction costs are low, and in practice compulsory reassignments will often be justified where the interested parties are numerous and transaction costs soar.

Dworkin offers an example to show the counterintuitive implications of this norm.[27] Derek is poor and sick, his sole comfort a book that he would grudgingly sell for $2 only to buy needed medicine. Amartya is fabulously wealthy. He would gladly pay $3 to add Derek's book to his library, on the off chance that he might one day glance at it. If the police confiscate Derek's book and give it to Amartya without requiring him to pay Derek

---

[27] *See* Dworkin (1985), 242–5, and Dworkin (1986), 286–8; *see also* Kronman (1980), 229–32.

for it, social wealth will increase. But in what sense, Dworkin asks, will justice be furthered or society improved?

Dworkin's point is that increased wealth is not itself desirable, and that implementation of a wealth-maximizing scheme must be defended, if defense is possible, by reference to more basic moral principles. Utilitarian considerations, or citizens' express or hypothetical consent, might vindicate it in the large, even if isolated instances of its application do not meet with intuitive approval;[28] but a mere increase in wealth, quite apart from these further considerations, is no reason at all to rejoice.

Dworkin's example, however, can also be turned to another purpose. It illustrates what many commentators consider one of the principal defects of wealth maximization as a social norm: its bias in favor of the rich when a good is used for consumption rather than production.[29] Assuming that the amount someone would be willing to pay for a right rises as his wealth increases—as is the case with most rights of any consequence, such as rights respecting the use of land, or rights to fill the air with noise or smoke, or to enjoin someone from doing so—then in contests over the assignment of an entitlement for consumption purposes, the rich are more likely to receive the right than the poor. The same is true when conflicts erupt between business enterprises, or between producers and consumers, to the extent that the rich purchase a disproportionately large slice of the goods or services such enterprises provide, or to the extent that they own a proportionately larger share of productive resources. This bias—Dworkin's example multiplied—significantly enhances the difficulty of justifying wealth maximization in an unadulterated form. To many, it can only appear unjust to allow personal wealth to influence the allocation of contested rights, rather than a proper way of rewarding diligence or frugality. Industrious individuals obtain their reward in the form of higher incomes; to confer on them an additional bonus, at the expense of those who choose to spend their time or earnings differently, seems grossly unfair.

What is especially troubling is that this bias tends to have a snowball effect, making wealthy beneficiaries yet richer, hence more likely to benefit from the bias the next time rights are contested, and so on without end. If wealth maximization were pursued relentlessly by an omniscient social guardian, and if compensation were never extracted from the recipient when a right was reassigned, then very shortly almost everything worth having, including labor rights and personal liberties (if they too were up for grabs), might belong to a single owner. Each pairwise comparison might augment the wealth of the rich while diminishing that of the poor, giving

---

[28] See below, section 9.3, for an examination of these defenses.

[29] *See, e.g.*, Baker (1975), 16–21; Bebchuk (1980), 682–4, for a more extended discussion of this problem.

the rich an even greater edge when the next item came on the block, accelerating the polarization of ownership until the distribution of entitlements was as lopsided as could be.

A collateral problem, of course, is the indeterminacy of the lucky tycoon's identity. Who ends up owning the world, if anyone does, depends upon the order in which the omniscient guardian makes pairwise comparisons. Even one of society's poorest members might retire as the modern Croesus if comparisons were made cleverly enough and his holdings increased gradually with successive transfers.[30] The ideal of wealth maximization itself furnishes no guide for arranging the queue.

To be sure, this eventuality is by no means a practical worry. Information is dear, and no populace would brook policies that exacerbated inequalities to this pronounced extent. But that observation is beside the point. The argument is not that the ideal of wealth maximization, imperfectly implemented, might not be blatantly offensive. The contention is rather that the ideal, in principle, is unsatisfactory. The cheaper information becomes, the more loathsome the system might also become. To render it acceptable, even when applied to an initially equal distribution of resources, constraints must be imported from without. Wealth maximization therefore cannot serve as a complete social norm, even given a just starting point.

It hardly suffices to stipulate, as Posner does, that compulsory transfers should be forbidden if transaction costs are low.[31] One must supply some principled reason for this restriction. Posner seems sometimes to suggest that the restriction originates not in some autonomous theory of justice, nor in the contingent fact that information regarding people's willingness to pay for a given right is often expensive and litigation surrounding uncompensated reassignments is apt to be common and costly (if legal challenges are permitted), but instead derives from the deleterious effect

---

[30] I assume that only pairwise comparisons between individuals are made. One could also imagine coalitions forming to stymie those whose wealth attained threatening proportions, sparking the formation of hostile factions to overcome these new collective forces, and so on. The range of possible scenarios only compounds the problem of indeterminacy.

[31] How high they must be before compulsory reassignments are justified is another question Posner fails to address. One might allow mandatory transfers of rights only when transaction costs exceeded the potential gains from trade, thereby preventing an efficient rearrangement of entitlements. Posner seems to lean toward this view when he says that "[m]uch of [the common] law seems designed . . . to allocate resources as actual markets would, in circumstances where the costs of market transactions are so high that the market is not a feasible method of allocation." *EJ* 62. However, alternative views, such as permitting forced transfers in cases where transaction costs, or transaction costs per person affected, are high along some absolute scale, might be even more attractive to someone who considered wealth maximization important. After all, if one were inclined to dispense with bargaining where the aggregate gains from reassigning a right to be free from pollution from homeowners to a factory total $3,000,000 and the cost of voluntary reassignment is $3,000,001, one should hardly be less averse to doing so when the cost of bargaining falls by $2.

that frequent or marked reshuffling of entitlements is likely to have on social wealth in the long run.[32] This suggestion, however, seems doubly misguided. First, the claim that the ideal's implementation in its extreme form would impede the maximization of wealth over time is false. For wealth, as Posner defines it, cannot be identified with a society's productive output, and it need not increase just because valuable services have been performed or valuable goods created. If an auto worker would rather doze in his backyard than stand another hour on the assembly line, then wealth is maximized by his going home. He apparently values the hour in his hammock more than someone is willing to pay for what he can produce in that time,[33] that is, his asking price for that hour exceeds employers' offer price. The fact that the omniscient guardian's reassignment of the labor right to the worker if it belonged to the employer would cause production to decline, if it is a fact, is therefore not objectionable from the perspective of wealth maximization. Nor should it be. To identify the maximization of wealth with the maximization of social output would be to condone forced labor camps and many of the worst excesses of Stalin's Five Year Plans. But unless such an identification is made, there is no reason, on the score of wealth maximization alone, to fault the omniscient guardian for not insisting on compensation when rights are transferred, just because transaction costs would not be prohibitive.[34]

The claim that a rule mandating or generally permitting uncompensated reassignments of entitlements in situations where transaction costs are comparatively low would diminish aggregate social wealth suffers from a second failing as well. Even if this proposition were correct, it would not support a total ban on rearranging entitlements without requiring payment when transaction costs are low. Just as a utilitarian can mount a plausible case for punishing murderers but cannot condemn the occasional secret murder that increases utility without instilling fear in others, so too the

---

[32] *See, e.g.* Posner (1985), 93.

[33] I ignore, for purposes of illustration, the fact that workers are often unable to bargain for wages equal to their marginal product, given transaction costs and the rigidities imposed by legislation and labor contracts.

[34] Posner might want to cast this argument in a different way, and say that a group of rational persons possessing equal allotments of valuable resources would, if asked, refuse consent to a regime that reallocated those resources without requiring compensation in situations where transaction costs were relatively low. The fact that they would refuse consent, the argument continues, proves that the creation of such a regime would not maximize wealth, inasmuch as rational persons who desired another system would *ipso facto* be willing to pay more to put another set of rules in place. This stratagem, however, would be akin to surrender. As Chapter 10 demonstrates, appeal to the rational consent of equally wealthy persons yields a legal order at odds with even the constrained form of wealth maximization that Posner considers intuitively appealing. Posner cannot secure the benefits of this argument without forfeiting other positions he seems unwilling to abandon. Posner now accepts this objection, recognizing that wealth maximization must be supplemented by an additional principle to block victimization. *See* Posner (1990), 375–9.

proponent of wealth maximization, if the preceding argument succeeded, might justify a rule against forced transfers in certain circumstances but could not denounce an isolated exception that spared parties the costs of haggling and left entirely unimpaired people's readiness to work, trade, and save. In these exceptional cases, if utility were not increased (as in Derek and Amartya's case), the question would remain why victimization is excusable when maximizing wealth. The ideal Posner advances again lacks the resources to answer it. It seems doubtful that any attractive ideal could.[35]

9.3. THE MORAL FOUNDATIONS OF WEALTH MAXIMIZATION

Posner attempts to defend wealth maximization as a normative ideal by marshalling two distinct classes of arguments. Half of his defense is illustrative and comparative. He seeks to show that the actions most conducive to maximizing wealth comport more closely with popular intuitions about what is desirable in particular circumstances than do those commanded by certain rival moral theories. The other half of his apology is constructive. Starting from the assumption that unanimous, rational consent to a policy by persons aware of their predilections, powers, and social status constitutes a sufficient justification of that policy, Posner purports to demonstrate that wealth maximization would enjoy nearly universal support. The following two subsections examine this pair of arguments. Although Posner's intuitive defense is unconvincing, his appeal to consent to justify wealth maximization is sound in principle. Posner's own argument from consent, however, is riddled with ambiguity. The second half of this section seeks to expose its gaps and indeterminacies, leaving their resolution for Chapter 10.

A. The Intuitive Appeal of Wealth Maximization

Posner's account of the relation between wealth maximization and utilitarian or deontological moral theories is obscure. At times he speaks of wealth maximization as a "blend" of rival philosophical traditions,[36] as

[35] In addition to needing an adequate grounding in fundamental moral principles, both to support its absolute restriction to cases involving high transaction costs and to justify its prescriptions in those cases, Posner's norm of wealth maximization needs a method for valuing lives, limbs, suffering and lost enjoyment. This problem is more vexing for a theory of wealth maximization than for most other theories of corrective justice, because limiting the value of somebody's life to what he would pay to preserve it—which for this theory seems the most natural solution—would yield counterintuitive results in many cases, even if that amount included his expected future income net of living expenses. Consider the predicament of the indigent pensioner. It appears that here too departures from the standard of wealth maximization may be warranted, perhaps through the recognition of certain personal rights that either are not waivable or violations of which furnish a right to compensation.

[36] *EJ* 66.

"constrained utilitarianism,"[37] or as "an ethical norm giv[ing] weight both to utility, though less heavily than utilitarianism does, and to consent, though perhaps less heavily than Kant himself would have done."[38] This conception of wealth maximization seems to permit its defense to piggyback on principle-based arguments (as opposed to blunt appeals to people's intuitive responses in selected cases) for those contending moral views, but it has the disadvantage of obliging its advocates to reconcile the deeper, often divergent moral rationales from which wealth maximization allegedly draws support. Other passages, however, along with Posner's failure to discuss the most prominent justifications of utilitarian and Kantian moral theories, suggest that the overlaps he notes are merely designed to exhibit wealth maximization's consonance with shared intuitions, particularly its divergence from one or more of those sometimes allied theories when their implications are hard to accept.[39] On this construction, wealth maximization has an independent base, and its defender need not be concerned with harmonizing the conflicting impulses of what to some extent are parallel moral theories.

Posner's scattered remarks on justification seem to indicate that he thinks he can have it both ways. He says, for example, that to the extent that wealth maximization is viewed as "constrained utilitarianism," "one can defend it by whatever arguments are available to defend utilitarianism."[40] Yet he never troubles to state, let alone uphold against criticism, the arguments that have been advanced on behalf of utilitarianism. The furthest he goes is to reject a variation on Rawls's original position, offered by Harsanyi and Hare,[41] that uses utility as a maximand, because "it opens the door to the claims of the nonproductive"[42]—a result Posner finds intuitively unacceptable. Nor does he explain how the rights he champions can be squared with whatever he takes the theoretical underpinnings of utilitarianism to be. Similarly, he appeals to a potpourri of rights that a largely undefined form of "Kantianism" allegedly implies, without explaining their genesis from more fundamental moral concepts or defusing their tensions one with another, not to mention their evident incompatibility with utilitarian prescriptions. In the absence, however, of such attempts to expound and reconcile the deeper rationales for the moral theories he

[37] *EJ* 87.

[38] *EJ* 98.

[39] See, for example, *EJ* 87, where, prior to introducing his argument based on hypothetical consent, Posner writes: "I have been more concerned with elucidating the concept of wealth maximization and contrasting it to utilitarianism than with justifying it systematically. So far the case has rested mainly on the somewhat narrow and negative ground that wealth maximization avoids some of the ethical difficulties posed by utility maximization."

[40] *EJ* 87.

[41] *See* Harsanyi (1955), and Hare (1974) and (1981), as well as section 2.2's criticisms of this approach to deriving moral principles from a model of fair and rational social choice.

[42] *EJ* 100.

casually invokes in support of his own, it seems that the most Posner can plausibly claim to have shown by comparing wealth maximization's implications with those of rival consequentialist and deontological theories is that wealth maximization's implications are intuitively agreeable. Perhaps someone willing to do more work could have it both ways (although the odds, in this case, would be stacked heavily against him), but Posner himself cannot. His superficial attempt to borrow the best of warring creeds without getting caught in the crossfire is a failure.

To the extent, moreover, that Posner does wish to avail himself of the arguments buttressing competing moral views by demonstrating that the policies most conducive to maximizing wealth advance utility or honor certain bedrock rights, it is unclear why the ideal of wealth maximization should itself stand as a moral beacon. As numerous critics have noted,[43] the more sensible course, for one pursuing this argumentative strategy, would be to concoct a mélange of attractive rights and goals and to look directly to that hybrid theory for moral guidance. There can be no justification for seeking moral direction from some separate theory, such as wealth maximization, whose practical implications only track the admittedly optimal composite theory's prescriptions imperfectly and, if appeals to intuition constitute its sole ground, merely coincidentally. Wealth maximization needs some independent moral ground if it is to command allegiance in its own right, unless one can show that efforts to maximize wealth are more likely to produce a just result than attempts to do justice directly. But the latter demonstration appears hopeless, for nothing remotely analogous to the paradox of hedonism, and no special problems of measurement or complexity, might compel the use of wealth as a surrogate for some more desirable end. The least circuitous path looks, as usual, the most inviting. Furthermore, the necessary independent justification, which might be furnished by collective consent at the cost of embedding wealth maximization in a broader theory of rights (thus exposing it to constraints impressed upon it by other elements of the system), surely cannot come from a simple demonstration that advocates of wealth maximization value outcomes that defenders of other theories also find congenial.

Nor is an independent justification likely to succeed except by relying on sophisticated notions of rational consent and political obligation, that is, the obligation to abide by collective choices, even those that impose duties one finds onerous, in a polity whose members justly share the benefits of political union. As the example of Derek and Amartya shows, an increase in wealth is not *ipso facto* an increase in *anything* valuable. Often transfers of entitlements that augment social wealth do deserve approbation, of

---

[43] *See, e.g.* Dworkin (1985), 249–55; Kronman (1980), 232–9.

course, but only because, in those instances, either they constitute Pareto improvements, with no party's position worsened and at least one party's happiness increased (as almost invariably happens when voluntary exchanges occur without significant negative externalities),[44] or they cause so large an increase in one party's well-being as morally to outweigh the comparatively slight, noncompensable loss suffered by others who are affected.[45] But then the increase in wealth is only incidental to what makes the transfer desirable; it adds nothing to the moral argument for ensuring its consummation.

Two further obstacles stand in the way of an independent justification of wealth maximization. The first is simply that its practical upshot in many cases, if Posner's elaboration of the ideal is accurate, is for many people repugnant. The denial of welfare rights to those handicapped or impoverished through no fault of their own,[46] the qualified approval of racial or religious segregation,[47] the blithe endorsement of untaxed inheritance,[48] and the encouragement of so-called "Calvinist" virtues[49]—all of these consequences seem more repellent than attractive.

The second objection, connected with the moral irrelevance of increases in wealth *per se* and the intuitive failings of wealth maximization regarded as the sole standard of distributive justice (given a just starting point fixed in some other way), is simply that the best theory of fair shares, as Part I of this book attempts to prove, is that offered by equality of fortune. If that claim is correct, then the goal of wealth maximization can only occupy a subordinate position within that theory (if it has a place at all). Wealth maximization cannot usurp its primacy. Because, moreover, equality of fortune is premised on an account of personal rights rather than on the importance of actualizing states of affairs not necessarily defined by reference to personal rights, wealth maximization can only hope to find

[44] *See* Kronman (1980), 235.

[45] Thus, in responding to Dworkin's objection, Posner supposes that the book is worth not $3 but $3,000 to Amartya, whereas Derek values it at only $2. He notes that when the numbers are so lopsided, "the transfer probably will increase the amount of happiness in society, even if Derek is not compensated." *EJ* 108. But even if one is willing to credit this utilitarian approach, Posner's reply misses the point. As Dworkin rightly rejoins, one can hardly turn aside a nettlesome objection to a theory's implications for a range of cases by imagining *different* cases to which the objection does not apply. *See* Dworkin (1983b), 295. Indeed, Posner's reply makes even plainer that it is only when wealth maximization results in a large increase in utility, or a small increase unaccompanied by a diminution in any party's welfare, that the ideal seems attractive. A mere increase in wealth, apart from these consequences, has no allure whatsoever.

[46] *See EJ* 76, 100; Posner (1985), 101. While continuing to acknowledge that wealth maximization leads to this result, Posner now refrains from saying whether he favors or opposes public compensation for the disadvantaged. *See* Posner (1990), 381.

[47] *See EJ* 85. Posner now appears to think wealth maximization deficient insofar as it permits suppressing a minority religious faith. *See* Posner (1990), 377–8.

[48] *See EJ* 82.

[49] *See EJ* 68.

vindication in the actual or presumed exercise of those rights.[50] If wealth maximization has any role to play in shaping the distribution and reallocation of entitlements in a just society, it is because the citizens of that society have consented or would rationally have consented to abide by its dictates, or because a supervening moral principle requires its adoption.

B. Justification by Consent

Justificatory appeals to consent are closely connected to arguments building on people's intuitive responses to a theory's implications, for one cannot plausibly maintain that people would consent to principles of distributive or corrective justice whose ramifications are disquieting. But while appeals to consent must meet the test of intuition in the results they yield, they cannot stop there. They must be accompanied by persuasive accounts of rational, collective choice, and explain why and to what extent the favored model of social choice vindicates the prescriptions alleged to flow from it. Part of that enterprise consists in stating and justifying the background set of entitlements against which choice occurs, as well as any constraints on information that the model may presuppose. Part consists in elucidating the relationship between appeals to consent, however characterized, and other types of justification the theory employs.

Posner fails to discharge virtually all of these preliminary tasks. He never explains how appeals to consent can coexist with arguments grounded in what he seems to consider the self-evident value of increases in utility, let alone offer a general account of normative justification. Posner does say that consent is "an ethical criterion congenial to the Kantian emphasis . . . on autonomy,"[51] and labels it "an adequate safeguard of the autonomy interest."[52] More light, however, is lacking. In particular, the nature and scope of the "autonomy interest" is never defined, nor are its relations to competing interests adumbrated. This last omission is especially serious, since Kant regarded rational autonomy as the single, exclusive, generative moral concept, and there is no obvious way to reconcile it, as the source of basic rights, with the foundational concepts of divergent ethical traditions, such as utility or organic unity. And while competing foundational

---

[50] This forms the basis of yet another argument against an instrumentalist defense of wealth maximization. For it is highly unlikely that any patterned theory, which specifies which distributions are just independently of how they came about, could successfully track the results of a theory that defined just outcomes in terms of the historically contingent exercise of rights over time. *See* Nozick (1974), 153–64; Dworkin (1985), 256–9. Of course, Posner is one step further from demonstrating such a match, for he never outlines the mixed deontological-consequentialist theory whose results wealth maximization supposedly shadows. No one has yet shown how to judge the accuracy of a copy without an original.

[51] *EJ* 89.

[52] *EJ* 96.

concepts might themselves be traced to some conception of autonomy if they can be derived by reference to some more basic notion of hypothetical choice, Posner explicitly rejects such a unified justification, at least with respect to utilitarian rationales for wealth maximization.[53] One is left with a plurality of normative principles and structural disarray.

Posner's account is also plagued by circularity and a curious redundancy. His aim is to defend wealth maximization by showing that rational persons would consent to its adoption as an overriding legislative and adjudicative principle. But the principles to which people would agree depend upon the distribution of entitlements at the time they are asked to choose, for people's holdings determine the extent to which they stand to gain or lose from the implementation of one or another principle. And the distribution of entitlements, Posner argues, is initially fixed by the wealth maximization principle itself. Thus the wealth maximization principle at least partly determines its own selection, and whatever argument is offered to justify it as the arbiter of initial shares seems to render the argument from consent at least partly superfluous.

Posner's apparent confusion can be dissipated, of course, if an independent moral theory is used to specify the distribution of rights and resources at the time collective choice is exercised. For the reasons given in section 9.1 above, reliance on such a theory is inevitable. Once an initial distribution has been specified, however, the question arises how one should conceive of choice in those circumstances. Posner says that one must simply "imagine actual people, deploying actual endowments of skill and energy and character, making choices under uncertainty."[54] He further assumes, with assertion taking the place of argument, that no matter what principles are adopted, people will be free to retain and bequeath the fruits of their labor subject to no more than minimal redistributive taxation, since mandatory compensation for poor genetic luck is in Posner's opinion "inconsistent with . . . Kantian notions of individuality."[55] Given these assumptions, if almost everyone would find it in his self-interest to assent to wealth-maximizing policies—however qualified, and whether or not attended by compensation for those hurt by comparison with what they would retain or receive under some (unspecified) theory of liability that functions in default of wealth maximization's favored theory—then wealth maximization, so diluted and refined, is justified.

Posner's argument from consent has some appeal. If the status quo can be changed so that at least some people benefit and no one is harmed, then such a change is undeniably desirable. Even if a few people are injured by the change, the losses they suffer might be morally outweighed by the gains

---

[53] *See EJ* 100.
[54] *EJ* 100.
[55] *EJ* 76.

to others, at least if those losses are small; alternatively, they might be viewed as an unwanted but often unavoidable incident of what is on balance a beneficial form of communal life, or perhaps dismissed as the unfortunate but justifiable result of a gamble the losers can be presumed to have made because of the large *expected* pay-off the policy promised. Chapter 10 builds on this root idea. In the remainder of this section, however, my aim is merely to expose the major ambiguities, assumptions, and problems that mark Posner's version of the argument from consent.

The principal difficulties one must face in mustering an argument from consent may be grouped under three heads. The first is specifying the status quo from which change is contemplated; the second is stating the conditions under which departures from the prevailing order are justified; and the third is ascertaining which of the permissible changes is best. Each of these categories of problems deserves closer inspection.

(i) Defining the Status Quo

Deriving a just initial allocation of entitlements from the principle of wealth maximization itself is, as section 9.1 noted, an impossible bootstrap operation. An independent principle of distributive justice must be invoked to establish the baseline. Similarly, an independent theory is needed to specify those measures essential to the maintenance of a just distribution of resources over time, in the absence of injurious actions that might occasion tort liability. In *The Economics of Justice*, Posner himself favors a libertarian order which permits the naturally talented and economically and socially fortunate to thrive without having to compensate those cheated by natural chance against which they were unable to insure, an order which allows the successful to pass along the products of their luck or industry to their friends or family and thus to magnify material disparities still further over the course of generations. One can, however, endorse more congenial distributive principles, such as those defended in the first part of this book. Finally, one needs either a background theory of corrective justice that is subject to consensual modification, or a method of resolving disagreements over the choice of a standard if none has priority. Posner's effort to justify wealth maximization by means of nearly universal consent appears to presuppose the existence of an alternative theory of tort liability which serves as the backdrop against which changes can be measured. But he never states the origins or content of the theory he assumes to be in place, thereby rendering it difficult to assess the propriety of departures from it when a significant minority might be expected to withhold its consent.[56]

---

[56] In his discussion of automobile accidents, Posner assumes, for the sake of illustration, that some theory of strict liability has been codified or otherwise accepted and that a

(ii) Defining Permissible Departures from the Status Quo

Under what conditions may extant liability rules be traded for new rules? Or if no rules are in place, how should one assess the merits of competing proposals? The first step in answering either of these questions is to specify the information available to those charged with choosing and the motivations that guide their choices. Posner takes people as he finds them, with divergent talents and interests, grants them knowledge of the capacities and predilections that they and others possess, and assumes that their choices are predominantly self-interested, with perhaps a tinge of altruism towards the needy and neglected. All that they lack is knowledge of the future. No veil of ignorance obscures their sense of who they are or what in particular they want, funnelling their choices into a utilitarian or Rawlsian mold. Posner's argument for these premises is simply that he abhors the consequences of allowing the selection of standards of corrective justice to turn on a more rarefied conception of rationality and personality, namely, redistribution of wealth from the productive and lucky to the unproductive and unfortunate.[57] Because this argument supposes, however, that the principles these idealized choosers select will govern the allocation of personal and property rights, not just the assignment of loss when injury occurs, one might deem it misplaced when applied—as it must be, if the theory of fair shares developed in Part I is taken for granted—solely to the selection of tort liability rules. Nevertheless, there are strong reasons, I shall argue, for adopting Posner's model of enlightened collective choice that are independent of his personal moral intuitions.

Is choice to be actual or presumed? To require an actual vote, Posner rightly notes, is impracticable. One must accept as binding the best answer to the following question: what rules would people agree upon if allowed to choose in the absence of the usual costs associated with debating and deciding?

A much more difficult question concerns the preconditions for the acceptability of liability rules. Must it be the case that everyone will almost certainly benefit from or at least remain equally well off under the

---

negligence standard must prove its superiority in order to supplant it. He later says, however, that his choice of strict liability as the default standard was "arbitrary," and that one could "equally well assume" that negligence is the reigning norm. *See EJ* 95-9. His example therefore affords no indication how he would confront the problem of devising a background theory against which to assess wealth maximization's blandishments. The same is true, for example, of the assignment of a right to control the use of air either to polluters or to people who wish to breathe unpolluted air. Posner says that he does not know on whom this right should be conferred. *See* Posner (1985), 92.

[57] *See EJ* 100.

proposed rules *vis-à-vis* the status quo or some alternative proposal? Or is it enough that each person's expected benefits equal or exceed his expected costs, even though in actuality some people will gain and some will lose by comparison with existing rules or a rival proposal? Or might rules clear the hurdle of acceptability when the sum of their expected gains exceeds their aggregate expected losses, despite the fact that some antecedently identifiable individuals will surely or probably be harmed by the change?

Posner never clearly distinguishes these questions. His remarks on automobile accident insurance suggest that he regards the second question as equivalent to the first if insurance is available against uncompensated personal losses and third-party liabilities. But it would be wrong to leap to that conclusion. Posner's example[58] obscures the fact that insurance cannot transform expected gains into actual gains if those affected remain or become self-insurers. If all motorists are identical in every relevant respect (e.g. are of the same age, display equal care, drive automobiles of the same manufacture and vintage), if all buy both first-party and third-party insurance under a negligence regime but will pay less for coverage than they would under a strict liability regime because the aggregate cost of processing and litigating claims is lower, then of course it follows that increased expected net benefits are automatically translated into actual net benefits, assuming that compensation is adequate[59] and equally likely when injury occurs. But actual gains need not trail expected gains if insurance is not universal. Suppose that one of Posner's drivers is extremely wealthy, that he prefers to risk having to pay out of pocket rather than buy insurance, that he would not have caused any accidents under the (by hypothesis) less efficient strict liability rule and does not do so under the negligence rule. Suppose, further, that he is himself the victim, under a negligence regime, of a freak accident caused by another motorist who took all reasonable precautions. Although the wealthy driver expected to benefit on the whole from the change in legal regime, he did not in fact do so. The question therefore remains: are expected gains that do not become actual gains nonetheless sufficient to render proposed liability rules acceptable? Does it make any difference if those who are actually made worse off because they insure themselves *could* have insured and thereby guaranteed themselves an actual benefit, even after paying their insurance premiums? Posner never explores these complications.

---

[58] *See EJ* 95.

[59] This proviso is needed because if compensation is sometimes inadequate—in the case of mortal injury, for example—and if a change in liability rules lowers insurance costs but, by lowering the cost of driving, induces additional use of the roads, thereby causing at least one additional fatality that would not have occurred under the former rule, then even though the expected benefits of the change outweigh the expected costs for everyone, at least one person will in actuality be made worse off by the change.

He does say, however, that a rule of corrective justice may be justified despite its not being in everyone's antecedent self-interest. "Only a fanatic," he claims, "would insist that unanimity be required to legitimize a social institution such as the negligence system."[60] But Posner never offers a justification for this utilitarian relaxation of the consent requirement. Nor does he so much as hint at how the certain (or expected) losses of some are to be weighed against the certain (or expected) gains to others in determining whether a particular proposal is acceptable overall. An adequate theory of corrective justice would have to address these concerns.

No matter what answers are given, however, wealth maximization, I hope to show below, would rarely command the necessary votes in any of the traditional domains of tort law so long as a non-wealth-maximizing legal regime is in place and something approaching unanimity is required to alter it. Even on the hypothesis that replacing strict liability for injuries resulting from automobile accidents with a negligence standard would reduce the costs of driving, Posner must concede that many pedestrians who do not drive might balk at the change. To be sure, many would benefit indirectly, as consumers, by the reduced costs of transportation. But the smaller the overall efficiency gains, and the more often they walk beside and across streets, and the less they drive, ride, or consume goods or services conveyed by motor vehicles, the less likely that they would assent. Posner adduces no empirical evidence indicating that only a "fanatic" would find the number of disappointed people so small that their wishes could be coolly disregarded.

Yet an example more favorable to Posner's project than that of reductions in automobile–pedestrian accident costs is hard to imagine. Bebchuk notes that legal enforcement of wealth-maximizing contractual rules would be welcomed by all, at least as a prospective modification of a less efficient order, because contracts are voluntary agreements and the more efficient the rules governing parties' relations, the more benefit the parties can expect to derive and divide between them.[61] But in most realms of conduct where tort liability is a salient concern, widespread approval of wealth-maximizing changes would never emerge. Think of the likely response of homeowners near a toxic chemicals factory if they were told that negligence was a more efficient liability standard than the present rule of strict liability for industrial accidents and then were asked whether they would support replacing the latter with the former. Or consider an

---

[60] *EJ* 97.

[61] *See* Bebchuk (1980), 676; *see also* Polinsky (1983), ch. 5. Of course, in the case of voluntary agreements, rational parties would themselves select wealth-maximizing terms and remedies for breach, whatever default rule was made into law. But it may be wise to embody efficient rules in law anyway in order to obviate the need for repeated reflection on optimal protections, thereby saving time and avoiding isolated mistakes.

employer's reaction to the proposal that he be held liable for all accidental injuries sustained by his employees in the course of their work, not just those resulting from his negligence. It is usually possible to identify discrete and often sizable groups of potential losers when changes are contemplated in the liability rules in force in a given society. Unless Posner's consent requirement is emasculated, it will almost never be satisfied. Holding the vote prior to the initial allocation of resources in a society, I argue below, does not appreciably improve wealth maximization's chances of success.

Even in cases where people are apt to both gain and lose from the consistent application of a rule over time, with aggregate social gains exceeding aggregate social losses, and where they are not obviously consigned to a group of net losers from the start, resistance to the inauguration of a wealth-maximizing policy would frequently occur. Its bias in favor of the affluent would plainly hamper its adoption. And while limiting the application of the wealth maximization principle, without compensation, to potential transfers where transaction costs are substantial might preclude a great many patently unjust reassignments of rights, it could not sever the self-reinforcing link between law and lucre present in all other situations. Nor would it dispose of the problem, more marked among the poor than among the rich, that people might not consent to wealth-maximizing policies, even when they expected to profit on balance, because they were risk-averse and there was some chance that they would suffer significant net losses against which they could not insure without exhausting the excess of their expected benefits over their expected costs.[62] Consent to applying the principle of wealth maximization to particular types of conduct considered in isolation from one another would surely be rare.

Some have argued, however, that if the principle were applied to a wide array of activities simultaneously, consent would readily be given, because each individual's losses from some applications would likely be offset by gains from others, permitting all to prosper from the change. Indeed, this appears to be Posner's considered view,[63] even though his examples involve the application of wealth-maximizing rules to a single activity. Certainly a defense of wealth maximization as a global principle has better odds of success than attempts to justify it piecemeal if the beneficiaries vary across activities. The biases just mentioned admittedly render the task

[62] *See* Bebchuk (1980), 705–6. As an example, consider the plight of homeowners who live near a factory that has the potential to be an obnoxious polluter but who also own large amounts of productive capital and who therefore expect—though everything depends upon what the factory next door does—to profit from the replacement of a strict liability regime for nuisances with a negligence regime.

[63] *See EJ* 94 n.18; *see also* Dworkin (1986), 301–9; *cf.* Michelman (1968) (advancing a parallel argument with respect to minor, uncompensated governmental takings of private property).

more difficult, but if certain possible applications that are prone to produce concentrated losses for a given group are not adopted, as Posner recommends,[64] or if compensation is made a mandatory concomitant of transfers of rights when it is cost-effective and can be targeted with sufficient accuracy,[65] the proposal shows promise. Whether that promise is realizable, and how the principle's reach must be circumscribed to realize it under contemporary conditions (given a just distribution of resources), are largely empirical questions, in answering which Posner offers neither data nor detailed speculations.

The final problem that must be surmounted in developing a theory of when wealth-maximizing departures from a just order are justifiable by virtue of hypothetical consent is that of defining the respective roles of the legislature and judiciary in its formulation and implementation. One might, for example, leave only factfinding in a specified range of cases to judges, reserving to the legislature the job of delimiting the sphere where the norm of wealth maximization holds sway and of determining when compensation should be required and how it should be calculated. Alternatively, one could vest considerable discretion in judges, allowing them to decide when the application of a wealth-maximizing norm is just and when compensation should attend the compulsory reassignment of property rights. Posner almost entirely ignores this issue, perhaps because he believes that legislators and judges have for some time, perhaps unbeknownst to themselves, been furthering the generation of wealth through their laws and decisions. The normative question, however, is not foreclosed by current practice and must be answered by one who would make of ours a more utopian world.

(iii) Choosing between Permissible Departures from the Status Quo

More than one proposal might pass whatever tests satisfactorily reflect defensible answers to the foregoing questions. The problem, then, is ranking them.

If everyone will actually benefit from the change, or can be expected to benefit from the change, how should the efficiency gains be divided among them? If the chosen rules cannot achieve this ideal division directly, should rules of compensation be adopted as well? At what point should transaction costs be considered sufficiently high to outweigh the argument for compensation? How should the aggregate gains that competing proposals offer be weighed against the degree to which the distribution of those gains is suboptimal?

---

[64] *See EJ* 101.
[65] *See* Polinsky (1983), chs. 2 and 14; Bebchuk (1980), 706–7.

If a proposed rule may be justified despite its imposing expected losses on antecedently identifiable persons, how should those losses be counted against the expected gains to others in judging the proposal's overall acceptability? To what extent should compensation be mandated when it requires forgoing enhanced efficiency?

Some, and perhaps all, of these questions must be addressed in selecting a wealth-maximizing policy in preference to the status quo. None are easy. Posner does not offer even the beginning of an answer.

10

Outline of a Theory of Corrective Justice

POSNER'S argument from consent springs from a sound intuition. Any legitimate departure from a just order must win the approval of all whose fortunes might be influenced by the change, with the arguable exception of people whose lot is not significantly worsened when the gain to others is considerable. Respect for individual rights and personal autonomy demands no less. Posner's own attempt to justify the principle of wealth maximization by way of consent, however, is a sere reed, its roots tentative and shallow. No backdrop against which to map proposed changes is provided, consent remains a shadowy notion, and criteria for selecting from among qualifying proposals never gain mention. Fortunately, Posner's mistakes and omissions furnish negative blueprints for construction.

10.1. SETTING THE STAGE

The setting in which proposed liability rules should be considered is formed partly by the theory of equality of fortune developed in Part I. Each person knows that he is initially entitled to an equally valuable bundle of resources, selected in the light of whatever property and liability rules are in force. He knows, moreover, that people's holdings are largely protected over time against the ravages of bad brute luck, including variations in people's earning power traceable to genetic differences, upbringing, and inherited wealth. He also recognizes, however, that inequalities in wealth and income will probably burgeon nevertheless, for it is impossible to eliminate the effects of brute luck entirely, and differences may arise justly as some work or consume more than their fellows or enjoy better or worse option luck. Those choosing principles of corrective justice are furthermore aware of their own proclivities and preferences, as well as those of others. They are not the spectral figures that populate Rawls's original position. They are ordinary, rational persons, convened to fashion rules of tort liability within a framework of equal shares before bidding for the resources and opportunities their shares comprise, knowing that the rules they choose will govern their use of the liberties and goods they acquire.

The proper setting for discussion, however, is not contoured exclusively by the theory of equality of fortune as it has thus far been sketched. The question whether people would consent to replace the status quo with rival liability rules assumes that a standard of corrective justice already exists, a principle that prevails by default should agreement fail to coalesce around an alternative plan. As we saw, Posner at times seems to think that he can dispense with this preliminary definition of a just baseline by teasing principles of corrective justice from the ideal of wealth maximization straightaway. In more cautious moments, however, he appears to recognize that a floor is needed if consent is to elevate. The delineation of a nonconsensual theory of corrective justice must precede the suggestion of something better.

That nonconsensual theory might not be based, of course, directly upon relevant moral considerations; it might instead be derived through some procedural mechanism defended by appeal to certain moral principles, even though the product of that procedural mechanism receives no direct support. Thus, one might imagine a situation in which no theory of corrective justice has precedence, and contend that whichever proposal garners some stipulated measure of support from a group of self-interested people should be adopted and that the initial allocation of rights should proceed on the understanding that the favored proposal will come into force once the common pool of resources has been divided. But while this alternative conception of the derivation of liability rules is coherent, it offends the fundamental notion of equality that underlies the theory of equality of fortune. For it would allow one segment of the community, be it a plurality or a majority (depending upon the procedure employed), to impose its preferences on the remainder to its own profit, tripping them at the start and thus handicapping them in the ensuing race for resources. The ideal of equal regard and equal authority would be forfeit were one group singled out to legislate for all, in virtue of the aspirations, abilities, or some other trait of its members. It would also be arbitrary to allow majoritarian procedures to settle liability rules but not rules that bear more obviously on the size of distributive shares. Why should an initial equal division be sacrosanct, but not the liability rules—which will alter the size of people's shares over time—against which it is made? The ideal of equality must shape all aspects of the distribution, or none at all.

The question therefore becomes: what unchosen conception of corrective justice, modifiable by consent (or perhaps by moral principles requiring sacrifices of some for others), seems most commensurate with the distributive theory of equality of fortune? The answer might seem obvious. Because the theory envisages the original distribution of resources as an auction in which all property rights are ideally put on the block separately, bid for, and thus acquired, it seems to follow that, at least as an initial matter, any violation of a right, whether intentional or inadvertent, triggers a right to redress on the part of the victim and a corresponding obligation to make amends on the part of the transgressor. That result seems all but inherent in the nature of property rights. It is, of course, a separate question whether a given person has purchased or received by way of gift a particular right to noninterference, or has taken rights subject to encumbrances or qualifications, such as a rider making ownership of a right subject to a wealth-maximizing or least-cost-avoider rule. If somebody does own a right that someone else has invaded, however, it seems almost axiomatic that the invader is bound to make the right-holder whole insofar as he can.[1]

Within the theory of equality of fortune, this conception of property rights and its attendant principle of correction is in many ways attractive. Its aim is the laudable one of ensuring the integrity of people's initial entitlements over time by protecting the value of property rights against fluctuations attributable to the actions, as distinct from the preferences, of other people regarding those rights, provided that the holders of those rights do not surrender the protections afforded by law by violating reasonable collective rules for the use of personal property or for the exercise of personal freedoms in public places. Its root idea is that in choosing the elements of his initial stock of resources, each person must bear the risk that their market price—the value that others place on those goods—will fall; but his enjoyment of those goods—the value that he ascribes to them independent of the value that others place on them—may not be diminished by the voluntary actions of other people insofar as they impinge on his possessions. Likewise, each person is to be shielded against physical and mental injury, so long as he does not stray beyond the edifice of rules erected to regulate social intercourse, even though the value of his capacities to others is subject to the vicissitudes of the labor market. Equality can only be preserved over time, the thought runs, if liability rules do not favor the productive over the indolent, the adventurous over the diffident, the rich over the poor. The only rules that satisfy this condition are rules that render absolute the property rights people acquire when common holdings are first apportioned (unless they waive them), and that

---

[1] Jules Coleman has pointed out that the question whether a person who has been harmed has a right to compensation is distinct from the question whether the person who caused the harm is obliged to provide part or all of whatever compensation the injured person is due. *See, e.g.* Coleman (1982) and (1983). The temptation to divorce the two questions is perhaps strongest when a number of people subjected the victim to the same risk of harm, but by chance only one of them caused the harm (many people drive above the speed limit while intoxicated but not all cause accidents), or when it is known that one of a set of persons caused the harm but the identity of the causal agent cannot be ascertained (two hunters fired, one bullet struck the victim). Some such cases might necessitate modification of the causal–corrective paradigm. I shall not explore that problem here, however, nor shall I undertake the difficult task of defining the causal relation that is ordinarily the prerequisite of tort liability, although section 11.4 touches on some of the problems Coleman's point raises in connection with collision cases. I merely flag these holes for later spadework.

compel compensation for any injury caused by encroachments upon them. The background theory is one of strict liability.

This view has considerable intuitive appeal. Somebody who has purchased a right to a certain quantity of clean water or a right to enjoy land free from noxious fumes, whether at public auction or from somebody who holds legitimate title, seems plainly entitled to recompense from someone who trenches upon it. If a person chooses to save part of his earnings and to enhance the value of whatever property his right to noninterference protects, then the augmented loss from interference is properly charged to the person who caused the loss, not to the one who chose to defer the enjoyment of his accumulated earnings under the umbrella of that right. Similarly, someone who abides by the rules of the road and the criminal law apparently should never have to suffer an uncompensated loss at the hands of those who violate those rules, whether by leaving their lane improperly (perhaps owing to mechanical failure) or by assaulting passersby; and the more expensive his car or the more future income he loses, the more the injurer owes. Any other rule would unjustly penalize people who, while acting within their rights, chose to labor longer or to use their earnings to purchase land or durable goods. Requiring those who wished to amass material possessions or to acquire valuable skills to pay more for the right to be free from injury at the hands of other people (rather than natural forces), whether at an original auction or through the later purchase of additional insurance, would betray the ideals of equal regard and freedom of choice that lie at the center of the theory of equality of fortune. Equality of resources can only be secured over time, it seems, by offering ironclad protections to all who remain within the bounds set by their justly acquired entitlements and whatever rules the community reasonably selects to regulate the stream of commerce and interpersonal dealings.

The weakness in this argument, however appealing the substantive theory it yields, is its incompleteness. The argument concedes that the collective good may license at least some restrictions on the initial allocation and subsequent transfer of property rights. Thus, some property may be set aside for communal ownership, rules of the road may be fashioned for public thoroughfares, zoning restrictions may be adopted, and antitrust laws may be enacted and enforced. Moreover, the state would apparently be justified in taking these measures even if unanimous agreement were unattainable on the reach of collective rights, laws governing the use of roads, or zoning regulations. But if the state may impose such restrictions on the initial distribution or subsequent transfer of property rights in pursuing some notion of collective advantage, what obstacle can there be to the state's constraining ownership (which in turn limits rights to recompense) in other ways? For example, why cannot the state decree, prior to the initial distribution, that wealth-maximizing rules of tort liability will be enforced because they will make the community better off on the whole, just as antitrust laws will be a collective boon, even though in some cases those who suffer injury or dispossession will be denied a right to recover? Strict liability attaches only to the extent that unconditional property rights are allowed to come into existence. Why assume that equality of fortune requires them to be the norm rather than the exception?

Answering this question properly requires stating and defending a theory of public good and collective choice that describes the situations in which deviations from an auction of *all* property rights among persons possessing equal bidding power are permitted or even morally mandated and in which limits on the transfer of justly acquired rights are defensible. The formulation of such a theory is a vitally important task which I am unable to discharge here. But it is essential to set forth, in at least a tentative and schematic way, the background against which a theory of that kind must be developed.

Equality of fortune supposes, most fundamentally, that within a sphere of rights protecting people's physical and mental integrity, individuals are initially entitled to equal shares of the community's resources. The property rights from which their shares are built, or which they later sell or give away, are not, however, bundled together unalterably. Instead, popular pairings of rights merely reflect common preferences, and entitlements are always separable at the behest of those choosing the composition of their baskets of resources. Water rights need not be tied to the land through which a river flows, for example, nor must rights to be free from loud noises or putrid odors attach to a parcel of real estate. Constraints on divisibility, though a practical necessity in any actual auction, would on this ideal plane constitute an objectionable compromise of people's liberty of decision.[2] Just as the amount of resources to which somebody is entitled is independent of his conception of the good life, except insofar as that conception issues in productive activities or risk-taking that results in larger or smaller holdings than others possess, so too the constitution of his holdings generally may not be bounded or dictated by what others believe would best advance his or their happiness or virtue.

It is against this backdrop that proposals for limiting the acquisition or transfer of ownership rights must be considered. And they must be considered not by etiolated persons fitted with stiff informational blinders, of the sort that figure in Rawls's original position or other ideal contractarian schemes. That way lies utilitarianism, majority tyranny, or at best the dominance of some dimension of personality, be it desires or an

---

[2] See above, section 2.4.

individual's penchant for risk-taking, to the exclusion of the deliberate choices of complete selves. They must be considered, rather, by persons aware of their abilities, predilections, and values, who respect one another's equal claims to resources and influence and who attempt to treat one another fairly. Before these judges, two types of proposals would in general win assent. The first are schemes that improve the position of some people without making others worse off relative to the baseline of equal division described above, either because no one stands to lose from their adoption or because those who would otherwise lose are somehow compensated. The second set of proposals that would gain approval, I argue (more controversially) below, are those whose adoption would yield substantial benefits to some people while disadvantaging others only slightly. Self-interest coupled with a disposition not to begrudge others gains in which one cannot share would motivate assent to the first set of proposals; acceptance of the moral duty to help others if one can benefit them significantly at little or no cost to oneself would cause people to embrace proposed policies belonging to both the first and second class.

In any actual legislative assembly, of course, even the best-intentioned of people would inevitably disagree over which of the many possible modifications of an all-inclusive auction to accept. There could well be tension in some cases between maximizing the size of aggregate gains and distributing gains more equally, particularly given the transaction costs associated with compensatory or redistributive payments. And people might differ in their predictions of the effects of proposed policies, as well as over the amount of cumulative disadvantage they believe it is morally permissible to inflict on one or more persons for the sake of a given gain to others. The details of zoning ordinances, rules of the road, and so forth would also likely spark many of the disagreements they do in our society today. But while these difficulties are real and important, and would have to be addressed by a comprehensive theory of the public weal and of public choice, they need not be disposed of here. For purposes of this outline, it suffices to assume that, on the basis of one of the two rationales just stated, some goods are held in common and permissible regulatory statutes exist. All other property rights, paired with a right to recompense for their violation, then remain to be allocated at an all-inclusive auction unless some qualification of this procedure wins approbation. The question is when, in general, fair-minded persons would agree to trade this unconstrained auction for one that limits the severability of property rights so as, in effect, to make liability for harm other than strict.

10.2. PERMISSIBLE DEPARTURES FROM THE STATUS QUO

Some conclusions are obvious. If compensation could be effected costlessly in the event of unwarranted injury, because insurance cost nothing, because litigation over the existence or amount of liability was nonexistent, because holdout and free-rider problems were only academic headaches, and because settling accounts was an instantaneous, trouble-free process, then a system of strict liability would serve admirably. And if some of these costs were present, as they inevitably are, but if they could be reduced by replacing strict liability with another standard, with the result that everyone gained on balance—either directly, as a consequence of the new liability rule alone, or mediately, by way of the shift in rule coupled with compensation of people who would otherwise lose by those who stood to profit from the new rule—then there could be no objection to the switch.[3]

This is the simple thought actuating those who favor a negligence rule in cases where people or enterprises impose reciprocal risks on one another, on the assumption that a negligence standard is as effective a curb on inefficient risk-taking as strict liability yet that it occasions a lesser sum of litigation, insurance, and transaction costs.[4] Charles Fried's notion of a lifetime risk budget, on which people may draw in imposing a risk of death on other people without incurring an obligation to compensate those who lose their lives, is one prominent example.[5] If all can be expected to subject others to approximately the same aggregate risk of mortal harm over time, and if first-party life insurance is cheaper in such cases than third-party liability insurance, with its attendant costs of settlement or litigation, then, Fried argues, everyone would favor the assignment of such a risk budget to all members of society. Ergo, its establishment would be just. Likewise, George Fletcher's contention[6] that victims should have no right to recover for harms flowing from risks that all members of a certain group impose reciprocally upon one another stems from the evident truth that a rule that improves everyone's situation relative to some other rule is preferable to the latter.

Both views share premises, of course, that might be contested.

---

[3] The question would naturally arise how the aggregate gains from any substitution ought to be distributed. For example, should all receive the same nominal savings? Or should personal gains be proportional to wealth? Or proportional to actual or expected transaction, litigation, or insurance costs? And once an ideal is formed, one faces the further question whether to attempt to redress any imbalance resulting from the new liability rule through some type of tax-and-subsidy policy, given the imprecision of such an attempt and the deadweight losses that invariably attend such levies and transfers. But the answer to the question whether strict liability should be replaced by a Pareto-superior alternative is uncontroversial.

[4] Whether a negligence rule would lower the sum of these costs in a given area of conduct is of course an empirical question. I argue below that a negligence rule would generally not be cheaper to administer than a rule of strict liability. See section 10.3.

[5] *See* Fried (1970), 189–200, 257–8.

[6] *See* Fletcher (1972).

Self-insurers, for example, might in fact be made worse off if a negligence standard supplanted strict liability even if their expected losses declined at the time the change was made, particularly if the harms resulting from the relevant set of risks were substantial and infrequent. But if, as seems proper, the appropriate concept of hypothetical consent is one defined in terms of expected rather than actual benefits, at least where the nature and magnitude of the potential losses are largely unaltered by the change in rule, then this upshot is scarcely disquieting.

More important, Fletcher's definition of a reciprocal risk as one that is not "greater in degree and different in order"[7] from that imposed by the other party is crucially ambiguous, and his thesis unacceptable if risk is defined in terms other than expected nominal loss. If, for instance, two motorists subjected one another to a 2% annual chance of a nonnegligent injury resulting in the loss of half the value of the victim's automobile, then the adoption of what is *arguendo* a more efficient negligence rule in place of strict liability would be welcomed by both if their cars were equally valuable, but would seem unjust and, from the standpoint of one of the drivers, quite undesirable if one owned a Volkswagen and the other a Rolls. Suitably understood, however, Fletcher's point, like Fried's, seems sound.[8]

Beyond it lies rougher terrain. Under what circumstances might the abandonment of strict liability for injury be justified when the institution of a different standard would yield aggregate gains, whether denominated in terms of utility or willingness to pay, that could not be translated into net expected or actual gains for every affected individual because compulsory compensation of the losers by the winners from the change of rules would eat up all of the aggregate gain that the change produced?

Assuming that those considering alternative liability rules are aware of their own and others' aspirations and abilities and seek a just result, the answer turns on whether expected or actual gains should be deemed adequate for rational consent, and, if the former, under what conditions; and when morality justifies the implementation of the new rule despite the actual or expected harms to be visited on those whose interests would be impaired by its adoption.

With respect to the great run of proposals, actual and expected gains or losses go hand in hand, so no distinction between them is necessary. They diverge, however, in two overlapping sets of cases: where people presently self-insure and their expected gains from the change in rules cannot

---

[7] Fletcher (1972), 542.

[8] Fried's proposed lifetime risk budget needs additional qualifications as well. For instance, the fact that somebody has remained a hermit most of his life, never exposing anyone else to risk of mortal harm, cannot license his exhausting his risk budget in a single fling by firing a gun blindfolded on a city street.

necessarily be converted into actual gains through the purchase of insurance because the costs of insurance exceed the expected gains; and where the change in rules subjects people to new risks that are not fully compensable monetarily, such as a risk of death or serious bodily injury.

The second set of cases appears small. Assuming for the sake of argument that a negligence standard is more efficient than strict liability in some context, there seems little reason to expect its adoption to have much impact on the types of risks that people face. The change in liability rules would not, for example, transform radically the risks that motorists encounter on the highways, or the hazards that homeowners face from adjacent property owners. By lowering the expected costs of driving or engaging in dangerous activities, the replacement of strict liability by a negligence rule might induce people to engage in those activities slightly more often, with a corresponding increase in the expected injuries they cause that cannot be compensated fully. But the change would probably be of negligible magnitude over the range of possible liability rules that warrant careful attention. Except perhaps in rare cases, it would not force one to distinguish between expected and actual gains in framing a theory of justificatory consent.

The first set of cases is probably somewhat larger, but no more troublesome. If one excludes cases where the change in rule would alter the size of the risk, because such cases fall under the foregoing heading and seldom arise, then in facing the question of consent, self-insurers would be asked to vote on a change that left the character of the risks they ran unaffected but reduced or did not alter their incidence. No one would have reason to cast a dissenting ballot.

The most interesting theoretical question, in deciding whether to modify the initial regime of strict liability for harm or to replace property entitlements carrying the right to enjoin intrusions with entitlements bearing only the right to compensation for resulting injuries, is the extent to which people have a moral duty, nonpolitical in origin,[9] to surrender some of their rights so that others might derive a substantial benefit.

My view, elaborated at greater length in Chapter 12, is that people do have a duty to sustain an uncompensated loss to aid others if the loss would be insubstantial and if the expected gain to at least one of the individual beneficiaries would be considerably greater; however, if the sacrifice would be large, or if the gain derived by each of the beneficiaries would not

[9] By "nonpolitical" I mean that the duty is not one that can be said to arise necessarily when people enter into a cooperative scheme from which they benefit and whose burdens they are obliged to share. It would beg the question to say that assent to some type of wealth-maximizing or utility-maximizing principle is a precondition to membership in a just polity. The question is whether people have a duty to make such sacrifices for the good of others— sacrifices that will by hypothesis never be reciprocated—*on the assumption that a just division of benefits and burdens already obtains.*

significantly outbalance the loss, no matter how many beneficiaries there might be, then the sacrifice is not morally compelled. Gain and loss are to be measured in terms of the importance of the benefit or sacrifice to the fulfillment of someone's aspirations and preferences. And importance is to be judged according to the place that a disinterested assessor would assign the contribution or loss in a person's overall plan of life, even though the hierarchy of ends that the plan comprises remains a purely subjective ordering of the potential donor or beneficiary. Thus, no reliance need be placed on an intersubjective comparison of the intensity of preferences, nor would judgments of relative importance be hostage to somebody's frequently biased estimation in time of conflict of the salience of some goal he desires to reach.

In addition to its facial appeal, this principle appears to explain and, when recognized, to reinforce our intuitions about the propriety of certain actions in concrete cases. Few would dispute that it is morally incumbent on a potential rescuer to save another person's life if he can do so at small cost to himself, regardless of whether he has reason to expect a reward; yet few would also think him similarly bound to attempt the rescue if he would thereby have to risk sizable material losses or the forfeiture of life or limb. As for cases in the middle, where the gains and losses are more evenly balanced, most would agree, I think, that sacrifices are not morally required when the gains to another are only marginally greater, provided that such sacrifices are not mandated by a scheme promising net benefits over time to all participants or specified by a more explicit agreement of reciprocal exchange.[10]

Determining the significance of a potential loss, and comparing it with the importance of some expected benefit to another person, are difficult acts of judgment which reasonable people are likely to perform differently, at least in borderline cases. But a more exact statement of the principle seems impossible.[11] Nor is this reason for despair. A modicum of indeterminacy at the edges is often unavoidable in the expression of moral

[10] My more controversial claim that the *number* of winners or losers is morally irrelevant is the subject of the whole of Chapter 12. That claim is qualified there in several important ways.

[11] In *Law's Empire*, Ronald Dworkin endorses a very similar principle of abstract duty, but he tries to give it greater definiteness by arguing that gains and losses should be measured in terms of a person's willingness to pay for what is gained or lost. *See* Dworkin (1986), 295–309. The invocation of a willingness-to-pay standard, however, is apt to furnish little guidance in the great mass of cases, as Dworkin himself seems to concede. The possibility that individual rights will be violated, he says, precludes the use of this hypothetical market measuring rod; but given Dworkin's expansive conception of rights, which includes the right not to suffer harm on account of the prejudices of others and the right to take actions necessary to protect oneself against grave threats to one's life or health, *ibid.* 307–8, despite the inconvenience and irritation those actions might occasion others, there seems a genuine danger that the qualification will engulf the rule and relegate the use of willingness to pay as a standard of comparison to a position of insignificance. This conclusion seems especially likely when one recalls that Dworkin's discussion is premised on the assumption that those asked to enter

rules. It appears, moreover, as Chapter 11 attempts to show, that little disagreement would arise over its application to areas with which tort law has historically been specially concerned, so that the threat of wildly discordant judgments is in fact an empty one.

Before pursuing more circumstantial inquiries, a few generalizations seem apposite. The first is that uncompensated forced transfers of entitlements would never be licensed in instances where transaction costs are low. If the aggregate prospective gains exceed the collateral costs of compensation, and if those costs are insubstantial, then no one can be expected to surrender his right to compensation. And if the prospective gains are so small as to be blocked by piddling transaction costs, they cannot generate a duty to sacrifice either. Wealth-maximizing principles derived in this way rather than as Posner attempts to deduce them would therefore never justify the confiscation of Derek's book so that it might grace Amartya's unread shelves, nor could it lead to a series of forced transfers in accordance with pairwise comparisons that might concentrate ownership of much of the world's material resources in a single person. The only cases in which forced transfers might be defensible are those where the disparity between gains and losses in the absence of compensation would be appreciable, where the losses would have a negligible impact on the lives of those who sustained them, and where even rough compensation would be inordinately expensive, in absolute terms and not just relative to the nominal value of the net gains. I am at a loss to name actual cases that might plausibly be said to meet this condition.

The argument, however, for replacing property rights to land, water, airspace, and many physical possessions that enable the owner to enjoin incursions with rights to nothing more than compensation should someone encroach upon those possessions is often forceful. This argument is particularly strong in cases where the costs of negotiating a fair price for permission to infringe dwarf the costs of having an impartial third party, such as a court, place a value on the harm and confer an enforceable right to compensation on the owner. The argument for creating a mechanism for valuation of which the prospective infringer who is willing to pay compensation can avail himself, instead of leaving settlement to the parties, is especially compelling if either a free-rider problem surfaces among a group of potential infringers or a holdout problem arises among those who would be injured, and if that problem threatens to preclude

hypothetical bids have roughly equal bank balances, *ibid.* 303, and that all are likely to benefit in the long run from a series of sacrifices and gains, *ibid.* 306. If one assumes, however, that wealth is unequally distributed and that sacrifices will go uncompensated—and the latter assumption, at least, is essential to the foregoing discussion—then Dworkin's limited endorsement of willingness to pay as a criterion does not clearly extend to the cases under review. In the vast majority of instances where comparative importance must be measured, there is no substitute for an appeal to reflective judgment.

collectively advantageous agreements that benefit everyone affected or that leave only a small minority slightly worse off while promising sizable gains to the rest. Most of these cases would probably involve nuisances,[12] and the reason for insisting on compensation is plain. If transaction costs are high or collective action problems are present, the explanation will generally be that some business concern, rather than a private individual, desires to visit harm on its neighbors or holders of downstream water rights, and if that is so, the gains will likely be diffused among consumers or owners of capital but the injury concentrated on private persons. In these circumstances, the latter lack a duty to sacrifice so that others may turn a profit, and rarely will it be reasonable to assume that all will benefit in the long run from a rule excusing compensation, unless perhaps the harms involved are scarcely noticeable. The collective benefits that flow from maintaining an efficient allocation of resources also militate in favor of requiring compensation.

The difficult remaining questions concern the proper method for distinguishing cases where such private appropriations should be permitted if compensation is paid from those where injunctive rights should not be subject to divestiture, and the way in which the value of harms should be determined. I argue below that this distinction should be based on the probability and above all the gravity of the potential harm, because the latter implicates the adequacy of compensation and the difficulty of monetizing an injury. Compensation should in any case equal the subjective value of the loss, that is, the injured party's asking price, to the extent that it can be established fairly reliably and without undue cost.

One issue that I shall not discuss below is the role that judges should play in determining when departures from a regime of strict liability or of adamantine property rights should be sanctioned. Because people initially fashioning principles of corrective justice would presumably prefer as much definiteness and advance notice to citizens as possible, they would likely prevent judges from laying down novel liability rules so far as they could, and restrict judges' discretion to the more mundane task of finding facts and dispensing remedies in accordance with guides supplied by the initial legislative assembly or its successors.[13] Judges would, however, almost surely be given greater leeway in ascertaining when people are entitled to injunctions rather than limited to a claim for damages, since such determinations often turn on highly variable facts and since precise

[12] See below, section 11.2.

[13] I ignore entirely the problems posed by legal transitions, that is, the replacement of one set of liability rules by another once society has been constituted, resources have been assigned, zoning ordinances have been passed, and plans have been formed on the expectation that certain rules will continue in force. For an indication of the complexity of these problems, *see, e.g.* Graetz (1977) and (1985); G. Schwartz (1983); Kaplow (1986); Ramseyer and Nakazato (1989).

guidelines for making such determinations cannot be issued in advance. But I shall not pursue questions of institutional competence further.

10.3. SOME GENERALIZATIONS ABOUT NEGLIGENCE AND STRICT LIABILITY

Because a negligence rule is the natural rival to strict liability in most contexts, it is worth noting, before considering their relative merits in several areas of special concern to tort law, that strict liability would often be the allocatively more efficient rule. It would therefore often be unnecessary to weigh the greater efficiency of a negligence rule against the more desirable distributive implications of strict liability.

Under both liability rules, of course, potential defendants would have an incentive to act with an optimal level of care, that is, an incentive to spend money or its equivalent to reduce the likelihood or severity of possible injury to the extent that the marginal benefits from such expenditures equaled the marginal costs of precautions,[14] assuming that courts were able to ascertain plaintiffs' injuries or the efficient level of care with a fair degree of precision. As far as their economic consequences are concerned, there are, as Landes and Posner note, but two major differences.[15]

The first involves the costs of administering the liability rule. To apply a negligence standard in a given case, a court or other adjudicative body must ascertain what level of care would have been optimal. Such determinations are in some cases expensive, not only for the parties, who must hire experts to testify and lawyers to argue, but also for the community insofar as they increase the cost of maintaining a public adjudicative system. A strict liability rule, by contrast, requires no such determination by the courts, even though it would force economic actors, as would a negligence rule, to perform their own cost-benefit calculus in deciding what to do. Nevertheless, strict liability will not necessarily result in lower administrative costs on the whole, Landes and Posner contend, because the costs of processing legal claims (other than the cost of determining optimal precautions) and of arranging settlement will be higher under a strict liability rule than under a negligence rule owing to the larger number of claims that would be filed. For certainly some potential plaintiffs who would be deterred from suing if they had to prove their injuries were caused by a defendant's negligent act or omission would sue if the other elements of their claim remained the same but they no longer had to establish the defendant's failure to exercise due care. Landes and Posner

---

[14] I assume throughout that negligence is defined as failure to make marginal expenditures on safety when such expenditures fall short of the marginal harm they would eliminate. The earliest judicial statement of this definition is generally considered to be Judge Learned Hand's opinion in *United States v. Carroll Towing Co.*, 159 F.2d 169 (2d Cir. 1947).

[15] *See* Landes and Posner (1981).

therefore conclude that it is impossible to say a priori which liability rule would result in greater administrative expenses.

This conclusion, however, appears precipitate. While it may have merit as a matter of abstract theory, the balance seems far less even once familiar facts about tort suits are taken into account. In a large preponderance of those cases where one can imagine a genuine choice between negligence and strict liability—such as cases involving harms resulting from highway accidents or the release of noxious substances—the bone of contention will be the definition of due care and the defendant's fulfillment of that standard if the extant liability rule renders that inquiry relevant.[16] If strict liability were the norm, more injured parties would doubtless recover, but there seems little reason to assume that lawsuits would multiply. Out-of-court settlements would be the rule. And while the assessment of damages might be contentious, possibly even quite costly, it would probably not be appreciably more costly than it would be under a regime where injured parties lacked a right to recover from injurers but fought with their insurers over the proper amount of reimbursement. A strict liability standard, moreover, could well reduce the aggregate costs of insurance by relieving potential plaintiffs of the trouble and expense of buying first-party insurance against nonnegligent harm in cases where they were likely to suffer harm, if at all, only at a potential defendant's hands and not at their own. One ought therefore to be skeptical of Landes and Posner's assertion that the costs of administering negligence and strict liability rules, while only determinable empirically, are apt to be similar. Strict liability is likely cheaper in the large.

The second principal economic difference between the two liability rules, according to Landes and Posner, is that, in practice though not in theory, if liability is strict, then a potential injurer has an incentive to consider whether it is economically prudent to engage in some activity at all on a given occasion, not merely what precautions he should take as a general matter if he does engage in that activity. If a negligence standard prevails, however, a defendant's activity level will tend to be unduly high, because the cost of monitoring it and weighing the expected harms and benefits from each action would be so expensive as to cause courts, and hence the potential injurers themselves, to ignore the problem of a defendant's activity level altogether, save in egregious cases.[17] If a factory,

---

[16] Two prominent exceptions to this rule are suits to recover for toxic torts or harmful pharmaceutical drugs where it is difficult to establish the cause of the harm in any given case. These cases would cease to serve as counterexamples, however, if the law dispensed with a strict showing of causation and limited recovery to that portion of the injury equal to the ratio of the percentage increase in the injury attributable to the toxin or drug in question over the background level of such injuries.

[17] *See* Landes and Posner (1981), 875–6; see also Polinsky (1983), 46–8; Shavell (1980). Of course, to the extent that potential injurers under a rule of strict liability purchase insurance

for example, installs a filter on its smokestack that keeps harmful emissions to an allocatively efficient level during normal use, and if courts neglect to examine defendants' activity levels in awarding damages, then the factory's owners would lack an economic reason to refrain from more intensive use of their facilities from time to time, despite aggravated and, by hypothesis, allocatively inefficient injury to adjacent property owners or those who inhale the smoke. But if liability were strict (and causation and harm easily demonstrable), then the factory's owners would keep production at their plant within efficient bounds. Likewise, motorists would pay proper attention to both the care, including the speed, with which they drove and the amount they drove if they were strictly liable for all the harm they caused to pedestrians, yet would not attend to their odometers if they were only liable for injuries they caused negligently, where negligence was defined with reference to care but not the value of the trip a driver was taking when an accident happened.

But it would be overly hasty to infer, Landes and Posner argue, that strict liability is the more allocatively efficient rule. For even assuming a defense of contributory negligence (in which negligence was defined without regard to activity level), potential plaintiffs under a strict liability rule would have no incentive to count the costs and benefits of increases or decreases in their activity level in deciding whether to act, since the value of their activity on a particular occasion would not affect their right to recover for injury, whereas under a negligence rule that failed to take account of defendants' activity levels, potential plaintiffs *would* have reason to consider the frequency with which they engaged in a given activity because they would bear the risk of injury caused by defendants who exercised due care. Whether strict liability or a negligence rule would be more efficient therefore depends upon whether wealth would be maximized by providing an incentive for defendants *or* for plaintiffs to regulate their activity levels. Hence, Landes and Posner conclude, strict liability cannot be said a priori to be superior.

Once again, however, an incontestable theoretical conclusion carries little punch in practice. The greater inefficiency usually stems in fact from the absence of a check on potential defendants' activity levels. In most nuisance cases involving noise or harmful discharges into water or the atmosphere, this is plainly so, since injured parties are often unable to

---

and premiums are not closely correlated with accident records, their incentive to refrain from inefficient conduct will be reduced. Diluted incentives of that kind, however, should be attributed to imperfections in the insurance market, not to a rule of strict liability. Ordinarily, they are eliminable to a considerable degree through coinsurance and deductibles, and in any event these faults are unlikely to be more profound under a regime of strict liability than under a negligence regime.

reduce the incidence of harm significantly by altering their activity levels.[18] And in most other cases, potential plaintiffs have potent disincentives to engage in dangerous activities with economically excessive frequency, even if they were entitled to compensation in the event of injury, for monetary compensation is rarely a complete substitute for pain and anguish, permanent physical harm, or death. In practice, the focus should generally be on controlling potential defendants' activity levels, which means that strict liability would usually prove the superior rule.

Two further points support a presumption in favor of the allocative efficiency of strict liability. First, a negligence rule is more likely to deter potential injurers to an excessive degree than a rule of strict liability if, as is mainly the case, there exists some uncertainty as to how a court will define due care in a particular situation. Because defendants under a negligence rule face a large discontinuity in liability at the point of optimal safety— one step beyond the mark causes liability to shoot up from zero to the full value of the injury—they will take care not to cross the line. If the line's location is hard to determine in advance, because judges or juries are somewhat unpredictable, then potential defendants will naturally err on the side of caution. Under a strict liability rule, by contrast, potential defendants will not be inclined to stop well shy of the point of optimal safety, because the difference for them between being just at that point and being slightly beyond it is immaterial. Hence, potential defendants are more likely to approximate efficient behavior under a rule of strict liability than under a negligence rule.

Second, a negligence rule is prone to be less efficient over time than strict liability if courts generally rely on customary practices and prior decisions in establishing a standard of due care, in lieu of performing a fresh calculation of marginal costs and benefits in each case that comes before them. Reliance on previous determinations or present practice will result in the imposition of an inefficient standard when the relevant costs and payoffs change and old ways become outmoded, and will probably produce a time lag in at least some instances. Strict liability, however, compels potential defendants to remain abreast of new developments; its sanctions—more hefty awards and forgone profits—are swift and certain. It is a standard, moreover, attuned automatically to the capacities of

---

[18] Injured parties may, however, be able to influence the harm they suffer. In such cases, the injurer's liability, as Susan Rose-Ackerman points out, should ordinarily be limited to the aggregate amount of cost-justified precautions in which potential victims should have invested, at least in cases where large transaction costs preclude negotiation between the parties. *See* Rose-Ackerman (1989). Whether potential victims should be permitted to recover the cost of precautions before injury occurs, or whether they should only be allowed to recover after the harmful or potentially harmful event has transpired, or whether some public regulatory alternative is most desirable, is, as Rose-Ackerman notes, a difficult question whose answer may vary with circumstances. *See ibid* 45–50.

individual defendants and the susceptibility of particular plaintiffs to injury. Resort to a broad standard of negligence, such as the locality rule in general medical practice, will likely be too lenient on some defendants, because courts are unwilling or unable at reasonable expense to particularize their application of the general rule. Here, too, strict liability wears a more attractive sheen.

11

Illustrations

THE previous chapter provided only a skeletal description of the theory of corrective justice that equality of fortune seems to imply. When property rights are initially assigned, I argued, the only just set of rules is one that holds people strictly liable for harm they cause willfully or unintentionally by violating those rights or some rule reasonably designed to facilitate public intercourse, such as laws establishing rights of way and permissible conduct in public places, except when they do so under duress.[1] Collective consent, however, understood as the informed, uncoerced agreement of people fully apprised of their individual and collective abilities and desires, rather than steeped in ignorance of who they are or what they want or what they can do, may justify modification of this principle of liability. Consent can be presumed, I said, if a proposed change would benefit some without making anyone else worse off, and if the change is superior, taking account both of its distributional consequences and its aggregate benefit, to competing proposals. In addition, morality permits altering the background rule if those who would inescapably lose, because compensation by those more fortunate is impossible or unduly costly, would not be gravely injured and if at least some people who would thereby gain were likely to profit substantially. Neither of these conditions, I argued preliminarily, would be met in cases where the costs of transferring rights were low, although there may be adequate reasons, as I hope to show below, to relegate injured parties to a damage remedy rather than injunctive relief for some nuisances. I concluded by listing several reasons for doubting that a negligence standard would usually be more efficient than strict liability.

This chapter examines several prominent areas of tort law and asks whether consent or the moral principle I described and endorsed could justify the substitution of a negligence rule for strict liability. These inquiries are illustrative, not comprehensive. Many special problems are not discussed for want of space, as are several large topics outside these legal domains. Most conspicuously, I say nothing about products liability, although it is traditionally classified as part of tort rather than contract law. In my view, a background rule of strict liability is generally inappropriate in regulating consensual exchanges between responsible adults, including product sales; in these cases, positive economic analysis, in conjunction

[1] The rationale for this exception is set forth below, pp. 248–52, and in Chapter 14.

with theories of individual rationality and of paternalism, and supplemented by extensive empirical research, is the proper guide to fashioning legal rules.[2]

Finally, I offer no remarks on the possibility of adopting wealth-maximizing rules across the board, primarily because that course has little to commend it. It would be an extraordinary coincidence if those persons who would be harmed by the introduction of a negligence rule in one area of tort law would be precisely those destined to benefit from its extension to some other area, so that its simultaneous application to both areas would earn approval when its application to one area would fail to win assent. The bias in favor of the affluent inherent in the ideal of wealth maximization would render this happy coincidence still more fantastical. An overarching ideal of wealth maximization does not deserve serious attention.

11.1. INTENTIONAL TORTS

Unprovoked, unwanted harm, when inflicted intentionally, intuitively yields the strongest right to compensation. Injurious assaults on someone's person or the willful destruction of his property uncontroversially gives rise to a right of redress in the absence of extenuating circumstances. Freedom from trespass against one's mind, body, or possessions, at the price of respecting the corresponding rights of others, is among the most basic liberties of a just polity. Somebody who deliberately trammels another's most valued entitlements manifests disrespect for his moral autonomy and betrays the terms of a fair scheme of social cooperation. Indeed, once one grants that a just order exists, it becomes almost tautological to say that any action that intentionally upsets that moral equilibrium generates a right to its restoration.[3] Collective consent to a modification of that rule could not conceivably be elicited, because no barriers, such as a collection problem or prohibitively high transaction costs, stand in the way of individual waivers of rights to reparation.

A victim's right to compensation in these circumstances clearly extends to the whole of the damage done, whether or not the person responsible

---

[2] In the absence of fraud and duress and given a just distribution of resources, the principal reasons for regulating exchanges are externalities, incomplete information, market imperfections, consumer irrationality, and parties' failure explicitly to allocate various risks, resulting in uncertainty and possibly expensive litigation. The extent to which these factors are present varies markedly with circumstances and with one's normative conception of rationality. And people's views on the legitimacy of overriding express assignments of risk depends in turn on their beliefs about autonomy and paternalism. These myriad and highly fact-specific issues require more extended discussion than I can manage here. An excellent recent treatment of this complex subject is A. Schwartz (1988).

[3] A similar view is expressed in Fletcher (1972), 550.

for the harm could reasonably have anticipated its severity. The venerable maxim that one takes one's victim as one finds him, however thin his skull happens to be, embodies a cardinal principle of justice: an innocent person should not suffer any permanent diminution in his wealth or welfare, to the extent losses can be repaired, by dint of another person's deliberate, harmful action without his consent. Not only is there no moral justification for laying reasonably unexpected losses to the victim's charge, and ample reason to compel the deliberate injurer to make his victim whole, but it is hard to imagine considerations of efficiency decreeing a different result. Allocative efficiency generally demands that the full costs of an activity be internalized and reflected in its price; the fact that those costs are unusually large in some cases hardly excuses payment, although it may be reason for an injurer to insure (if insurance is permitted and available, which it ordinarily is not when harm is intentional) in order to smooth out his liabilities over time.

Whether punitive damages should ever be awarded to victims of intentional harms in addition to compensation, whether the obligation to pay damages for such torts should not be subject to discharge in bankruptcy in contrast to obligations to reimburse those injured accidentally, and whether a longer statute of limitations should (contrary to current practice) exist for intentional tort actions than for other personal injury suits are questions of public policy that different communities may answer differently, depending upon their beliefs about the efficacy and fairness of alternative solutions. There is little point in forming hypothetical generalizations about these matters. Nor will I take up the question how liability should be apportioned when an intentional injury is causally overdetermined, as when one person maliciously clubs to death somebody about to die from a lethal poison administered by his cohort, or how it should be allotted when the injury is caused jointly by two or more people, as when a pair of burglars ransack a house. Instead, I offer some remarks about the relations between intent, voluntariness, consent, and the duty of potential plaintiffs to protect themselves.

Black-letter tort law counts harm as intentional if it results, in some suitably direct way, from an act (or perhaps an omission) the agent knew or should have known to be a proscribed invasion of the victim's right. That the tortfeasor did not desire the harm's occurrence is legally irrelevant to his liability, even though certain moralists, such as partisans of the doctrine of double effect, consider the agent's desires crucial to determinations of his moral culpability. In one sense, almost all actionable injuries are therefore intentional, even if caused accidentally, for the tortfeasor in a nuisance suit or a collision case invariably intends to behave in a way that he knows or ought to know might hurt others or damage their property without their consent. What distinguishes intentional torts from these other harms, making remedies and exemplary damages seem more appropriate, is the agent's actual or legally presumed *certainty* that the victim's (or somebody's) rights will be abridged, coupled with the fact that the injurious action usually could not have been expected to be socially beneficial and may have been performed from malice or reckless disregard for the interests of those harmed, as with most cases of battery or conversion.

Nevertheless, injury coupled with actual or attributed intent to violate someone's rights is neither a necessary nor a sufficient condition of tort liability. It is not necessary inasmuch as minors and mentally impaired adults are ordinarily held liable for the harms they cause,[4] regardless of whether they knew or were even capable of knowing that their actions would overstep permissible bounds. It is not sufficient, because someone who intentionally harmed another person might escape liability if he acted under duress or hypnosis and had not brought the consequences of those states upon himself. Both qualifications suggest that voluntariness rather than intent is the basis for liability under existing law. Would it remain so in a just state?

The economic argument for holding children and mentally incompetent adults liable for their torts is that it provides an incentive for their guardians to control their conduct, whether by means of physical restraints or education, and that in general it is cheaper for guardians to police their charges than for potential victims to take precautions. These factual claims seem reasonable in most contexts, but even if they proved incorrect, the moral argument for vesting guardians with responsibility would trump a contrary calculus of relative costs. Children, after all, do not spring from the sky spontaneously, like tornados, hazards for which no one is to blame. They owe their birth to identifiable persons, who in giving them life perforce assume responsibility for raising them and providing them with a fair share of resources when they come of age.[5] There is no moral reason to force others to subsidize their upbringing by shifting to them the risk that somebody else's child will harm them or their property, nor could one expect widespread consent to this reversal of responsibility.

Mentally impaired adults present a separate problem. Like all persons born into a just society, they are entitled to a certain amount of care and

---

[4] Children are generally judged in accordance with a reasonable person's expectations of the care that children should display when they participate in activities typically engaged in by minors their age, but they are held to the standards applicable to adults when they act in ways that only adults normally do, such as driving an automobile. Motoring accidents constitute the largest class of tort claims involving minors. See, e.g. *Daniels v. Evans*, 107 N.H. 407, 224 A.2d 63 (1966) (19-year-old motorcyclist held to adult standard of care); *Goss v. Allen*, 70 N.J. 442, 360 A.2d 388 (1976) (17-year-old beginning skier held to standard appropriate to youths his age rather than adult standard, because skiing generally does not endanger others, minors routinely participate, and no permit was required).

[5] See above, Chapter 7.

resources from their parents. Upon attaining majority, it falls to the state, as the community's representative, to care for them with the funds that parents are obliged to provide all their children according to the principles defended in Chapter 7, unless some person or organization voluntarily assumes responsibility for them. If additional money is needed, contributions are owed by all, as compensation for their bad brute luck. The same rule applies to those who become incompetent later in life, except that a fraction of their then current holdings would first be appropriated for their care.

If care for these adults is provided by the state, then the state should find the least expensive means to supply it compatible with a just distribution of the costs of doing so. It has two options. Either the state could assume the risk of any harm caused by mentally incompetent adults. Or it could place that risk on potential victims. (Arguably, the state could only do so if it also provided potential victims with the funds to insure, since it would be unjust to compel persons who happened to be injured by mentally impaired adults to bear a disproportionately large share of the cost of caring for them. But since the state would have to obtain the funds from the very same people through taxes, the result would be a wash.) The first option amounts, in effect, to compulsory state insurance, the second to state quiescence and a regime where individuals may, but need not, protect themselves. Which would be preferable would depend mainly upon the cost of first-party insurance by comparison with state insurance and the justifiability of a paternalistic requirement to insure because potential victims might not apprehend or fully appreciate the risks to which they were exposed by incompetent adults and would irrationally forgo insurance. A similar calculus would be needed with respect to mentally impaired adults in private care.

However, not only is intentional harm unnecessary to assign liability to its cause: it is also insufficient. Of course, someone who strikes an assailant in self-defense, without using unnecessary force, need not fear liability for whatever injury he inflicts. Indeed, blows delivered in self-defense might not even be deemed intentional harms, for they involve no invasion of the assailant's rights if one views him as having forfeited his freedom from harm by threatening or attacking first. But even the infliction of injury on a perfectly innocent individual does not presently constitute a tort,[6] be he someone the injurer reasonably but erroneously believed threatened him with imminent physical injury[7] or a bystander struck mistakenly in an attempt to repel an apparent attack.[8] Can this rule be squared with the

---

[6] *See generally* Prosser and Keeton (1984), 124–9, § 19.

[7] See, e.g. *Courvoisier v. Raymond*, 23 Colo. 113, 47 P. 284 (1896).

[8] See, e.g. *Morris v. Platt*, 32 Conn. 75 (1864).

general principle that necessity supplies no exemption from liability[9] and with a background norm making an injurer strictly liable for whatever harm results from his intentional violation of another's rights?

Richard Epstein thinks not. Epstein contends that unless the victim himself assaulted the injurer in such a way that a reasonable man would defend himself, the victim has a right to recover. *Morris v. Platt*, he says, was wrongly decided: innocent third parties should be able to sue the immediate cause of their injuries, although if the injurer acted reasonably he should have a right to recover a like amount from the person who provoked him.[10] Likewise, claims of self-defense should be judged solely in light of the threat the victim apparently posed, and not be influenced by surrounding events that might have made a particular defendant trigger-happy.[11] Nor should threats or compulsion by a third party constitute a valid defense: if B shoots C at the instigation of A, who was holding a pistol to B's head, then C should have a right of action against B as well as A (though B should be able to collect from A, if he is not judgment-proof, were C to collect from B). If A is unable to pay, then one of two innocents —B or C—must be out of pocket, and in Epstein's view "it is fairer to require the defendant to bear the loss because he had the hard choice of harming or being harmed when . . . the plaintiff had no choice at all."[12]

---

[9] See e.g. *Vincent v. Lake Erie Transp. Co.*, 109 Minn. 456, 124 N.W. 221 (1910) (shipowner liable for damage to dock during storm caused by his moored vessel); *Taylor v. Chesapeake & Ohio Ry.*, 84 W. Va. 442, 100 S.E. 218 (1919) (compensation owed for damage caused by defendant's shunting floodwaters on plaintiff's land); *see also* Restatement (Second) of Torts § 263.

[10] *See* Epstein (1973), 159.

[11] Epstein therefore thinks that the Colorado Supreme Court erred in *Courvoisier* by allowing the jury to consider how a reasonable shopowner would have responded in the midst of a riot after having been robbed twice, instead of requiring the jury, as the lower court did, to employ an objective standard that made no reference to the unique circumstances of the case in determining whether the defendant might have perceived himself as threatened. *See* Epstein (1973), 173. Unfortunately, Epstein nowhere says how this objective standard should be framed or what information about a given individual (sex? age? beliefs? prior experiences?) should be considered in determining whether he acted reasonably. Would it have made sense to ask, in *Courvoisier*, how a reasonable shopowner would have responded had the plaintiff acted as he did at midday in a peaceful town? Even though the man he shot was in fact a policeman sent to quell the riot, well aware that fear was rampant and tempers short?

[12] Epstein (1974), 169. Epstein does not consider the possibility of having B and C split the losses. Prosser and Keeton claim that compulsion, in the form of a threat by a third party, is currently an inadequate defense, both to criminal charges and to civil liability. *See* Prosser and Keeton (1984), 129. They do not, however, cite any cases to support their assertion about civil liability, nor do they attempt to reconcile this rule, which they apparently endorse, with their claim that a non-negligent bus driver who intentionally runs down one group of pedestrians rather than another when brake failure prevents his stopping is not liable for the resulting deaths. *See ibid.* 148. Whether *moral* blame or *criminal* liability should attach if one person kills or harms another under threat of serious personal injury is a question I take up in Chapter 14.

This case, he believes, is perfectly analogous to *Vincent*; private necessity furnishes no excuse from liability for damage resulting from the defendant's actions.[13] All that matters is that the defendant caused the victim's injuries without being physically forced or reasonably frightened into doing so by the victim himself.

Epstein's view is consistent, yet hardly compelling. Certainly somebody who is assaulted or who reasonably believes himself or his property to be threatened with serious injury should not incur liability for harm he inflicts on his apparent attacker in fending him off. Collective consent to that rule can be presumed. But it begs the question to say, as Epstein does, that to recognize compulsion or private necessity as a defense to civil liability in other cases is to allow the injurer "to shift the costs of his own problems onto the shoulders of the plaintiff."[14] Why are they *his* problems rather than those of the innocent victim he shot by mistake or at the behest of another when his life or fortune hung in the balance? If the injurer's car had been sucked up by a twister and deposited on the plaintiff's house half a mile away, or if his hand had been held and his finger pressed when he fired the shot, Epstein would not hold him liable. Why should the result be any different if the compulsion exerted on him was only slightly less direct, provided that his response was a reasonable one and did not manifest less care than one could expect of a person in his predicament?

To aver, moreover, that no moral reason exists to saddle one innocent rather than another with the loss is not necessarily to declare *Vincent* mistaken. Most would agree that somebody who buys a boat assumes the risk that it will be wrecked in a storm; if he seeks to lessen that risk by using someone else's property to shield his own, exposing that property to greater danger than it would otherwise have faced,[15] then he must bear the

---

[13] Presumably Epstein would say the same of the murderers' liability to the decedent's heirs in *Regina v. Dudley & Stephens*, 14 Q.B. 273 (1884), where starving crewmen killed a cabin boy for food rather than die themselves along with him, since it would be implausible to claim that the boy *threatened* the defendants by *not* sacrificing himself so that they might live.

[14] Epstein (1974), 169; *see also* Epstein (1973), 173.

[15] Under current law, the dockowner would have borne the risk that vessels in port, but not tethered to his dock, would be driven into it by unusually high waves or wind, thereby damaging it. The rule appears to be that when somebody's chattels, rightfully located on his own property or the public domain and presenting no special hazard, are brought into contact with someone else's property by unexpected natural causes, such as floods, earthquakes, or cyclones, then the chattels' owner bears the risk of their own destruction but not that of harm they may cause to the property or persons of other people. The justification for this rule is presumably that the principal cause of the harm in such cases is nature, not the voluntary actions of another person. But if the natural disaster is foreseeable, and thus one against which people could insure, then it is unclear why this counts as a reason to abandon strict liability, given that reasonable use of one's property occasions liability when some minor natural accident—a bug in one's eye or the fall of a stone onto the road—causes one to injure another person. A better rationale, if its assumptions are correct, is that first-party insurance in such instances would be cheaper on the whole, because it would eliminate potential litigation and difficult problems of proof of causation; that it would provide greater security,

loss if the shield is splintered. Those who merely go about their business, however, cannot similarly be said to have assumed the risk of being assailed on busy streets or seized in their homes and forced to hurt others on pain of serious harm to themselves. Consistency therefore does not require the outcome Epstein defends.

Although Epstein fails to adduce any reason to make the injurer bear the loss if his assailant cannot pay and if he acted reasonably under compulsion or in self-defense, rather than let the loss lie with the victim or divide it between them, there is nevertheless at least one efficiency argument available to him. By shifting the loss to the injurer if his attacker is unable to compensate the ultimate victim, the law would supply him with an incentive to take all reasonable precautions to avoid unnecessary injury to innocent parties. Potential victims would lose one incentive to stay out of firing range, but the remaining incentive—the avoidance of physical injury —should be sufficient. This argument, Epstein might continue, is admittedly not very forceful, since those who find themselves in the injurer's straits might not ponder their potential civil liability, in the unlikely event that they knew the applicable rule. And in any case their concern for innocent third parties, or lack thereof, would probably determine the amount of care they took, not whatever additional financial incentives are thrown into the hopper. Moreover, the reasonableness of the injurer's conduct could be adjudged by a finder of fact, albeit at some cost. But a weak reason, he might say, is still better than none; a feather tips an even balance.

The balance, however, is not quite even. Although injuries received in this way are not archetypal instances of bad brute luck, since disability and life insurance are available and could be extended to cover such eventualities, they are unusual. It therefore seems unjust to place the risk of not insuring on only one of the innocents involved. In the absence of any moral reason uniformly to assign the risk to only one of them, and lacking strong efficiency-based arguments for doing so, the right course appears to be to split any losses between them that remain once the responsible party's assets have been exhausted. In fact, this proposal hardly seems weaker on efficiency grounds than Epstein's suggestion, since it would still provide an incentive to the potential injurer—blunted as it would be in both cases by concern for his personal safety and any third-party liability

because the owner of the object that caused the injury might not have the means to compensate the injured party if his own property has been destroyed and he has neglected to buy sufficient insurance; and that collective consent to the rule would be forthcoming, because the prospective gains and losses, excluding savings in transaction and litigation costs, would roughly cancel out: the affluent have more property at risk, but also more property that might damage others' possessions. In the very rare case of truly unforeseeable disasters against which insurance was unavailable, the general provisions for handling bad brute luck set forth in Part I apply.

insurance he may have purchased—to exercise caution. In addition, it would provide an incentive to potential victims (if one were needed) to keep themselves or their possessions out of harm's way, and should reduce the costs of litigation by comparison with Epstein's favored rule, because injurers would only have half as much at stake.

If the principal concern is to distribute the burden among innocents, however, why confine the harm to only these two parties, rather than spread it among all members of the community? The simple answer is that this has, in effect, been done. As I argued in Chapter 4, making insurance universal but allowing people to opt out if they choose is tantamount to dispensing with mandatory insurance and permitting people to choose whatever coverage they want. Unless one believes there are persuasive paternalistic reasons for forcing people to insure against injuries delivered or received under compulsion or by mistake when the injurer has taken reasonable means to protect himself, one might as well let the loss lie with the parties, if only because doing so supplies incentives that might promote prudent conduct in at least a slim subset of the relevant cases and marginally reduces the costs of settlement. Doubtless these reasons would in most circumstances sound far from overwhelming. But strength is a function of the competition, and alternative suggestions appear frailer still.

Thus far the discussion has focused on the duty of injurers to make amends for harms inflicted intentionally on obviously nonconsenting victims. In actuality, of course, the plaintiff's alleged lack of consent might be disputed. Suits by patients against physicians for allegedly unauthorized procedures,[16] or by participants in athletic contests against the organizers[17] or other players,[18] provide abundant examples. Ascertaining whether consent has been given is, however, too fact-specific an inquiry to be usefully discussed here; a survey of various contexts in which consent might be given, and the appropriate presumptions to apply to each, would shed too little light on the general principles under review to repay attention. A more manageable question is whether a potential victim whose lack of consent has been expressed or could reasonably be inferred is obliged to take steps to protect himself from intentional harm or to warn potential

[16] See e.g. *Mohr v. Williams*, 95 Minn. 261, 104 N.W. 12 (1905) (successful action for assault and battery against physician who operated on plaintiff's left ear rather than his right ear because the left ear was more diseased, since doctor had only obtained consent to operate on the right ear).
[17] See e.g. *Hudson v. Craft*, 33 Cal. 2d 654, 204 P.2d 1 (1949) (successful suit against promoters for damages sustained by willing participant in illegal boxing match). But see *Hart v. Geysel*, 159 Wash. 632, 294 P. 570 (1930) (no liability for death of boxer in illegal prize fight); Restatement (Second) of Torts § 60.
[18] See e.g. *Hackbart v. Cincinnati Bengals*, 601 F.2d 516 (10th Cir. 1979) (intentional injury in violation of official players' rules held compensable); *Nabozny v. Barnhill*, 31 Ill. App. 3d 212, 215, 334 N.E.2d 258, 260–1 (1975) ("a player is liable for injury in a tort action if his conduct is such that it is either deliberate, wilful or with a reckless disregard for the safety of the other player so as to cause injury to that player").

assailants of his acute susceptibility to injury. The general answer, foreshadowing a similar query with respect to nuisances, and harking back to one sufficient condition for modifying the background norm of strict liability, is that a potential victim has no such obligation unless he could prevent considerable harm to himself—which would translate into a large judgment against the person who caused his injury—at comparatively and absolutely little cost to himself.[19] Of course, people who are prone to injury, such as hemophiliacs, will ordinarily take pains to guard themselves in public, since the rules of social intercourse do not require extraordinary vigilance and accidental injury might occur for which they could not obtain compensation. If monetary compensation were an incomplete remedy for injury, moreover, people would usually take precautions, even if they could count on recompense for the harm that befell them. But such measures are not morally required, nor can the law justly impose such obligations without providing a corresponding subsidy, merely to save the money of those who might intentionally trespass on their rights.

11.2. NUISANCES

Within the confines of equality of fortune, what the law commonly recognizes as a nuisance gives rise to two questions. When would rational, well-informed persons, prior to the distribution of what they knew would be equally valuable shares whose constitution each person would freely determine, collectively consent to a rule denying a right of redress for incursions on land and water rights? And in cases where they deemed compensation warranted, would they make available an injunctive remedy or only a damage remedy?[20]

The simplest case is that in which the transaction costs associated with the transfer of a right are low, yet the injury that will occur in the absence

---

[19] The extent to which this moral duty can ground a comparative negligence rule is an interesting question I shall not explore here. It bears emphasis, however, that allocative efficiency is not the only possible foundation of such a rule.

[20] A separate question, from which I abstract, is when such persons would agree upon zoning regulations prior to the original allocation of resources. Restrictions on the uses to which certain pieces of real property could be put might win collective assent for several reasons. They could be chosen to prevent possibly shortsighted and arguably unfair bidding, as when one person forgoes the purchase of a right to be free from noxious gases because the owners of some neighboring plots have or will buy such a right and thereby shield him costlessly from potential hazards (unless, of course, they decide to sell those rights to a would-be polluter). Restrictions might also reduce wasteful bargaining over the sale of rights in an ongoing society, as industrial processes and residential preferences change. And they might usefully shorten bidding if an auction were actually held. Because the choice of zoning regulations would depend on the configuration of desires in a specific society, and because it implicates the difficult problem of determining morally proper rules for collective decisionmaking, which I shall not discuss, I leave unanswered the question whether zoning restrictions would constrain the original allocation of resources.

of its transfer is substantial. Blasting operations that will cause a building on a neighboring plot to topple, or production processes that will result in the release of a powerfully malodorous gas over a single piece of property with a single inhabitant, are paradigmatic examples. Clearly the background requirement of compensation for infringement would not be abandoned in such cases, because it would not be in everyone's long-term interest to dispense with it. The costs of doing so would be concentrated, the benefits small (because transaction costs would by hypothesis be low) and diffuse, accruing primarily to the rich (since most such cases would involve the imposition of harm by business enterprises, often on people using land for consumption purposes, and the ownership of capital will always remain primarily a perquisite of wealth). Rational, risk-averse persons would never assent to a rule allowing forced transfers of real property and water rights without compensation when transaction costs were low, even if the transfers were wealth-maximizing, for the same reason that they would not sanction the wealth-maximizing theft of personal possessions without payment.

Nor would it be appropriate to arm owners solely with a damage remedy, again for reasons parallel to those forbidding forced sales of private property or personal rights (e.g. rights not to labor or not to grant sexual favors). Sometimes the owner would not relinquish the right at any price; to consign him to damages after the fact would be to leave him defenseless against irreparable injury. Moreover, even if the original owner would be prepared to sell the right for a specified price, it would often be very difficult, given his strong incentive to inflate his demands, and at any rate expensive, both for the litigants and for society (if it footed the bill for courts), to determine what his asking price would have been before the right had been taken and he was left with a suit for damages.

In addition, it seems unfair to limit the owner to the amount for which he would have settled had that been the highest offer he received for the right he in fact relinquished involuntarily. In a market setting, where a unique good is up for sale, the seller and potential buyers ordinarily haggle over where the price should be set along the line running from the lowest amount the seller would accept to the highest amount a buyer would pay. If the owner of a right to real or personal property were compelled by the foregoing method of calculating damages to sell it, in effect, for his rock-bottom price, then he would be cheated of whatever share of the surplus he would have wrung from the buyer in reaching an agreement. If that were so, then there would be a rapid disappearance of buyers, in the colloquial sense of the word: all would take first, and only later ask what they owed. Markets for goods in very limited supply would dry up. This deficiency could be corrected by having courts establish what would have been the confiscator's highest offer price before he violated the right or appropriated the good for his own use and then splitting the difference between that price and the original owner's lowest asking price between the parties. But this solution is doubly problematic: first, because it would compound the problem of valuation by requiring two imprecise assessments in place of one; and second, because there is no guarantee that the parties would have split the surplus evenly had they been left to set a price on their own. If transaction costs are low, either absolutely or relative to the value of the rights involved, the simplest, fairest solution is to let interested parties negotiate their own exchanges. And the only way to ensure this result is to give owners a right to enjoin impending seizures of their goods or violations of their land and water rights. To be sure, equipping owners with an injunctive remedy creates the possibility that a mutually beneficial exchange will be thwarted by strategic bargaining on the part of potential buyers and sellers. But this is a risk society routinely runs in barring forced sales, and the gains from doing so ordinarily far outweigh the costs.

The second case, also relatively easy, is that in which the intrusion is slight, transaction costs comparatively high, and the intrusion of a kind that almost everyone makes at one time or another in roughly the same degree. The law properly refuses to grant damages, let alone injunctions, in case of such harms, in tune with the maxim "live and let live." Because virtually everyone benefits from a rule that permits noisy, smelly, or smoky activities that impose minimal inconvenience or discomfort on neighbors, at the cost of having to endure small disturbances they in turn create, collective consent can be presumed. The trouble of obtaining the consent of a multitude of individuals beforehand would thereby be eliminated, as would suits whose costs would exceed the possible recovery (and which would therefore only be initiated out of spite, or to discourage repeated abuses). The reciprocal nature of such activities ensures that victims receive in-kind compensation, in the form of a license to impose like discomfort on others in pursuit of their own aims.[21] But even if reciprocity were absent, damages should not be allowed, in view of the insubstantial nature of the harm and the relatively greater cost of judicial dispute resolution.[22] Judges should not have to spend time imposing fines for backyard barbecues.

What of hypersensitive individuals? If they impose on their neighbors the same manner of harm as their neighbors impose on them, then it seems safe to assume that the cost of engaging in the relevant activities, if separate deals had to be struck, would be relatively uniform. In those circumstances, hypersensitive individuals would have no claim to special relief, apart from whatever compensation they might be owed for

[21] A more detailed version of this argument may be found in Epstein (1979a), 82–7.

[22] A slight harm, oft repeated, may grow to significant dimensions. In such cases the harm should be made actionable, in the absence of reciprocal injury.

congenital debilities or injuries against which they could not have insured. But what if reciprocity is lacking, because they do not engage in any manner of disturbing conduct, yet are inconvenienced or upset by the behavior of those who do? The general rule under existing law is that hypersensitive plaintiffs cannot recover anything in such situations. The standard for actionable wrongs is set by the reactions of a normal person in the relevant locality.[23] At first glance, however, this rule seems hard to reconcile with the general principle that significant harms *are* routinely actionable if reciprocity does not obtain, because universal agreement to forgo one's original right to sue if one's rights are significantly abridged would never materialize. Why should the fact that most people would scarcely be bothered by a nonreciprocal invasion prevent the lone person who is disturbed from obtaining redress?

The answer is straightforward. A vast number of rules, such as rules of the road, that are geared to the capabilities of a normal person (or pitched somewhat below to accommodate virtually everyone) are necessary if social life is to flourish. If those unable to meet those standards are not responsible for their inability to do so, then they deserve compensation for the bad brute luck they have suffered, assuming that they did not incur their disability after they became adults and waived their right to insurance. If their disadvantage stems from their own choices, however, then no remedy is open to them: they must assume the cost of their own decisions. The same principles apply to hypersensitive plaintiffs in nuisance cases. If their malady stems from causes beyond their control, then they are entitled to compensation directly from their fellow citizens, again assuming that they did not surrender their right to compensation by forgoing insurance against the cause of their disability after they attained adulthood. To impose the costs exclusively on those who chanced to be their neighbors, and whose actions stayed within generally permissible limits, would offend our notion of justice, particularly if the hypersensitive individual entered their locale after they had already made their home there or if they settled in his locale without notice of his condition (which would probably be expensive to provide).[24] But if, by contrast, hypersensitive individuals are such by choice rather than chance, then it seems only fitting to make them bear the consequences of their own decisions. It is as though they developed expensive tastes in wine or food which gave them higher grocery bills. Thus, the established rule appears correct, with the

[23] *See* Prosser and Keeton (1984), 627–8; Restatement (Second) of Torts §821 F, comment d.

[24] The reply that no unfairness would exist because everyone could insure is unconvincing, since few would in fact insure in view of the low antecedent risk of relatively slight liability and the comparatively excessive transaction costs involved. Making compensation part of the general scheme for allaying the effects of bad brute luck would greatly reduce the total expense of cost-sharing without sacrificing fairness.

caveat that hypersensitive individuals who are not to blame for their susceptibility to greater than ordinary discomfort are entitled to collective compensation in certain cases. It goes without saying that landholders who engage in sensitive *activities* would lack a colorable claim to compensatory damages from those whose activities are disturbing yet within normal tolerance (unless they had earlier purchased such a right), inasmuch as their susceptibility to injury flows from their deliberate decision to initiate delicate operations without insuring themselves or buying freedom from disturbance.[25]

Existing law allows the amount and nature of harm that may be done to nearby landowners to be set in one of two ways: by zoning ordinances or by existing uses within a given area. The propriety of establishing zones prior to the initial distribution of resources, or of altering them later, with or without compensation, are questions beyond the scope of this book, although I think that the creation of zones, at least prior to the original distribution, would be permissible and often desirable. The power of one or more owners to weaken the protections available to other present or future landholders, however, is much more questionable. The so-called locality rule is founded on the notion that damages should not be awarded if all landowners in a certain locale reciprocally impose roughly the same hardships on one another, because each already enjoys implicit compensation and no purpose would be served by countenancing a stream of offsetting claims and counterclaims, or by requiring parties to shoulder the costs of reaching explicit agreements. It effectively allows those owners to assert freedom from liability for injuries inflicted on a new owner (or long-time owner who did not make a timely protest as the character of the area changed) who does *not* subject his neighbors to comparable annoyances, on the ground that he "came to the nuisance" (or sued too late). This result is hard to sustain in light of the majority rule that the plaintiff's coming to the nuisance is no defense, because to recognize such a defense would be to permit those landowners who first developed their property to restrict the uses to which neighboring tracts might be put—possibly diminishing their value—by engaging in activities whose byproducts, such as noise and smoke, render adjacent property unsuitable for some purposes.[26] The

---

[25] The law is in accord in most American jurisdictions. See e.g. *Belmar Drive-In Theater v. Illinois State Toll Highway Comm'n*, 34 Ill. 2d 544, 216 N.E.2d 788 (1966) (no recovery when highway service center's lights prevented showing of drive-in movies); *Amphitheaters, Inc. v. Portland Meadows*, 184 Or. 336, 198 P.2d 847 (1947) (same).

[26] See e.g. *Ensign v. Walls*, 323 Mich. 49, 34 N.W.2d 549 (1948) (longstanding use of property to breed and board dogs enjoined when neighborhood changed and new owners complained); *Campbell v. Seaman*, 63 N.Y. 568, 584 (1876) ("One cannot erect a nuisance upon his land adjoining vacant lands owned by another and thus measurably control the uses to which his neighbor's land may in the future be subjected"). But see *Spur Indus. v. Del E. Webb Development Co.*, 108 Ariz. 178, 494 P.2d 700 (1972); *Bove v. Donner-Hanna Coke Corp.*, 236 A.D. 37, 41–2, 258 N.Y.S. 229, 234 (1932).

strongest argument that can be made on behalf of the locality rule, with its associated defense of "coming to the nuisance," is that its abolition would create uncertainty concerning the costs of pursuing various noisome projects unless those who did so either bought insurance or purchased the remedial rights of neighboring landowners; but either of these courses of action would defeat the purpose of the rule, which is to mitigate the expense to the parties (and ultimately to consumers and workers) of concluding formal agreements or availing themselves of legal remedies. Some have argued, moreover, that rejection of the locality rule would be inefficient. If the first user could not affirmatively defend by noting that the second user suing him came to the nuisance, then potential second users, the argument goes, would have an incentive to make wasteful investments in order to collect damages.[27]

Both of these arguments fall short. The second argument, like the analogous argument in support of the prior appropriation doctrine with respect to water rights, lacks merit where rights to pollute, to cause other disturbances, or to use water can be purchased beforehand or protected by insurance, for recognition of this defense would create an incentive, a priori equally powerful, to rush in with wasteful investments in the hope or expectation of being paid to cease the annoying activities (or have one's water rights purchased), or at least to establish a presence that would enable the aggrieved owner to prevent diminution of the value of his property by suing for damages. On efficiency grounds there is no reason to prefer the locality rule. And on moral grounds it fails, because the defense of "coming to the nuisance" would allow some landowners to reduce the value of others' holdings without compensation, at least if the latter did not object promptly, and such a rule, which would ordinarily operate to the benefit of businesses and the detriment of homeowners and thus in general favor the rich, would never command nearly universal assent. The locality rule, moreover, would preclude an owner who once imposed the same higher order of disturbance on others as they did on him from asserting his right to damages in perpetuity, so long as most others continued to engage in those disturbing activities, even if he ceased his operations and wished to use his land more tranquilly. That result seems unjust to him (unless the locality rule, in conjunction with the activities of neighboring owners, increased the value of his property), whereas the converse would not be unjust to others: it is only right—and wealth-maximizing—to make them internalize the full costs of their operations, which means paying in cash what they previously paid indirectly by putting up with the now defunct disturbance. If a looser standard of nuisance is to apply to a certain area, it should be done by contract or, what may often be more efficient, by legislation.

[27] *See* Baxter and Altree (1972).

Consider, finally, nuisances that result in nonnegligible harm and thus warrant some remedy, but that affect large numbers of persons simultaneously, thereby making negotiations between injurer and victims expensive. In such cases there may be reason to deny victims the right to an injunctive remedy, at least if the injury inflicted is not beyond the reach of monetary compensation when judged from the victims' perspective,[28] even though they retain the right to an injunction when the harm they suffer is serious and transaction costs are low. The primary problem with permitting each victim to enjoin actions which the perpetrator is willing to pay more to continue than injured persons would demand in recompense is that each person has an incentive to withhold his consent until the others have agreed on a price, in an effort to extract as much of the difference between the injurer's offer price and the sellers' combined asking prices as he can. Negotiations might therefore consume much time and could well prove futile unless some mechanism for collective choice were available to trump the temporizing tendency of individual rationality. Such a mechanism would furthermore be in everyone's antecedent self-interest, if everyone were guaranteed his fair share—but no more—of the surplus generated by the mass sale of rights. A legal rule specifying a damage remedy in such situations, or a procedure for collective decisionmaking coupled with certain substantive constraints, would achieve this end. Automatic application of the rule would also remove the costs that would attend, and might prevent, the choice of a common approach to a nuisance affecting a large number of people.

What rule should govern? There seem two main options. The first would be to guarantee all injured parties at least an amount sufficient to restore them to their previous indifference curve, but to allow the actual price, representing the division of the surplus generated by the transfer, to be determined by negotiations between the buyer and representatives of the sellers, perhaps subject to majoritarian or supermajoritarian ratification by the sellers themselves. The drawbacks to this approach are: that it might require courts or other tribunals to put a price tag on the harm that individuals suffer if disputes arose, assuming that figure were to serve as a baseline (multiplied by some number greater than or equal to one) for compensation; that it might prove cumbersome and costly, particularly if a vote had to be taken; and that it might fail to yield a mutually beneficial agreement as a result of one or more of the parties' bargaining strategies. Its salient virtue is that it leaves to the parties the task of dividing the spoils, just as though negotiations were proceeding between two persons.

The second option would be to specify beforehand how the surplus was to

[28] In most cases where this assumption fails, as when lethal gases are intentionally discharged upwind of residential neighborhoods, criminal penalties would probably be appropriate, along with legal and equitable relief.

be shared in any case where the party causing the nuisance (or perhaps one of the plaintiffs who complained that the collective action problem deprived him and others of a beneficial exchange) requested that the state employ and enforce the designated valuation procedure. The surplus could either be assigned exclusively to the buyer, with the sellers getting damages equal to their injuries; exclusively to the sellers, with the injurer just breaking even; or to both sellers and buyers, in some proportion fixed in advance. The first formula would require courts to value the injury to a large number of persons, a task all the more daunting if damages were subject to future revision. The second might at first glance seem only to require that courts ascertain the buyer's highest offer price, which in the case of business enterprises might be approximated with some precision; but in fact the harm suffered by each of the individual sellers would have to be measured as well, in order to ensure that no one was badly harmed by the deal and to determine both the size of the surplus and its proper division among the sellers. The third formula would call for the very same calculations as the second; it would merely set aside some supernormal profit for the buyer. Because the buyer's best offer price would be fairly easy to discover by comparison with the sellers' asking prices, there seems little to separate the three versions of this second option, so far as administrative convenience is concerned, and little, too, to distinguish all three from the first option.

If people were just as likely to be buyers as sellers, and would in fact be both several times in their lives, the choice among these three formulas would also be arbitrary on the score of justice. But they are not. Nuisances of this type afflict a small subset of the population, and do so infrequently. And whereas the poor are apt to be fairly represented among the group of sellers—perhaps even overrepresented, if most nuisances blight poorer neighborhoods bordering industrial areas—they are likely to be under-represented among the buyers, because the buyers would consist primarily of owners of capital and derivatively of consumers, in both of which groups the affluent are overrepresented. These general considerations militate in favor of the third course—a division of the gains—with the dividing line drawn closer to the buyer's top offer price than the opposite pole if, as in the United States, wealth is distributed unjustly. It would probably be wise, however, to aim for a point short of the buyer's highest offer price, to ensure that the buyer also benefits and is not deterred from invoking a valuation process that may ultimately deny him a market return on his investment. The one shortcoming of this approach, in contrast to the first option, is that the division is established in advance by the state, not left for the parties to hammer out themselves. But the savings in time and money and the greater certainty of reaching an agreement[29] under this compromise

[29] Polinsky argues that unless liability equals actual damages in cases where a damage remedy is available but an injunctive remedy is not, stubborn bargaining strategies may block

version of the second option would probably, once the empirical data were in, render it the most attractive suggestion. It is, of course, not without costs, and those costs might block what would otherwise be a transfer of entitlements that left everyone better off, even if the valuation process were streamlined along the lines of class actions to save money. But the implementation of any theoretically attractive course encounters friction.

The foregoing proposals all define the injured parties' losses in terms of their lowest asking price. However, courts typically measure damages instead by changes in market value, where the market price is defined by what the highest bidder (not including the current owner) would pay for the right with and without the nuisance. This conventional measure of damages, however, is sometimes unjust. Just because no one would pay more than $5,000 for a portrait of Ms. X is no reason to grant her a maximum of $5,000 in damages for its destruction if she would not have sold the canvas for under $20,000. Indeed, suppose she had originally paid $10,000 for the painting. The same conclusion follows with respect to rights to use and enjoy real property. Measurement might be difficult in practice, but doubts about hitting the right number are no reason not to strive for the best guess possible.

What should be done if virtually everyone would gladly accept proffered compensation for some disturbance, yet a few would refuse any amount of compensation if they had the power to do so because they were unwilling to leave a cherished plot of earth, had all the material means they desired, and would be happiest if they did not have to abide disturbance? The situation this question contemplates is, of course, of marginal concern. The problem would only arise if such persons held property before the nuisance began, since in other cases the previous owners would have been compensated for the continuing harm and the property would have been sold on the understanding (or so the law should presume) that the injury would not abate. And such uncompromising stalwarts would seldom be seen. But should they stand in the way of transactions that would yield large benefits all around, then it does not seem overly harsh to ask them to rest content with a generous damage payment and some small annoyance for the sake of the larger collective good. Such sacrifices seem a rare but inescapable evil of organized social life, as perhaps wartime conscription is. The moral imperative to accept minor losses if necessary to render substantial benefits to others applies here with as much force as it does in other contexts.

Nuisance law confronts a number of additional difficulties. Most of

an efficient outcome. *See* Polinsky (1983), 19–20. His argument overlooks the possibility of effectively precluding the bargaining strategies he describes by compelling the parties to split the surplus generated by agreement according to a ratio fixed in advance by law.

them, however, are largely empirical in nature, their answers turning on the expected costs and benefits of the available options in a given case. While detailed inquiries of this kind are beyond the bounds of this chapter, the theoretical framework for resolving them should now be fairly plain. Its extension to abnormally dangerous activities is easily accomplished.

11.3. ABNORMALLY DANGEROUS ACTIVITIES

Liability has routinely been imposed without proof of negligence at common law for harm arising from unusually dangerous activities, at least when the harm is of the type that renders the activity causing it unusually dangerous. The classification of activities as abnormally dangerous, however, has varied over time and jurisdiction, depending upon law-makers' and judges' favored bases for predicating liability. The famous case of *Rylands v. Fletcher*, for example—the fountainhead of many of the more recent formulations of the standard of strict liability for abnormally dangerous activities—produced two different theories of liability and two corresponding rules. Justice Blackburn, writing in the Exchequer Chamber, asserted that "the true rule of law is that the person who for his own purposes brings on his land and collects and keeps there anything likely to do mischief if it escapes, must keep it at his peril, and if he does not do so is prima facie answerable for all the damage which is the natural consequence of its escape."[30] But Lord Cairns, in affirming the decision for the House of Lords, narrowed Justice Blackburn's rule, holding instead that liability exists without fault only when it results from some "non-natural" use of the injurer's land, as opposed to "any purpose for which it might in the ordinary course of the enjoyment of land be used."[31] Only because the defendant's construction of the reservoir that flooded the plaintiff's mine was a singular occurrence in that locale at that time was the defendant found answerable for damages.

Case law on both sides of the Atlantic has tended to follow Lord Cairns's formulation of the principle, restricting liability in the absence of negligence to dangerous conditions and activities that are deemed inappropriate or unnatural in light of the circumstances surrounding their occurrence.[32] The error in this approach should by now be evident. The proper rule is that of Justice Blackburn, with a bow to the spirit behind, if

---

[30] *Fletcher v. Rylands*, L.R. 1 Ex. 265, 279–80 (1866). This statement of the law was accepted verbatim, without qualification, by Lord Cranworth in his concurring opinion in the House of Lords. See *Rylands v. Fletcher*, L.R. 3 H.L. 330, 340–2 (1868).

[31] *Rylands v. Fletcher*, L.R. 3 H.L. 330, 338 (1868). Lord Cairns's opinion is at best ambiguous, however, for immediately after introducing the distinction between "natural" and "non-natural" uses, he quotes Justice Blackburn's statement of the rule and says that he "entirely concur[s]" with it. *See ibid.* at 339–40.

[32] *See* Prosser and Keeton (1984), 546–51.

not a nod in favor of implementing, Lord Cairns's distinction between natural and non-natural uses in a few exceptional cases.

The background principle defended above is that people are liable for all harms of more than minimal gravity caused by their voluntary actions, whether intentional or accidental, if those actions result in the violation of some legally protected right. This principle is slightly broader than Justice Blackburn's, for it applies to all actions that alter a plot of land, such that when natural forces operate on the altered area, harm ensues to owners of neighboring lots. The engine of destruction need not be created by *adding* to one's property; subtractions may be equally blameworthy, as when someone lowers a natural dike and causes flooding. But with this minor correction, the rule enunciated by Justice Blackburn is sound. The mere fact that serious harm results is sufficient for liability; that an activity has higher expected casualties than most forms of behavior in a given area, whether because the harms to which it gives rise (when it does) are substantial or because it injures with remarkable frequency, is irrelevant to the question whether compensation is owed except when reciprocity furnishes in-kind compensation sufficient to forestall suits for damages when the harmful activity is within the scope of the rule.

Nor can one conceive of something approaching universal consent to a modification of this principle. The germ of truth in Lord Cairns's view that even especially risky activities cannot result in liability in the absence of fault if they are "natural" to a region is that when people impose nearly reciprocal risks on one another, there is no point in requiring compensation for injury. Individuals should be allowed to buy first-party insurance if they desire protection, instead of having to purchase, or risk the non-purchase of, third-person liability insurance, with its presumably greater claim resolution costs.[33]

But the germ is only that. Perfect reciprocity rarely obtains, and unless the risks that the victim and the injurer imposed on one another were nearly equivalent, compensation must be paid, else no potential loser would consent to even this small modification. Equivalence, moreover, must be defined in terms of the expected *nominal* loss to the victim if even this limited exception is to win assent. The standard of liability may not be changed from strict liability to negligence, for example, merely because each of two neighbors performs blasting operations that pose a one-in-ten risk of lowering the value of the adjacent property by a half: it is also necessary that the two properties be of equal value. Otherwise, the neighbor who has much more to lose would not agree to exchange his right to compensation for the other person's waiver of his right to damages

---

[33] *See* Fletcher (1972), 541–2, 547–8.

should the first person injure him, unless he is an altruist or a fool.[34] But once reciprocity is defined in terms of equal expected nominal losses over some relatively short span of time, the chances of this exception taking hold are small. In fact, it would probably be wise to dispose of the exception and to make liability strict in all cases where substantial harm results, because the exception would apply so rarely, because the savings in claim resolution costs would likely be minuscule, and because the parties to whom the exception applied would often be uncertain prior to an injury and suit that it did apply, requiring them to buy more complex and more expensive insurance that covered either third-party damages or first-party losses, depending on the court's ruling with respect to the exception's applicability (unless they concluded an agreement stipulating their respective liabilities in advance). If potential litigants wished to arrange a more economical division of liability themselves, they would remain free to do so; the rarity of reciprocity means that the parties would ordinarily be few in number, so high transaction costs should not be an insuperable impediment if, as seems extraordinarily unlikely, the savings promised to be large.

The only interesting question with respect to dangerous activities is when injunctive relief should be available, in addition to damages after injury has occurred. If potential defendants are rational, they will avail themselves of all cost-effective precautions under a strict liability regime. Even if they are myopic, subjecting potential victims to greater risks than it is in their financial interests to do, there seems no reason to grant equitable relief to potential plaintiffs so long as monetary damages are adequate and their payment is relatively certain, either because the potential injurer's wealth far exceeds his potential liability or because he has ample insurance. A necessary condition of equitable relief must, as usual, be the prospect of irreparable harm, that is, the loss of something, such as life or health, for which cash is an imperfect substitute.

The prospect of irreparable harm, however, does not seem a sufficient condition of injunctive relief. Many activities in which people responsibly

[34] The case law altogether ignores this distinction between the *types* of risk to which parties subject one another and the *expected loss* they impose. For example, the rule excusing nonnegligent defendants from liability for fire damage to neighboring buildings when fire which was not the product of some abnormally dangerous activity escapes from their property (*see* Prosser and Keeton (1984), 544) places those who have more to lose at an unjust disadvantage. Although they are able to expose others to the same manner of risk, they are penalized for saving their earnings in the form of tangible objects or real estate rather than spending it or squirreling it away in some fireproof vault. Similarly, in *Turner v. Big Lake Oil Corporation*, 128 Tex. 155, 96 S.W.2d 221 (1936), the Texas Supreme Court held that a rancher whose watering holes were polluted and grazing lands destroyed by the escape of salt water from ponds the defendant constructed to operate his oil wells was not entitled to damages unless the defendant was negligent in constructing and maintaining those ponds, despite the fact that the rancher's watering holes posed no comparable danger—though they too might have overflowed—to the defendant or anyone else.

engage, from lighting logs in fireplaces to flying an airplane, could cause irreparable harm to others through an unexpected sequence of events, even if the risk is quite small. No one suggests banning them all: social and individual life would soon grind to a halt or suffer significant impoverishment. The problem is drawing a line between those combinations of harms and probabilities that people should be forced to tolerate by dint of the benefits they yield, and those from which potential plaintiffs are entitled to demand advance protection. If the harms were certain and substantial, then they would ordinarily be enjoinable, often under a nuisance theory, even if they were not irreparable. But there exists a wide middle space between the poles of certain occurrence and certain nonoccurrence, just as there is a gamut of possible harms varying in gravity and possible benefits varying in importance. Striking the balance seems unavoidably an exercise in judgment, ideally to be made by the legislature, with courts ensuring consistency both in the choice and in the application of criteria for decision. The possibility of especially serious harms that are not fully compensable should probably be given special weight in performing the calculus. To say more, however, would require investigating a range of conduct in some detail and devising a host of particularized rules to govern behavior in that domain. That project, valuable though it is, would carry well beyond this inquiry.

11.4. COLLISION CASES

Collisions occur because at least one of the parties broke a rule governing use of the roadways or airspace, assuming that the applicable rules are consistent and complete, in the sense that if everyone observed them scrupulously, no injurious contact could conceivably occur. Sometimes rules are broken negligently, as when drunk drivers race about at excessive speeds. Sometimes, however, violations occur despite a driver's or pilot's having taken all cost-justified precautions, because, for example, a bolt snaps, a heart stops beating, or an instrument malfunctions despite regular inspections. According to the background theory of strict liability sketched above, the nature of a violation that causes a multi-party accident is irrelevant to the amount of compensation owed. The offending party or parties must pay, without regard to the apparent triviality of their offense or the extent of the injuries they caused. Liability is absolute and unlimited, provided the other party is innocent of wrongdoing and did not fail to mitigate damages when it was easy to do so.

If more than one party broke a rule leading to the collision, liability must be apportioned. Numerous formulas for apportionment are conceivable, no one of which seems clearly superior in light of the rationale for choosing strict liability as the baseline. One might begin by making the negligent party liable for all damages if only one party was negligent. If more than one party was negligent in some causally relevant way,[35] then liability could be allocated among the negligent parties in accordance with some notion of comparative negligence.[36]

1. If neither party was negligent but both broke some rule,[37] then each party could be made to assume its own losses, as it would have had to do if no other party had been involved, or as it would have had to do under a negligence system.

2. Or each party could be made to assume the *other* party's losses, as would have been the case had the other party not broken a rule too.

3. Or total liabilities could be split evenly between the parties, given the apparent arbitrariness of choosing either of the first two proposals in preference to the other and the necessity of ascertaining the harm both parties suffered under both of them, so that an even division would entail no additional cost.

4. Or each of the parties could be forced to pay an amount equal to the aggregate damages of *both* in order to achieve optimal deterrence, with payments in excess of actual damages (that is, an amount equal to actual damages or half the combined payments) going to the state, for eventual even redistribution throughout the community.[38]

[35] I shall not discuss the merits of rival conceptions of proximate causation, a theory of which this view presupposes, but simply assume that decisions are made on the basis of the most tenable theory.

[36] For example, one could apportion liability in accordance with the ratio of one party's negligence to another party's negligence, where negligence is defined as the percentage excess, at the margin, of the expected injury from a party's action or omission over the cost of reducing that expected injury. To illustrate, let x equal the ratio, at the margin, of the expected injury (or, more precisely, the sum of the possible injuries multiplied by their respective probabilities) to the burden on the first party of further precautions, minus one. And let y equal the corresponding figure for the second party. Thus, $x = i/cx - 1$, and $y = i/cy - 1$, where i represents the expected injury at the margin and c the marginal cost of further precautions for the respective parties. (Because i necessarily exceeds c if a party is negligent, x and y will always be positive.) The first party's comparative negligence, and corresponding share of the total liabilities, would then be $x/(x + y)$, and the second party's $y/(x + y)$. If, for example, the first party's marginal ratio of expected losses to costs of prevention was $1.3 : 1$, and the second party's $1.1 : 1$, then $x = 0.3$ and $y = 0.1$. Thus, the first negligent party would have to assume 75% of the resultant liabilities, while the second negligent party picked up the remaining 25%. Although this appears an intuitively appealing conception of comparative negligence, determining numerically the relevant rates in an actual case might prove difficult, as well as costly for both the parties and the legal system. Of course, it would always be open to the parties to save themselves expense by stipulating their comparative negligence based on preliminary calculations.

[37] The following proposals could be applied even if one or more parties were negligent, if one thought that a distinction between negligent and nonnegligent offenders was inappropriate, given its irrelevance to the assignment of liability if only one party to the collision broke an applicable rule in some causally relevant way, or if one believed that the marginal advantages it offered, both moral and economic, could not justify the higher claim resolution costs it would entail. The rule stated in the preceding sentence would then be ignored.

[38] The obvious drawback to this proposal is that the state would have to monitor all settlements when collisions occurred, lest it (and the public generally) be cheated of its share of the damages, even if the parties preferred to settle quickly and cheaply without going through the elaborate calculations and measurements the government would mandate.

5. Or courts could be left to divide liability for actual damages in conformity with whatever equitable principles they developed, giving primary weight, presumably, to some conception of relative fault or comparative causal contribution.

6. Or each party's liability could, as Epstein recommends, be equal to the reduction in total damages that would have occurred had that party not breached some statutorily imposed duty but the other party had acted as in fact it did, with the division of the remainder, if any, contingent on the kinetic energy each of the parties would have contributed to the collision had it not breached its statutorily imposed duty;[39] if the sum of the reductions in damages that would have occurred if one party had not breached its duty while the other party had acted as it did exceeds total actual damages, then actual damages should be apportioned, I suppose, according to the ratio of the reductions that would have occurred had the parties not breached their respective duties.[40]

The problem with Epstein's proposal is not only that the counterfactual determinations it requires would be difficult to make with any precision. A more serious difficulty is that both the emphasis he places on breach of a specific statutory requirement and his suggestion that residual liability be divided according to the kinetic energy of the colliding vehicles seem misdirected. Epstein apparently intends the class of statutory requirements to be narrower than the class of all rules of the road—to include speed limits, for example, but not the rule requiring cars to remain in their lanes if the cause of a car's leaving its lane is a sudden blowout against which the driver could not reasonably (i.e. cost-effectively) have guarded. This restriction, however, seems arbitrary: why not extend the counterfactual avoidance test to the breach of all rules governing use of public roads?

---

[39] *See* Epstein (1974), 179–81. Epstein provides no numerical examples, but I take it that his liability rule would operate as follows. Suppose that A and B were both causally responsible, in an appropriate way, for their collision, and that both suffered injuries valued at $5,000. Suppose that if A had not been speeding, A's injury would have been only $3,000 and B's $2,000. Suppose that B did not breach a statutory duty. Then A would be liable straightaway for $5,000 (10,000 − (5,000 − 3,000) − (5,000 − 2,000)), that is, for the difference between the parties' actual damages and the damages they would have suffered had A not breached his duty. The remaining $5,000 in liabilities would be divided according to what would have been the kinetic energies of the two cars had A not been speeding. If the ratio of A's kinetic energy (the mass of A's vehicle multiplied by the square of its velocity, in this case the speed limit) to B's kinetic energy would have been 3 : 2, then A would be answerable for 60% of the remaining $5,000 in liabilities and B would be liable for the other $2,000. In sum, A would be stuck with his own $5,000 loss and have to pay B $3,000 toward B's own loss of $5,000.

[40] Epstein himself never discusses this possibility; I have simply attempted to extrapolate from his discussion of simpler cases. Thus, to return to the example of the preceding note, if both A and B had been speeding, and if damages would have fallen by $5,000 had A not been speeding, as stipulated in that example, and if they would have fallen by $10,000 had B not been speeding (the accident would not have occurred), then A, on this extension of the rule, would be liable for one-third of the actual damages—10,000 × (5,000/(5,000 + 10,000))—and B would be liable for the other two-thirds. Hence, B would have to pay $1,666 to A.

Epstein's reliance on kinetic energies to allocate liabilities also seems misplaced: if one of the vehicles whose driver was guilty of some infraction was at a standstill, or moving *away* from the vehicle that struck his, should that driver's share of the residual damages be zero or negative (resulting in a rebate on what he had to pay under the avoidance test)? It seems more sensible to apportion residual damages, once the (unrestricted) counterfactual avoidance test has been applied, according to one of the first five formulas. The problem of measurement would remain.

Which of these possible rules is best? The proposal that seems theoretically (if only marginally) most just is a variation on Epstein's that is sensitive to the foregoing criticisms. If neither party was negligent, then each party's liability would be equal to the amount by which total damages would have been reduced had he not broken some rule of the road; if the amount by which total damages would have been reduced exceeds actual damages (which might happen if the preceding calculus were performed by more than one nonnegligent party that violated some rule), then actual damages would be apportioned according to the ratios of the counterfactual reductions associated with each party. If only one party was negligent, then both morality and efficiency argue for his assuming complete liability. Finally, if more than one party acted negligently, then comparative negligence seems the most just rule.

The complications that would attend the implementation of this rule in cases where no party was negligent but two or more parties broke some traffic ordinance, however, seem sufficient reason to set it aside in such cases and to require each party in violation of some ordinance to bear his own losses and to pay an equal share of any damages owed a victim who did not transgress a relevant rule. Cases in which one or more parties were negligent could be handled as explained in the preceding paragraph.

Requiring parties who violated an applicable rule to bear their own losses in cases where no party was negligent is, of course, *morally* as arbitrary as making them bear each other's losses or splitting total losses between them. But it would probably be cheaper administratively than those two alternatives, since it would remove the need for more than one legal action to settle claims and since it would eliminate litigation over the extent of damages. Nor would it create the administrative complications that would attend the collection of excess damages for later redistribution, ostensibly on grounds of overall economy although probably with counterproductive results. Assuming, therefore, that this proposal should be taken as the just background rule, the question is whether there exists a Pareto-superior alternative to it, or at least a competing standard of liability that offers sizable gains to some persons without subjecting the rest to more than offsetting aggregate losses or significant individual losses.

Two alternatives frequently find defenders. The first is a universal negligence standard, with no liability for accidents resulting from the violation of some highway or airway rule unless the offender failed to take all precautions whose expected benefits to everyone affected exceeded their cost to him. The second is a first-party, no-fault rule, which would make unintentional injurers and victims alike liable for whatever injuries they sustained, however serious they were and regardless of who was to blame.

At first glance, neither proposal appears a promising candidate. The worm in both is that, although motorists or pilots expose one another to the same types of risk, they do not face identical losses should those risks materialize. Some people drive Porsches, others putter about on mopeds, still others drive freight trucks. A little Cessna can knock a Boeing 747 from the sky just as readily as the reverse. Some of those killed in collisions had lofty ambitions and earning potential, whereas others had already retired. Unanimous or even very widespread consent to the exchange of a strict liability rule for one that placed the onus of insurance on nonoffenders in some or all cases would apparently only be given at knifepoint. A large class of persons has too much to lose.

This initial verdict, however, must be set aside if the savings in administrative and claim resolution costs, along with the reduced costs of accidents and accident prevention, are likely to outweigh the expected losses to some people flowing from either or both proposals, leaving everyone advantaged all things considered. Likewise, if such savings, supplemented by additional compensation furnished by those who stand the most to gain, would leave the initial detractors of those proposals indifferent between them and strict liability, then there may be reason to switch. Are huge savings of this sort likely?

Consider, first, collisions between motor vehicles. Under a strict liability regime, almost all motorists would buy both third-party liability insurance and first-party coverage for injuries sustained in single- or multi-vehicle accidents caused by their having broken some highway rule, whether through negligence or misfortune.[41] During settlement negotiations or lawsuits in multi-vehicle collision cases, argument would center on one or more of three issues: which party or parties committed an offense, thereby causing the accident to occur; how fault should be apportioned, if more than one party is blameworthy; and how great the damages were to each party injured at least partly through the fault of another.

Under a negligence rule, both third-party and first-party insurance would again be virtual necessities, so that in this respect there would be no reduction in insurance costs. To be sure, by extending the reach of first-party

---

[41] There may be good reasons, both of justice—ensuring that victims are compensated—and paternalism, for mandating the purchase of a certain minimum amount of both types of insurance.

insurance to cases where no party was negligent and only the party other than the injured first-party insurer unintentionally violated some rule, the change in liability rule might reduce the cost of processing claims for compensation by eliminating inter-party disputes over the magnitude of injury in such cases. Disputes between the insured and his own insurance company are apt to be less acrimonious, it is generally thought, and certainly less likely to result in litigation. A negligence rule might also enhance consumer choice by allowing the insured party to decide what kind of coinsurance or how large a deductible to include in his first-party insurance policy, although this change is unlikely to yield any net benefits, inasmuch as the same risk-assuming, cost-reducing options would be available as part of the third-party liability policies replaced by first-party coverage. The sole advantage promised by the negligence rule is therefore a partial reduction in litigation and claim resolution costs—only partial, because legal disputes might still arise over whether the single rule-violator was negligent—across one band of cases.

The disadvantages of a negligence rule, however, are at least equally weighty. In addition to the legal issues likely to arise in a suit under a strict liability regime in cases involving one apparent rule-violator who was arguably nonnegligent, the question what standard of care should apply, and whether the defendant met it, would also have to be faced. As I noted in section 10.3, the resolution of those issues is likely, in practice, to carry higher costs than any reduction in expense attributable to a diminution in the number of legal claims. And overdeterrence might result if the definition of negligent conduct is hazy over the relevant run of cases—as it surely is with regard to conduct on the highway. Because both potential plaintiffs and potential defendants engage in the same activity, the salutary effects of strict liability on motorists' activity level *qua* potential defendants would be offset by the reduced attention they would pay to their activity level *qua* potential plaintiffs. But the lack of this further advantage notwithstanding, strict liability appears unlikely to prove a noticeably less efficient rule in motor vehicle collision cases. The large savings that would be necessary to allow a negligence standard to overcome the injustice it would effect by disfavoring those who put more at risk are simply not present.

In a modified form, however, the no-fault proposal fares much better. Advocates of such proposals regularly carve out a partial tort exception: negligent, reckless, or intentional conduct generates liability if it causes harm of sufficient gravity. Thus, the deterrent to inefficient conduct afforded by both strict liability and negligence rules is retained in serious cases. Recovery in those cases, moreover, is not limited to some fixed amount, as often happens under workers' compensation statutes, but extends to the full of actual damages, thereby ensuring that those who are badly injured receive just recompense. The principal attraction of such no-fault plans is that they eliminate litigation over the fact of negligence (under a negligence standard) and the valuation of harm (under both negligence and strict liability rules) in cases where the amount at stake is small, by requiring motorists to purchase their own insurance, or risk not buying coverage, up to the specified amount.[42] The main drawback is that motorists' incentive to take due care is reduced in situations where injury might occur below the threshold amount but not above it (unless recovery under the partial tort exception is limited to actual damages minus the threshold amount, in which case this shortcoming would always be present, albeit to a negligible extent in cases where serious injury might result from some action). For in such situations, negligent motorists would only be liable for their own injuries, not the harm they visited on others as well. Nevertheless, although the significance of this reduced deterrent could only be ascertained through empirical investigation, given the likelihood that first-party coverage would contain large deductibles or a generous measure of coinsurance, and given the inevitable trouble and annoyance associated with filing claims and having repairs performed, a weakened deterrent would probably not result in a substantial increase in collisions.

Could the prospective savings outbalance the injustices that ordinarily attend departures from strict liability? The answer would depend on the size of the gains and the extent of the injustice, both of which would, though only to some degree as regards the latter, be empirical issues. But if the threshold beyond which liability became strict were set low enough not to work a significant disadvantage to those with more at risk, yet high enough to encompass most harms resulting from minor accidents, then collective consent to the no-fault rule, taken as a partial substitute for the background rule of strict liability, could be presumed. Setting the threshold, of course, would require judicious balancing: the higher the threshold, the greater the savings in litigation and insurance costs, but also the greater the danger of injustice to those who drove more expensive or fragile cars or who were more susceptible to small personal injuries. Whether an acceptable equilibrium could be found would turn on the facts.[43]

[42] The law could still require drivers to purchase insurance against first-party losses or third-party tort liability above that amount, for their own good or for that of those they injure.

[43] Other possible cost-saving modifications of the strict liability rule warrant consideration, such as fixed payment schedules for various types of injuries or limitations on awards for pain, suffering, or other intangible injuries. Unfortunately, it appears impossible to reach general conclusions with regard to them. If one starts from the assumption that pain and suffering should be compensable, then any limitation on recovery will result in some injustice. But people might be willing antecedently to trade the risk of injustice for lower litigation and insurance costs. Everything depends on the particular limitations proposed, the likely savings, variations in the disutility of certain harms between people, and the distribution of attitudes towards risk with respect to incomplete compensation for the injuries covered by the plan.

The case of midair collisions, by contrast, is easy. Consent would not be given to the abandonment of strict liability, in whole or in part. Only serious claims would arise from midair crashes; hence, no savings could be gleaned through a limited no-fault rule by eliminating inter-party disputes over petty claims.

Consent would also be withheld from the substitution of a negligence rule or a limited no-fault rule for strict liability in collisions involving motorists and pedestrians. Cost savings, if they materialized, would likely be insubstantial, particularly because a strict liability rule would alone check potential defendants' activity levels (if insurance premiums closely followed accident rates or contained large deductibles), and the activity level of drivers is of greater concern than that of pedestrians. Litigation would continue over the fact of negligence (under a negligence standard) and, in some cases, over the amount of injury (under no-fault and negligence rules). And pedestrians would have to purchase additional insurance against loss of life, loss of salary, and medical expenses, at least under a negligence rule, which would largely offset decreases in the cost of drivers' third-party liability coverage. The number of inter-party claims, moreover, would not be appreciably reduced under a limited no-fault rule, since most accidents involving pedestrians result in injuries that would greatly exceed any acceptable threshold. So the proffered gains, if there were any, would be inconsiderable. In addition, the change in liability rule would not impact evenly on all citizens. Many people are predominantly pedestrians, and though they might benefit indirectly from the small reduction in transportation costs, that indirect benefit would certainly fall short of the disproportionate loss they would have to bear.[44] Hence, the rule of strict liability would only be modified by consensus, if at all, in the case of motor vehicle collisions resulting in harms of relatively small value.

In defending the moral propriety of a regime of strict liability, with exceptions for no-fault automobile collision insurance up to a limited amount and for a negligence standard in certain situations where parties impose reciprocal risks on one another, I have assumed that the distribution of resources in the community to which that regime would apply is otherwise just. That assumption, however, appears less crucial to this chapter's recommendations than to those contained in Chapters 7 and 8. Even if the distributions of wealth and income were unjust, as they now are in the United States and Britain, the foregoing principles of tort law ought probably to be implemented. For wealth maximization is an even less attractive ideal in a world marred by greater disparities in holdings

---

[44] *See* Bebchuk (1980), 673–4 (criticizing Posner's defense of a negligence rule to govern automobile accidents involving pedestrians).

than justice permits, in light of its bias in favor of the affluent and its tendency to widen the gulf between rich and poor over time. And a negligence standard, while no more—and probably less—efficient than strict liability in most of the traditional domains of tort law, seems less just. Unless circumstances dictate otherwise or some other option is more attractive than those considered, strict liability should in most cases remain not only the background standard but the adopted rule.

PART III

SAVING AND TAKING
LIFE

12

Do Numbers Count when Saving Lives?

IF a plurality of persons is in mortal peril and somebody can rescue one or more but not all of them with roughly the same effort, how should he decide whom to save? This question forms the hub of the next two chapters. The final chapter of Part III turns from choices among those facing imminent death to the problem of killing someone not himself in immediate danger in order to save persons who are threatened by death or who would otherwise benefit from his demise.

Reasons for favoring one group of potential survivors over other groups may usefully be divided into three categories. First, there are those based on properties of the individuals composing the various groups that are not contingent on their membership in those groups, such as their age, the number of their dependents, and the expected quality of their future life. Chapter 13 examines reasons of this kind. Second, there are reasons derivative of the rescuer's relations to the endangered persons. From the perspective of morality, perhaps the most important factors shaping these relations are the rescuer's personal concerns and affections, as well as any special obligations he has assumed (through his acceptance, for example, of a public office with prescribed duties) to help some rather than others. Although I touch upon reasons of this sort below when considering the moral relevance of the number of people who could be saved by one action rather than another, I do not discuss them at length. Third, there are reasons for favoring one group that refer to properties of the groups among which the rescuer must choose that cannot be reduced to properties that individuals possess independently of their membership in those groups. The only such property that deserves serious attention, I assume, is that of being larger than other groups of imperiled persons. Other conceivable reasons for preferential consideration, such as one group's containing more Caucasians or Catholics, seem either to be morally irrelevant or to offend the principle that people ought to be accorded equal regard when life-or-death decisions are made unless personal concerns of the chooser take precedence.

Be that as it may, this chapter concentrates on the question whether one group's being more numerous than another gives rise to a duty or an obligation to save the lives of its members in preference to those of persons belonging to the smaller group if it is impossible to rescue everyone. This question has received much attention in recent years, and I shall begin by reviewing the salient arguments for the moral irrelevance of numbers in section 12.1, before turning to some of the more forceful objections to this position in section 12.2. Section 12.3 examines several arguments for the claim that numbers matter. Although intuition suggests that numbers are morally relevant, the arguments most commonly advanced in support of that contention are, upon close inspection, gravely flawed. Section 12.4 attempts to repair their deficiencies by defending the view that rescuers ought to save as many lives as they can, special concerns and obligations apart, without relying on the premise that it is objectively worse if more people die than if fewer perish.

12.1. THE CASE FOR THE MORAL IRRELEVANCE OF NUMBERS

Because people usually place a premium on staying alive, they often ensure that sufficient resources are available to rescue them all should their lives be endangered. However, because most people do not deem it worthwhile to ensure against every untoward possibility, preferring to run various risks rather than spend the sums necessary to eliminate them altogether, and because some enjoy activities whose thrills are inseparable from their dangers, it sometimes happens that life-saving resources are too scarce to keep all the unlucky from death's door. Philippa Foot offered the example of a doctor whose supply of an expensive drug is only sufficient to save either one patient, who needs a massive dose, or five other patients, whose individual needs are more modest, but not all six.[1] Similar cases arise when hospitals are forced to cope with more accident victims than they can save, some of whom require more resources than others, or when clinics must decide whether to assign their limited number of renal dialysis machines to a small number of chronic patients or to reserve them for patients who need treatment only temporarily, thereby allowing the clinics to save more lives over the long run. Shortages of rescue equipment when large numbers of people are trapped by fire, or when a violent squall vents its fury on fishing boats and passenger ferries alike, illustrate the same difficulty.

Choices between lives may of course result from causes other than the voluntary assumption of risk. Sometimes they are forced on people willy-nilly. Military commanders in a defensive war, for instance, may have to abandon one set of soldiers to the enemy's fire in order to save others. Churchill confronted a similar choice in 1940 when he refused to notify the populace of Coventry of an impending air raid rather than betray knowledge of the German codes that might save more lives in the future. Officials may have to decide how to respond to an ultimatum from terrorists threatening to murder several hostages unless someone who will

---

[1] *See* Foot (1967).

certainly be killed, probably painfully, is exchanged for them. The question all these cases pose is whether there exists a moral reason to save more rather than less numerous groups when circumstances preclude the rescue of all.

Elizabeth Anscombe, in her brief reply to Foot, asserted that the widespread assumption that numbers count is unwarranted.[2] If a doctor uses his entire supply of a drug to save one patient, who needs all of it to remain alive, rather than five patients, each of whom requires one-fifth as much, then he cannot be reproached for his choice, Anscombe said, "unless the preference signalizes some ignoble contempt" for the individuals left to die. Likewise, if a crowd is stranded on one rock, if a single person is perched on another, and if a sailor can only reach one of the shrinking isles before the tide engulfs them both, then he cannot be rebuked if he spurns the multitude and lifts the lone individual from the rising flood. For who is wronged, Anscombe asks, if one person is plucked from the jaws of death rather than several others? None of the larger band can claim that the doctor or rescuer owed *him* the drug or a place in the boat. If these scarce resources were left idle when they could easily have been used to save lives, then *everyone* awaiting rescue could lodge a complaint, for great need was present, the means for alleviating it at hand, and the opportunity lost through callous indifference. But so long as the drug or the boat was put to good use, Anscombe says, the decision to save one instead of five is not open to moral criticism.

Unfortunately, Anscombe's article is chary of argument. She never states the premises from which her conclusions derive, nor does she attempt to meet possible objections or answer obvious questions. Why, for example, if "because they are more" is, as Anscombe concedes, a "good" and "perfectly intelligible" reason for saving the larger group, is it not a decisive reason if one's own interests are not substantially implicated and the impact of one's choice on others is overwhelmingly important, determining who lives and who dies? Why is it enough if one does *some* good when one could do yet *more* good at no greater cost to oneself?

Other questions jump quickly to mind. Why can a member of the larger group not claim that the doctor owes him the drug simply because his life could be purchased at less cost than the more needy patient's life, freeing resources that could in turn save even more lives? Under what conditions could someone claim that he rather than someone else was owed a seat in the boat or a vital injection? Does it make a difference if the captain of the boat is a Coast Guard officer rather than a private yachtsman, or if the drug that the physician may administer is public property and the six potential

---

[2] *See* Anscombe (1967). Anscombe is replying to Foot (1967). Charles Fried expresses his agreement with Anscombe's conclusion in Fried (1978), 219.

beneficiaries are all participants in some national health insurance scheme? Would there be anything amiss if the doctor or boatowner saved his friends first? And if numbers do not count, how should one choose between the two groups? Ought the doctor to flip a coin in deciding whether to save five or one, thereby giving each person a one-in-two chance of surviving? Or does treating them as equals entail giving the single person a one-in-six chance and the group of five a five-in-six chance, since flipping a coin might be thought to imply that each of the five is only one-fifth as deserving of concern or only one-fifth as valuable as the sixth?[3] Anscombe offers no answers.

John Taurek does. He presents three arguments for the conclusion that it is not morally incumbent on someone to save the larger of two groups of endangered individuals, special obligations apart.[4] Taurek's first argument runs:

(1) If someone's friend was in mortal peril, he would be morally permitted to save him rather than five strangers.

(2) The fact that one of the endangered persons is someone's friend is a fact too insignificant to affect the latter's obligations or duties.

(3) Ergo, if someone must choose between saving one and saving five, he is morally permitted to save the one, even if the one is not his friend.[5]

Premises (1) and (2) require support. The first may be defended by appealing either to intuition directly or to the third argument below. Since it strikes me as intuitively correct, and since it would probably command general assent, I shall assume that it is true. The second premise, however, is extremely implausible. Although some utilitarians aver that one's obligations are unaffected by the fact that one loves or cares about particular persons—one ought always to maximize utility, regardless of whose utility it is—they would almost certainly reject the first premise. Most of those who accept the first premise believe that certain duties and permissions are agent-relative. Complete impartiality is not required when one's own welfare or that of one's friends is at stake, but in all other cases where people's salient interests are involved impartiality is obligatory. If

---

[3] Frances Kamm contends that assigning chances of survival according to numbers is both consistent with the assumption that lives are not objectively valuable and fairer than a simple coin-flip when groups differ in size. *See* Kamm (1985), 180–6; see below, pp. 286–90. Her considered view, however, is that the larger group ought automatically to be saved. See below, p. 302 n. 31.

[4] *See* Taurek (1977). In untangling the strands of Taurek's arguments, set out rather haphazardly in his article, I have benefited from Derek Parfit's critique of them in Parfit (1978).

[5] Taurek (1977), 295–9.

this view is correct, however, then the second premise is unsound, and the first and second together cannot sustain Taurek's conclusion.[6]

Taurek's second argument is as follows:

(1) If someone had to choose between saving his own life and saving the lives of five other people, he would be morally permitted to save himself.

(2) If it is permissible for someone to save himself rather than certain other people, it must be permissible for anyone else to save that person rather than those others, whether or not the rescuer's welfare would be affected by the choice.

(3) Hence, it is permissible to save one person rather than five if one must choose between them, whether or not one would lose anything of value oneself if one made the opposite choice.

Assume, once again, that the first premise is true. (It is obviously more plausible than the first premise of Taurek's first argument.) Taurek's conclusion then follows only if the second premise is credible. Its infirmity, however, is patent. Like the second premise of the first argument, it is tantamount to a denial that there exist agent-relative permissions. In this case, however, the claim is even more doubtful, because even someone who thought that a person could not morally favor his friends over strangers might well agree that he may put his own life ahead of others' lives.

Taurek advances a third argument, however, which at once justifies the first premises of both of the preceding arguments and which concludes, more strongly than they, that the relative sizes of imperiled groups are of no moral consequence when deciding whose lives to save, special obligations apart. This argument runs:

(1) In the absence of special obligations, the only moral reason to prevent an outcome is that the outcome would be worse than some alternative state of affairs one could bring about by preventing that outcome.

(2) The deaths of any number of persons would not be a worse outcome than the deaths of any other number of persons [assuming that one of the sets of persons, the badness of whose deaths is being compared, is not a subset of another].[7]

---

[6] Notice, incidentally, that the first argument Taurek offers cannot establish the moral irrelevance of numbers as it stands. One might accept premise (1), but deny that a person may save the life of his friend rather than the lives of a *great many* more others. Indeed, that is a common view. An additional argument for the complete irrelevance of numbers is therefore necessary.

[7] The clause in brackets is my addition. Taurek might well accept the qualification (though see below, n. 9). It would allow him to disown the view, provisionally ascribed to him in Parfit (1978), 291, that no outcome is objectively worse than another. Taurek could then claim that, if one outcome is bad for particular people, and if a second outcome is at least as bad for each

(3) Hence, there is no moral reason to prevent the deaths of one set of persons rather than the deaths of another set, provided that the second set is not a subset of the first.

Taurek makes no effort to buttress his first premise. He apparently thinks it self-evidently true. Since none of his critics has questioned it, and since I do not think it seriously flawed,[8] I shall not discuss it further.

The bone of contention is, of course, the second premise. The gist of Taurek's defense of it is his claim that it is impossible to "give a satisfactory account of the meaning" of impersonal value judgments, such as the assertion that it would be objectively worse if some were to die and others to live rather than the reverse. "I do not wish to make [such a claim]," Taurek says, "unless I am prepared to qualify it by explaining to whom or for whom or relative to what purpose it is or would be a worse thing."[9] Would a drought in the Sahel, he might ask, necessarily be a greater tragedy, other things equal, than an earthquake in Anatolia that took fewer lives?

Taurek imagines someone attempting to convince an individual to give up the drug he needs to stay alive in order to save five other persons by arguing, for instance, that it would be a worse thing for the five to die than for him to perish because a larger sum of future happiness or intrinsic value would pass from the world. He concludes—reasonably—that these arguments would sound strained, even absurd, if voiced by an allegedly disinterested party, contemptible if made by one of the five. The losses

of those people but worse for one or more of them, then the second outcome is worse than the first. Thus, while one cannot say that X's suffering harm H is objectively better or worse than Y and Z's each suffering harm H, one can say that X's suffering harm H is better than X and Y's each suffering harm H. Parfit assumes that Taurek would accept this proviso. *Ibid.*

[8] I would suggest one slight revision. Many writers distinguish obligations from natural duties on the basis of people's voluntary acquisition of the former. *See e.g.* Simmons (1979), 7–28; Brandt (1964). If one thinks this distinction helpful, then one would want to amend the initial clause to read: "In the absence of special obligations and natural duties . . . . " Taurek may have intended "obligation" to cover natural duties as well as obligations proper.

[9] Taurek (1977), 304. In this passage, Taurek seems to endorse the view that no outcome is objectively worse than another. As I noted above, n. 7, Taurek might want to qualify his claim. Of course, he might contend instead that no outcome is objectively worse than any other, but that if someone is faced with a choice between two actions that are equally costly from his own point of view, one of which would bring about a state of affairs that is not worse for anyone than the state of affairs that the alternative action would effect but that is better for at least one person, then he has a *duty* to perform the action that leaves at least one person better off. One might think this thesis problematic because it leaves unexplained why one has the duty it posits, when the most natural explanation for the existence of such a duty is that its fulfillment would bring about an objectively better state of affairs. Taurek might reject this suggestion, however, and explain the imperative by reference to a moral person's equal concern for all who will be affected by his actions. Someone who empathized with everyone affected would naturally choose that action that benefited one person without harming anyone else. As a practical matter, of course, it does not matter which of these views (or some other functionally equivalent view) Taurek endorses.

people suffer are always their own losses, dependent upon what they, as separate individuals, value. There is no super-person who experiences the lot of them, nor, Taurek argues, can people's gains and losses be summed morally.

My way of thinking about these trade-off situations consists, essentially, in seriously considering what will be lost or suffered by this one person if I do not prevent it, and in comparing the significance of that *for him* with what would be lost or suffered by anyone else if I do not prevent it. This reflects a refusal to take seriously in these situations any notion of the sum of two persons' separate losses. To me this appears a quite natural extension of the way in which most would view analogous trade-off situations involving differential losses to those involved . . . . [10]

If six valuable objects are threatened by fire and someone cannot save them all, it is doubtless rational for him to retrieve as many of the most costly pieces as he can from the flames. But people, Taurek thinks, are not like clocks and crystal:

[W]hen I am moved to rescue human beings from harm in situations of the kind described, I cannot bring myself to think of them in just this way. I empathize with them. My concern for what happens to them is grounded chiefly in the realization that each of them is, as I would be in his place, terribly concerned about what happens to him. It is not my way to think of them as each having a certain *objective* value, determined however it is we determine the objective value of things, and then to make some estimate of the combined value of the five as against the one. If it were not for the fact that these objects were creatures much like me, for whom what happens to them is of great importance, I doubt that I would take much interest in their preservation. . . .

And so it is in the original situation. . . . Each faces the loss of something among the things he values most. His loss means something to me only, or chiefly, because of what it means to him. It is the loss to the individual that matters to me, not the loss of the individual. But should any one of these five lose his life, his loss is no greater loss to him because, as it happens, four others (or forty-nine others) lose theirs as well. And neither he nor anyone else loses anything of greater value to him than does [the one individual not among the five], should [he] lose his life. Five individuals each losing his life does not add up to anyone's experiencing a loss five times greater than the loss suffered by any one of the five. [11]

This seems to me an attractive view. Life is precious—for most of us the most precious of possessions—and the loss of any life worth living lessens the universe (whatever gains it might yield simultaneously). To acknowledge, however, that the continuation of a desirable life is in most instances a good which generates a duty to preserve it if one can do so at moderate cost to oneself is by no means to concede that the benefits one furnishes people can be measured, added, and compared. Each person values his

[10] Taurek (1977), 307–8.
[11] Taurek (1977), 306–7.

own life, but no one values the aggregate of people's lives in the same way that each person does his own existence, because no one lives them all serially or simultaneously. People sometimes sympathize with one another, of course, and to that extent the loss of one is a loss to many. But rarely is suffering fully shared, especially between strangers. And in the end we die alone. When someone passes away, he usually loses what he values most; when several people die, however, nobody loses more than does any one of them. The same is true of anguish, pain, or like misfortunes. Interpersonal comparisons of the evils that befall people are often possible, but it is simply a mistake, a mistake that in some ways parallels the central flaw of utilitarianism, to claim that different people's lesser evils can be added together to produce something that is morally worse than the individually greater evil another person suffers alone. And nowhere is this truth more evident than when lives hang in the balance. There is no way to measure the loss of a multitude against the loss of one individual. From an objective vantage point, the number of persons who suffer injury is irrelevant to the decision whom to spare. What matters is the magnitude of the loss to those threatened with the greatest injuries; it does not matter at all whether they stand alone or with the crowd.

It may seem odd, I suppose, that morality should permit, perhaps even require, pairwise comparisons of the harm two individuals stand to suffer when deciding which harm to avert if one can only turn aside the loss threatening one of the two people, yet bar addition of the harms that a plurality of people might suffer when deciding which group of people to help. If I understand his position, Taurek is untroubled by this apparent fact because he denies the possibility of any objective interpersonal comparison of evils. If the harms confronting two people are vastly different, natural sympathy will probably lead one (it would lead Taurek) to help the person who stands to suffer the much more grievous loss, and it will probably cause one to focus on the worst harms threatening individuals in two competing groups without prompting one to sum the harms threatening each group's members. But it cannot, in this view, yield any duties to assist one individual, or one group, rather than another.

This may be the correct account. The strength of our intuition that it is incumbent on us to prevent the loss of one person's arm rather than spare a different person a small bruise might properly be ascribed to instinctive or culturally instilled or fortified empathy. Perhaps this conclusion can be further buttressed by an argument from collective consent of the sort advanced in section 12.4 to vindicate the equally popular intuition that numbers count. Nevertheless, I have serious reservations regarding what appears to be Taurek's stance. For example, fairness imposes constraints on choice, as I explain below, that Taurek ignores. And my confidence in extending the collective consent argument of section 12.4 to the problem of interpersonal comparisons is appreciably weaker than my conviction that it solves the problem of numbers when individuals belonging to different-sized groups are threatened with the same harm. It seems to me, for example, that one ought to save one person's arm at the price of another person's bruise even if collective assent has not been given to a general rule of comparison that yields that result, and even if one has not formed an intention to act from such a principle before one must choose. Perhaps it is simply an irreducible fact about the moral universe that objective pairwise comparisons of harms are possible (at least when the disparity is striking) but that harms are not morally additive over groups of persons. While that view might also be hard for many people to accept, it seems less difficult to countenance than the assertion that the basis for pairwise judgments, and perhaps all choices between persons, is solely emotive.

Arguing for the position that the harms different people suffer cannot be summed for the purpose of moral decisionmaking, however, as against one that reifies evils and that sees people as morally constrained to minimize debits on the universe's balance sheet, is difficult in the abstract, for neither view is obviously wrongheaded at that rarefied level. Although Taurek's approach seems to me deeply appealing, others may react differently to the juxtaposition. The argument must therefore extend to a comparison between the ramifications of the two positions. Taurek contends, and there seems no reason to dispute, that exclusive focus on how a situation appears from the point of view of each person whose life is in jeopardy, together with the moral irrelevance of the combined losses of groups of individuals, entails that it is always permissible for someone to save himself or a friend rather than any number of other people threatened with an equally grievous loss, provided that special duties or obligations do not come into play. One who shared this view could admit that somebody's concern for others might lead him to lay down his own life or abandon a friend if he could thereby keep many more others alive. But even if such a sacrifice were praiseworthy, it would never be morally required.

If someone had to choose between two groups of strangers confronting an identical threat, then one who accepted this argument might follow one of three paths. Taurek himself would flip a coin, no matter how greatly the two groups differed in size. Because "each person's potential loss has the same significance to [him], only as a loss to that person alone," Taurek would give each person the same fifty-fifty chance of survival.[12] Any other method of choice that attempted to treat people equally would, he correctly says, require an impossible moral addition of the losses suffered by different persons.

A second approach, if one does not believe (as Taurek may not) that

---

[12] Taurek (1977), 307; *see ibid.* 303.

fairness mandates the first course, would be to favor the group one knows or has reason to think will contribute most to whatever one regards as important, such as the arts, medical research, or economic prosperity. If one knew nothing about the individual characteristics of the groups' members, then someone who held this view would rationally save the larger group, because he would thereby maximize the odds of preserving the potential contributors whose work he values. Once again, however, he would not be *obligated* to rescue the larger group, since many individual losses do not add up morally to one colossal loss that tilts the balance of duty in their favor. He might, on a whim, choose the smaller group instead without fear of moral censure.

The chief shortcoming of this second approach is that fairness matters. When one lacks a marked personal concern for the welfare of those who are endangered, one's duty to accord them equal regard plainly outweighs one's slim hope that by saving the larger number, one will contribute more significantly to projects of which one approves. If one acknowledges that one owes other people (and perhaps even some nonhuman mammals) noninterference with their bodies and possessions and at times small sacrifices simply in view of the fact that they are self-conscious creatures like oneself whose lives may go better or worse from their own perspective, then one can hardly deny the moral necessity of forgoing a slight possible benefit to accord those people the equal chance of survival that they, as equal moral subjects, deserve.

Frances Kamm favors a third method of choice. In her view, fairness and the equal regard one owes to those whose lives are imperiled implies, at the very least, that one assign chances of survival proportional to the number of people in each of the groups from among which one must choose.[13] She denies that if the choice were between three people and six, both groups should have a one-in-two chance of survival; instead, she contends, the first group should have a one-third chance while the second should be twice as likely to be rescued.

Kamm offers two arguments for this conclusion. Her first argument appeals to an uncongenial conception of equal treatment. Kamm asserts that, even if lives lack objective worth, one should pay some attention to numbers because treating people as equals always means giving some weight to the fact that somebody prefers a certain outcome. If the fact that somebody prefers a particular result does not alter the way one decides which result to bring about, then he is denied the equal consideration to which he is morally entitled. Kamm explains:

[13] In fact, Kamm goes further and argues that one should save the larger group forthwith. See below, p. 302 n. 31. She begins, however, by arguing that the assignment of chances proportional to numbers is preferable to Taurek's suggestion that a coin be flipped, no matter how markedly the two groups differ in size. *See* Kamm (1985), 181, 184–6. Gregory Kavka also thinks the proportionality rule an improvement over equal odds for groups irrespective of their size. *See* Kavka (1979), 293.

[W]e will not have succeeded in counting his preference for a certain state of affairs if the fact that he prefers it makes no difference in the process of deciding which state to bring about. His preferring will make no difference in this process of deciding if we would proceed in the same way whether or not he had this preference, even when recognition of his preference could help his cause. This will be so if we follow the policy Taurek recommends and toss a coin. For this policy would lead us to do the same thing whether it is a case of one in opposition to five, or one in opposition to a single other person's preference. If we count only objects of preferences in this way, then a person's preference will be superfluous whenever one other person shares it.[14]

Kamm never says, however, why there is a denial of equal treatment if a person's preference will not affect the way in which one chooses survivors when that person belongs to one of the endangered groups. Certainly her conclusion follows if one assumes that treating people as equals entails doling out chances according to numbers. But it in no way helps to elucidate or justify that conception of equal treatment. It merely states an implication of a view adopted for some *other* reason.

What that reason might be is obscure. If one starts from Taurek's assumption that lives do not possess objective value, that what matters is the loss *to* each person, and if one assumes (as I do throughout, leaving comparisons of the value of different people's lives for Chapter 13) that losses of life are equal and, as Kamm does for the sake of argument, that their value cannot be summed morally, then it seems to follow, as Taurek says, that extending equal regard to others means giving each the same chance of survival, irrespective of how many stand alongside or against him. Assigning chances proportional to numbers only seems justified on the assumption that lives, or preferences, do possess objective worth, and to be—as in Kamm's case it is—an indefensible halfway house along the road to choosing directly (rather than merely assigning chances) in accordance with numbers.

Kamm's argument that a process for selecting actions affecting some person denies him equal treatment if the process is such that his preference does not, in every case, influence the probability that a certain action will be chosen is perplexing for yet another reason: Kamm's favored method of choice—majority rule—also renders a person's preference superfluous if he happens to be in the minority or if he finds himself in a majority greater than one. Kamm notes that "even in majority rule an individual may be superfluous," but she thinks that majority rule is not hobbled by the objection she offers against coin-tossing because "each 'excess' member of the majority knows that if his side had not yet won, he would have been used to balance an opponent. It is only when he does not care whether or not he is thus used (that is, when the object of his preference has won) that he is not thus used."[15]

---

[14] Kamm (1985), 181.   [15] Kamm (1985), 182.

This reply, however, is unavailing. Under the coin-toss rule, each member of a group of more than one person also knows that, had he found himself alone, his presence would have made a difference. It is only when he does not care whether his presence is taken into account (that is, when he has already been assured the equal chance to which he is entitled) that his presence is not taken into account. The parallel is exact.

Kamm might rejoin, I suppose, that in the latter case, someone *would* prefer to have his preference count for something, rather than find himself relegated to a mere one chance in two; to say that he "does not care" whether his presence is taken into account is therefore incorrect.

This rejoinder also fails, however, because it simply begs the question. The reason a member of the majority does not care whether his vote is counted under a system of majority rule is either: (*a*) because he thinks majority rule is a morally admirable procedure, and the majority of which he is a part would prevail whether or not his vote were counted; or (*b*) because he wants his preference to win, whether or not majority rule is morally unimpeachable, and he would achieve what he wanted whether or not his vote were counted. Kamm cannot, however, intend the second possible construction of her claim, because it would not hold equally of a member of the *minority*. The vote of every member of the minority is, in Kamm's terms, "superfluous," and the reason that minority members do not care that their votes make no difference cannot be that they will get what they want anyway, but rather that they believe that majority rule deserves moral approbation. (By the same token, it is not true that under the coin-toss rule, every person whose preference is "superfluous" would like to have "superfluous" preferences counted: a member of the *smaller* group would be *worse* off if chances were assigned in proportion to numbers.) But if interpretation (*a*) represents the proper construction of Kamm's claim, then it reduces to the tautology that someone who thought majority rule morally proper would not find majority rule morally objectionable. The same is true, however, of the coin-toss rule. Thus, Kamm's argument that the coin-toss rule fails to treat people as equals because it sometimes renders their preferences "superfluous" might be used with equal force against the majority rule she prefers—if, that is, there were some non-question-begging reason for thinking that rule sound, which there is not.

Kamm's second argument for favoring chances proportional to numbers over Taurek's proposal to give each group the same chance of salvation runs as follows. Assume, with Taurek, that if six people are in mortal danger and if the rescue squad can only reach one in time, then each should be given a one-in-six chance of outliving the ordeal. Suppose, however, that two are able to agree, and do agree, to return to save each other if either of their numbers comes up, and that, as luck would have it, they cannot possibly save any of the other four. Surely, Kamm says, it is not unfair to let the pair pool their chances through an agreement of this kind, thereby increasing each of their odds to one-in-three, since none of the other four would thereby suffer a reduced chance of surviving. But then, Kamm says, people should always be allowed to aggregate their chances, since their doing so would never harm those unable to join the pool. Whether or not they could and would rescue one another pursuant to an agreement if they won the rescue lottery is irrelevant. Hence, if by chance more people find themselves in one group than in another, they too should be permitted to aggregate their individual chances, which of course they would almost invariably do. One might say that fate has pooled their chances for them automatically. Ergo, a group's prospect of rescue should vary with the number of its members, assuming (what Kamm later maintains is false) that there are no convincing arguments for majority rule in such cases.[16]

The rotten timber supporting Kamm's conclusion is her assumption that pooling is always morally permissible where circumstances render it feasible and where those who band together do not purposely and impermissibly exclude other endangered people from their group. (Indeed, only pronounced dislike or perhaps strong moral disapprobation could lead them to act in this way, since group members would always enhance their own prospect of survival by adding to their number.) What right do people have to combine their chances so that they receive more consideration than those who lack allies? If each person's life matters equally to the rescuer, and if lives lack an objective value capable of moral summation, then each should still receive the same chance of survival.

Kamm reaches a different result because she loses sight of this fundamental implication of Taurek's view. Her example makes this slip seem natural. She starts from the assumption that only one of six can possibly be saved. In that case, each should be granted a one-in-six chance of being rescued. She then postulates a *change* in circumstances. Through some fortuitous occurrence, two people can save each other if either of them is saved, but neither can help the other four if he is rescued. In thinking about this altered scenario, one is apt to focus on the two who are able to improve their lot by reaching an agreement and to assume, since the others cannot sign on and since their chances are not diminished relative to what they were before the two made their deal, that the remaining four cannot be harmed by any agreement the two manage to reach. This assumption, however, is incorrect. If the two agree, then the rescuer is, in effect, confronting a choice between *five* groups—four with one member each, one with two—not six. If numbers are irrelevant, and if each person is entitled to the same consideration and thus the same chance

[16] *See* Kamm (1985), 185–6.

of staying alive, then he should assign each *group* an equal, one-in-five chance of survival. Relative to *this* baseline, which Kamm assumes *arguendo* is proper, allowing two to pool their chances without reducing their odds *would* injure the other four, since it would relegate each of the others to a one-in-six chance when each ought to be given a one-in-five chance. When the number of groups changes, whether through natural accident or voluntary action, the baseline shifts too. In Kamm's example, the rescuer then faces the paradigm case of unequally sized groups, and his response must be, as before, to assign each group a like chance of salvation. Kamm's conclusion only follows if one rejects the notion of equal treatment implicit in Taurek's view; Taurek's view does not, as Kamm suggests, entail its own negation. But Kamm supplies no reason for spurning Taurek's conception of equal treatment that is consistent with the premise that the value of lives cannot be morally summed; and as the foregoing response to her first objection makes plain, it appears that no convincing reason can be given without jettisoning assumptions she at least claims for the sake of argument to share.

There is, I think, a second reason why Kamm's argument is so seductive. Varying her example slightly makes the point plainer. Suppose, once again, that only two of the six can return to help one another, but that doing so would be so perilous as to constitute a supererogatory act. Assume, for instance, that the two could make a pact to help each other, that half the time such help is completely efficacious, in the sense that both will live, but that half the time the rescuer will die in the course of saving the other person. Should the two be permitted to pool their chances in this case and thus to raise their individual post-agreement chances from one in six to three in twelve? Unlike Kamm's case, neither would be obliged, in the absence of an agreement, to try to save the other if his number were chosen, and neither would make such an effort at great risk to himself unless pooling were permitted by means of such agreements and unless he entered into one. If such agreements were banned or rendered nugatory by altering individuals' odds of rescue to offset them—in this case, by assigning each of the two a two-in-sixteen chance, and each of the isolated four a three-in-sixteen chance—then there would be a greater loss of life in the long run. And this result will probably strike most people as disquieting.

If, however, in the face of this intuitive uneasiness one recalls that lives do not possess objective value and that treating people as equals means looking at their plight from their several perspectives and giving each the same chance to emerge with his life, then this implication of Taurek's view should not, on reflection, be unsettling. What it does supply is a spur to create a convention or to facilitate a community-wide agreement that permits pooling in such cases because everyone's antecedent chances of survival would thereby be improved. Indeed, that thought, as I argue in section 12.4, should lead one to favor a policy of saving the greater number straightaway when groups differ in size. This hypothetical example does not, however, weaken Taurek's position in the absence of such a convention or agreement.

It warrants emphasis that a coin-toss is only morally imperative if no special duties or obligations supervene. If the person forced to choose were bound by a promise or some other obligation to save a particular individual or collection of persons, then his choice would not be morally indifferent. He might then be compelled to dispense with a coin-flip if strangers' lives were at stake, and perhaps even to set aside his personal concerns as well. Similarly, if the person controlling the scarce life-saving resource did not own it but acted, instead, as the owner's delegate, then he would be duty-bound to behave in accordance with whatever policy the owner specified. If he were a public official, for example, and if public policy forbade his giving precedence to friends and required him to save the larger number, then that is what he ought to do.[17]

12.2. OBJECTIONS TO THE CLAIM THAT NUMBERS DO NOT MATTER

Taurek's argument for the moral irrelevance of numbers and his advocacy of random choice between imperiled groups have not gone unchallenged. In this section I examine several objections to Taurek's view, none of which succeeds.

The first objection questions Taurek's reason for choosing randomly between two groups of unequal size when no special considerations are in play, rather than his claim that it is objectively no worse if some die in place of others, however unequal their numbers. It attacks his conception of fairness, rather than his view of the nature and limits of moral duty.

Taurek argues that if each member of the two groups apparently stands to lose the same amount by dying, and if one takes an equal interest in the well-being of each of them, then one ought to grant each person the same chance of survival. Hence, one should choose randomly from among competing groups, after assigning each group the same odds of prevailing. If the choice is between two sets of people, one might as well flip a coin.

But, the objection runs, why make the moment when the rescuer comes on the scene the critical moment, so far as chance is concerned? Is not a

---

[17] This is, in fact, the duty of most public officials whose job is to rescue people in danger, such as Coast Guard personnel, firefighters, and police officers. Military commanders are assigned a similar responsibility, as of course are public officials charged with instituting *preventive* life-saving measures, such as highway guardrails or lighting. The notable and curious exception are doctors dispensing publicly subsidized health services, who in most cases are not required or prodded to maximize the number of lives or quality-adjusted-life-years they save.

coin-flip a pointless re-run of the natural lottery that determined membership in the two groups? Might it even be an unfair method of choosing survivors, akin to forcing everyone to wager his life a second time, once the wheel has already been spun? Why not save the larger group without further ado?

These questions do not constitute a single objection to Taurek's recommendation, since they are unaccompanied by an alternative proposal from which they could be shown to flow. Perhaps they are best seen as requests for clarification. In any event, they ought not to embarrass someone who shares Taurek's view. The problem they pose is that of establishing that one chance event properly determines the allocation of benefits and losses while another does not. No doubt it would be objectionable if, once all the interested parties had agreed that a certain coin-flip would be decisive and the coin was flipped, someone came along and announced that he was nullifying the earlier result and flipping the coin again. Similarly, if those whose lives are in danger chose a procedure for selection beforehand and if the rescuer refused to abide by their decision, his action might be criticized. In both cases, he would be declaring people's agreements void—without right, if they were made fairly and responsibly —and defeating their legitimate expectations. But someone who flips a coin when those in peril did not enter into a prior agreement establishing a different rule of selection, or who does so justifiably unaware of any plan they devised, is not similarly culpable. Since Taurek assumes that the rescuer is not bound by any established rule of selection, the method of choice he recommends is indeed fair. It does not constitute a second spin of the wheel, because neither he nor, so far as he was reasonably aware, those in danger designated an earlier spin as the first spin.

Assuming, however, that the rescuer is reasonably ignorant of any agreement reached by those whom he might save and that he did not formerly announce that he would choose according to a certain criterion should this situation arise, does it matter morally what selection procedure he employs? Taurek may believe that it does not, for his casual defense of random selection is contingent on the rescuer's having equal concern for those facing death, and his language suggests that if equal sympathy is lacking, the rescuer may choose according to his predilections because no one has a right to be saved when lives are in competition. This conclusion, however, whether or not Taurek accepts it, is not implied by the thesis that the deaths of some people are not objectively worse than the deaths of others. And most people would reject it. In the absence of a contrary obligation, it does seem permissible to favor those for whom one has special affection or respect. But where the choice is between strangers, fairness mandates random selection. Allowing prejudices or petty preferences to determine who lives and who dies violates the rights of those discriminated against to equal regard from their fellow citizens in matters that are of cardinal importance to them but that do not concern their fellow citizens significantly. It denies their equality as moral subjects.

This contention, of course, is not immune to challenge. If a white man is not obliged to give blacks equal access to his private tennis court, one might ask, why is he obliged to grant them an equal chance of obtaining the use of his yacht or his medicine chest if the lives of whites are also jeopardized and he cannot help everyone? Such objections can be parried, I believe, by invoking the intuitively appealing thesis that one owes strict impartiality to others when their fundamental interests are at stake, but that the degree of impartiality one owes them diminishes when their concerns are less substantial and one's own welfare is more seriously affected. I shall not pursue this dispute here, however. The question now is whether a rescuer might just as well make his choice of the lucky group depend on a random event (such as a coin-flip) that takes place after the lines have been drawn and people are trying to outshout one another for assistance, as on some characteristic of the groups or their members, chosen in an unbiased manner, that depends on events antecedent to or concomitant with the formation of the two groups.

Provided that the latter characteristic is chosen arbitrarily and not because the rescuer has an unreasoned contempt for those who have or lack that characteristic through no fault of their own, and provided that members of the two groups bear equal responsibility for their predicament,[18] choosing survivors according to some attribute that they or the groups possess is unobjectionable. In fact, it is tantamount to tossing a

[18] When blame can be assigned unequally, the argument for equal treatment is considerably weakened. Suppose that the one person who needs the large dose of a drug to survive suffers from a liver ailment which, unlike the five who each need one-fifth as much, he knowingly aggravated through his excessive consumption of alcohol. Or suppose that six persons are trapped by a fire (five in one room, one in another), that there is only time to save the one or the five, and that the lone person's negligence caused the blaze. In cases such as these, random selection seems inappropriate: one ought to save the innocent first.

Although this point is not relevant to the choice of survivors, it may be worth noting that, even where moral blameworthiness is equal, there may be reasons for not selecting beneficiaries randomly. Suppose, for example, that retribution is not a legitimate aim of punishment, that all who attempt a particular crime are morally culpable to the same degree, whether or not they succeed, and that optimal deterrence can be achieved, given the costs of imprisonment (including forgone production by those in prison and those guarding them), by punishing a fraction of apprehended felons more severely than the rest. Assume, further, that unequal sentences are neither unjust nor unfair if citizens are apprised of the policy in advance and the maximum penalties are not unduly harsh (an assumption that may be false and that I shall not attempt to defend). Should recipients of the heavier sentences be chosen randomly from among those who attempted the crime? Perhaps not. Although their moral desert may be equal, it might be wiser to apply the sterner sanctions to those who tried and succeeded before applying them to those who tried and failed, on the supposition that, in general, successful felons pose a greater danger to society and their incarceration or execution is likely to prevent future crimes more effectively than the incarceration or execution of bunglers.

coin, either when the rescuer strides onto the scene or as he speeds to the debacle, knowing that he will only be able to assist one of the two groups. There is no difference between pairing groups with the two sides of a coin and flipping it to determine which group one will save and writing some characteristic that only one of the groups possesses on a slip of paper, writing its negation on the other side, and flipping it to choose the survivors. Any trait picked at random will provide a fair basis for selection.

Of course, there are reasons for flipping or spinning *something*, be it a roulette wheel, a coin, or some other object whose equal sides have been matched with the two groups, rather than deciding according to the first criterion that pops into one's head. First, there is the practical need for a simple system of selection. If the choice is to turn on some characteristic of a group or its members, then the rescuer must be able to ascertain which group scores highest on his chosen scale; if that characteristic is not readily apparent, then it may not be possible, or it may require too much time or energy, to glean the information necessary to apply the selected standard. If the standard refers, for example, to the percentage of cricket fans or left-handed women in two large groups, then it could not guide the rescuer's efforts unless he were able to learn a good deal about those who were desperately in need before he committed himself, and the acquisition of this information may not be possible or wise. Under the circumstances, a coin-flip or some criterion that can be applied easily would be better.

There is, however, a second, more important, reason for relying on some random event that is independent of one's preferences, such as a coin-flip, rather than on the impulsive choice of a criterion, if one is not bound by a settled policy of action. If one "randomly" seizes on some simple standard to determine who shall live, particularly if one has already glimpsed the people in peril, one may be influenced by an unconscious bias or tendency that unfairly lends members of one group a greater chance of survival than members of the other. Needless to say, if no hidden bias mars one's choice, then this method of picking the decisive characteristic is unimpeachable. It is just like picking the winner's name out of a drum. But if the characteristic is one that might reflect unjustifiable disdain for people of a certain kind, and if some other criterion comes to mind that cannot possibly suffer from this failing or if there is time to flip a coin, then it seems advisable to let the latter settle the matter. Better to play safe than risk unfairness. The equal regard we owe our fellow citizens when their paramount interests are at stake demands no less of us.

But consider the following objection. It is not the case that *any* characteristic, if chosen randomly, would serve as well as any other. Making survival depend on unalterable features of persons' identities or on their habits, preferences, or desires offends the fundamental axiom that people ought not to be disadvantaged in the distribution of rewards and benefits, special considerations apart, because of what they cannot help being or because their tastes or conceptions of the good are of one sort rather than another. Indeed, choice according to criteria of this kind, someone might claim, is akin to passing a law *ex post facto* or, what is at least equally odious, one that penalizes people for traits they cannot help having. For the essential feature of an *ex post facto* law is that it deprives a person of some good because of an action he performed at a time when he could not possibly have known that the action in question would work to his legal detriment. But precisely the same effect is achieved, it might be said, by any criterion for selection that makes survival depend upon some arbitrarily chosen characteristic of a group's members that it lay within their capacity to alter, such as the color of their socks. The same is true of any characteristic of a group, such as its having the most women or children, which, had the affected persons been informed of the criterion, could have influenced the actions they performed that led up to their membership in one or the other group. Those who face loss of life because some such criterion was adopted will naturally ask the rescuer (not without some exasperation), "Why didn't you tell me?" Similarly, a law that penalizes people for characteristics they cannot help having is repugnant because it gives them no chance to escape punishment through their voluntary behavior. But a criterion for selection that makes life and death hang on personal characteristics that lie beyond people's control, such as their sex, height, or ancestry, is equally unfair, someone might argue, even if the trait were chosen because it first occurred to the rescuer and not because he thought it a badge of inferiority. Those discriminated against by the criterion would rightly exclaim: "But I couldn't help it!" Hence, the objection concludes, if a criterion of either of these two types is used, those it condemns to death will die unfairly. One arbitrarily chosen criterion is *not* as good as any other.

This objection, however, is easily met, because the analogy it draws with unjust legislation collapses on closer inspection. What is objectionable about a law that disadvantages someone for actions he performed before it was enacted or for immutable personal attributes is that it deprives him of something to which he has a right without his having transgressed a rule that he knew or should have known and that he could have observed had he so willed. But the choice of survivors in accordance with randomly selected criteria that mention someone's intentional behavior at an earlier time or traits he cannot help having does not deny those who are left to perish of something to which they have a right while unfairly allowing others to keep what they should have received. When two groups are imperiled and one alone can be saved, the members of both only have a right, in the absence of a previously established contrary policy, that a fair method of selection be employed, not a right (which could never be honored in all cases) that they, and by implication everyone similarly situated, be saved. As I argued above, however, any criterion chosen at random is fair and serves as well as another; all are equivalent to making the toss of a coin decisive. The charge of unfairness is therefore mistaken.

Jonathan Glover has advanced a second objection to the claim that numbers are morally irrelevant in choosing survivors.[19] This claim has the consequence, Glover notes, that one ought always to save one life rather than none, if that can be done at small cost to oneself, but that if one can save either one life or two but not both, it is permissible to save the one. Hence, if A and B are stranded on separate rocks on Monday and one can save one of them, then one should do so. And if C alone is stranded on Tuesday, one ought to save him as well. But if C had been stranded with either A or B on Monday, one would not be blameworthy, if the foregoing claim is correct, if one passed up C and his partner for the lone individual. "This moderate view of the irrelevance of numbers," Glover says, "seems linked to the unacceptable view that saving lives consecutively is more worthwhile than saving lives simultaneously. (The alternative assumption is that the rightness of saving a life has nothing to do with any value placed on the life which is saved.)"[20] Although Glover does not argue against the alternative assumption directly, he clearly deems it erroneous.

The problem with Glover's argument is that one of these two assumptions is *not*, as he claims, a "necessary feature" of the claim that numbers lack moral relevance when saving lives. Certainly the claim that saving lives all at once is less worthwhile than saving the same number over time is outrageous. And the alternative claim that the rightness of saving a life has nothing to do with its "desirable outcome" or with "any value placed on the life which is saved" (Glover apparently thinks these two expressions synonymous) sounds faintly absurd. But those who share Taurek's view need not make either assumption. They might contend that one is obliged to save a life because it is desirable, at least from the point of view of the person one might save, to go on living, and because the value of continued life to that person outweighs one's right to remain immersed in one's less important affairs, thereby creating a duty of assistance. They can, however, simultaneously reject the notion that saving a life entails the preservation of a certain quantity of value capable of being added to the value of other states of affairs for purposes of normative appraisal. It therefore need not be true that the more lives one saves, whether concurrently or consecutively, the more good one does. Lives, they might contend, simply do not have the kind of objective value that bits of

[19] *See* Glover (1977), 208–9. Glover's objection is cast as a reply to Anscombe (1967) rather than Taurek. John Harris echoes Glover's objection in Harris (1980), 71–2.

[20] Glover (1977), 209. On page 208, Glover says that the "alternative assumption" is that "the rightness of saving a life has nothing to do with its desirable outcome."

machinery do, which makes it rational to salvage the most costly items when a number of pieces are jeopardized. Lives are only valuable to particular persons, often equally so. One who would display equal concern towards those persons must therefore grant them an equal chance of survival.

Brian Barry offers a third objection. In criticizing Anscombe's view that a doctor or boatowner may not be reproached if he uses his entire supply of a rare drug or his boat to save one person when he could have saved five others, because none of the five could claim that he had been wronged, Barry writes:

> Why should we not say, however, that it would be wrong to save fewer lives rather than more? It seems to me spurious to argue that the drug and the boat were not wasted: they were wasted in the sense that they were not used to the best advantage. Suppose the doctor treated one of the five patients with an adequate dose of the drug and poured the remaining four-fifths of it down the sink. If giving all the drug to one patient would have been all right, is there anything wrong with that? If so, why? In both cases one person is saved when five might have been. Or suppose that the man with the boat goes to the rocks with lots of people and takes off just one person picked at random. He is surely wasting life-saving space in the boat—as much as—but no more than—if he went to the rock on which just one person is stranded and rescued that person. The question "Who is wronged?" thus is irrelevant. We need not show that anyone is wronged before we can say that it would have been better to use the life-saving resource to save more lives.[21]

Barry's final point is well taken, and I shall return to it below. His main argument, however, need not trouble Anscombe or Taurek. For the charge of wastefulness only carries conviction if one presupposes what the latter deny, namely, that lives have an objective worth that allows their value to be summed in deciding whom to save. Once this assumption has been dropped, Barry's argument loses its sting. Nothing is wasted if the one who is stranded by himself is rescued instead of several others, because in either case something of incomparable worth—a life of unparalleled value to the person who leads it—is preserved. The boatowner *would* deserve rebuke if he declined to save a life at the cost of some small gain to himself or to someone he loves, because morality requires that we make small sacrifices if they would produce great gains for others.[22] And something *would* be wasted if the boatowner steered his craft to the more populous rock and hoisted but one person to safety, leaving the others to

---

[21] Barry (1979), 637.

[22] Although not pertinent to the present discussion, it does not follow that, if many people can individually make barely noticeable sacrifices that together produce a sizable gain for another person, then they are bound to do so. By contributing one dollar each, a million people could make the recipient much better off, but there is no reason why he, rather than one of the million, should benefit. If all were treated equally, then each person would give a million times and receive once, leaving everyone where they started.

face the rising tide. The boat still had plenty of room, and it would have cost the captain nothing to wait another minute while a few more people clambered aboard. Someone who believes that the moral value of lives is not morally comparable need not deny that if one state of affairs is Pareto-superior to another, then it is better in some objective sense. Somebody who can bring about the second at no more cost to himself than the first is morally culpable if he neglects to do so. But so long as one insists that people's lives have value chiefly insofar as they are prized by the individuals whose lives they are, and that it is not worse, in some cosmic sense, if a host of people perishes rather than a single individual not among that number, then Barry cannot urge his objection without begging the question.

Nevertheless, begging the question is not always a sin. At some point, most moral disputes end in the assertion of incompatible normative propositions, none of which can be defended by appealing to still more fundamental evaluative premises or imperatives. This might be such a point. As Barry notes, just because no one can claim that he has been wronged does not mean that no wrong has been done. Derek Parfit has argued forcefully, for example, that certain actions with disastrous consequences for the welfare of future generations cannot be condemned on the ground that they wrong particular persons, for those persons who lead impoverished lives as a result of them would not exist if they had not been performed.[23] The same is true of any action that both causes someone to come into being and causes him to have less desirable traits or capacities than someone else one might have caused to exist would have had. Moral arguments against conditioning children to conceive of themselves as superior or inferior to other classes of persons before their personalities have acquired some solidity (if there are any compelling ones, as opposed to arguments based solely on the agent's personal preferences), or arguments against creating a Brave New World of persons who are perfectly content with their lot but who attach no value to personal autonomy, beauty, or the advancement of man's understanding of himself and the world,[24] must apparently be founded on the badness or undesirability of the states of affairs they bring about rather than on whether people can sensibly complain about what was or was not done to them. Perhaps not saving the many is another example of an action that is wrong but that does not wrong specific individuals. Or, more likely, perhaps one can show that members of the larger group *do* have a right to assistance, or that, even if they lack such a right, they ought nevertheless to

---

[23] *See* Parfit (1982) and (1986), 854–62. Parfit's argument is criticized in Woodward (1986) and (1987), and in Hanser (1990).

[24] Glover discusses objections of this kind to particular types of genetic engineering and behavior control in Glover (1984), chs. 12 and 13.

receive precedence. In any event, the case for what Glover calls "the maximizing policy"—"other things being equal, we ought to intervene in a non-random way if the result will be a smaller loss of life"[25]—deserves to be heard.

12.3. SOME LEADING ARGUMENTS ON BEHALF OF THE MAXIMIZING POLICY

The first point often made by defenders of the maximizing policy is that it need not presuppose the inane view that the sufferings of several people amount to a greater sum of suffering than the suffering of any one of those people *because* the total amount is experienced by some super-person who partakes of the sufferings of the individual sufferers. Taurek might be suggesting (though he need not be) that the maximizing policy rests on this assumption when he refers to "our collective or total pain, whatever that is supposed to be," and says: "[S]uffering is not additive in this way. The discomfort of each of a large number of individuals experiencing a minor headache does not add up to anyone's experiencing a migraine."[26] As Parfit has remarked, however, "[t]hose who believe that suffering is 'additive' do not believe that many lesser pains might be the same as one greater pain. What they believe is that the lesser pains might together be as bad."[27] Just as it is worse if somebody suffers from headaches on two successive days rather than on only one, so too, proponents of the maximizing policy argue, it is worse if two people suffer from headaches rather than one, regardless of the identities of the individuals. Although this claim might be mistaken, it is certainly not incoherent.

A second point worth noting, before considering positive arguments for the maximizing policy, is that it is too facile to argue, as Anscombe and Taurek at times appear to do, that the physician or the boat's captain do no wrong if they save one rather than five because they violate no one's rights, and that they violate no one's rights because they own the scarce life-saving resource in question. Ownership can be hedged about with duties and restrictions, and people commonly lack complete freedom to do whatever they wish with their possessions. Not only can people be forced to sell their property if the public good demands, or to contribute their time and energy to collective projects if need is sufficiently great, as in the case of wartime conscription. It is a commonplace that the absence of legal prosecution does not entail that moral reprobation is inappropriate. Charity may be a

---

[25] Glover (1977), 206.

[26] Taurek (1977), 308–9. Taurek also says: "Five individuals each losing his life does not add up to anyone's experiencing a loss five times greater than the loss suffered by any one of the five." Ibid. 307.

[27] Parfit (1978), 293. *See also* Scheffler (1982*a*), ch. 5; Hart (1979), § III; Nagel (1975), 142–3.

duty if another person is in extreme want and a gift would not cost the donor dearly, even if the law does not command it. Further argument is needed to demonstrate that members of the larger group of potential victims do not have a parallel claim to the goods or labor of those who might save them; their clamorous protests cannot be silenced by glibly reminding them that they do not hold title to what they need to survive.

In addition to these negative points, advocates of the maximizing policy typically rely on three arguments in making their positive case. The first is a blunt appeal to intuition. Perhaps it is just barely excusable to choose randomly when it is one life versus five (though even this claim is doubtful). But suppose that there were not five but five hundred people who could be saved if the solitary man were left to perish. Is it reasonable to flip a coin when the numbers are so lopsided? If one only had time to dig free one of two groups of miners trapped by a cave-in, should one even hesitate if one could save twenty rather than two? Would it not be reprehensibly stupid to erect a highway barrier along some remote country road, where one motorist will die every twenty years without it, rather than along a heavily used urban freeway where a motorist will die every month in its absence? Examples of this kind, proponents of the maximizing policy submit, will convince most people that their view is correct. Certainly there is no denying that the intuitions on which they rely are widely shared.

The second argument frequently made is bottomed on the assertion that lives, or life-years, or the satisfaction of preferences, or the existence of some conscious state, has objective value susceptible to interpersonal addition. Because people have a duty to conserve or enhance the amount of objective value in the world so far as they are able, and because the maximizing policy achieves this purpose, the argument runs, it is incumbent on us to endorse it. Both Glover and Barry appear to embrace this consequentialist reasoning.[28]

An exhaustive account of this argument's shortcomings lies beyond the bounds of this chapter, indeed of this book. All that I can do here is

---

[28] John Sanders accepts it in part in Sanders (1988). Because each human life is valuable and because the value of lives can be summed, he contends, the number of lives at stake should influence life-saving decisions. Sanders does not fully accept Glover and Barry's view, however, because he believes that the relative losses *to* different people should also shape life-saving decisions. Sanders seems to think that the second factor dominates when the sizes of competing groups do not differ greatly, thus making a coin-flip appropriate, but that the first factor becomes increasingly important as the disparity in numbers grows, making choice according to number morally imperative when one group is much larger than another. I shall not assess the coherence of this compromise view, though it seems to rest on an odd and, to my mind, unattractive conception of moral value. Why the objective importance of lives, for example, should have no effect *at all* on an imperiled person's odds of being saved when the sizes of competing groups are roughly the same, but suddenly, once the divergence in size passes a certain point, becomes controlling, is one perplexing question Sanders does not discuss.

indicate some of its weaknesses, without probing them or considering defenses. The first problem is that this consequentialist view would (without ad hoc qualifications) produce counterintuitive results in a great many instances, even if it yields an intuitively satisfactory outcome in this particular case. If popular measures of objective value were used, for example, this view might mandate the human-capital approach to saving lives[29] or some close cousin, requiring that the productive, the young, or the naturally buoyant be saved before the rest, even if those further back in the queue are not responsible for their incapacity and have thus far led more impoverished lives than those ahead of them through no fault of their own. More generally, consequentialist reasoning of this kind is difficult to support without endorsing utilitarianism or some kindred moral theory, several of the principal failings of which have already been sketched. Its implementation would inevitably magnify the effects of unequal fortune, rather than mitigate them, as a just theory of social and individual duty would. This view also has the unappealing consequence, unless circumscribed by the incongruous recognition of agent-relative prerogatives or tempered by some theory that the relevant maximand will best be achieved by striving for something else, that someone ought to save the larger number even when he or his loved ones find themselves in the minority.

The other major problem with this approach is its implausibility as a grand theory of morality. The notion that individuals, born into the world with their own concerns and affections, are obliged to spend their days maximizing some abstract quantum appears utterly fantastical except as part of a particularly unattractive theological *Weltanschauung*. Moreover, even if consequentialism can be rendered palatable by requiring the maximization of objective value only when one's actions can prevent a substantial loss or cause a considerable gain and when one's personal concerns and affections are not significantly implicated, and even if this can

---

[29] The assumption that people can be assigned some sort of objective value apparently underlies the "human-capital" or "livelihood" approach to valuing lives when choosing between competing public policies. *See e.g.* Zeckhauser and Shepherd (1976). According to this approach, the value of a person's life is the discounted present value of his future production, or future production minus consumption. The unacceptability of this measure of value for purposes of social investment decisions is plain. As critics have noted (*see e.g.* Acton (1976)), the human-capital approach presupposes either that citizens are properly viewed as chattel of the state and that the state ought to invest in resources to save its human herd only to the extent that enhanced production exceeds the state's outlay, or that the proper objective of public policy is to maximize gross national product. Neither assumption has anything to commend it. For what is the state but the chattel themselves? And why vaunt the means to happiness over happiness itself?

In addition, the human-capital approach bids a government discriminate in favor of the young and well-salaried when dispensing life-saving resources, generally to the detriment, at present, of women, minorities, and the aged. This bias in favor of unearned privileges or of those who simply choose to labor at more lucrative occupations, if not the bias in favor of the young, hardly counts in its favor.

be done without incoherence, the view is open to the objection stated in section 12.1, that whatever objective value can be ascribed to the prevention of harm (if any can) cannot be summed morally, even if it does allow one morally to assess actions based on their effects on any *two* people.

The third argument for the maximizing policy rests on an alleged analogy between the choice of survivors and democratic decisionmaking in recurring political contexts. Just as people's personal preferences[30] should be given equal weight in choosing public policies that violate nobody's moral rights, it might be said, so their personal preferences for continued life should be given equal weight in deciding whom to save. If there would be something odd about flipping a coin to decide whether legislation should be guided by majority or minority preferences, would there not be something equally odd about tossing one when a majority of those whose lives are in jeopardy, each of whom deserves the same regard, clearly favors one action rather than another? Similarly, if people have a duty of fraternity to do what is best for their fellow citizens, weighing their wishes equally when the actions between which they are choosing are equally good from their own point of view, are they not bound, as Kamm suggests, to save the greater number?[31]

Despite its superficial allure, the argument pales on close inspection. For there exists a crucial difference between what equal respect entails with regard to the routine choice of public or personal actions that affect others significantly and what it implies in situations where the state or a citizen must choose between imperiled individuals. In selecting public policies over which opinion is split, the majority is given its way, but only on the assumption (at least on the normatively contestable conception of democracy I presuppose) that everyone will find himself in the majority on matters of importance to him as frequently as everyone else, or at least that

[30] See above, subsection 2.2.A; *see also* Dworkin (1977), 234 ff., 275 ff., 357–8; Dworkin (1985), 365–72.

[31] This politically inspired notion of equal treatment seems to explain Kamm's preference for assigning chances according to numbers over assigning each person the same chance of survival, as well as her preference for majority rule over the assignment of chances according to numbers. *See* Kamm (1985), 181, 187–8. She further claims that majority rule "seems to better express the equality of opposing individuals, and hence to be fairer" than assigning odds in proportion to numbers, because the latter "calls upon . . . some unequal factor outside of [individuals] (as in a coin toss)." *Ibid.* 187–8. To the extent that this additional argument is separable from Kamm's appeal to the notion of equal treatment implicit in democratic procedures, however, it is obviously question-begging. Whether a coin-toss is an "unequal factor" that fails to reflect "the equality of opposing individuals" transparently depends upon the conception of personal equality one deems normatively important. If one shares Taurek's conviction that the losses different people sustain when they die are equal and cannot be summed for purposes of moral deliberation and judgment, then one must disagree. Only a random choice in which each *person* is given the same chance to live faithfully mirrors people's equal moral status.

everyone will on balance benefit personally from majoritarian decision-making to approximately the same degree because many heads are often better than fewer. Were the majority always composed of the same people, who therefore profited disproportionately from collective projects, majority rule would be unjust. Likewise, if in choosing between actions that are equally attractive from his perspective someone bowed to the balance of preferences, and if the beneficiaries of his actions were always the same, then he might be criticized for *not* giving equal regard to the needs or desires of those of his fellows towards whom he had no special affection, assuming that the actions of others did not right the imbalance caused by his own: justice requires that all be advantaged to roughly the same degree over time. Hence, the distribution of benefits in accordance with the will of the majority is only justifiable insofar as it is a means to the more basic aim of delivering maximum equal benefits to all. The flaw in the analogy between majoritarian decisionmaking and the maximizing policy is therefore apparent, for choices between lives cannot possibly be viewed as links in a long chain of decisions from which all will profit equally. They involve the assignment of an indivisible benefit which, for many of those concerned, will occur only once. In such situations, as opposed to conflicts that recur, fairness demands that each person receive an equal chance of obtaining that benefit. There is therefore nothing odd about flipping a coin to decide which of two groups vying for survival will be saved, though there would be in allocating the advantages of most collective endeavors. On the contrary, a coin-flip is precisely that device that a just state, or a just person, would use to steer his actions.

So the third argument for the maximizing policy fails, along with the second. Yet the intuitions on which the first argument rests are difficult to surrender, even if one admits that it is not objectively worse if many people die than if a different, smaller group perishes and even if one concedes that no analogy holds between majority rule and a choice between different lots of lives. Moreover, many state officials are in fact bound, most would say rightly, to save as many lives as possible when not all can be rescued, if not for the reasons given, then because the citizenry has agreed, or would have agreed, to codify the maximizing policy. Would legislation to that effect, or action in conformity with the maximizing policy on the rationale that everyone would have agreed to it beforehand, really be unfair to those left to die without having been given any chance of survival? Might similar reasons oblige a private individual to adopt the maximizing policy as well, at least when his own interests are unaffected by his choice? Do numbers count after all, even if lives lack objective worth and people in peril deserve equal consideration?

12.4. A DEONTOLOGICAL DEFENSE OF THE MAXIMIZING POLICY

It is possible to reconcile our intuition that numbers matter with the claim that the world goes no worse if one group of people passes away than if another, different group meets its end. And in doing so we need not deny that somebody forced to choose between two sets of lives in the absence of a settled policy for selecting survivors fails to decide fairly if he saves the larger number straightaway, instead of choosing people randomly.

The reconciliation comes from construing the formation of an intention to act in a way that increases everyone's antecedent chance of survival as universally beneficial, even if the conditions that would call forth that action never happen to obtain. Regarding a conditional benefit as a present advantage is plainly reasonable: a prepaid insurance policy, for example, is not worthless simply because the recipient has no immediate claim to dividends. Thus, if by resolving to choose in accordance with the maximizing policy before one is actually faced with a choice between lives one confers a benefit on everyone by improving their odds of being saved should their lives be in jeopardy, and if one has a duty, however weak, to extend benefits to others if one can do so at negligible cost to oneself, then one ought to frame an intention to save the greater number when the lives of people about whom one does not especially care or towards whom one has no special obligations are at stake. To be sure, the present value of the benefit one thereby confers on others is minuscule, given the small likelihood that their lives will be in danger in circumstances where one will have to choose to save but one of two or more unequally sized groups of people. But since the provision of that benefit is costless, one ought nevertheless to form the intention to rescue more rather than fewer.

Having formed that intention, one should then save the greater number if one is actually confronted with such a choice. To pull back and flip a coin would be to nullify the benefits one meant and ought to confer, for antecedent benefits exist only to the extent that the resolution one formed guides one's actions at the appropriate time. To toss a coin would also be to act contrary to one's self-interest, to the (very slight) extent that one's own chance of survival is improved if others choose according to the maximizing policy and if one's refusal to do so weakens their resolve or reduces the number of other people who have a resolve to let the relative sizes of groups determine their choice when they must decide.

Choosing in accordance with the maximizing policy involves no unfairness, for everyone's antecedent chance of survival is increased equally by one's intention to save the larger group. And the stricture against nonrandom choice is met by making the crucial chance event governing choice the process leading to the formation of the two groups rather than the spin of a wheel, the toss of a coin, or the unbiased selection of some other criterion once groups are formed. If one neglected to adopt the maximizing policy before one was faced with a choice between groups of different size and one then decided to save the larger number, one's decision might be open to criticism (I shall return to this problem below) if one could not have decided to save the smaller number with equal probability, for members of the smaller group might then be denied an equal chance of survival. However, if one resolved to follow the maximizing policy in advance, the charge of unfairness would clearly be inappropriate, for the criterion of relative size embodies no unjustifiable disdain and does not result in anyone's having less chance of survival than someone else. Selection according to size is as fair as Taurek's suggested coin-flip.

This argument applies to both individuals and governments. The state has a duty to treat its citizens as equals and to advance their interests as far as possible for a given sum of money. Since the maximizing policy benefits everyone equally and since taxpayers do not shoulder unreasonable costs if public officials save as many lives as possible rather than toss a coin when faced with a choice between endangered groups, government officials should be enjoined to save the greater number, provided that members of the larger group are no more to blame for their plight than are members of the smaller group. Formal legislative approval of the policy appears unnecessary to render its adoption morally permissible or its implementation imperative, for it is obviously in everyone's self-interest that it be put into effect. But governments ought to enshrine it in law anyway, to discourage officials from deviating from it to the advantage of their friends or favorites and to induce citizens to make the policy their own.

For the reasons stated above, people in their private capacity ought to resolve to save the larger number too, at least when doing so would not entail betraying some special obligation or attachment. If one believes that citizens are obliged, albeit to a lesser extent than those who hold public office, to act in accordance with the just and fairly adopted policies of their government when doing so would cost them little or nothing, then their obligation to follow the maximizing rule might be stronger still.[32] In fact, if this belief is correct, and if the maximizing policy has been embraced officially, then it might be argued that even people who formed no intention to rescue the larger group before they were confronted with a choice between different numbers of lives ought to save the greater

[32] Whether citizens in fact have such an obligation is a difficult question. The government's adoption of affirmative action programs, for example, is not generally thought to oblige private employers to establish similar programs. Whether the analogy is sound, however, is questionable. Typically, the view that employers need not follow suit is twinned with the belief that affirmative action programs carry costs for employers in at least some instances, either because they reduce productivity or because they occasion dissatisfaction. No similar cost is associated with adopting the maximizing policy.

number, rather than toss a coin. For citizens, in this view, should follow the official course if it is morally permissible and carries little or no cost, and those in the smaller group would not be treated unfairly if rescuers did honor the government's rule, inasmuch as they had reason to expect that any rescuer who happened along would save a larger group before he saved a smaller one.

It is tempting to go one step further and argue that, even if neither an individual nor his government has adopted the maximizing policy before a choice between unequally sized groups arises, the person poised to make the rescue ought to save the larger group rather than select survivors at random because all of those endangered *would have agreed* to the maximizing rule before they found themselves in their unenviable predicament, had they been given a chance to do so. The fact that no agreement was struck because a suitable opportunity was lacking, that no maximizing convention has sprung up, and that the government neglected to instruct its officials to save as many lives as possible (and thereby to lay a similar charge on its citizens, if the argument mentioned in the preceding paragraph is correct), is irrelevant, it might be said, because unanimous hypothetical assent to a policy is as good as actual consent. Both bind with equal force. Indeed, in enacting the maximizing rule, the state would itself be relying on the presumption that everyone would agree to that rule. So what wrong is done to those left to die if a citizen or an official chooses survivors on that same rationale, even if no convention or agreement or official presumption of agreement arose or was made or was announced beforehand?

This is, I repeat, a tempting argument. The hypothetical agreement it contemplates is not one that takes place behind a thick veil of ignorance, which might commit its defenders to utilitarianism or some other objectionable moral theory, but one that denies people no knowledge save information about the future. It cannot be used to constrain people's freedom of choice or action, for it insists that their actual preferences—not those that they would have if they were more prudent, or less depraved, or unaware of their personal characteristics or beliefs—should determine how they are treated.

Making the proper procedure for selecting survivors turn on the preferences people have before they become aware of their later good or bad luck, moreover, yields an intuitively satisfying account—at least at first blush—of both governmental and individual obligations. Government officials and private citizens who have no interest in the welfare of those in peril would be expected to save the larger group unfailingly, since impartiality can be demanded of state officials in their public roles and since this policy would maximize people's antecedent chance of survival without requiring them to make sacrifices, in the event that the choice of survivors were theirs, that they would be unwilling to make.

Private rescuers who are themselves among the smaller group, or who are especially concerned about the survival of one or more of its members, would not be expected to save the larger group automatically at great cost to themselves or to people whose existence they value, because they would never have sincerely agreed to this condition, even though not doing so would slightly lessen their antecedent chance of survival. Rather, those with special interests would be permitted to give extra weight to their personal concerns in deciding which group to save, though presumably the permissibility of favoring one lot of persons because of one's special regard for someone who belongs to it would not be absolute, but would depend upon the importance of one's attachment to that person and on the difference in the size of the two groups. People would agree to make some sacrifices for the sake of improving their chance of being saved and the prospects of people about whom they care, but there are limits to what they could realistically promise to do. Because it would be unfair to hold some to a more exacting standard than others, the minimum level of sacrifice required would be set by the preferences or capacities of those least willing to let numbers override their personal interests when they are rescuers.[33]

Although this argument for attaching importance to the size of competing groups in the absence of a prior resolution to do so is forceful, and although its implications for personal and governmental choice are intuitively attractive, I hesitate to endorse it. Obligations can arise through actual consent or through participation in a conventional pattern of behavior from which one benefits, but not—or at least not ordinarily— through something as impalpable as hypothetical consent. If somebody proclaimed a $10 bet that he would pull an ace from a deck of cards, shuffled the cards, made his selection blindly, and then found an ace in his hand, he could not come to me and demand that I pay him $10 if I never agreed to bet, even though I would in fact have accepted his invitation if I had been asked and even though I was certain that he was not lying.

Nor does it seem that the instant case forms an exception to this rule, if exceptions in fact exist. Suppose that someone chanced upon two groups of vastly unequal size, only one of which he could save. Suppose that he spied a friend among the smaller party, so that saving the larger group would entail some sacrifice on his part. Finally, suppose that it is not objectively

[33] This conclusion is not inconsistent with my earlier claim that one ought generally to do one's duty, even if others neglect theirs, and that doing one's duty might in some circumstances entail doing more than what would have been one's proportionate share if others had acted morally. See above, Chapter 8, n. 37. The adoption of some version of the maximizing policy is only obligatory if the slight benefit it would confer on others significantly outweighs the cost to oneself and those one loves. The marginal decrease in the antecedent benefit to others of building in an exception for one's friends, however, would certainly not be so substantial by comparison with the cost of not doing so as to render such an exception morally forbidden. One therefore has no duty to apply the maximizing policy without regard to the identities of those whose lives are at stake.

worse that more die rather than fewer, and that no convention exists requiring rescuers to set friendship aside when the disparity in numbers is large, so that the rescuer could not be said to derive antecedent benefit from everyone's intention to respect such a convention and thus be bound to honor it himself, even if he never benefited from the convention by being saved instead of others when his life was in danger. In these circumstances, the rescuer does not appear obliged to let his friend perish, even if he would have preferred that such a convention were operative before he had to choose. He is not obliged to follow a rule that he and others would have chosen to govern their behavior if in fact no agreement occurred and others do not obey it. Actual agreements, whether explicit or tacit (in the form of acquiescence in a practice from which one profits), are morally decisive in this case; hypothetical ones, it appears, are not. Unlike governments, which have a duty to treat all citizens with equal concern and to maximize the number of lives saved insofar as that can be done without injustice or unfairness, private citizens are not generally thought to be morally bound to choose that policy from among those that are fair and just that would hypothetically attract the most enthusiasm.

Suppose, however, that the rescuer had no friends among the two groups and would as gladly rescue one as the other. Would he be treating members of the smaller group unfairly if he did not decide ahead of time to save the larger group but now saved them straightaway, arguing that members of the smaller group deserve no chance of survival because they would have endorsed the maximizing policy beforehand? Or would he wrong members of the larger group if he did the opposite and flipped a coin instead of allowing everyone's prior preference for the maximizing policy to determine who survives?

The answers to these questions seem to depend, as does the proper course in the previous hypothetical case, on the conventions that actually govern such choices in the rescuer's society. If virtually everyone saves the larger group when they have no strong personal interests in the survival of a member of the smaller group, and if it is generally expected that they will, then it seems that members of the smaller group would not be treated unfairly if someone with no settled policy of his own saved the larger group without flipping a coin first. They would only be getting the treatment that they had anticipated and of which they approved. Indeed, if the rescuer did flip a coin, he might merit criticism, if not for unfairness, then because he was obliged to respect a collectively advantageous convention from which he himself benefited antecedently.

If, however, there is no established policy, or if the rule is to choose a group at random rather than to save as many lives as possible, then it might seem unfair of the rescuer to pick the larger group if he has not formed an intention to do so prior to his confronting the choice. There would be nothing wrong with his adopting the maximizing policy before making a decision of this kind, even if the usual procedure were to toss a coin, since the maximizing policy violates no one's rights and since it is to everyone's antecedent advantage, whether or not they realize it. Indeed, for the reasons stated above, he has a duty to form that intention. But to resolve to save the larger number once the groups have been formed would, it seems, be unfair to members of the smaller group, who did not want or expect choice according to number and who in any case have a right to a decision that meets the test of randomness.

Of course, these subtle worries about what would be right or fair in the absence of a prior disposition to save the greater number or an official government policy to that end could be banished to the realm of idle speculation by resolving to act on it now, before we are called upon to choose. And that resolution is one each of us should make, at least with respect to situations where strangers are in distress. When the lives of those we love are at stake, we need not save the larger group or choose randomly if the preceding arguments are correct, for the world goes no worse, in any morally relevant sense, if the group that does not include our friends is left to die, and we cannot be expected to give everyone the small antecedent benefit that adoption of a strict maximizing policy affords when that would entail an offsetting sacrifice now and perhaps a considerable sacrifice later. If there is a convention in one's society according to which numbers always deserve some if not decisive weight, then one might possibly be obliged to take the difference in the sizes of the two groups into account even here because of the antecedent benefits one derived from the convention. In my estimation, however, the benefits of such a convention would likely be so trivial as to generate no such obligation if a convention of that kind existed, and they would probably be so small by comparison with the expected cost of the convention as to render its creation irrational. But as there is no convention of this type in our own society, the problem one would pose if it existed is of greater theoretical interest than it is of practical concern.[34]

---

[34] The preceding discussion is confined solely to choices between lives. Chapter 14 extends the reasoning underlying the maximizing policy to decisions whether to kill some people or nonhuman mammals in order to save others from death or lesser harms. But it could also be extended to other choices between groups of people where the possible harms confronting members of the various groups are less serious than death, whether those harms are the same or different either within or among groups.

13

The Relevance of Personal
Characteristics to Choices between Lives

SHOULD certain personal characteristics of individuals facing imminent death, such as their age or the size of their family, incline someone to save the life of one person rather than another if he cannot save both? If so, which characteristics ought to influence choices between lives, and under what circumstances? This chapter attempts to answer these questions. The next chapter then asks whether the results reached here and in Chapters 8 and 12 justify killing some people or animals to benefit others.

13.1. TROUBLESOME CASES

In determining whether various personal qualities are morally relevant to choices between lives, it helps to begin by listing the different types of case where life-saving decisions might be based on them. Too often the question which characteristics (if any) should guide selection is posed in the abstract, on the unspoken assumption, apparently, that all who dispense scarce life-saving resources are bound to judge according to the same criteria. Those seeking an answer discuss a particular situation in detail, and then conclude that the solution to that case should apply to all conceivable choices between lives. However, unless one is a rather unsophisticated consequentialist who believes that individuals, government officials, and voluntary associations ought everywhere and always to deliberate in exactly the same manner, there is no reason to start from this assumption. Instead, one should first examine concrete choices between imperiled individuals to ascertain whether the same moral responsibilities come to the fore every time such decisions must be made. A cursory review reveals important differences among possible cases.

Decisions between lives may be divided into two categories: those that doctors and public officials make fairly routinely in allocating medical resources; and those that arise unexpectedly in the context of what one might call emergencies. In the first and larger class of cases, the scarcity of life-saving resources may have one of two causes. Most often it results from people's prior decisions not to bring more of the necessary resources into being, because they deemed the expense of doing so prohibitive by comparison with the extra safety those precautions would yield. Examples include shortages of costly mechanical devices in hospitals, such as heart-lung machines; insufficient quantities of expensive drugs; and the limited availability of various health care facilities, such as burn treatment centers or mobile coronary units. In these cases, the necessary resources could have been made available, thereby obviating a choice between potential survivors; but given the price of protection, people preferred to gamble. Sometimes, however, the dearth of medical resources comes about naturally, rather than as the result of people's morally permissible decisions. The prime example is the shortage of spare organs for transplantation notwithstanding the mandatory harvesting of cadaver organs.

Choices between lives in emergencies form a diverse lot.[1] They range from those firefighters occasionally have to make when carrying people from burning buildings, to decisions soldiers confront in wartime, to the question of who should be given the last life preserver when, through chance or negligence, there are not enough to go around as the ship dips slowly beneath the waves. Sometimes these decisions must be taken by government officials, sometimes by those who are themselves endangered, sometimes by private individuals from a position of comparative safety. In a few cases, established conventions guide selection; in most others, no rule was agreed upon by those threatened with extinction before disaster struck, and custom fails to make choice any easier. At times, the scarcity of life-saving goods can be traced to decisions not to take all possible precautions because of the cost that added safety would entail, as when plasma and physicians are in short supply following the derailment of a passenger train, or when rescue workers are unable to reach all of the trapped miners before their strength and oxygen give out. In other instances, the shortage may more accurately be described as unintended and unavoidable, and may be attributed to chance or the machinations of others, as when choices between people arise in a war begun by another state's unjust aggression. To be sure, one might claim that even in this last group of cases, the difficulty emerges because of the conscious assumption of risk: surrender can often purchase freedom from choices between citizens' lives, if at the cost of other freedoms and property. But cases where life-saving resources are known to be inadequate to save everyone if an accident occurs and nothing is done to augment them differ significantly in the voluntariness with which risks are borne from cases where, despite

---

[1] It is, of course, sometimes impossible to take personal characteristics into account when deciding whom to save, even if it is desirable to do so, for the requisite information may be lacking or time may be too short to assess the rivals' merits. Imagine rescuers forced to decide immediately upon their arrival at the scene of disaster whom to pull from the icy water or whom to snatch from the approaching flames. But often enough is known about potential victims to enable decisionmakers to consider their personal characteristics if morality so requires.

every effort to ensure the survival of all in the event of calamity, the selection of beneficiaries from among a larger pool of potential survivors cannot be eschewed. Thus, the spectrum of cases in which choices between lives might be made on the basis of personal qualities is extremely wide.

Unhappily, most of the solutions that have been proposed to the problem of choosing between lives have all but ignored the diversity of situations in which the problem must be faced. And the majority of advocates have contented themselves with unelaborated assertions.[2] There is little choice but to build from scratch. Contrary to what is almost a stock assumption among commentators, I shall argue that the relevance of personal characteristics to choices between lives varies, depending upon who is choosing and why life-saving resources are in short supply. Of the two types of medical cases described above, choices necessitated by dint of previous decisions not to purchase quantities of the scarce goods sufficient to accommodate everyone who needs them to stay alive ought to be handled differently from choices rendered inevitable by unforeseeable natural scarcity. And the various emergency cases raise problems of their own. I discuss these topics respectively in the next three sections.

---

[2] For example, Beauchamp and Childress, in arguing for the random selection of survivors, reject the use of other criteria for choice because, they baldly assert, nonrandom criteria "seem arbitrarily selected and also tend to reduce persons to their socially-valued roles. Furthermore, they do not incorporate justice in the form of equality, equal access, and equal opportunity" as satisfactorily as an entirely random selection procedure does. Beauchamp and Childress (1979), 196. But they do not expand on any of these charges. Instead, they simply assume that the case for a queuing or lottery system has been proved.

Likewise, Katz recommends choosing by lot from among those patients who would maximize "the therapeutic utility of a scarce medical resource," because "there is no morally acceptable basis for making judgments of relative desert." Katz (1973), 403. He refrains, however, from stating how the "therapeutic utility" of scarce medical resources should be measured and what constitutes an "acceptable moral basis" for making judgments about anything. He also does not consider objections and alternatives to his view.

John Kilner, after setting forth his recommendations for allocating scarce medical resources with little normative defense, simply asserts in a footnote, without argument, that choices between eligible patients facing imminent death should be made by lottery. *See* Kilner (1990), 230 n.8.

Finally, Nicholas Rescher, in an influential article, sets forth five criteria for selection for creating a pool approximately 30–50% larger than the number eligible for therapy. His five criteria are: (1) the therapy's relative likelihood of success; (2) the length of time the patient can be expected to live if granted treatment; (3) the patient's family role; (4) his prospective contribution to society; and (5) the services he has already rendered to others. Once the members of this group have been identified, he says, beneficiaries should be chosen by lot. *See* Rescher (1969). His justification of these criteria, however, relies almost entirely on appeals to self-evidence and undefended notions of equity and social investment in human capital. Nor can Rescher reconcile successfully his invocation of criteria and his ultimate repudiation of them in the random selection of survivors from among those in the pool: if his five criteria are indeed justified, then one ought, I should think, to judge as best one can in accordance with them, not throw up one's hands at the end. Moreover, if patients accepted those criteria, as Rescher must assume, then it is hard to see why they would favor random selection at the final stage instead of doctors' conscientious attempt to choose in conformity with those criteria.

13.2. JUSTICE, MEDICAL INSURANCE, AND EXPENSIVE LIFE-SAVING RESOURCES

The most common and frequently debated choices between people's lives are made by doctors whose supplies of drugs or costly equipment are insufficient to meet expected demand. The bulk of the theories on offer apparently assume that these scarce resources are the property of hospitals or some public authority, that patients have no right to them, and that those who own them ought to choose recipients according to disparate moral criteria whose relevance is self-evident. These assumptions, however, are undefended and indefensible. Certainly situations do arise, most often in what I earlier labeled emergencies, where those who face death do not themselves own, or have moral or legal title to, the resources essential to their continued existence. If equality of fortune represents the ideal of justice, however, in a perfect world this would not be true of scarce medical resources whose quantity is limited by choice rather than natural circumstance.

Before turning to the implications of equality of fortune for the allocation of such resources, it seems helpful to trace the ramifications of the hypothetical insurance approach described in sections 4.2.B and 6.1. Although the two theories yield identical prescriptions in the case of adults and similar prescriptions in the case of minors, they arrive at their common destination via different paths, and treading each of those routes in turn may help one choose between the two theories.

A. The Hypothetical Insurance Approach

According to the hypothetical insurance approach, those who suffer from substantial bad brute luck against which they lacked an opportunity to insure deserve compensation equivalent to the benefits of the insurance policy they would have purchased if they had been able to do so and if they had had equal resources at their disposal with which to buy it. Where the opportunity to insure is present, people may use their just holdings either to buy insurance or not, as they choose; it is for them to decide how much to gamble with fortune. If luck proves unkind, then the dividends to which they are entitled depend upon the amount of insurance they elected to buy, the terms of which are primarily a function of the incidence of particular types of misfortune and the riskiness of their behavior.

With the exception of medical resources whose underabundance has natural rather than human causes, the implications of this theory for the availability of health care and the distribution of scarce goods are straightforward. Persons who suffered from congenital disabilities or from serious illness or accidents before they reached the age of responsibility, when the burden of buying health insurance fell on their shoulders, would be treated according to the terms of the health insurance policy they would presumably have bought if cognizant of the statistical chance of their suffering from these infirmities and injuries and of their probable effects on their lives, both with and without the corrective treatment that medical science could provide. Purchase of the same policy would be attributed to all, since individuation would be impossible when those whose hypothetical choices were considered lacked the mental capacity, experience, and settled desires to choose responsibly. Adults would be obliged to pay for this policy in return for the protection it afforded them while young, according to the hypothetical terms to which a representative individual would have agreed.[3]

Once somebody has attained the modicum of reason and experience necessary for him to make responsible decisions about his own health insurance, choosing a certain level of security at a certain cost is ideally his own affair, although in practice there may be good paternalistic reasons for requiring him to purchase a minimum amount of insurance. The rates individuals pay will depend upon seven factors: (1) the cost of various types of medical care; (2) the frequency of certain health problems and their correlation, if any, with different kinds of behavior; (3) the riskiness of a

---

[3] What those terms would have been is a difficult question. Two possibilities seem attractive. According to the first proposal, each person must, as an adult, pay back the premiums on his hypothetical policy, either out of his allotted share of resources when he comes of age or out of later earnings. Since each person received the same coverage, each owes the same amount. The second proposal takes over Dworkin's reasoning for the graduated benefits and taxes of his "underemployment" insurance. Those entering into a hypothetical insurance agreement, it might be claimed, would tie adults' premiums to their actual incomes, so that the rich, who can usually better afford insurance, would pay more for their previous protection than the poor.

Both views draw support from other elements of the insurance approach to bad brute luck, but for that very reason neither proposal seems entirely consonant with it. In defense of the first view, one might argue that if adults should have to pay for the health insurance coverage they receive, with no breaks for the poor or surcharges on the rich, then consistency seems to require that the same principle be applied to hypothetical health insurance policies. Yet bad health seems, at least initially, to be indistinguishable from other types of bad brute luck that afflict minors, and thus properly integrated with "underemployment" and handicap insurance to produce comprehensive graduated rates, as the second proposal recommends. Perhaps the strongest argument on behalf of the first view derives from the principle that the ignorance under which hypothetical insurance purchases are made should not be greater than necessary to preserve the fairness of those insurance decisions. It is impossible to safeguard fairness in the choice of insurance against not being able to earn a certain salary without depriving purchasers of knowledge of their earning power. But it is not necessary to withhold information about their future salaries from those buying catastrophic health insurance, except insofar as those salaries are dependent on the insurance they buy (and to that extent "underemployment" insurance would provide coverage). If this claim is correct, then graduated rates would never emerge, because those who would be harmed by their choice over flat rates would not assent to them. The chief problem with this argument is that it attributes individualized knowledge of their future salaries to minors, when such knowledge is an impossibility and, if it were possible, would probably result in different people insuring to *different* extents, whereas the hypothetical insurance approach insists on treating all minors alike.

person's actions; (4) his willingness to pay for various treatments, knowing the benefits they typically yield; (5) his aversion to risks of various kinds; (6) the cost of administering the insurance program, including the cost of monitoring behavior and resolving contested claims; and (7) the competitiveness of the insurance industry, along with the profits that insurance firms make. Those who run a greater risk of suffering some misfortune because they voluntarily engage in actions that are known to raise their chances of experiencing ill health or injury will, in a free market for insurance, face a higher schedule of rates because the prospect of their collecting on their insurance exceeds the mean. However, justice requires that no one pay higher premiums because his genetic inheritance, his childhood injuries (unless his parents are responsible and should assume liability for additional premiums occasioned by those injuries), or diseases for which he was not responsible or which he did not voluntarily run an abnormally great risk of contracting endow him with an unusually high likelihood of requiring treatment while an adult. No one should be penalized because he was the victim of bad brute luck against which he could not have protected himself. One of the tax credit, tax deduction, or subsidy plans described in section 4.1 could be used to prevent unjust discrimination in insurance rates.

Expensive live-saving technologies do not pose a special problem for this theory. As with cheaper treatments, availability is a matter of supply and demand. Those who are unwilling to pay the higher premiums necessary to gain access to expensive equipment or costly drugs simply do not receive them if their luck turns sour and they find themselves in need, unless of course they are able and willing to pay the full cost of the treatments (as opposed to that fraction of the cost represented by insurance premiums). Nor does this result seem unjust. If equality of resources prevails and the prices charged for essential goods are not extortionate,[4] then whatever distribution results from private exchanges is just, even if it entails that some will die who might have been saved were others more magnanimous. Life is, after all, an inherently risky business. Those who decide to trust to fortune, rather than incur the expense of insurance, must accept the consequences.

---

[4] The pricing problem is far too large to set out here, let alone resolve. It implicates the regulation of monopolies and the establishment of patents, both of which seem inevitable in a competitive, efficient health care industry, and the proper allocation of the costs of developing drugs, machines, and techniques that will benefit large numbers of people both now and in future times. (Future benefits or present externalities might ground an argument for some public subsidization of research and development, which the state might in turn recoup from indirect or future beneficiaries.) I simply take for granted here that morality sets a limit to what someone can charge for information, products, or services that are crucial to the continued well-being of others. Probably few would quarrel with this general principle, though disagreement would likely arise over its application in concrete cases.

The market would—and should—determine who among those similarly insured (or equally uninsured) would receive some scarce life-saving treatment if demand temporarily exceeded supply and all who qualified for treatment could not be given it. Whether various personal characteristics would be relevant to choices between lives would, on this theory, thus depend on whether people would choose to make them so. One can only speculate as to those qualities on which people would want the choice to turn.

Some conjectures are fairly certain. Several characteristics often cited as morally significant—such as a person's family role, the number of people who depend on him, his past services or potential contribution to the community, and his moral character—would doubtless play no part in such decisions, because it would not be in the interests of the overwhelming majority of persons to make such factors determinative. In a free insurance market, policies that attached importance to such attributes, even if only in the extremely rare event of a life-or-death conflict, would fail to attract those against whom they discriminated. The latter would flock to insurance companies that did not make such distinctions, isolating those who would benefit from ascribing importance to such attributes and leaving them with no advantage whatsoever. Hence, insurance companies would have no incentive to write such clauses into the policies they offered. In fact, to the extent that recruiting a large number of policy-holders meant higher profits for insurance companies and greater security for their customers, both insurance companies and policy-holders would have an incentive to omit such clauses.

Criteria for selection to which it would be in almost everyone's antecedent interest to assent would gain inclusion. For example, one could expect virtually unanimous agreement on a clause that forbade granting treatment, in the event of a shortage, to somebody with an extremely bad prognosis if treated. If someone competing for a life-saving treatment had but a paltry chance of recovery or was likely, if he survived, to lead a very restricted, painful, or otherwise miserable existence, then he would have to go to the end of the queue, since such a rule would improve all policy-holders' antecedent chances of leading long, worthwhile lives. Indeed, if the cost of treating such a person, even if he faced no competition for some scarce resource, added noticeably to the cost of insurance, it is unlikely that many people would opt for protection against such an eventuality.

Another example would be a clause denying priority, in the case of a tie, to the very elderly. Obviously this clause would run counter to the interests of those who are far advanced in years, but people would probably deem it prudent to agree to this clause when they were young at the price of being disadvantaged later, assuming that lifetime policies were available and popular. If policies normally ran for shorter periods of time, however, then it is unlikely that older policy-holders would assent to the clause unless they were granted a sufficient discount for doing so.

What would be done if there were a clash among persons who escaped exclusion by criteria like the foregoing? The natural solution, which the market would probably adopt, seems to be choice according to some random selection procedure, with each policy-holder having an equal chance of receiving treatment. Perhaps a policy of "first come, first treated" would be deemed sufficiently random to satisfy this condition, to the extent that it was feasible. If the immediate treatment of those in need increased their chances of recovery, it would apparently be in everyone's interest to favor it when an excessive number of patients did not present themselves for treatment simultaneously or there were no reason to believe that a rush of patients would soon occur.

One could also imagine insurance companies (or health maintenance organizations) offering a priority surcharge, which would guarantee preferential treatment to the purchaser if his life were at stake at the same time as someone else's and if both could not be saved—assuming, of course, that the other person had not himself paid the supplement, in which case random choice would again become necessary. It seems doubtful, however, that policies incorporating this feature would be popular unless the amount collected in supplemental payments were considerable enough to allow firms to lower appreciably the price of a policy that did not guarantee priority in the event of shortfalls. Otherwise, those who did not qualify for special consideration would turn for coverage to insurance companies that treated all their policy-holders equally, since they could thereby increase their chances of survival without paying higher premiums.

Another strategy that firms could try, though it would probably be too expensive to succeed if conflicts were rare, would be to offer all policy-holders who bought insurance over a particular range of services the same chance of obtaining them if those people were in need, but to buy extra machines, drugs, or needed services and to make them available to those who lost out in the first lottery for treatment if they purchased a second, supplemental policy beforehand. And of course policies that offered differential insurance rates would also be possible, enabling people to attune their policies to their aversion to risk. Uniformity need not prevail in a free insurance market. I suspect, however, that schemes that used the rule of "first come, first treated," that chose randomly in the case of a tie, and that varied only in their level of coverage would attract the most members.

One final point that deserves mention is that social worth or prospective contribution to society could become a criterion for selection even if no insurance policy mentioned it. If the public good required that one person be treated before others when a conflict occurred, and if the government is justified in abrogating contracts in order to promote the public interest, as it does when it drafts people to mount a successful war effort, then it would apparently be within its rights in requiring hospitals to give priority to certain people, whether or not they had purchased private insurance granting them precedence. The stock example is putting the national leader's health first in time of crisis. It is difficult, however, to imagine other cases involving the civilian population in peacetime where distinctions made on the basis of social worth would be tolerated by a free populace, let alone approved, apart perhaps from official discrimination against certain classes of criminals. A government that treated its citizens as equals could not favor anyone simply because more people cared for him than for somebody else or because his conception of the good was more widely shared. An individual could only be favored if he were so likely to make an important contribution to the personal welfare of many more people that he were rightly regarded as a public good and virtually everyone would have agreed beforehand that he ought not to be held to his own decisions regarding insurance and risky conduct. In effect, his insurance purchases would be subsidized, or provided as part of his compensation, because of the positive externalities that flowed from his work. Although subsidized health insurance is common in government service, it seems unlikely that citizens would tolerate it widely in the case of expensive coverage with respect to scarce life-saving resources.

B. Equality of Fortune

According to the hypothetical insurance approach, personal characteristics are relevant to choices between lives where a dearth of life-saving resources derives from people's actual or hypothetical decisions only if policy-holders so elect or, in the case of minors, if they would so have elected. Equality of fortune returns a different answer as an initial matter, although once autonomy is given its due the two theories' prescriptions are indistinguishable in the case of responsible adults, if not in the case of minors. Unless adults choose to waive its requirements in return for the greater autonomy that the purchase of catastrophic health insurance in a free market provides—as they may be presumed to do—justice requires that health plans supply a comparatively high minimum level of coverage and that, other things equal, they favor the younger of two persons widely separated in age if only one can be helped.

Recall that the cardinal principle underlying the theory is that people receive equal bundles of resources and that the effects of brute luck be spread around as equally as possible, so long as this can be done without imposing unreasonable hardships on the more fortunate. With regard to health care, this implies that minor ailments, which are fairly evenly distributed and which are in general so closely bound up with people's voluntary behavior that in many cases it is impossible to tease elements of brute luck apart from instances of option luck, do not warrant mandatory redistribution; people are free to deal with their smaller health problems as they choose, whether by joining an insurance scheme or by paying their expenses out of pocket. Major misfortunes, however, do call for compensation. Those who by chance are stricken with severely debilitating diseases or who by accident suffer terrible injuries or handicaps while behaving in ways that were not especially risky deserve medical treatment and other goods during and possibly after their convalescence at the expense of those who were spared these ills, in order to restore, so far as possible, the distribution of resources that prevailed prior to the onset of misfortune, so long as those who were lucky are not required to make unreasonably large contributions to help the less fortunate.

No doubt people will disagree about what constitutes an excessive or unreasonable demand on those who have always fared well. In Chapter 8, I suggested that the compulsory donation of a kidney or a cornea would probably not fall under this rubric. But the point is arguable, and differences in judgment might exist as to what financial contributions overstep the limit. There are problems, too, in determining how much the compensation to which someone would ordinarily be entitled ought to be reduced because of abnormally risky conduct on his part, leaving someone who chooses to take various chances with the option of settling for less compensation than the rest if his luck deserts him or of making up the difference through the purchase of private insurance. But the initial implications of equality of fortune for health care are clear. A certain amount of medical treatment and compensation is owed to those who suffer bad brute luck to a marked degree (and facing imminent death through disease or accident is an uncontroversial instance of exceptionally bad luck, at least when someone is young or middle-aged), with the possibility left open of buying additional health insurance above the minimum set by justice if one so chooses.

What relevance do personal qualities have to choices between lives? Here one must ask which personal features reflect uncompensated differences in the brute luck hitherto enjoyed by those whose lives are at stake. In a just society, where individual instances of exceptionally bad brute luck were dealt with as they arose, the only personal characteristic that would fit this description is age. Factors often thought morally relevant to choices between potential survivors, such as a virtuous character, someone's past or prospective work on behalf of the community, and the number of children or friends he has who would be adversely affected by his death, may be ignored, for they do not reflect uncompensated differences in the brute luck that came the potential survivor's way. They therefore have no bearing on the justice of treating one seriously ill or injured person rather than another. To be sure, someone's contribution to the community may constitute a good reason for giving him priority if his welfare were crucial to the common good; but that reason traces its ancestry to the consent of those who form a political unit, not to fundamental principles of justice.

This is not to say, of course, that from the standpoint of the community, people's obligations on the score of justice are unaffected by the aforementioned characteristics. For example, if the head of a large family is denied treatment, then the assistance owed to his survivors may greatly exceed that which justice would require of the community if he left behind a smaller family. The point is merely that choices between persons cannot rightly be based on these criteria.

One might dispute this claim by arguing that all of these factors are relevant under different labels, inasmuch as the bad luck that befalls family, friends, and fellow citizens through somebody's death ought to enter the balance in deciding whom to save.

But this counterargument fails for a variety of reasons. First, with the exception of his children, almost all those who would stand to lose most by someone's death are persons who associated with him voluntarily. Their loss might therefore be seen as primarily an instance of bad *option* luck, and thus as irrelevant to the justice of the choice between people's lives. Second, it is extremely difficult to gauge the effect of someone's death on others, especially since this calculation must be made over time and include effects on future as well as present persons. The indeterminacy involved in any estimate of this kind is reason for discounting the importance assigned to it. The fact that *young* children lose a parent—almost all of us lose our parents, so their death is not *ipso facto* an instance of bad brute luck—does not necessarily entail (though it frequently will) that they have suffered from bad brute luck. Widows or widowers often remarry, and not all parents provide ample emotional support or influence their children's development positively. In any event, the long-term differences will often be negligible—except in rare cases, such as the death of a national leader, to which special considerations might apply anyway—because financial compensation will be afforded the unlucky survivors. Third, and most important, the bad brute luck that might come to *others* through someone's death is no reason for saving *him* in preference to someone else. As Chapter 12 explains, numbers as such are not morally relevant to choices between lives. They become important in certain situations because it is in everyone's antecedent interest to make them so. But here it is obviously *not* in everyone's interest to make the welfare of people other than the potential victims relevant to choices between lives. That is why they would not figure in insurance policies if health care were a purely private affair.

They equally have no place in choosing survivors outside cases covered by private insurance.

The ages of those among whom choice is necessary, however, must be taken into account if a life-saving decision is to be just, assuming that the young do not gratuitously waive their right to preferential treatment when their lives are in competition with the lives of elderly persons. If one person has lived for considerably longer than another before both find themselves competing for the same scarce life-saving resource, and if neither was brought to this pass by engaging in especially risky behavior, through his own negligence, or by intentionally injuring himself, then the first has, in general, already been blessed with more good brute luck than the second. Justice may therefore require giving some preference to the latter so that the brute luck each receives over a lifetime may be more nearly equal. But the size of the gap between their ages is supremely important. If one person is 60 years of age, the other 20, and if both can be expected to live until 70 if treated, then there seems to be a clear case for choosing the 20-year-old. The older person is fortunate to have lived a fairly long life, and the younger person could not be said to be a great deal luckier if he were saved, since in the end the younger person with a life expectancy of another 50 years would probably live only ten years more than the older person, and those additional ten years would not fall in what most people think of as the prime of life.[5] If the gap is somewhat smaller, however (say, a 50-year-old versus a 30-year-old), then the case for giving preference to the younger person is decidedly weaker, especially if both have the same life expectancy of 75 years. While it is true that one has already had the good fortune to live several years longer (in this case, 20) and will, if saved, increase that difference still further (to 45), saving the other will not just even things out but will turn the tables and give *him* a hefty advantage (25 years). It is not obvious that justice mandates intervention to swing the pendulum of relative good brute luck from one pole to the other.[6] If the gap is tiny, of course, then justice has nothing whatever to say.

If the younger man could *not* expect to live as long as the older one, then

---

[5] This argument assumes that even if the view of personal identity advanced by Hume and ably defended by Derek Parfit is correct, psychological links between past and future selves are not so weak as to justify treating people as though their lifespans were less long than lifespans of the bodies that house them. To ignore or even to discount differences in age on the ground that personalities, convictions, and ambitions change over time would be highly counterintuitive.

[6] One alternative to choosing completely randomly when the gap in ages is small or moderate in size is to make potential recipients' chances an inverse function of that proportion of a normal life they have already lived. In theory this proposal might be attractive if people's lifespans were roughly equal, but in practice it might be unworkable, especially if potential recipients began to quibble over the assignment of odds, the calculations and selection procedure, and alleged differences in the past opportunities available to both. It may be best to settle for an approximately just result.

the argument for helping him is accordingly strengthened, so far as the equalization of brute ، luck is concerned. Some might think this an unattractive implication of the theory. Should not the number of years a person has remaining be an independent factor in choosing between lives?

Two replies are possible. First, if the younger person were expected to die soon or to live a short, miserable life if treated, then there would, as I argue below, be a strong presumption against helping him instead of the older man, since it would be in everyone's antecedent interest to adopt a policy that denied care, in case of conflict, to somebody with a poor prognosis. Second, there are forceful reasons for concentrating on years lived to the exclusion of years left if the two potential survivors are the same age or if the younger of the two would, if saved, not live as long as the older one already has, assuming that one rejects the utilitarian view that people are obliged to maximize the amount of happiness or the number of satisfied desires that decorate human history. Each person has but one life to live—a proposition no less profound for being tautologous. The time remaining to him, even if much less than the years to which another can look forward, is still likely to be a good deal more valuable to him than the latter's happiness. If this is so, and if each is faced with the loss of everything he has, then in choosing between them it seems proper to ask what course would be fair to each, in light of their responsibility for their predicaments and the luck that has already come their way, rather than to let one's decision be guided by the bounty the future promises them. If the choice were between two persons, both 30 years of age, one a human being and the other a member of some alien species who, if saved, would probably live several hundred more years, would one feel bound to pick the second?

Perhaps it is also worth mentioning that it is *time*, rather than past experiences, achievements, or happiness, that is crucial in this connection. What matters is that people receive roughly the same opportunities (if compensation for other instances of bad brute luck has already been paid); what they make of them is their own affair.[7]

How much weight should be given to differences in age and to life expectancy is a matter of judgment. While decisions in extreme cases (identical twins, an octogenarian versus a healthy teenager) are unproblematic, the large range of intermediate cases might provoke sharp disagreements. When opinion is fairly evenly divided, authorities should probably not allow differences in age to play a role in assigning scarce life-

---

[7] This statement is not entirely accurate, because compensation for bad brute luck cannot always completely cancel the misfortune somebody has suffered. Nevertheless, it would be impracticable to try to correct for these deficiencies further by giving more weight to victims of imperfectly compensable bad brute luck, given the difficulty of measurement and likely disagreements over weighting.

saving goods. The fact that medical problems are often closely tied to voluntary actions, both on individual occasions and over the longer term through habitual behavior, and that those forced to choose are generally unable to determine the extent of someone's responsibility for his plight, argue against permitting small or moderate differences in age to become determinative. Those who find even the slightest attention to age counterintuitive should recall that according to the theory of equality of fortune, adults may alter the terms of compensation if they so desire, and that if the choice were theirs, they would almost certainly vote, when young or middle-aged, to discriminate against the elderly if every imperiled person could not be saved. Exactly the same result, as we saw, would be reached on the insurance approach described in subsection A. So the two theories arrive at the same place in the case of adults, though equality of fortune takes a longer route to that end.

By parallel reasoning, equality of fortune would allow people to agree to deny treatment to someone who is much less likely to benefit from care, either because his chances of recovery are meager or because, should he survive, the likelihood of his leading an extremely impoverished existence is high. Since it would be in everyone's antecedent interest to give precedence to those with much more favorable prognoses, equality of fortune would in practice return the right verdict. It would also do so in every other case where a criterion for choice would find a place in all insurance policies because it would be prudent for everyone to assent to its inclusion.

Indeed, because equality of fortune accords ample scope to personal autonomy, it would dictate a free market in insurance for adults, as section 4.1 explains. Thus, it would arrive at the same result as the first proposal. Adults' chances of receiving care would be left to the market, with the consequence that a policy of "first come, first treated" would be adopted, at least within each health maintenance organization or insurance group if no centralized plan emerged. If more people than could be accommodated appeared simultaneously for treatment, then recipients would be chosen randomly from among those who, through their insurance policies, qualified for a treatment that could not be given to all, except if their prognoses were singularly poor, if they were quite aged when younger persons also qualified, or if some other restriction were written into their policies. Both theories would also allow people to buy extra private insurance against the possibility of their not being chosen, and both acknowledge the right of the government to override existing arrangements in dire circumstances. The sole difference between the theories concerns their treatment of minors. Under the theory of equality of fortune, minors would be entitled to whatever compensation was necessary to place them on an equal footing with their peers, provided that excessive sacrifices were not demanded of those spared major health problems, and everyone would be required, without exception, to contribute equally to its provision. The hypothetical insurance approach, by contrast, might provide less comprehensive care. As before, this seems a point in equality of fortune's favor.

13.3. JUSTICE AND THE ALLOCATION OF CADAVER ORGANS

The second type of medical situation in which choices between lives are necessary and can be made on the basis of personal characteristics arises when a shortage of life-saving goods results not from people's decisions to invest in fewer resources than are needed to save everyone but from natural scarcity. The outstanding example is the choice between potential recipients of an organ available for transplantation when artificial substitutes do not exist or do not perform as well as living organs.[8] Such a choice might arise, of course, even if the supply of cadaver organs were usually sufficient to meet existing needs and even if the arguments of Chapter 8 are correct. It might be necessary to choose between minors' lives if a rare shortfall occurred, for example. And choices might also be necessary between adults in the case of organs that cannot be taken from living donors without killing them, since voluntary organ transfer schemes would not arise with respect to those organs. In addition, through happenstance more persons might require transplants than could be supplied, especially if a freak accident injured large numbers of people or if hospital facilities were limited, tissue-typing were a problem, cadaver organs could not be stockpiled for long periods of time to cope with sudden increases in demand, and, in the case of kidneys, no system for selecting unwilling donors had been established because the supply of cadaver organs was almost always adequate and too few renal dialysis machines were available to keep alive all of the accident victims who needed one. Even in an ideal state, choices between potential recipients of cadaver organs might therefore be necessary because all could not be accommodated.

How should cadaver organs be allocated when demand exceeds supply? Two answers to this question seem compatible with the ideal of equality of fortune.

A. Random Selection

Under the first plan, cadaver organs would be collected by the state and

---

[8] Inadequate supplies of drugs, genetically engineered material, or animal or fetal tissue that cannot be synthesized or obtained in larger quantities, perhaps owing to government regulation, would also illustrate the problem.

regarded as common property which the deceased held in trust during his lifetime. They would then be assigned in such a way as to equalize the bad brute luck that potential recipients experienced, except to the extent that people would unanimously favor some modification of that criterion for assignment. Hence, those who bore some responsibility for their needy condition would find their chances of receiving an organ discounted in proportion to their fault or the riskiness of the conduct that resulted in their needy state (unless a simpler but less precise adjustment were administratively necessary). Similarly, the aged would be disadvantaged, as explained in the preceding section. And people with extremely gloomy prognoses would stand at the end of the line because it would be in everyone's antecedent self-interest to put them there. Once the odds had been modified in these ways, available organs would be allocated randomly.

B. Allocation by Auction

The second plan also starts from the assumption that scarce cadaver organs should be viewed as additions to the pool of resources to be divided equally once people's bad brute luck has been taken into account. But it departs from the first proposal in carrying the notion of an updated auction forward to the distribution of scarce cadaver organs and in claiming that cadaver organs should therefore be assigned to the highest bidders when they are allocated. On this interpretation of the theory of equality of fortune, those in need should be seen as having not an equal right to the one available organ, but as having an equal right to bid for it. Just as the purchase of other types of insurance against bad brute luck should be left to adults shopping in a free insurance market, so should protection against this rare misfortune, with victims of bad brute luck in childhood who are more likely to need transplants receiving a tax deduction or credit to help them buy insurance or an organ when in need. Those who pay the most walk away with their lives. This is in fact what happens in a just state when expensive medical treatments are needed that only some people can afford or which they had the foresight to insure against needing when others chose to gamble. There is no anomaly in following the same course with respect to human tissue.[9]

If this second approach is correct, then a distinction must be made between cases where the need for cadaver organs regularly outstrips availability and tissue-typing is a minor concern, so that the number of cadaver organs and the number of potential recipients in any given year can be predicted with a fair degree of certainty, and cases where conflicts

---

[9] I once again say nothing about possible paternalistic justifications for requirements that all citizens buy the same, or a minimum, amount of insurance.

among potential recipients seldom occur because the supply of cadaver organs is usually more than adequate to meet everyone's needs or because the difficulties involved in matching tissues and storing organs for transplantation are so formidable that seldom could more than one of those requiring a transplant benefit from an organ recently removed from someone who died.

(i) Predictable Shortages

Where demand normally exceeds supply[10] and where tissue-typing is not a significant problem, cadaver organs should, on this second formulation of the theory, be auctioned off among people in need. But because competition for such organs would be fierce and because even the winners would often be nearly bankrupt if they received an organ, people who might have need of an organ would pay firms in advance to bid on their behalf in the event that they do. Competition among these firms, assuming that time permitted an auction, would result in a fixed price per cadaver organ that reflected people's willingness to pay in advance for access to a scarce organ should they need one, and thus a concomitant price for an antecedent right to such an organ. The price of a particular right would depend upon people's odds of needing a transplant, the fraction of potential recipients who could be accommodated, and people's willingness to pay to reduce their chances of dying. Since it is unjust to penalize someone whose chances of needing a transplant are above average through no fault of his own, only those who engaged in risky behavior would have to pay more (after taxes) for an antecedent right to a cadaver organ, with the difference between the cost to them and the cost to an average person a function of the riskiness of their behavior; conversely, if someone reduced his chances of needing a transplant through his voluntary actions, then the cost of such an antecedent right to him would be lower.

If the government wished to mirror this market solution without requiring the time-consuming and unnecessary charade of an actual auction, it could do so by selling tickets which, if its predictions were correct, would guarantee each purchaser a transplant organ if he needed one, and charging buyers different prices for the tickets, depending upon how much their actions improved or worsened their odds of needing a transplant. The number of tickets sold would equal the number of organs that were expected to become available divided by an average purchaser's chance of needing one; the average price of a ticket would be a function of people's aversion to risk, their wealth, the perilousness of their behavior, and the number of tickets relative to the number of people in the relevant

---

[10] A regular shortfall should occur only rarely, if at all, if cadaver organs are harvested as a matter of course, as Chapter 8 advocates.

population. (Thus, if an average purchaser's chance of needing a particular type of organ were 1/1,000 and 1,000 such organs were available annually, then the government would sell 1,000,000 tickets. If the population were 5,000,000, then 1 in 5 people would be able to buy tickets eliminating a 1/1,000 chance of their dying that year for lack of a transplant, and the price would be set by the demand for such tickets under the stated conditions.) Tickets would go on sale at fixed intervals—every year or two, say—in order to give people as much scope for decision as possible. (People might want to buy tickets when they were young, but be more inclined to pass up the purchase once they had grown old.) Frequent sales would also allow the government to adjust the price charged to individuals whose conduct had become more or less dangerous since the preceding sale. In addition, they would permit the price to reflect changes in the size of the community, the number of cadaver organs available, medical technology (e.g. the development of artificial organs), and popular preferences. Tickets would of course be nontransferable, or only transferable under government supervision, since the price of a ticket would be tailored to an individual's behavior and personal qualities. The difference between the amount collected from the sale of tickets and the cost of the cadaver organ extraction program, which would probably be large, should apparently be viewed as an addition to the pool of resources available to all in the ongoing auction, and therefore divided equally among the population.[11]

This ideal solution to the first kind of problem could be put into practice forthwith if only adults needed the organs, perhaps with some refinements. (For example, if potential recipients with poor prognoses were denied transplants, the government could lower the price of tickets; because almost everyone would favor this amendment, it would probably be adopted.) These musings would furthermore be idle if only minors needed the specific cadaver organs in question (as might be true of organs belonging to small children), in which case their assignment would be made, in the event of conflict, according to whatever rule would be chosen if all minors knew their identities and their odds, on average, of needing a

---

[11] A market approach to allocating transplant organs is defended in Hansmann (1989), 79–83. Hansmann's proposal differs from the one outlined here primarily because Hansmann favors using the market to fix the supply of transplant organs as well as to distribute them. He would therefore leave both supply and distribution to health insurance companies, which would create a futures market in cadaver organs. Schwindt and Vining (1986) offer a similar proposal. Although these recommendations might well be superior to policies now implemented in the United States and Western Europe, I would not endorse them in an ideal world so far as the supply of organs is concerned. As Chapter 8 explains, equality of fortune rejects the notion that people have property rights in their organs that permit them to control the disposition of those organs after they have been removed from their bodies or after they are dead. Equality of fortune would also require some intervention in the market to compensate people who face an above-average risk of needing a transplant through no fault of their own.

transplant. (Presumably a lottery among all potential recipients who did not have bad prognoses would result.) But problems would arise when both adults and minors could use the cadaver organs that became available. If all minors must be treated alike, then the question becomes: are we to assume that all those who are under age and who could benefit from a transplant would have bought a ticket and charge them accordingly when they become adults? If we do, then it seems that we are being unfair to the many who would doubtless have gambled with fortune and not have bought a ticket, assuming that attitudes towards risk are distributed as haphazardly among the young as among adults. We would apparently be unfair to adults as well, since this suggestion would increase the prices they would have to pay for tickets by taking a certain number of organs off the market without reducing demand. So should we assume instead that *no* minors would have bought tickets? This too seems unfair, for many minors would surely have purchased tickets if attitudes towards risk were distributed equally among all age groups. It would condemn many minors in need of transplants to an unjust death, while lowering the price of tickets to adults and giving them an unfair advantage *vis-à-vis* the young.

There are at least two ways of resolving this problem. The first starts from the assumption that all minors must receive the same treatment, since one cannot assume that one child is more risk-averse than another, and asks whether it would or would not be rational for everyone to buy a ticket if they as adults would later have to pay for it. And it concludes that all minors *should* be regarded as having purchased tickets, both because such tickets would generally be an especially attractive buy for minors with many years ahead of them and because it assumes that the injustice of forcing someone to pay for a ticket he would not have bought is less than the injustice of denying tickets to all persons who are under age and thus of consigning some of them to death unjustly. Hence, all minors who could use cadaver organs from which adults might benefit instead would receive them if they were in need, which would in effect guarantee everyone a full set of organs at 18 or 21 years of age if there were enough organs for all minors who needed them. Adults' chances of buying an antecedent right to an organ would be limited to whatever quantity was left over once all of the needy minors had been accommodated.

This solution, however, suffers from two apparent shortcomings. The first is that it would entail providing transplants to minors whose prognoses were dismal at the cost of denying them to adults whose prognoses were excellent. This result seems counterintuitive, both in its own right and because, if the competition for organs were confined exclusively to either minors or adults, those with poor prognoses would almost certainly be excluded, since it would be in everyone's antecedent self-interest to adopt this restriction. Its second apparent failing is that it seems unfair, because it would accord minors more protection against certain species of bad brute luck than adults would receive, even though there is nothing in the theory of equality of fortune that could justify preferential treatment for minors unless the age gap were large.

The second possible solution tries to mend these flaws. It points out that both difficulties arise because of the initial supposition that minors must all be treated as having bought a ticket or as not having bought one. Why, it asks, should one make this assumption? Attitudes towards risk would presumably vary as much among the young as among their elders. One may therefore infer that minors, as a group, are as risk-averse as adults, as a group. (Or, if one thinks it proper to identify the inchoate selves that minors are with the selves that they will be when they come of age rather than with some average of the selves that they will be over the whole of their lifetimes, then one may infer that minors, as a group, are as risk-averse as *young* adults, as a group.) On the basis of this inference, one may conclude that minors, as a group, would have purchased the same number of tickets in proportion to the number of organs they needed as would adults (or young adults) as a group. Hence, the same percentage of minors in need of organs should qualify for transplants as the percentage of adults (or young adults) who would qualify for transplants if the population and the number of potential recipients remained the same but all minors were assumed to be adults (or young adults) and a sale of tickets were held. This in turn would entail that only a certain percentage of needy minors' lives would be saved, just as only a certain percentage of needy adults' (or young adults') lives would be saved; presumably survivors would be chosen at random from among the set of minors who required cadaver organs that adults could also use, since more exact information about their preferences would be unavailable and a market solution unworkable.

This result, the second solution's defenders would argue, is not unfair; on the contrary, it would erase the bias in favor of the young that marks the first solution, thereby allowing it to escape the second objection above. If, moreover, minors, as a group, were assigned fewer organs than they, as a group, could use, then they would have to allocate them according to whatever rule would be chosen if they knew only their statistical chance of needing an organ, and the fair and sensible rule to select, under these circumstances, is one that would discriminate against minors with poor prognoses but give everyone else an equal chance of receiving a transplant. Hence, the second solution would evade the first objection as well. It therefore seems superior to the first proposal, although its merit relative to that of the first, non-auction approach to the allocation of scarce cadaver organs is more debatable. If this solution is indeed correct, where demand exceeds supply and tissue-typing presents no great obstacle, cadaver organs that can be used by both minors and adults ought to be distributed among minors who are potential recipients on a random basis, once those with bad prognoses are excluded, and they ought to be allocated among adults who need them according to the ticket scheme sketched above, which also discriminates against those with poor prognoses, both groups receiving that percentage of the total number of cadaver organs equal to the percentage of the total number of potential recipients they contain.

(ii) Unpredictable Shortages

How should transplant organs be allocated in the more common case of organs whose supply does not predictably fall short of demand? If only one suitable recipient presents himself and the organ cannot be stored to help someone else, the decision is simple: he should be given the organ, and required to pay the cost of its extraction and transplantation, for which purpose his medical insurance should suffice (if he bought any). When a conflict does arise, however, the ticket scheme described above would obviously be inappropriate, for the unpredictability of these conflicts precludes the antecedent sale of a guaranteed right to an organ. But perhaps a related scheme could be inaugurated. One could imagine the government selling rights to preferential treatment in the event that a conflict occurs, perhaps of varying degrees of strength (so that a first-order right triumphs over no right at all, but a more expensive second-order right trumps a first-order right, and so on), and then assigning organs according to the rights people possess. If a tie resulted, then either a recipient could be chosen randomly from among those who had the same highest-order right, or the state could allow the tied right-holders to bid for the organ. Since it seems likely, however, that an overwhelming majority would favor random selection to an auction in case of a tie, and since if conflicts of this kind were very rare almost no one would buy more preferential treatment than the rest, random selection would probably become the rule in such cases. If it did, and if everyone favored a rule discriminating against potential recipients with little chance of a successful recovery if treated, then those with especially bad prognoses would, as in the first case, be denied equal consideration when not everyone could be saved. It might seem that this plan would yield counterintuitive results in the case of a conflict between someone with a poor prognosis who bought a preferential right and someone with fine prospects who did not, since it seems that the first should be given precedence. However, if the government only sold preferential rights which would be of use to holders when their chances of recovery were not abysmal, on the rationale that all purchasers and nonpurchasers would favor conditional rights of this kind, then an intuitively satisfactory outcome would emerge. (More likely, administrative expenses would compel the government to forgo the sale of preferential rights, and simply choose randomly from among those with fair prognoses.)

C. A Comparison of the Two Plans

At what points do the two plans described in this section—one appealing directly to considerations of justice, the other to an auction—diverge over the allocation of cadaver organs in insufficient supply? First, the non-auction plan would give priority to the younger of two persons separated widely in years, for reasons stated in section 13.2, whereas the second would not, unless some rationale could be found for refusing to sell tickets to older persons. Second, in cases where the demand for cadaver organs exceeded the supply by a predictable amount, the auction plan would yield a market solution to the problem of distribution where adults (though not children) are concerned, whereas the first proposal appears committed to random selection, unless of course all adults agreed to institute a ticket scheme of the sort described above. Since cases of this kind appear far less likely to arise than unpredictable conflicts if cadaver organs were extracted by the state as a matter of course, the most important practical difference between the two theories is the first, and this disagreement would only separate them in a small minority of the handful of conflicts that would likely occur. Their differing effects on the distribution of wealth and income would be trifling as well. Hence, the practical importance of choosing between these two competing interpretations of the ideal of equality of fortune is inconsiderable.

13.4. EMERGENCIES

The set of possible choices between lives in what I labeled emergencies is highly heterogeneous, as the examples of section 13.1 reveal. Nevertheless, the question whether personal characteristics, when they are known, should guide such choices can be answered quickly by reference to the arguments and distinctions of the last two sections.

First, it is necessary to distinguish cases where a rule of selection was understood to apply or was agreed upon beforehand by those in mortal peril from cases where none was. In cases of the first sort (e.g. on military campaigns, in mine cave-ins), the rule should obviously be decisive, as all those affected have given their consent. In cases of the second kind, further distinctions are necessary.

One might begin by distinguishing cases where medical authorities must decide who is to receive medical attention—after a train wreck, say—from all the rest. Here the choice of recipients should be governed by the terms of people's health plans, assuming that those terms are known or easily discoverable. If they are not, but if (as seems likely) most people purchased similar policies with respect to the types of treatment contemplated, then medical authorities should probably be guided by the presumption that everyone in need of assistance holds a policy incorporating those terms. If people's insurance policies differed significantly with regard to the life-saving treatments being considered, and if it were impossible to discover the type of policy a particular victim held, then recipients should probably be chosen randomly, unless potential recipients' prognoses or ages differed substantially. The same is true of nonmedical decisions taken in the absence of a rule that has been agreed upon beforehand, such as choices between the lives of those trapped in burning buildings or floundering in icy water.

It should be borne in mind as well that the relative sizes of groups of potential survivors are relevant to these choices, and that numbers are apt to provide a weightier reason for favoring some rather than others when triage is necessary than are various personal qualities. Whether numbers were decisive would turn, of course, on people's antecedent preferences concerning the rate of exchange between age, quality of life, and the size of competing groups.

The rule of decision would also depend on who must choose. If the rescuer were a state official or a private individual with no personal interest in the survival of any of those endangered, then he would be obliged to hew strictly to an impartial course. Selection would have to be random, unless prognoses or ages diverged markedly, since no ticket plan could be devised to cope with emergencies. However, if the rescuer were a private individual whose own life were at stake or who had to choose between the life of a friend or loved one and the lives of strangers, then it seems permissible for him to put his own loyalties and affections first. The obligation to behave impartially has limits.

14

Killing People or Animals to Benefit Others

Is it ever morally permissible to kill another human being or an animal in order to benefit oneself or somebody else? The last two chapters inquired whether the relative sizes of groups destined to die unless helped, or the personal characteristics of their members, are morally significant in deciding whom to save. I concluded that, barring explicit agreements or conventions to the contrary, and prescinding from the most important interests of private individuals forced to choose survivors, several factors—including numbers, likelihood of survival, culpability, probable quality of future life, age, and perhaps the public interest—might be morally relevant to choices between lives, at least when the differences between potential beneficiaries are in these respects considerable. The question this chapter addresses is whether these features of groups or persons license or even require the killing of some people or animals so that others may continue living or enjoy a more pleasant existence.

14.1. INTRODUCTORY REMARKS

Several distinctions and exclusions are necessary to lend manageable dimensions to this discussion. First, I shall consider only cases where killing deprives a creature possessing, or capable of possessing and having possessed,[1] sufficient self-awareness to be said to lose something by dying of what would have been a desirable existence had it continued to live. I assume without argument that self-awareness is a matter of degree, largely dependent upon a creature's capacity and propensity to link its past and future from its own perspective and to distinguish its actual state from possible states via memory, imagination, and desire. Below a certain point, the connections between the beliefs, desires, and experiences of a creature at different times from its own point of view are too tenuous to allow one to say that a self exists for whom death, as opposed to the suffering that often attends death, is an evil.[2] Drawing the line between creatures that are

[1] This disjunctive condition is designed to ensure that a human being or an animal that was self-conscious, but is now comatose or in a state of suspended animation, does not lose its right to life if it could be restored to a self-conscious state that it would prefer to nonexistence.
[2] For a detailed statement of many of the considerations that support this position, see Michael Tooley's masterful book *Abortion and Infanticide*, esp. ch. 5.

harmed by death in this sense and creatures that are not is difficult. Its placement depends upon the relevant behavioral and neurophysiological evidence, the interpretation of which has generated much disagreement, as well as the extent to which one is obliged to give a creature the benefit of the doubt in uncertain cases. In my judgment, all mammals belong above that line, except for very young infants and some older human beings and animals suffering from cognitive deficiencies.[3] But I recognize that others would divide the animal kingdom and the various stages of human development differently. In any case, I shall not discuss the slaughter of nonmammalian animals, human abortion, or infanticide. Because the creature, fetus, or infant killed cannot properly be said to suffer harm if its life is shortened, causing its death painlessly cannot be reprehensible, in my opinion, so long as others are not thereby aggrieved.[4]

Second, no attention shall be given to cases where the person killed freely consented to his death. Whether it is permissible or obligatory to take the life of someone who wills his death only because of the erroneous but unshakable conviction that it is morally incumbent upon him to die, and whether a person's consent is truly voluntary in a given case, are interesting and important questions. So, too, is the problem of justifying suicide or self-sacrifice in cases where a person's identity would change or his views concerning the prudence or propriety of his consenting to die would alter were he to remain alive.[5] But the answers to these questions lie outside the scope of this chapter. The following pages accordingly contain no mention of suicide, voluntary euthanasia, or situations where altruistic individuals ask to be killed so that others may live.

Third, I shall say nothing about killing in wartime or in the course of resisting a brutal or unjust regime. The killing of illicit aggressors, if necessary to stop them, seems usually to be permissible, although the vexing task of devising an acceptable theory of *jus ad bellum* for the contemporary world and of detailing the conditions under which political assassinations are justified is far too large to take up here. The formulation of a theory of *jus in bello*, with its problematic distinctions between

[3] Two defenders of animals' rights concur with this view. Both Singer and Regan believe that fowl and psychologically more primitive animals lack the self-consciousness necessary to give them a right to life; higher mammals, such as primates and cetaceans, easily pass the test, they contend, while doubts about whether other mammals meet the standard should be resolved in their favor, given the moral danger of setting the hurdle too high. *See* Singer (1979*a*), chs. 4 and 5; Singer (1979*b*), 153; Regan (1983).

[4] In making this assertion, I do not mean to suggest that popular methods of raising, trapping, or slaughtering nonmammalian animals are irreproachable. To the extent that those methods cause pain, they are morally objectionable, although in some cases those harms may be morally outweighed by benefits to others. Most modern poultry and fur "factories" merit disapproval under this standard. Nor should these cursory remarks be taken to condone unrestricted abortion or infanticide.

[5] *See* Buchanan (1988).

combatants and civilians, guilty and innocent, excessive and allowable uses of force, must also await another occasion. I share the common view that mutually beneficial conventions ought ordinarily to be respected where they exist and fostered where they do not; that the differential treatment of soldiers and civilians is among them, even in the modern age of "total" war; and that it is at times morally obligatory to run the risk of greater harm to oneself or one's countrymen in order to reduce the harm one inflicts on others, including iniquitous aggressors. But specifying when killing is permissible in wartime is too formidable an enterprise to carry out here. Nor shall I take up the issue of capital punishment. The sufficiency of retribution, reform, deterrence, and prevention as justifications, both theoretically and empirically, requires special treatment.

This chapter concentrates, instead, on the permissibility of killing innocents in peacetime who, at the time of their deaths, do not willingly offer their lives to benefit others. Beginning with the question whether it is morally permissible in a just society to kill innocent people, such as elderly hospital patients, to advance others' welfare, I shall defend a variant of Chapter 12's maximizing policy in the context of public law enforcement, but argue against its extension to most other domains. I shall then consider the justifiability of killing persons belonging to alien groups to help members of one's own society. This discussion includes a moral assessment of the slaughter of nonhuman mammals for therapeutic, educational, and nutritional purposes, as well as remarks on the exploitation of foreign peoples. I conclude with some reflections on the desirability of sending most of the world's carnivores the way of *Tyrannosaurus rex*.

14.2. PERMISSIBLE KILLING IN A JUST SOCIETY

Almost all members of our moral community would agree that it is wrong to cause serious physical injury or a significant, uncompensable loss of property to an innocent person for one's own profit or to prevent some trivial harm to oneself or others. The greater the prospective injury or loss to the innocent person, the more probable or considerable must be the harm to oneself or others to justify shifting the expected injury or loss to him. For many people and animals, death is the ultimate evil. If a creature possesses sufficient self-awareness to lose what it recognizes (or has recognized and may continue to recognize), however dimly, as *its* future by dying, and if its future is on balance a desirable one, then a powerful reason is necessary to justify imposing this overwhelming and irremediable loss upon it. In this sense, all creatures that can, from their perspective, be harmed by death enjoy a right to life.

Justifying these assertions by reference to more basic moral principles is for most of us neither necessary nor possible: they have the status of moral axioms. That normal human beings and, at least to a limited extent, higher animals have a right to life is self-evident. Not only is this principle intuitively appealing in the abstract, but it coheres with our convictions about the permissibility of killing in actual and hypothetical situations. Both consequentialist and deontological theories accept it without demur. The debate revolves around the strength, rather than the existence, of such creatures' right to life.[6]

Some declare that at least a human being's right to life is absolute, provided that he has not forfeited the protection due him by willfully endangering others. The nontrivial rights of one person may not be infringed to forestall violations of the rights of others, even if the latter are cumulatively more weighty in the sense that, if one had to choose between preventing someone else from violating the first or the second set of rights, one ought to block the second invasion. Robert Nozick is often cited as a spokesman for this uncompromising stance,[7] and Charles Fried seems to echo Nozick's denunciation of "rights consequentialism" when he says that he does not know how to answer the question whether he "would be willing to kill an innocent person to save the whole of humanity from excruciating suffering and death," although in the end Fried deems the slaughter of innocents permissible if necessary to hinder a truly "catastrophic"

---

[6] Philosophers who believe that moral rules, like legal rules, have their origin in actual agreements among members of a society and that their protections do not extend to nonmembers (*see e.g.* Mackie (1977); Harman (1977)), or who contend that moral principles can only be justified by demonstrating that there are compelling egoistic reasons for adopting them (*see e.g.* Narveson (1977); Gauthier (1986)), would not be so easily appeased. The former would require proof of existing conventions backed by sanctions, which should be simple to furnish in most cases involving the killing of human beings, if not of animals. The latter would demand some reason to think that concern for the welfare of *all* others and a strong disinclination to kill them or make them suffer are among the set of dispositions and attitudes the inculcation of which will lead, with a higher probability than any other set, to a flourishing life, given one's needs and desires and the dispositions and attitudes of the people with whom one lives. For some people, such as psychopaths, perhaps no such reason can be given. But there are sound egoistic reasons why most of us should develop a genuine respect for other people, even if it would not necessarily be prudent to include nonhuman mammals within our circle of moral concern. A fine account of those reasons is given in Kavka (1985); *see also* Singer (1979a), ch. 10; Mackie (1977), 193–5.

[7] It is difficult to say whether this characterization of Nozick's view is accurate. Nozick's blanket repudiation of a "utilitarianism of rights" in *Anarchy, State, and Utopia* suggests that all rights, even comparatively minor ones, are absolute. On this reading, Nozick's theory would forbid the infringement of some unimportant right, such as the right to freedom from slightly injurious assaults, even if necessary to foil someone else's murderous designs, unless perhaps compensation is later paid. This unyielding view is certainly unacceptable. Nozick's remarks on value and the foundations of ethics in *Philosophical Explanations*, however, point to a more flexible position. If the purpose of rights is to conserve value, and if the correct measure of value is organic unity, then it appears possible that transgressing someone's less cherished rights, if an inevitable consequence of curbing some terrible evil, might be necessary to increase the world's organic unity and thus be excused or justified by the resulting addition in value. Unfortunately, Nozick has not expounded his views in sufficient detail to enable one to say how he would resolve this issue.

outcome.[8] Roman Catholic moralists, approaching absolutism from the assailant's side, typically speak of the unconditional wrongness of killing rather than announce an inviolable right to life, although they too shun counterintuitive results by permitting killings that are not themselves willed as means or ends so long as they are the consequence of otherwise permissible actions and the evil done is not disproportionate to the good achieved.[9]

Most people, however, think that a person's right to life is weaker still. They would agree that, other things equal, it is wrong to thwart any creature's desires, however humble, and that frustrating someone's wish for continued existence is rarely defensible, but contend that a person's right to life may have to give way before other ends that people value and other rights they are bound to protect. The world need not hang by a thread before killing can be justified. If innocents must die in the course of capturing criminals or terrorists who, if left unapprehended, will spread fear and death to many more, then we must reconcile ourselves to shedding innocent blood. If political violence is necessary to preserve the lives or liberties of a large number of people and if some blameless persons will invariably be caught in the crossfire (the child chained to Hitler's wrist), then one ought not to shrink from making unwilling martyrs of them. If one obese explorer is caught in the entrance to a cave and the rest of the party can only save themselves from the rising floodwaters by blowing their chubby companion free with a stick of dynamite,[10] or if four men are adrift in a dinghy and all will starve unless one is killed to provide a meal for the other three,[11] then it is better that one die—even if he would otherwise survive the disaster—than the rest perish. It may even be right, some would claim, to hand over an innocent man to an angry mob to prevent several lynchings,[12] or to kill old, dying, or comatose patients in order to obtain transplant organs to save others. Though always strong, they submit, the right to life is not always supreme.

My own view is both more and less radical than the justification usually given for the prescriptions sketched in the preceding paragraph. I would reject as intuitively unappealing the utilitarian notion that one may, indeed should, weigh against one another the expected number, length, and quality of lives that will be lived if one pursues alternative courses of

[8] Fried (1978), 31.
[9] Defenders of the doctrine of double effect have displayed a wealth of ingenuity in reconciling the principle's prescriptions with the plain man's intuitions. *See e.g.* Geddes (1973) and Hanink (1975). The malleability of intentional descriptions provides fertile soil for disputes.
[10] See Foot (1967).
[11] See *Regina v. Dudley & Stephens*, [1884] 14 Q.B.D. 273. For an intriguing discussion of this problem, see Fuller (1949).
[12] *See* McCloskey (1957), 468–9; Smart and Williams (1973), 69–73.

action, and that one may or should kill if the morally relevant quanta can be maximized in that way. If one abstracts from the potential killer's personal concerns and applicable laws and conventions, and if one assumes that a possible innocent victim would lead a desirable life if spared, then the potential victim has a right to life that the welfare of all who might benefit from his death, however large their number, cannot override. The value of people's lives, as I argued in the last two chapters, does not admit of moral summation, and only certain pairwise comparisons justify favoring one over another. To that extent, I side with the absolutists. This admission, however, does not entail that it is always wrong to kill someone to help others. If the person slain loses little or nothing by dying, or if he earlier joined in a scheme that licenses some killings to maximize participants' chances of living long, fulfilling lives, then his murder would not be reprehensible if others thereby gained.

I shall explore the consequences for the permissibility of killing of Chapter 12's maximizing policy and Chapter 13's conclusions regarding insurance schemes and the quality of survivors' lives in the next two subsections respectively. Subsection C discusses the extent to which a threat to someone's own interests or the welfare of people about whom he cares excuses his killing innocent persons to remove or mitigate the peril. Needless to say, cases where killing is possible may and often will involve considerations examined in more than one subsection. Rarely, however, will the principles defended here conflict in practice; to the extent that they do, intuitive judgment alone can say where the balance lies in particular cases.

A. Killing to Reduce Total Deaths

The most common justification for taking innocent life is that killing is necessary to save yet more lives. However, two sets of cases must be distinguished. First, there are situations where killing is Pareto-optimal: unless somebody is killed, *both he and others* will perish. Bernard Williams's hypothetical case of a South American archaeologist forced to choose between watching Pedro's bullies murder twenty Indians and shooting one himself to obtain the release of the other nineteen falls into this category.[13] The propriety of killing in these situations appears plain, notwithstanding Williams's hesitation. The main problem these cases pose is that of selecting the victim fairly, particularly in circumstances where it is unclear whether killing is in fact essential to save lives. If all will surely die unless someone is killed, then the decisionmaker should choose the victim randomly if he is not among the class of those who might die, except to the extent that potential victims' culpability or expected quality of life differ

---

[13] *See* Smart and Williams (1973), 98–9.

significantly. (Whether potential victims are obliged to comply with fair procedures if they themselves must decide who will die is another question, which I consider in subsection C.)

But what if the death of all is not clearly inevitable? Suppose that some will not agree to draw straws because they doubt the necessity of killing—rescuers might soon find the survivors of the plane crash or a lifeboat's emaciated crew—or because they believe that others will die natural deaths before they do and before they are too weak to profit from their comrades' deaths. Should they be made unwilling participants in a survival lottery?

The answer, I think, is "No." The proper course, if their doubts or beliefs are reasonable,[14] is to exempt them from the lottery, unless perhaps, as I discuss in subsection C below, the decision must be made by those who are imperiled and morality cannot rightly demand consideration of others' rights and interests in truly desperate circumstances. No one can be forced to waive his right to refuse to risk or sacrifice his life where it is possible to identify those who will not waive and where their refusal would not be unfair to others (as would be the case, for instance, in the situation described in the preceding note, or perhaps if soldiers were needed to fight in a just war). To be sure, there is some danger that those opting out will become free riders. They might hope that the lottery's survivors will share their food, fuel, or whatever, with them, without their having had to run the risk of becoming the unwilling contributor. But that result should not be disconcerting. The survivors have no duty to succor the holdouts, even if their grisly bounty could easily support the nonparticipants as well. Those who decline to take their chances in the lottery perforce assume the risk that those who cast lots will show scant generosity later. If some of the survivors take pity on them, they are indeed fortunate; but they have no more claim to help than if the others had declined to play Russian roulette and decided to accept their fate passively.[15]

The second kind of case in which killing would maximize the number of

[14] If their doubts or beliefs are unreasonable, then allowing them to opt out would in *some* situations permit them to obtain an unfair benefit. If it were plain, for example, that one and only one member of the group need die, that the rest would be saved automatically if and only if a sacrificial victim offered himself, and that the victim must consent to being killed, either by participating in a lottery or volunteering straightaway (in order to rule out murder by one or more potential victims to save themselves), then no one could fairly refuse to run the same risk as the others of becoming the victim. Participation may rightly be made mandatory in such situations.

[15] Notice that a lottery is one means by which the weak or ailing can turn the tables on the more robust, or at least place them on an equal footing by inducing them to participate in the draw (assuming that the latter do not use their natural advantage to take by force what they are not entitled to take fairly). For a lottery among those likely to die natural deaths before the others (and thus to provide them with sustenance) could extend their life expectancies beyond that of the strongest and healthiest member of the imperiled group, denying him the edge he would have had if nature had been allowed to choose.

people left alive involves the murder of someone who would *not* die if no one were killed, in order to prevent the deaths of two or more other persons. Killing in such situations is reprehensible if, as I believe, people have a right to life, unless agreements or conventions one is bound to honor dictate a contrary result, or unless perhaps the killer can only thereby save himself or those he loves from grave danger he or they did not bring on themselves. That more will die rather than fewer is morally a matter of indifference. The universe is in no way diminished if three lives are snuffed out instead of two different lives. Each of those who dies loses everything he has, and it is impossible to sum those losses morally because there does not exist a single person who may suffer all of the threatened evils and who must choose between them. In the absence of collective assent to a maximizing rule, one would be no less blameless if one killed a lone individual to save a hundred others than if one slew the hundred to save the one.

As in the case of choosing to rescue one of two imperiled groups, however, the adoption of a maximizing policy could well be prudent, at least if its application were limited to certain situations. But given the importance of a person's right to life, participation in a maximizing scheme should remain strictly voluntary, unless allowing people to opt out of such a scheme would be impractical or impose an undue burden or risk on others. In peacetime, formal maximizing schemes would, with possible rare exceptions mentioned below, only find advocates in two very different contexts: the resistance of dangerous criminal activity, and compulsory organ donation and transplant. The two situations warrant separate scrutiny, since they present opposing paradigms of instances where mandatory and voluntary participation is desirable.

Authorizing public officials battling crime or terrorism to take innocent life if necessary to keep more innocent people alive may be justified in much the same way as Chapter 12's maximizing policy with respect to life-saving. Assuming that no one is more likely to be taken hostage or to find himself in close proximity to fugitive lawbreakers than any other, the adoption of a maximizing policy permitting the killing of innocent people would be fair to all and advance everyone's antecedent self-interest. General consent could be presumed, or approval could be sought at the polls (either through a referendum, or through the election of represent- atives who favored such a policy) if one deemed explicit assent essential to legitimize such a policy. Of course, in actuality some people would be more likely to fall before their protectors' bullets than others: an isolated rancher in Wyoming runs less of a risk than a worker at J.F.K. Airport. But in general those most likely to die unwitting victims are also those most likely to profit from the introduction of a maximizing scheme. Risks and rewards generally go hand in hand. And in this case, not only would it not be feasible to allow people who did not wish to participate to opt out, because they could not be readily identified when authorities were forced to respond quickly to a threat, but it would also be unfair to others. Those who opted out would ride free on the policy favored by the collectively prudent majority. Moreover, if their identities became known, as might easily occur if lists were circulated among policemen and other government employees, then terrorists or criminals seeking shields would only take nonparticipants as hostages. Nonparticipants could thus expose their fellow citizens to greater risks. (Opting out would probably not inflate their own risks, because criminals who took the trouble to select human armor by consulting lists of nonparticipants would probably handle their involuntary helpers gingerly—not only because dead hostages are worse than useless, but also because ill treatment would likely cause the number of nonparticipants to dwindle.) Mandatory participation in a maximizing scheme would alone be feasible and just.

Needless to say, such a scheme would need several safeguards. Because it would be dangerous and unsettling to vest all citizens with the right to kill whenever they firmly believed that they would thereby save more lives than they would take and that no alternative action could save more, the right to kill in accordance with the maximizing policy should be restricted to selected public servants, except in highly unusual circumstances.[16] Since law enforcement officials would be involved in virtually all of the cases where it might come into play, this condition would entail few costs. Regulations limiting the use of lethal force should be enacted and procedures should be established for taking and reviewing decisions likely to lead to the death of an innocent person, in order to minimize abuses and imprudent choices by public officials. Because the stakes are so high and because it may be difficult to ascertain whether, if one forgoes an opportunity to kill or capture a terrorist because innocents will probably die in the course of the raid, more will be slain by the hunted before one has a chance to kill or apprehend him than the difference between the number of innocents who can be expected to die if one makes one's bid now rather than later, such decisions should probably be made collectively if time permits and be subject to routine reassessment by a supervisory body.

A maximizing policy that allows the killing of innocents in fighting criminals or terrorists may therefore be justifiable, although there will rarely be cause to act on it in a just state. By contrast, a compulsory maximizing policy that permits the killing of one person so that his organs or the equipment that sustains him may be used to save two or more others has little to commend it. John Harris has argued that a mandatory survival

---

[16] I discuss a few such emergencies below at pp. 344–7.

lottery among terminal patients,[17] in which the loser would be killed and his heart, kidneys, lungs, and other valuable parts shared among the needy winners, would constitute a significant improvement over current practice. But his reasoning is elusive. Harris seems to think that if a plan of this kind would increase the average lifespan by, for example, reducing the number of decedents, then a just government should hasten to implement it. Thus, if it were possible to cure two people suffering from some fatal disease by giving them a potion made from the minced brain of a murder victim (the brains of people who died natural deaths just would not do), then no one could fault a plan to select victims at random whenever two people contracted this disease. Similarly, if it were possible to extract organs from living people and to recondition them, then unwilling donors should be rounded up and their organs wrenched from them, Harris says, to benefit more numerous recipients. No rational person, he seems to think, would shun participation. Hence, the state may rightly compel all to join in the lottery.[18]

Harris errs on several counts, however. Even if one assumes that a survival lottery would prolong people's life expectancies, which it would probably do only if the afflictions in question did not strike the elderly in disproportionate numbers or a persons' odds in the lottery worsened with age, fairness certainly does not require one. The order of natural death could generally be used to determine who became a donor and who a recipient if cadaver organs were in insufficient supply. No fresh lottery would be needed. If for some reason (there appears to be none in practice) only live donors would serve, they could be taken in the order in which their vital signs waned irreversibly. Why not let the Fates spin the wheel? The problem cannot be that if one let nature choose the victims, the number of lives saved would not be maximized because those on their deathbeds sometimes have fewer reusable organs than more virile patients. For if the person destined to die next only had three of the six transplantable organs (heart, lungs, pancreas, liver, two kidneys) on which life might depend, whereas another sick patient had four, nothing would be gained by killing the second patient and giving three of his organs to the first patient, leaving one for another recipient, rather than taking two organs from the first patient when he died and giving one organ to the second patient, also leaving one organ for a third person in need.

[17] *See* Harris (1980), 82. In Harris (1975), he argued that *all* potential donors, not only those with a short time to live, should be included in the survival lottery. Harris apparently altered his stance in response to objections that his more inclusive scheme would prove impractical, merely trade one group of survivors for another without enhancing the fairness of the choice, and possibly reduce the level of public health at the margin by preying primarily on the healthy to aid those whose condition was most dire. *See* Singer (1977*b*) (criticizing Harris's initial proposal).

[18] *See* Harris (1980), 82.

Of course, organs are not interchangeable, and one can imagine cases where the number of lives saved could only be maximized by departing from the natural order of death. Suppose, for example, that there were three terminal patients, one of whom had a bad heart and two of whom suffered from renal disease and needed one kidney each without having any kidneys to donate themselves. If one of the latter two patients passed away first, he could supply a heart for the first patient but offer no help to the other patient who needed a kidney, who would therefore die as well. But if the patient with the bad heart were killed for his kidneys, two patients could be kept alive instead of one.[19] In that event, however, there would be no *lottery* among the dying patients. A maximizing policy would be in effect and nature would select the victim. Add a second patient with heart disease but at least one healthy kidney and one can once again take donors as they die naturally: two will die no matter what the natural order of death.

But why not resort to a maximizing policy in situations like the one just described, even if one cannot plausibly say that the victims were chosen by lot? The answer is simply that a compulsory maximizing scheme is unnecessary, indeed unjust, when a voluntary scheme is workable and a person's decision to join or not join would not unfairly burden those who choose differently.[20] And here the feasibility of a voluntary arrangement is beyond doubt. There would be no difficulty identifying those who chose, either when healthy or when terminally ill, to allow doctors to kill participants in the scheme if necessary to maximize the number of lives saved. Nor would someone's decision not to participate allow him to become a free rider, as would someone who opted out of a maximizing scheme designed to lessen the number of lives lost to dangerous criminals. By refusing to participate, he would forgo all gain. Rendering participation voluntary would also not deprive anyone of something to which he was entitled. Conversely, mandatory participation would infringe the right to life of those who desired to not join and who were called upon to sacrifice. It would be akin to imposing a maximizing policy on those in need of scarce life-saving equipment or drugs after their allocation had been determined by people's prior choices with respect to health insurance. If the

[19] This example—apparently the only one where the order of death would matter—would be unrealistic in many affluent societies. People whose kidneys give out can usually be kept alive temporarily by hemodialysis. If they would not die if denied an *immediate* transplant, and if donated organs would eventually become available (as would be the case if cadaver donations were mandatory, or if the other policies defended in Chapter 8 were implemented), then the case described would not present a moral dilemma.

[20] Whether voluntary schemes would attract participants is a separate question. Optimism, inattention to potential occurrences that would almost certainly not take place in one's life, the expense, and fear that membership might reduce the quality of medical care one would receive could easily keep people from signing up. The voluntariness of the decision leading to membership might also become a subject of litigation.

distribution of resources is just, their rearrangement to save lives cannot be condoned.

In this instance, a paternalistic requirement that all subscribe would be particularly outrageous, inasmuch as participation would not be in everyone's antecedent self-interest, let alone equally so. People's chances of contracting various fatal illnesses or becoming accident victims are not independent of their free choices. Chain smokers and rock climbers understand the dangers they face. Because the risks to which they are subject turn partly on people's voluntary actions, forcing all to face the same odds of becoming an unwilling donor would be patently unfair to those who prudently kept their chances of organ failure low and who would not have agreed to become a member of a maximizing scheme on the same terms as less careful participants. The odds could, of course, be corrected. But the complexity, expense, and potential for error (both in calculating the odds and in monitoring behavior) that such corrections would entail would render the scheme less attractive, particularly to those who purposely ran the fewest risks and guarded their health most closely.

Even those who bear the same risks, moreover, might have different attitudes towards participation. Some people dying of heart disease might gladly gamble with the time remaining to them in exchange for some chance of receiving a transplant, while others might prefer to finish out their days and then sleep, rather than risk immediate death to win an indefinitely long but dreary reprieve. Some might also decline to join for religious or moral reasons, and there seems no good reason why, in a liberal state that does not favor certain conceptions of the good or certain religious dogmas over others, they should be dragooned into doing so. Mandatory participation by ailing patients or the population at large in an organ transplant scheme that minimized deaths would therefore be a violation of right, not its embodiment.

Before considering the moral significance of differences between the quality of potential victims' and beneficiaries' lives, it seems useful to highlight the ways in which this account diverges from Judith Jarvis Thomson's inviting approach to these issues.[21] Thomson starts from two assumptions, both of which seem correct. First, she assumes that if one could switch a runaway trolley that would otherwise run over five workmen onto another track, where only one person is at work, one may do so, thereby killing the one in order to save five others. Second, she assumes that a doctor may not kill a healthy patient in order to obtain organs to save the lives of five other patients. In order to reconcile these two assumptions, she argues, one must further assume that people have a right not to be killed, that this right cannot be overridden *simply* because doing so would lead to an increase in utility, but that *sometimes* this right can be

[21] *See* Thomson (1985).

transgressed if enhanced utility would result. The problem is delimiting the last set of cases in an intuitively plausible way. Thomson suggests that what distinguishes cases where a maximizing policy may permissibly be followed from cases where it may not is that cases of the former class involve a threat to the larger group that can be diverted to the smaller group without changing the nature of the threat.[22] Thus, the runaway trolley may be shunted onto a side track, because the threat it will then pose to the lone workman will be the same as the threat it now presents to the five. But a physician may not take the life of a healthy patient in order to save five other patients suffering from various life-threatening ailments.

Unfortunately, Thomson never explains why the invariant nature of the threat has moral import. Why should the fact that some lethal force can be deflected from a larger to a smaller group license killing, whereas the fact that one must extinguish the smaller group by some means other than that which threatens the larger group does not? Thomson embraces this principle because it yields what she considers attractive prescriptions in the cases she considers. But the principle itself seems bereft of support.

I suggest that the intuitive appeal of Thomson's principle has two sources. First, people would almost invariably find it in their antecedent self-interest to authorize one another to kill in emergency situations where lives can be saved merely by deflecting a pre-existing threat. This limited extension of the maximizing policy to situations where time does not permit public officials to be called in to decide whether or not to kill rests on the same ground as public officials' authorization to take innocent life if necessary to capture or kill dangerous criminals. In cases where someone would have to create some new danger to one or more people in order to save a larger group from a different threat, however, popular assent to extending the maximizing policy might not be forthcoming. Lack of trust in other people's judgment and doubt concerning their ability to implement their plans, coupled with the fact that members of the larger group may be endangered as a result of their voluntary actions or that mandatory schemes are unnecessary because voluntary ones are possible (as in the organ transplant case), might induce people to forbid one another from acting to save the larger number, unless perhaps the numbers were lopsided. Alternatively, a polity might permit citizens to kill in order to maximize the preservation of innocent life, provided that they are able to show after the fact that their actions were reasonably necessary to save the lives of more people who were not responsible for their plight than they cost. The Anglo-American common-law defense of "necessity" or "choice-of-evils" plays precisely this role in some jurisdictions when raised by someone charged with homicide.

The second reason Thomson's view is appealing is that virtually

[22] Thomson (1985), 1403, 1407.

everyone would agree that a physician may not murder one patient in no danger of dying in order to obtain the body parts essential to save five others. But one need not embrace Thomson's approach to accommodate this conviction. Because voluntary risk pools are possible, and because there is no sufficient reason for mandating participation, doctors lack license to kill one patient in order to rescue several others. The fact that the lethal force would differ in the case of the five patients suffering from disease and the healthy person who might be killed to save them, whereas it would remain the same in the trolley case, is not the only, or indeed the crucial, distinction between them.

Because the relevant question, in assessing the moral propriety of a possible action, is what conduct people have determined or would find to be in their antecedent self-interest, not whether the means of death would be invariant, the view I have advanced would sometimes dictate a result different from that specified by Thomson's principle. For example, if the person by the trolley tracks had his hand on a detonator rather than a switch, and if he could either blow up the passengerless trolley, killing one person at work near the dynamite charge, or let it run down the five workmen, then on my view it would almost certainly be permissible for the bystander to push the detonator if the five were not to blame for the trolley's trajectory. If, as seems likely, people have consented, either explicitly or implicitly, to bystanders' exploding trains in such circumstances—say, by licensing public officials to do so in identical situations, or by making a "choice-of-evils" defense available there—then the bystander may proceed without flipping a coin. Thomson's approach, however, would preclude use of the detonator while permitting use of the switch, because exploding the trolley would alter the means of death while diverting it onto another track would not. Her distinction has no basis in reason or intuition.

The two theories might diverge in another case Thomson describes— though whether or not they would depends on how the facts of the case are filled out. Thomson imagines a situation in which five immobile convalescents will be crushed by a ceiling about to give way, unless someone turns on some motor-powered support to keep the ceiling from collapsing. If someone turns on the machine, however, it will emit toxic fumes that will surely kill a sixth convalescent in the adjacent room.[23] Thomson thinks it obvious that hospital personnel may not use the machine, because doing so would kill the sixth person by a different means from that threatening the five.

I find this a harder case. Whether someone may switch on the machine seems to me to depend on his professional role and relationship to the convalescents, on how the situation came about, on what the patients' expectations were on entering their rooms and on entering the hospital, and on what his fellow citizens have expressly or tacitly authorized him to do in such an emergency. What the moral permissibility of turning on the machine does *not* depend on, however, is whether it would alter the cause of death. Suppose that the ceiling were about to fall because there was a heavy weight atop it, that one could not remove the weight, but that one could shift it to a spot above the sixth person's room, so that he would die instead. Thomson would apparently allow one to shift the weight, but not turn on the machine. It seems to me that the two cases should be approached in the same way, by making identical inquiries. Most likely there would emerge no moral difference between the two actions—which is, I think, what intuition tells us too.[24]

B. *Relative Quality of Victims' and Beneficiaries' Lives*

A second consideration often deemed relevant to the morality of killing is the value to the victim and others of the life he would have lived had he not been killed, by comparison with the benefits that others can have been expected to enjoy as a result of his death. Although this consideration should shape all decisions involving the loss of innocent life, it comes to the fore in three types of cases apt to arise in a just state in peacetime: the possible killing of a patient who is elderly or who has a poor prognosis to obtain an organ to save a patient who is significantly younger or whose chances of a fuller recovery are appreciably better; the possible murder of one person to supply benefits other than life, such as the satisfaction of revenge or freedom from the burden of caring for an ailing or incompetent relative; and the possible slaughter of animals for food, clothing, or health-related experimentation or training. The case of animals is discussed in section 14.4; the first two cases may be resolved in short order.

Under the theory of equality of fortune described in Chapter 13, whether various personal characteristics, such as a patient's prognosis, should determine who will be saved when resources are scarce depends upon the insurance arrangements into which people have voluntarily

---

[24] These examples could be multiplied. To provide yet another illustration: Thomson thinks it impermissible to kill one person at a villain's behest, even if he will kill five other people if one refuses to do his bidding, because the threat one would present to the one would differ from that which the villain presents to the five. Thomson (1985), 1413–14. Again, her resolution of this case based on the variation of the threat strikes me as misguided. If one were absolutely certain that the villain would do as he says (perhaps he has had himself hypnotized, or he has never lied in the past in numerous similar situations), then he seems analogous to a runaway trolley that can only be halted by exploding a charge that is certain to kill an innocent workman beside the track. And that case does not seem significantly different from the case of a bystander at the switch who is forced to choose between five and one. The difficult task is deciding how likely the villain is to make good his threat, and determining what one's fellow citizens have authorized one to do. One cannot avoid answering these questions by noting that death would come by different routes in the two cases.

entered. Large differences in age would justify saving the younger of two
potential beneficiaries, even in the absence of explicit assent to such a
policy. But people would almost certainly have sanctioned such a policy
when they were young had they been consulted, because it would have
advanced their antecedent self-interest. That policy is therefore essentially
voluntary as well.

As one moves from decisions about whom to save to decisions whether
to kill, the importance of consent becomes stronger still. At stake is not
only the allocation of privately owned resources in accordance with
contractual arrangements, or someone's comparative claim to assistance
based on the relatively good or bad brute luck he has enjoyed, but also a
person's right not to be seriously harmed to promote someone else's
interests. Under no circumstances may morality exact excessive sacrifices
of people, or countenance the imposition of severe, irremediable losses
upon them, except perhaps by those under extreme duress. Chapter 8
argued that the compulsory donation of a kidney might be justified in the
highly unlikely event that cadaver organs and voluntary donations could
not meet demand and a transplant was necessary to save a life, because the
loss of an organ would rarely force someone to alter his lifestyle radically
and because someone denied a donation would certainly die. Loss of life
itself, however, is an incomparably greater injury than loss of a kidney.
Quite apart from the practical difficulties that would attend the murder of
old or sickly people to keep younger or healthier ones alive, such as
determined resistance by the would-be victims and their friends, and quite
apart from the negative impact such a policy would have on the doctor–
patient relationship and on the well-being of elderly people who were
deterred from seeking medical care, killing people no longer in their prime
to harvest their organs would be unjustifiable unless they had consented to
bear the risk of being called in exchange for an earlier assurance of aid
should they have needed assistance. Given the considerable dependence of
need on willful conduct and the objections many would have to
participation, few would probably join.[25]

[25] Killing irreversibly comatose patients to save other patients is another matter. A policy
licensing the killing of those who have permanently lost their ratiocinative faculties and self-
awareness to keep others from death would be in everyone's antecedent self-interest, for the
gains to beneficiaries would be substantial whereas no injury would befall the donor, who, by
hypothesis, has already ceased to exist as a person whose life can go better or worse from his
perspective. A similar conclusion may arguably be drawn with respect to persons who, though
still conscious, are bereft of self-control and their cognitive capacities and who, if they were
able to reflect on their future with any clarity, would prefer the oblivion of death to continued
torment and degrading reliance on others. Perhaps the same should be said of fetuses that will
be born dead or that will almost certainly live only a short and painful life. *See* Note (1988),
"Death Unto Life: Anencephalic Infants as Organ Donors."

Determining when these conditions are satisfied in the case of conscious persons would
often be more difficult than ascertaining when the loss of higher brain functions is irreversible.
But such decisions, however difficult, should probably be made in the rare event that
sufficient cadaver organs were unavailable and none could be taken from irreversibly
comatose patients.

A fortiori killing one person to supply another with benefits less salient than life itself is morally intolerable unless the victim licensed his murder under conditions that promised no greater benefit to others than the good he surrendered. Describing a plan that meets this test and that might prove attractive to a reasonable person is nigh impossible. No one would authorize his enemies to slay him so that they might gloat over his destruction, or issue an invitation to the poor to kill him for cash. A parent might conceivably grant his children permission to take his life if he grew markedly senile, making him a burden on those he loved. But such authorizations would probably be issued infrequently and acted upon even less often.[26] In other cases where altruism might lead someone to lay down his life for others, suicide would usually be possible and killing therefore unnecessary. But in a just society it is hard to imagine situations in which such exchanges might arise.

C. *Killing under Duress*

In addition to the number and quality of lives that killing might save, the identity of the beneficiary is potentially relevant to the permissibility of taking innocent life. It is, I submit, excusable to kill an innocent person to prevent the death or serious injury of oneself or somebody one loves, even if it would be wrong for a disinterested third party to act similarly. If, as in Nozick's fanciful example,[27] one will be crushed by the falling body of someone who is likely to survive the plunge unless one disintegrates him with one's ray gun, or if one can only extricate oneself from the rubble of a toppled building where one will bleed to death before help arrives by dislodging a beam, the movement of which will cause cinder blocks to cascade on someone nearby who lies unconscious but unhurt, one may take an innocent life to save one's own. Similarly, it would be permissible for the trapped explorers in Foot's example[28] to blow to bits the rotund rambler blocking the sole exit from the cave once the floodwaters had risen so high that they could wait no longer for help, even if the fat man's head was outside the cave and he was in no danger of drowning in the lake forming at his feet. Whether the innocent person who would be killed himself poses a deadly threat, as a madman or child with live ammunition might, or whether the innocent person is merely a bystander who would inevitably perish if one saved oneself from mortal danger—say, by destroying a bomber aircraft containing a small child—is irrelevant. It is furthermore irrelevant how many innocent persons one would have to kill to save oneself or somebody one loves dearly if one is not to blame for the

---

[26] Authorizations of this kind may even be morally impermissible if the senile person is a self sufficiently distinct from his former self to render the former self's grant of authority a license to murder a *different* person.

[27] *See* Nozick (1974), 34–5.

[28] *See* Foot (1967).

necessity of making this choice, even though an unrelated third party might have a duty to choose differently and even to frustrate one's defensive action if he has the power to do so. Thus, it would be excusable to murder a blameless man, or several innocent people, at the behest of an underworld leader if one would be murdered or badly maimed if one refused and if one was in no way responsible for being in a position where one had to choose between those two evils.[29]

The reason for this divorce between the obligations of a person facing death and those of disinterested officials or individuals is not difficult to fathom. Although the state and its officials have an obligation not to favor one citizen over another except when a maximizing policy of the sort described in Chapter 12 and subsection A of this chapter is in force, one cannot demand that private individuals act with like neutrality when they or their friends are threatened with annihilation. Somebody faced with the

---

[29] I essentially agree with Phillip Montague's views on self-defense, as set forth in Montague (1983) and (1989). (Sanford Kadish adopts a similar, though less detailed, position in Kadish (1976).) Montague argues that would-be victims have a right to use whatever force is necessary to defend themselves against a deadly threat caused intentionally, recklessly, or negligently by an aggressor, assuming that no innocent persons would thereby be injured, and that it makes no difference how many culpable aggressors the would-be victim would have to slay to save himself. He further argues that disinterested third parties are duty-bound to kill such aggressors if they possess the power to do so. I have no quarrel with this position or Montague's defense of it.

I disagree, however, with Montague's handling of cases involving *innocent* persons, whether they themselves constitute a lethal threat, as in Nozick's falling body example, or whether they are bystanders who would unavoidably die if the would-be victim acted to save himself. Because neither the would-be victim nor the innocent aggressor or bystander is, by hypothesis, blameworthy, a third party forced to choose between them would not, as Montague recognizes, be obliged to save the would-be victim; indeed, if a maximizing policy applied here, if the innocent aggressors or bystanders outnumbered the would-be victims, and if personal relationships played no role in the decision, the third party would be morally constrained to save the innocent aggressors or bystanders.

I fail to see, however, why the would-be victim should be similarly constrained. Montague asserts that he would be (*see* Montague (1981), 212; Montague (1983), 31), but he does not explain why this should be so. If a would-be victim may defend himself against a single innocent aggressor by killing that aggressor without flipping a coin, as Montague concedes that he may, then I perceive no reason why adding to the number of innocent aggressors or bystanders should materially alter the would-be victim's moral duties. For the reasons stated in Chapter 12, numbers in themselves lack moral significance, and for the reasons stated in text, assent to a maximizing policy would not extend to the case of self-defense. Perhaps Montague thinks that all innocent persons have a right to life, that all innocent lives are equally valuable (while the lives of culpable individuals are, somewhat oddly, entirely devoid of value), and that we have a duty to conserve value by maximizing the number of innocent lives preserved, even if we must die to do so. If Montague holds this view, however, then he must explain why the would-be victim facing a single innocent threat or facing the prospect of killing a single innocent bystander need not choose randomly between his own life and the other person's life. He must further explain why it is not incumbent on someone who could save two or more lives by surrendering his vital organs to do so, and, derivatively, why a physician who could kill him to save the others may not do so. It is hard to see how Montague might respond to these objections if he holds the view I suggested. But it is equally hard to see how he might defend his position without recourse to that view.

loss of what he prizes most dearly cannot be expected to make an enormous sacrifice for the good of others about whom he cares but little. As an empirical matter, people will put their own welfare and that of their loved ones first when they are imperiled, notwithstanding the rights of others. And this empirical fact supports (if it does not require) a normative conclusion, for one cannot fairly demand more of someone than he can give, and one cannot fairly demand greater self-renunciation from some than one does from others. A rule bidding scrupulous respect for the rights of others at the cost of death or grave injury is one few would honor and none would agree to as part of a practicable moral code. Of course, those who yield too readily to threats, or who subject others to great risk of severe harm in order to avoid some minor injury, merit the strongest censure. But extreme duress may excuse the infringement of others' rights, provided that the endangered party is not responsible for his predicament.

If this last proviso is to be defended, however, the argument for this agent-relative permission cannot be bottomed entirely on the impossibility of general compliance with a more exacting account of moral duty. For the captain who carelessly rammed the sinking ship on an ice floe is no more likely to want or be able to pass up the last life jacket than is one of the innocent passengers. The argument must therefore rest, if this qualification seems worth maintaining, on a fundamental right to preserve one's life or the lives of people one loves at the cost of others' lives *except* when the person one would thereby save is responsible for the deadly threat. Because this qualification seems to me intuitively compelling, and because I am unable to think of any other moral principles that are inconsistent with it and that I am not prepared to abandon, I am inclined to support this qualification. Whatever Hobbes may have thought, the guilty felon who assaults the prison guard is morally in the wrong, just as the sailor who turns his knife on his shipmates after losing the lifeboat lottery deserves reprobation. It would be one thing if three of the four survivors at sea decided to kill the fourth without allowing him to draw a straw on the same terms as the rest; in that case, he would surely be within his rights in resisting. But if he agreed to a fair procedure for selecting a victim, then he cannot justly complain if he fails to beat the odds. Whether it would be efficacious to punish someone for refusing to abide by a fair result, and whether a penalty may justly be imposed even if it will not deter, are separate issues. It is worth noting that at least in situations where the survivors are almost certain to be taken into custody, a mandatory death sentence might well prevent unjust killings (unless the authorities were unable to ascertain what occurred owing to a conspiracy of lies or silence) and that monetary penalties might be justified as compensatory measures, even if such penalties were powerless to stay someone's hand.

The more difficult question is whether one must refrain from killing if the other people trapped in the cave, or starving amid the snowy wastes, or confined to the lost lifeboat, are unwilling to cast lots, perhaps because one will probably be the first to die naturally, or whether one even has to offer those who share one's plight an equal chance to emerge with their lives. As the *Titanic* sinks, must one flip a coin before wresting the last life jacket from an infirm fellow passenger? If one grabs the last life jacket first, must one offer to flip a coin if a jacketless passenger comes along later? Different people may have sharply opposing intuitions about how these questions should be answered. But if the principle enunciated above is correct, then all merit negative answers. If the peril is great, one need not accept death passively or give oneself no more chance of surviving than those who are similarly situated. Altruism or perfect impartiality may be noble, but both far exceed the moral minimum.

In fine, the only time that the killing of innocent people is permissible in a just society is: in nonmedical contexts, when necessary to save more or younger lives than are taken and when no one could rationally oppose a policy licensing such killings prior to its implementation; under extreme duress, when that is the sole way to save oneself or somebody one loves; and in order to obtain needed transplant organs from people who are irreversibly comatose or clinging to lives that they themselves would acknowledge are worse than pointless if they were able to assess their plight rationally.

14.3. KILLING OUTSIDERS

Do the moral rules that constrain killing in a just state also limit the killing of innocents by people who are not members of the same state or governed by the same conventions as the potential victim? This section and the next consider the moral propriety of killing in cases where the slaughter of outsiders, whether people or nonhuman animals, would benefit the killer or members of his community. Section 14.5 discusses the killing of some outsiders to benefit other outsiders.

Situations in which it might be profitable to kill people who do not belong to one's political or social community involve both distant future generations and weak contemporaries. For instance, it might be in our interests and in the interests of our children to build a large number of nuclear reactors to generate electricity, even though it was impossible to dispose of radioactive waste and even though the waste would almost certainly kill a great many people (more than we would consider acceptable if they had to be drawn from the existing population) through accidents or inadequate storage facilities during the hundred thousand years needed for it to decay into harmless substances. Or we might find it profitable to release toxic pollutants into the air or water in amounts that will eventually prove lethal to later generations; or to use products or processes that thin the ozone layer, eventually resulting in additional cases of cancer; or to destroy tropical forests, with the consequence that plant or animal species that might have yielded curative drugs are eradicated.[30] Similar opportunities might exist with respect to foreigners. In most cases, of course, the danger of retaliation and the advantages of establishing mutually beneficial conventions would restrain a potential aggressor's hand, just as concern for our posterity and fear of early accidents might prevent the hypothesized nuclear reactors from being built. But suppose that no promises have been given and that certain outsiders are unable to visit reprisals on their executioners. Is there any reason not to round them up to use as subjects in lethal experiments from which they will never benefit but which are essential to develop drugs to cure members of one's own community?[31] Why not simply slay them for their gold, as Cortés did? Or hunt them for food or fun?

Apart, perhaps, from the small minority of people who believe that duties and obligations are rooted exclusively in actual conventions and that morality can gain no foothold where reciprocal benefits are impossible,[32] all would probably agree that it is impermissible to kill or seriously injure an innocent person unless the infliction of that evil is necessary to prevent substantial harm to oneself or others about whom one is specially concerned, where that harm is neither merited, nor caused by the likely victim, nor justified by the fairness of a scheme for selecting victims in accordance with a policy to which one has consented. Killing or injuring someone for trivial ends is wrong, even if he is an outsider unable to strike back. Every person possesses a right to life in virtue of his self-awareness and his desire to continue living which, if not waived or forfeited, morally repels attempts on his life except by those who are themselves confronted by grave injury or death through no fault of their own, or who come to the aid of persons so threatened with whom they have special relationships.

But are membership in a community and the potential for beneficial

---

[30] More imaginative but less realistic examples are discussed in Routley and Routley (1978).

[31] The line between insiders and outsiders need not be drawn geographically. A community might decide not to count unwanted infants among its members, particularly if they suffered from severe mental or physical disabilities and were likely, over time, to strain the community's coffers. May they be used as research subjects, even if they possess a rudimentary self-consciousness, in much the same way as some have proposed—*see e.g.* Harris (1983)—cutting up unconscious, unwanted fetuses for tissue transplants?

[32] *See e.g.* Gauthier (1986), 285–7. Some who share this view might assent to the principle stated in text because they believe that the optimal set of dispositions almost invariably gives rise to sympathy for the downtrodden, whoever they might be, and because they think it impossible to hone one's sentiments so discriminately that a person's political or social affiliation alone causes one's concern to blink on or off.

relations entirely irrelevant to the decision whether to kill? Doubtless many people would think the claim of irrelevance absurd. The vast majority of European and American colonial settlers of the last two centuries, for example, would have thought nothing of trading the lives of a hundred aborigines for one of their own. And the appalling indifference of citizens of wealthy nations today to disease and starvation in poorer countries suggests that a person's geographic and cultural isolation entail huge differences in his moral entitlements. Where lives are at issue there is nothing wrong with playing favorites, the thought runs, even if unimportant objectives may never justify killing innocent outsiders.

This view strikes me as horribly misguided. The strength of a person's right to be left alive and uninjured seems completely independent of whether he shares more affiliations (apart from deep personal affection) with the person who might end his days than does the person who would profit from his death. To be sure, if the question is whom to save, rather than whether to kill, and if the imperiled foreigners do not show the same solicitude to members of one's own group as they do to their fellows, then one need not automatically save a larger group of foreigners over a smaller group of one's own countrymen. The rationale for acting in accordance with a maximizing policy is that it advances the interests of its adherents, and under these circumstances one's interests would not be served by treating everyone alike. Given that numbers are irrelevant, any fair procedure for choice will do; and given the outsiders' refusal to treat everyone the same, it would not be unfair for one to favor one's own, thereby aligning principle with self-interest. But killing some people to help others is another matter. Just as one may not kill a member of one's own community, in the absence of duress or the victim's consent to a maximizing policy of the sort described in the preceding section, so one may not kill an outsider to advance the aims of those who share the stamp on one's passport. A person's right to life turns solely on his past conduct (including his prior agreements) and his level of self-consciousness; where he chanced to be born or settle is irrelevant.

This point is difficult to argue convincingly, however, because it is so basic. In attempting to persuade, sometimes all one can do is describe a situation where principles diverge and hope that, when their consequences have been laid bare, the reader or listener will agree that the position one advocates possesses the greatest intuitive resonance. That pass has not been reached here, for there remains more to the argument than blunt appeals to intuition. Much could be said about rationality, self-interest, the history of morals, and the object or aims of morality (if indeed morality can truly be said to have a point), not to mention the significance that these theories or facts do or should have for how we order our lives. I shall not scratch those issues here, because they are too large to discuss fully or convincingly in a few pages. Instead, I offer a thought-experiment which I hope many people will find dispositive.

Consider the circumstances under which the case for exploiting defenseless outsiders may be strongest. A new form of chemotherapy might save thousands of lives. Tests must be performed on human beings, since computer modeling and preliminary tests on animals have been inconclusive. These initial human experiments, however, might well be fatal. They might also be fruitless. Those who might benefit from the new treatment can be expected to live another two or three years if nothing is done. They will probably die sooner if subjected to unsuccessful therapy. If it would be wrong—as I assume it would be—to perform the tests on members of one's own community without their consent, and if few volunteered, would it be permissible to experiment on outsiders who would not willingly participate but who could not offer effective resistance?

I cannot believe that it would be. If human test subjects were needed, there might be reason to select severely mentally retarded patients who might benefit from the new therapy, assuming that a person's right to life depends upon the degree to which he is self-conscious and that the wrongness of killing declines as the expected improvement in the beneficiary's life increases and the difference widens between the quality of the victim's and beneficiary's lives, the length of time they would have lived, and the number of years they have lived. But whether the difference between the loss to the victim and the gain to the beneficiary would be sufficiently large in this case to overcome the retarded person's right to life —and I am inclined to think that the difference would *not* suffice to justify using involuntary experimental subjects—there seems no sound moral justification for forcibly enlisting outsiders when members of one's own community refuse to step forward. An innocent's home or allegiance cannot strengthen or erode his right to life. It is equally inconsequential that other members of the outsiders' society, though probably not the hapless test subjects themselves, will benefit from the therapeutic advance if indeed one occurs, unless that fact would have induced the test subjects to consent. If an insufficient number of people think the possible cure worth the risk of an even earlier death, then the experiments ought not to be performed. If the free-rider problem prevents potential beneficiaries from choosing subjects from among the ranks of those who would volunteer for a lottery if everyone else went along, then that is simply an uncorrectable misfortune. People live and die as individuals, not as cells within an organism whose welfare transcends their own. Quite apart from the incidental benefits of a policy of voluntarism, such as greater caution and consideration on the part of researchers, the moral abomination of killing one person to extend a potential benefit to one or more persons whose lot does not differ from his own condemns the proposal. The citizenship of the victim cannot render bad means to a good end legitimate.

14.4. KILLING ANIMALS FOR HUMAN GAIN

The argument of the preceding section has important implications for our treatment of nonhuman animals. If the right of innocent persons not to suffer serious injury or death is independent of their membership in a given community, so that it extends to adult foreigners no less than to unwanted handicapped children born on a community's soil but spurned by its members, and if animals possess such a right (whatever its comparative strength), then their inability to reciprocate human actions and to form a community with us is irrelevant to the duty we owe them to refrain from trenching upon their rights to continued life and bodily integrity. I assume (though I shall not argue here) that a creature possesses a right to life insofar as it is harmed by death, and that death harms a creature to the extent that it is self-conscious, in some measure aware of itself as an enduring subject with a future, and to the extent that death deprives it of a stream of experiences it would prefer to nonexistence if it were fully aware of what the future held for it and sufficiently composed and rational to express a preference responsibly. This conventional view can alone accommodate our respect for autonomy and our convictions regarding the circumstances under which death is rightly shunned. Moreover, it postulates a direct, intelligible link between the evil of death and a creature's right to be spared its infliction. I further contend, without reviewing the behavioral and neurophysiological evidence here, that animals well up the phylogenetic tree—at least all mammals, if one gives animals the benefit of the doubt in borderline cases—are sufficiently aware of themselves as agents and temporally continuous subjects of experiences for death to constitute a loss to them from their point of view, notwithstanding their apparent inability to speak except in very rudimentary fashion.[33]

These assumptions and the conclusion of the preceding section imply that nonhuman mammals possess a right to life that human beings may not legitimately ignore merely because nonhuman mammals are not and cannot be active participants in a cooperative social scheme. Yet billions of nonhuman mammals are killed each year for food, sport, clothing, cosmetics, and the often dubious benefits of medical, industrial, and

---

[33] For a discussion of the significance of linguistic ability to ascriptions of self-consciousness, *see* Davidson (1975); Frey (1980); Bishop (1980); Regan (1983), ch. 2; Griffin (1984); and references cited therein.

psychological research.[34] It is, of course, easy to *explain* the slaughter by reference to callousness, greed, and unthinking acceptance of traditional practices and attitudes. But is it possible to *justify* the interminable queue to the slaughterhouse and laboratory, assuming that mammals whose lives are taken are usually much the worse for being killed?

Only one argument for the differential treatment of nonhuman mammals and human beings for the purposes for which animals are commonly used is consistent with the preceding assumptions. At best, however, it constitutes only a partial apology for the mass slaughter now occurring. When the interests of different persons conflict, one might plausibly argue, somebody forced to choose between the two should consider the gains and losses to each from alternative courses of action. The natural and positive rights of the prospective victim and beneficiary may constrain choice in a given instance, but in some cases they will not be dispositive; a claimed right to some benefit, or not to suffer some disadvantage, may add weight to one pan of the scales without necessarily tipping the balance. Although all mammals, including human beings, ordinarily suffer a serious loss when killed, the value of what they lose varies widely, depending upon the articulateness of their self-awareness, their ability to plan, recall, and deliberate, the number and quality of experiences death steals from them, and the lives they have already enjoyed. These disparities may be so substantial in some situations as to allow the most important rights of one class of persons to be overridden by the needs and desires of those leading richer lives, or lives with longer, more satisfying futures. Thus, it seems obvious that if one had to choose between stopping a herd of sheep from rushing over a cliff and saving their healthy shepherd from falling to the rocks below, one should rescue the shepherd without hesitation. Similarly, if an explorer will die unless a polar bear is killed to provide him with food, heat, or shelter, then the bear should be dispatched forthwith. A nonhuman mammal's right to continued life and freedom from suffering, although important, may in some cases be trumped by the contrary interests of more intelligent beings.

This view of the relative force of peoples' and animals' moral claims boasts intuitive plausibility. But the balancing test it advances will not always smile on people's desires. A nonhuman mammal's life may ordinarily be taken to save the life of a human being, assuming that the human being will probably gain more than a momentary reprieve from death. Even lethal experiments on nonhuman mammals might be vindicated if this view is correct, provided that no substitutes exist and that

---

[34] In the United States alone, between 17 and 22 million animals are killed annually in the course of research and testing, 85% of which are rats or mice. National Research Council (1988), 18. All told, over 5 billion animals are killed each year in the United States for food, clothing, and other purposes. *Ibid.* 2. Mammals constitute a sizable fraction of that total.

the experiments do indeed promise noticeable benefits (as many experiments currently do not[35]) to people or higher animals. A nonhuman mammal's life might even be taken to spare a human being significant suffering, not just to keep him alive. But this argument cannot justify killing nonhuman mammals for food, sport, clothing, or other unimportant ends under prevailing farm and laboratory conditions when alternative sources of satisfaction or sustenance are readily available. In cases such as these, the animals' loss of what is most precious to them—their lives— cannot be compelled for the sake of people's casual pleasures. A wish for stylish leather slacks or a steak dinner, redundant toxicity testing or the joy of seeing an animal mauled after a rugged chase, cannot license depriving a mammal of years of relative contentment—or what for most would be, on balance, desirable lives if they were allowed to live in the wild after their own fashion, rather than subjected to the agonizing confinement of factory farms[36]—at least when their human executioners fail to compensate the victims in advance by providing a more secure and comfortable environment than the scrub and woodlands afford. Slaughtering healthy animals to provide specimens for educational dissection, or running them through fatal, often painful, psychological experiments, similarly fail the test of adequate need where rights to life are at stake. To claim that the lower quality of nonhuman mammals' lives justifies discounting their interests so drastically that the satisfaction of even insignificant human desires takes precedence over their most salient rights would be to eviscerate entirely the ascription of rights to them.

The unacceptability of assigning such flimsy negative entitlements to nonhuman mammals is particularly evident when one recalls that the moral rights of human infants and those suffering from severe mental disabilities are no greater than those of nonhuman mammals with a like degree of cognitive competence. If it would be wrong to kill babies and imbeciles for scholarly or other purposes because it would invade their rights (as opposed to the rights of those who love them), then it would be equally wrong to butcher cattle or chimpanzees for those ends. Of course, even if neither animals nor human beings with similar mental capacities have sufficiently weighty *rights* to stymie their slaughter for food or the slaking of scientific curiosity, one might decline to take the lives of the human beings because one *sympathizes* with them more readily than one does with beasts, or because one simply cares more about members of one's own species. But one could not object on moral grounds to somebody's looking

---

[35] *See e.g.* Pratt (1976) and (1980); Ryder (1975).

[36] Sobering accounts of the conditions under which most domestic animals are raised in the United States and Britain may be found in Mason and Singer (1980) and Singer (1977*a*).

elsewhere for his victims if his preferences ran the other way and no legal limitations stood in his path.[37]

In particular, the fact that human infants, unlike the severely mentally retarded, will in time acquire, if they are not slain, the experiential and ratiocinative capacities necessary to afford them a more solid right to life than nonhuman mammals is irrelevant to their present moral status. That someone may possess some moral claim in the future is no reason to treat him as though he possessed that claim now, just as the fact that we will all die some day is no excuse for someone's acting as though our bodies were already lifeless shells. Moreover, adoption of the view that people's moral rights depend upon their potential properties commits one, as Michael Tooley has shown, to recognizing as immoral not only infanticide but also, in many contexts, abortion and a person's failure to procreate.[38] Most people are unwilling to acknowledge these implications upon reflection. An animal's right to life is on a par with that of human beings possessing a similar level of intelligence and a comparable capacity for self-reflection (unless the human being has acquired a stronger claim to non-interference as a result of its prior display of greater mental powers and self-awareness). What may not legitimately be done to the one may not be done to the other. Membership in a particular species is no more relevant to a creature's right to life than membership in a given human community. If intuitively there are moral limits on the harms one may inflict on mentally handicapped and very young people, those cords bind equally snugly with respect to their nonhuman peers.

Nor can one defend a less solicitous attitude towards nonhuman mammals' welfare by arguing that animals killed for food, clothing, or information would not have been born but for people's desire to use them for these ends, and that because some life is better than none, nonhuman mammals so killed cannot complain of their premature demise. Not only is it a mistake to regard existence as a boon, since failure to bestow it does

[37] Although the moral right to life of certain nonhuman mammals and some human beings may be identical, a community that accepted this proposition might nevertheless reasonably forbid the killing of human beings but not animals in situations where both groups' right to life may be overridden by superior human interests. The fact that some normal people would object vociferously to the killing of other human beings on religious or emotional grounds might be thought sufficient for drawing this distinction. (The extent to which such external preferences should be heeded is questionable, however. Should opposition to executing whites but not blacks matter when administering capital punishment?) More persuasively, the danger of mistakenly killing a human being whose capacities entitled him to greater protection might be deemed too great to allow any killings at all, given the difficulty of discriminating among infants and mentally retarded children or adults and the cost of instituting adequate safeguards.

[38] For a wealth of detailed argumentation in support of this claim, *see* Tooley (1983), 175–241. Summarizing Tooley's excellent discussion of these complex issues would carry me too far afield.

not make anyone's life go less well than it would otherwise have gone, but acceptance of the argument has highly counterintuitive consequences. It would, for example, apparently permit people who would only have children on the proviso that they be allowed to use them as experimental subjects, or slaves, or meat, to carry out their despicable plan, on the absurd rationale that they would thereby be doing their wards a favor. Depending upon one's reasons for regarding increases in population approvingly or disapprovingly and whether one thinks it obligatory to confer large benefits on others when one can do so at much smaller cost to oneself, acknowledging existence as a boon may further issue in a duty to procreate, perhaps even to fill the world as full as possible with creatures whose lives are on balance worth living, regardless of the resulting decline in current living standards.[39] Few would find these implications acceptable. The slaughter of nonhuman mammals under present conditions also cannot be vindicated by their presumed consent. The legitimacy of the maximizing policy described in Chapter 12 and in section 14.2 is premised on the assumption that those who are killed or left to die under the policy consented or would rationally have consented to its implementation beforehand, fully aware of their personal circumstances, because that policy improved their chance of surviving into old age. In the case of factory farms or vivisection from which the test subjects are unlikely to benefit, however, that justification is unavailable because no rational mammal would sanction its own murder for the good of human beings.[40] Appeals to the choices that rational subjects, some of whom were human beings and some of whom were nonhuman animals, would make if ignorant of their identities are similarly unavailing, for they amount to an endorsement of some type of utilitarian calculus and its concomitant denial of rights capable of blocking or skewing a simple comparison of gains and losses. If subsection 2.2.A's refutation of this position is compelling, then it cannot be resurrected here.

The conclusion that nonhuman mammals may not be killed to furnish

---

[39] The difficulty of stopping short of this "repugnant conclusion" is explained in Parfit (1982).

[40] Perhaps one could imagine rational, antecedent consent by certain animals to the use of animals like themselves in experiments that would benefit such animals to a marked degree, thereby making our random selection of test subjects justifiable because it would be prudent for animals to run the risk of being chosen. But this argument, if sound, could never justify the slaughter of animals for purely human gain. And it would vindicate few actual experiments for the good of animals, because test subjects are rarely chosen randomly. Usually, they are bred for that very purpose, and it is inconceivable that a rhesus monkey raised in and for the laboratory would find the proposed hypothetical wager a wise one. Nor can this problem be sidestepped by moving the date of hypothetical consent prior to conception, for that would altogether emasculate the idea that *specific* living creatures would rationally agree to waive their right to life in certain situations. If such arguments were permitted, there would be no stopping short of utilitarianism, the shortcomings of which have already been enumerated.

small benefits to human beings or other animals, unless perhaps they are compensated earlier for the loss inflicted on them, therefore appears the most generous result (from the perspective of human beings) that is consistent with the assumptions with which this section began. Of course, the confirmed egoist, who denies the existence of normative truths, or someone who sets little store by consistency, need not embrace this result. The same is true of those who think that actual contracts or conventions alone have normative force, or those who believe that contracts between rational and competent human beings should serve as the moral paradigm and that animals, infants, and impaired human beings enjoy the rights that would be vouchsafed by such an agreement only in an extended and weaker sense. They may admit that other people possess rights to life and bodily integrity, both because they find it prudent to espouse prevailing views and because they have come to think this ascription of entitlements natural over the course of their education and indoctrination into a contemporary Western culture. They may also find this view compatible with the sympathies and affections they have developed for other people. Thus, the desires and inhibitions someone has acquired, the scope of which is difficult to delimit so precisely as always to advance his personal ends, and the formal and informal punishments meted out to nonconformists, may induce him not only to respect other people's persons and property, but also to denounce the ill treatment of infants and defenseless peoples in other lands. But he need not take a similar line with respect to animals, even if he believes that current forms of animal husbandry and the slaughter of young animals inflict grievous harm upon the victims. Cruelty and the pointless infliction of pain he may condemn, his feelings molded by his emotional reaction to the unnecessary suffering of human beings. But he need not go further and pronounce the killing of animals wrong even when it serves human ends—particularly his own. The slaughter of animals, one may imagine, is something he has always taken for granted. It does not bother him now. He knows, moreover, that the deaths of tens of millions of nonhuman mammals annually are unlikely to trouble him if he does not brood over their slaughter, for he does not identify instinctively with animals in the way he does with people. If he has reason to believe that broadening his sympathies to encompass the whole of sentient creation, or at least its more intelligent part, will not make his life any happier but in all likelihood only earn him the reputation of a crank, then his interests are clearly best served by a refusal to reflect and by preservation of the status quo.

Someone who conveniently believes that obligation tracks affection therefore need not be disturbed by the preceding argument. He may blithely exclude animals from his moral universe so long as no sanctions attach. I conjecture, however, that his approach to moral questions is one that few of us would approve. To adopt it is to concede that the enslavement of outsiders is not inherently wrong and that apartheid is not necessarily abhorrent: their propriety depends entirely on which side of the stick one is on. It is to admit that psychopathic killers or sadistic prison guards lack any reason, apart from fear of reprisals, to desist from dismembering helpless human beings if they have no desire to halt the killing. It is to consign the resolution of moral matters to the domain of feeling and force. The price of adopting this view would for most of us be excessively high.

The claim that a nonhuman mammal's right to life may only be overridden, in the absence of compensation, to secure important benefits or to ward off significant harm to people or other animals is thus the most favorable stance, from human beings' point of view, that one can conscientiously accept. Of course, some people may think that nonhuman mammals' claims are more powerful than I have suggested. They might instead deny that rights ever lower their guard before the interests of creatures with superior intelligence and self-awareness. The view outlined above does seem to imply, for example, that if a race of aliens from some distant galaxy had brains of phenomenal complexity, making their lives so much richer and more intriguing than our lives could possibly be that they stood to us as we stand to most other mammals, then they need have no qualms about killing us to produce life-saving serums for themselves or to use us in lethal experiments that promise them especially large rewards. Some may find this implication hard to credit; many people, myself included, would accept it rather than deny our right to kill nonhuman mammals to meet pressing human needs, or disavow the importance of consistency, or make moral rights turn entirely on the existence of social conventions backed by sanctions. One might argue, of course, that the parallel is flawed because once some threshold of cognitive competence is passed (and all normal people pass it), a creature qualifies for equal consideration with all other beings that have exceeded that mark, whereas those that fail to qualify—nonhuman animals, for example—are rightly treated as second-class moral citizens. But I can think of no tenable principle for dividing the continuum of consciousness in an intuitively appealing place. I am therefore disinclined to dismiss this argument from example as unsound, rather than merely drawing comfort from knowing that it is quite farfetched.

The view that it is generally wrong to kill nonhuman mammals for food, apparel, sport, and research under existing conditions does not imply that their slaughter would be immoral under changed circumstances. If people provided them with better living conditions than they would enjoy in the wild[41]—a constant source of food, protection from the elements, disease,

---

[41] Romanticized accounts of frolicsome cubs and contented fawns notwithstanding, wild animals often suffer severe deprivations and lead abbreviated, sometimes agonizing, lives.

and predators—then the benefits they supplied to the animals might excuse killing them when they grew old, for it would arguably be rational for some nonhuman mammals to trade their declining years and what might otherwise be a slow and painful death for a more secure and bountiful life.

People might disagree, to be sure, over the proper baseline to use in comparing the lots of farm and feral animals. Pigs kept in man-made enclosures in Saskatchewan might not survive a winter if freed there, or if released in a warmer but overpopulated region. Animals bred to dependence on antibiotics or unable to fend for themselves because selective reproduction has given them painfully large udders or stripped them of fur would find the gate to the forest scarcely more tantalizing than the door to the abattoir.[42] People might also disagree over which bargains a given animal would strike if it were rational and able to communicate with its captors, and over whether the limit to moral acceptability is in this context defined by the minimum terms that an animal would accept or by some point between that lower bound and human beings' best offer. More important, perhaps, why we are not obliged to improve animals' circumstances *without* killing them, as with human beings in need, rather than trade benefits for lives, is far from clear. What is plain is that meat, skins, and test animals obtained in accordance with the strictures I have outlined would be much more expensive than they presently are.

14.5. SHOULD WE KILL OFF THE CARNIVORES?

Suppose that a mammal is harmed when killed to the extent that it is deprived of a desirable existence, and that suffering is inherently evil, whether endured by human beings or by animals. Suppose further that a state of affairs is only valuable to the extent that it comports with the fully informed, settled preferences of creatures that figure in it or know of it, and that only the rights of other sentient beings morally constrain, directly or derivatively, the actions of responsible persons. Suppose also that one does not benefit a sentient or self-conscious being merely by bringing it into existence, and that one's obligations to effect, to hinder, or not to interfere with such a being's acquisition of consciousness stem exclusively

---

Wild songbirds, for example, rarely live more than one or two years, whereas most survive for ten years or longer in captivity. *See* Dawkins (1980), 52–5.

[42] Should the basis for measuring improvements to an animal's life therefore be the life that an animal bred with *different* attributes would lead in suitably defined surroundings? That approach appears to abandon the present focus (which alone seems morally defensible) on what a determinate, existing animal would rationally choose. If one rejects it, however, then the importance of defining the environmental baseline becomes more acute. Its rejection, moreover, opens up the possibility of genetically engineering animals whose lives would barely be worth living from their own perspectives in the most favorable "natural" setting one can imagine, allowing their human creators to minimize the benefits they would have to confer on those animals in order to justify slaughtering them for human gain.

from one's obligations or duties to other sentient or self-conscious beings, whether now alive or to be born. Finally, suppose that if one can save a nonhuman mammal from an undesirable death or spare an animal suffering at little cost to oneself, then one has a prima facie duty to do so, just as one ought to forestall the death or anguish of another human being if one can do so without great hardship. Thus, if a community is able to protect at negligible cost a large collection of animals from the ravages of floods, droughts, or fires, or from the depredations of inhumane trappers, then it should bring the animals under its aegis.

All of these assumptions are reasonable, even popular. Societies for the prevention of cruelty to animals abound in the United States and Britain; procreation is rarely considered a duty; people who had their healthy pets put away to spare them worry or kennel charges while on holiday would be thought heartless or daft;[43] the collapse of a beautiful cavern that no being would ever behold cannot be cause for regret. Yet these assumptions yield what many would consider an untoward result. They imply a duty to ensure that the earth's carnivores, at least the wild ones, die off, provided that we can do so without undue effort or ecological disaster. For if death by fire or pole ax is a bad end to bovine existence, so is death by a lion's jaw. Any time that a nonhuman mammal is killed in the wild when it would otherwise have gone on living a life that was better than nonexistence from its perspective, and any time that an animal causes another pain or discomfort, morally significant injury occurs. Such injury, moreover, is avoidable. Were predators eliminated, it would never come to pass. We therefore seem obliged to render those predators extinct.

One cannot justify nonintervention by arguing that because numbers are irrelevant when saving lives, and because one is faced with a choice between innocents—tigers, after all, cannot help themselves, just as sheep do not chew grass by choice—one need not favor prey over predators. It is true that one may not be bound simply to flip the scales of life and death. But under the circumstances one *does* seem obliged to prevent predators from reproducing, thereby ensuring their eventual annihilation. Sterilization would not be tantamount to preferring one life to another. It would deprive one generation of predators of the supposed joys of rearing young and of their offspring's companionship and assistance when they grow old, in order to save the lives and spare the suffering of countless herbivores who will exist in the future and who would have been killed or hurt if predators were still on the prowl. Given the disparity between the losses involved, it therefore seems that one ought to save the would-be quarry at a much smaller cost to present carnivores if one can do so without undue strain and if the ecological ramifications are not calamitous (e.g. a

---

[43] See Michael Lockwood's discussion of "Disposapup Ltd." in Lockwood (1979), 168.

population explosion of Thomson's gazelles precipitated by the elimination of cheetahs, followed by their mass starvation). If an average predator's loss from not being allowed to procreate, in terms of less desirable experiences and a shortened life, were equal to or exceeded the loss predators typically inflict on individual herbivore victims, then we would be justified in sitting on the sidelines. But comparative harms do not seem to stack up that way.

Carnivores, of course, need not be made to vanish altogether. If people wished to observe them, or were somehow gladdened by the knowledge that these ferocious beasts were still lurking about, then some could be kept in zoos or wildlife preserves, where they would be placed on a vegetarian diet (if that were possible) or fed the carcasses of animals that had died natural deaths, animals that lose nothing by dying, or animals that had been killed painlessly after a comfortable life on a farm. And ecological disasters need not ensue if herbivore populations could be controlled at scant expense. In the case of large animals whose meat or skins were in demand, such as zebra or antelope, this may even prove commercially profitable. (Where animals that might subsequently multiply are vermin, however, the cost of protection might exceed what people are morally bound to shoulder.)

I find this argument disturbing. Like many people, I have a strong desire to let life on the savannah unfold much as it always has, to allow wild animals to pursue the projects for which nature has fitted them, free from human intrusion. I would especially hate to see the great cats follow their saber-toothed ancestors into oblivion, save for a few pampered but frustrated specimens in artificial enclosures. But it is difficult to construct a convincing argument for the claim that it would be wrong to strip the wilderness of its more savage denizens, or that, though permissible, it is not obligatory to do so under any conditions. The fact that a murderer has dashing good looks or pleases crowds is not a sufficient reason to suspend his prison sentence; movie stars are not exempt from the criminal law.

There are, to be sure, contingent reasons for not intervening on behalf of the hunted. Well-intentioned extermination efforts may do more harm than good. Their cost, moreover, may be too high, given competing moral concerns. But suppose we lived to see a more prosperous age, when the earth had been scoured of injustice, when no one was in want of a commodious life, and when detailed studies had been completed and measures devised to forestall the possibly infelicitous effects of removing one link in the natural food chain. Suppose, further, that the cost of cleansing a nature still red in tooth and claw were trifling by comparison with our amplified resources. Would we not be obliged to act as nature's policemen and carry out the sterilizations? Would it be permissible for someone to begin now, if he had the knowledge, will, and wherewithal?

In attempting to defend a negative reply, one might argue that where one group of outsiders preys upon another and our interests or preferences would not be served by putting a stop to the killing, then we have no duty to intervene. But suppose that the outsiders in question were human beings who were powerless to affect our fortunes—neighboring clans in some faraway land—and that the evils that one group perpetrated against its peaceable neighbor included torture and murder. Would it really be a matter of moral indifference whether or not we stepped in to halt the bloodshed if we easily could? If we knew that cannibalism and human sacrifice were practiced on kidnapped victims by some Stone Age tribe in New Guinea and were somewhat taken with the idea of having the remote past preserved in our midst, just as we were inclined to leave the Serengeti untouched, would it nonetheless be morally permissible to pander to this preference when innocent lives were being lost? But if we are obliged to right such wrongs, then why should the obligation disappear when analogous atrocities occur in the animal kingdom? Certainly a nonhuman mammal's life is worth less than the life of a normal human being, and animals that fall prey to their natural enemies are often old, sick, or injured, and thus losing lives of still lesser value, possibly being spared a slower, more agonizing death. Nonhuman mammals past their prime, however, could be dispatched less painfully—poachers would frequently be happy to do the dirty work—and their lives are not entirely devoid of moral importance. Nonhuman mammals' inability to offer us assistance in turn can hardly be decisive either, if we have a duty to aid helpless human beings far removed from us in time or space. Hence, if the cost of intervention is low enough, there appears no excuse for remaining a spectator.

Another possible reply would be to claim that all self-conscious beings have a right to reproduce, even if the exercise of that right inevitably harms other innocent creatures. One cannot rightly demand that anyone sacrifice the many goods that flow from having offspring just because others will suffer large losses in consequence. But is this claim convincing? Suppose that certain kinds of violent criminal behavior were genetically transmitted from human parents to their progeny, so that the latter were certain to rob, rape, or murder unless kept under close surveillance or confinement. Surely it would not be reprehensible to prevent such people from reproducing if it would cost the community dearly to keep their children under close watch or lock and key. Nor does the permissibility of restraints turn on our right to defend ourselves. For suppose that the problem arose, once again, in a remote tribal village and that the potential victims were unable to protect themselves because they lacked means to prevent procreation other than a prohibition on sexual intercourse and infanticide, both of which they thought wrong and the first of which they could not enforce. No moral rule would bar our intervening to help those unable to help themselves when the harms with which they were threatened were much greater than the constraints we would impose on those who would otherwise imperil their lives.

Nevertheless, one might contend that we are not *obliged* to intervene even if we *may* do so. If this claim were correct, then we would not be bound to keep the carnivores at bay, although we might trim their numbers if we were so disposed. But this assertion rings hollow when the harm that death brings is so considerable and the pains of not reproducing comparatively negligible, especially for nonhuman mammals that part with their young at an early age and bear few litters. If inexpensive birth control measures were available, one could not stand idle with an unclouded conscience.

Thus, the only sound reasons for inaction are contingent ones: the more urgent concerns of at least a billion human beings and the danger of uprooting one evil only to plant several more. These reasons will undoubtedly suffice for many years to come. But if they paled with passing decades, or if the costs of extermination would be borne voluntarily by those who wished to bring the carnage to a close, then the entire weight of the argument for inaction would shift to the contrary preferences of those who favored the status quo. Because such fleet and frail desires cannot support that burden where human cruelty or injustice is involved, they appear unable to carry that load in the case of animals. I find this result unsettling, but see no way to avoid it without sacrificing consistency or admitting that moral duties depend solely on social sanctions and an agent's predilections. And neither of these alternatives seems to me any more congenial.

Envoi

PERHAPS the most unsettling effect of writing or reading a work of moral philosophy is a sense of weightlessness. Convictions one thought solid—sometimes even quite fundamental convictions—dissolve beneath one's feet, and those that retain substance often seem less sturdy or strangely transformed when set against a novel background. Seeing one's moral theory, or a set of more particular beliefs, as one theory or set among many frequently evokes doubt as to its correctness; and the experience of abandoning upon scrutiny some of the convictions one took for granted, together with the recognition that other convictions might meet the same fate if one thought persistently enough, may enhance that unease. In addition, a heightened awareness of the dependence of moral theories on our intuitions about what is right in certain real or hypothetical cases, the insecurity or faintness of many of the intuitions on which we rely, and the ease with which principles can be tailored or modified to accommodate misgivings or recalcitrant beliefs, tend to worsen the vertigo. More disturbing still perhaps is the powerful attraction, for many people, of diametrically opposed theories—Hobbesian contractarianism and justice as impartial consideration, utilitarianism and egoism—between which their allegiance vacillates or, if it stops short of apostasy, nevertheless softens under the glow of an attractive suitor. It might seem that moral reflection invariably snares the opposite of what it stalks, that it destroys rather than fortifies, substitituting uncertainty or moral listlessness for purposeful conviction. If that is so, then why indulge?

It may be contrary to professional self-interest for me to say so, but I doubt whether ethical inquiry is always beneficial. For some people, its effects appear largely pernicious, as when it induces a casual relativism that undermines a person's desire to act justly or to cultivate individual or collective virtues. But this observation comes at the very end of this book, rather than as a bold-face warning on the cover, because the danger of enervation seems to me slight with respect to people who care sufficiently about thinking coherently and acting rightly to struggle through a book of this kind. Moral argument may be unsatisfying—sometimes it seems to reduce to nothing more than opposed assertions and finger-pointing—especially when it takes the form of appeals to intuition or to the self-evidence of overarching principles. And indecision—about the relative force of various claims, about the legitimacy of making exceptions to otherwise unpunctured rules, about the correctness of the bedrock theses one espouses—is an unavoidable concomitant of this exercise. Like most people who have grappled with these problems, I have often wished that there were some way to go behind the clash of discordant intuitions or principles to resolve argumentative deadlock, some sure path to consensus. And even now I retain very strong doubts, for example, about the claims I have ventured regarding organ transplants, and about whether the approach I adopted to compensating for differences in people's unearned talents is the proper extension of the basic principles I endorse, let alone of any real utility. But there seems to me no substitute for the usual, often frustrating, attempts to expose the counterintuitive character of opposing arguments, the invocation of appealing principles that cannot be given any deeper grounding, the repeated reliance on the alleged importance of consistency and coherence.

None of these burrs, however, seems to me an adequate reason to forsake moral inquiry. For many, myself included, a clear understanding of our moral predicament is itself of substantial inherent value, as well as a powerful solace. The tolerance and habits of mind such thinking often fosters, moreover, are much more than incidental benefits. There seems to me no cure for uncertainty that is not worse than the affliction, both for the individual who chooses moral hibernation and for the society to which he belongs. And the uncertainty that trails reflection is by no means pervasive. In fact, philosophical analysis of the kind I described may be the sole route to the only confidence worth having—an enlightened certitude that generally enables one to act with assurance, whatever doubts might huddle at the edges of one's conscience. That confidence, for some of us at least, is well worth its price.

BIBLIOGRAPHY

ACKERMAN, B. (1980), *Social Justice in the Liberal State*, New Haven: Yale University Press.

ACTON, J. P. (1976), "Measuring the Monetary Value of Lifesaving Programs," 40 *Law and Contemporary Problems* no. 4, 46–72.

AKE, C. (1975), "Justice as Equality," 5 *Philosophy and Public Affairs* 69–89.

ALEXANDER, L. (1985), "Pursuing the Good—Indirectly," 95 *Ethics* 315–32.

—— and SCHWARZSCHILD, M. (1987), "Liberalism, Neutrality, and Equality of Welfare vs. Equality of Resources," 16 *Philosophy and Public Affairs* 85–110.

ANDREWS, W. (1974), "A Consumption-Type or Cash Flow Personal Income Tax," 87 *Harvard Law Review* 1113–88.

—— (1975), "Fairness and the Personal Income Tax: A Reply to Professor Warren," 88 *Harvard Law Review* 947–58.

ANSCOMBE, G. E. M. (1967), "Who Is Wronged?" 5 *Oxford Review* 16–17.

ARNESON, R. (1989), "Equality and Equality of Opportunity for Welfare," 56 *Philosophical Studies* 77–93.

BAKER, C. E. (1975), "The Ideology of the Economic Analysis of Law," 5 *Philosophy and Public Affairs* 3–48. ·

—— (1980), "Starting Points in Economic Analysis of Law," 8 *Hofstra Law Review* 939–72.

BARRY, B. (1973), *The Liberal Theory of Justice*, Oxford: Oxford University Press.

—— (1979), "And Who Is My Neighbor?" 88 *Yale Law Journal* 629–58.

—— (1989), *Theories of Justice*, Berkeley: University of California Press.

BAXTER, W., and ALTREE, L. (1972), "Legal Aspects of Airport Noise," 15 *Journal of Law and Economics* 1–113.

BAYLES, M. (1978), "The Price of Life," 89 *Ethics* 20–34.

BEAUCHAMP, T., and CHILDRESS, J. (1979), *Principles of Biomedical Ethics*, New York: Oxford University Press.

—— and Perlin, S. (eds.) (1978), *Ethical Issues in Death and Dying*, Englewood Cliffs, N.J.: Prentice-Hall.

BEBCHUK, L. (1980), "The Pursuit of a Bigger Pie: Can Everyone Expect a Bigger Slice?" 8 *Hofstra Law Review* 671–709.

BENNETT, J. (1978), "Whatever the Consequences," 26 *Analysis* 83–102.

—— (1980), "Accountability," in *Philosophical Subjects: Essays presented to P. F. Strawson* (ed. Z. Van Straaten), Oxford: Oxford University Press.

BENSON, J. (1978), "Duty and the Beast," 53 *Philosophy* 177–92.

BISHOP, J. (1980), "More Thought on Thought and Talk," 89 *Mind* 1–16.

BLACKBURN, S. (1971), "Moral Realism," in *Morality and Moral Reasoning* (ed. J. Casey), London: Methuen.

—— (1980), "Truth, Realism, and the Regulation of Theory," 5 *Midwest Studies in Philosophy* 353–71.

—— (1981), "Rule-Following and Moral Realism," in *Wittgenstein: To Follow a Rule* (ed. S. Holtzman and C. Leich), London: Routledge & Kegan Paul.

BLUMSTEIN, J. (1976), "Constitutional Perspectives on Governmental Decisions Affecting Human Life and Health," 40 *Law and Contemporary Problems* no. 4, 231–305.

BOGART J. (1985), "Lockean Provisos and State of Nature Theories," 95 *Ethics* 828–36.

BRANDT, R. B. (1959), *Ethical Theory*, Englewood Cliffs, N.J.: Prentice-Hall.

—— (1964), "The Concepts of Obligation and Duty," 73 *Mind* 364–93.

—— (1979), *A Theory of the Good and the Right*, Oxford: Oxford University Press.

BRODY, B. (1983), "Redistribution without Egalitarianism," 1 *Social Philosophy and Policy* 71–87.

BROOME, J. (1978), "Choice and Value in Economics," 1978 *Oxford Economic Papers* 313–33.

—— (1981), "On Valuing Life in Economics," unpublished Discussion Paper No. 87/81, March 1981.

—— (1984), "Selecting People Randomly," 95 *Ethics* 38–55.

BUCHANAN, A. (1984), "The Right to a Decent Minimum of Health Care," 13 *Philosophy and Public Affairs* 55–78.

—— (1988), "Advance Directives and the Personal Identity Problem," 17 *Philosophy and Public Affairs* 277–302.

—— (1990), "Justice as Reciprocity versus Subject-Centered Justice," 19 *Philosophy and Public Affairs* 253–74.

CALABRESI, G. (1970), *The Costs of Accidents: A Legal and Economic Analysis*, New Haven: Yale University Press.

—— and HIRSHOFF, J. (1972), "Toward a Test for Strict Liability in Torts," 81 *Yale Law Journal* 1055–85.

CHILDRESS, J. (1982), *Who Should Decide? Paternalism in Health Care*, New York: Oxford University Press.

—— (1989), "Ethical Criteria for Procuring and Distributing Organs for Transplantation," 14 *Journal of Health Politics, Policy and Law* 87–113.

COHEN, G. A. (1986), "Self-Ownership, World-Ownership, and Equality," in *Justice and Equality Here and Now* (ed. F. Lucash), Ithaca: Cornell University Press.

—— (1989), "On the Currency of Egalitarian Justice," 99 *Ethics* 906–44.

COLEMAN, J. (1975), "Justice and Reciprocity in Tort Theory," 14 *Western Ontario Law Review* 105–18.

—— (1976), "The Morality of Strict Liability," 18 *William and Mary Law Review* 259–86.

—— (1980), "Efficiency, Utility and Wealth Maximization," 8 *Hofstra Law Review* 509–51.

—— (1982), "Moral Theories of Torts: Their Scope and Limits: Part I," 1 *Law and Philosophy* 371–90.

—— (1983), "Moral Theories of Torts: Their Scope and Limits: Part II," 2 *Law and Philosophy* 5–36.

—— (1984), "Economics and the Law: A Critical Review of the Foundations of the Economic Approach to Law," 94 *Ethics* 649–79.

DANIELS, N. (ed.) (1974), *Reading Rawls*, New York: Basic Books.

—— (1979), "Wide Reflective Equilibrium and Theory Acceptance in Ethics," 76 *Journal of Philosophy* 256–82.

—— (1980), "Reflective Equilibrium and Archimedean Points," 10 *Canadian Journal of Philosophy* 83–103.

—— (1981), "Health-Care Needs and Distributive Justice," 10 *Philosophy and Public Affairs* 146–79.

—— (1985), "Fair Equality of Opportunity and Decent Minimums: A Reply to Buchanan," 14 *Philosophy and Public Affairs* 106–10.

DASGUPTA, P. (1982), "Utilitarianism, Information and Rights," in Sen and Williams (1982).

DAVIDSON, D. (1975), "Thought and Talk," in *Mind and Language* (ed. S. Guttenplan), Oxford: Oxford University Press.

DAWKINS, M. (1980), *Animal Suffering*, London: Chapman & Hall.

DE GREGORI, T. (1979), "Market Morality: Robert Nozick and the Question of Economic Justice," 38 *American Journal of Economics and Sociology* 17–30.

DENNETT, D. (1984), *Elbow Room*, Cambridge, Mass.: Bradford Books.

DEVINE, P. (1978), *The Ethics of Homicide*, Ithaca: Cornell University Press.

DICK, J. (1975), "How to Justify a Distribution of Earnings," 4 *Philosophy and Public Affairs* 248–72.

DINELLO, D. (1971), "On Killing and Letting Die," 31 *Analysis* 83–6.

DUFF, R. A. (1973), "Intentionally Killing the Innocent," 34 *Analysis* 16–19.

DWORKIN, R. (1977), *Taking Rights Seriously*, London: Duckworth.

—— (1981*a*), "What is Equality? Part 1: Equality of Welfare," 10 *Philosophy and Public Affairs* 185–246.

—— (1981*b*), "What is Equality? Part 2: Equality of Resources," 10 *Philosophy and Public Affairs* 283–345.

—— (1983*a*), "Comment on Narveson: In Defense of Equality," 1 *Social Philosophy and Policy* 24–40.

—— (1983*b*), "A Reply by Ronald Dworkin," in *Ronald Dworkin and Contemporary Jurisprudence* (ed. M. Cohen), Totowa, N. J.: Rowman & Allanheld.

—— (1985), *A Matter of Principle*, Cambridge, Mass.: Harvard University Press.

—— (1986), *Law's Empire*, Cambridge, Mass.: Harvard University Press.

—— (1987), "What Is Equality? Part 3: The Place of Liberty," 73 *Iowa Law Review* 1–54.

EPSTEIN, R. (1973), "A Theory of Strict Liability," 2 *Journal of Legal Studies* 151–204.

—— (1974), "Defenses and Subsequent Pleas in a System of Strict Liability," 3 *Journal of Legal Studies* 165–215.

—— (1975), "Intentional Harms," 4 *Journal of Legal Studies* 391–442.

—— (1979*a*), "Nuisance Law: Corrective Justice and its Utilitarian Constraints," 8 *Journal of Legal Studies* 49–102.

—— (1979*b*), "Causation and Corrective Justice: Reply to Two Critics," 8 *Journal of Legal Studies* 477–504.

—— (1985), *Takings: Private Property and the Power of Eminent Domain*, Cambridge, Mass.: Harvard University Press.

FEINBERG, J. (1980), *Rights, Justice, and the Bounds of Liberty*, Princeton: Princeton University Press.

FEINBERG, J. (1986), *Harm to Self*, New York: Oxford University Press.

FIRTH, R. (1952), "Ethical Absolutism and the Ideal Observer," 12 *Philosophy and Phenomenological Research* 317–45.

FLETCHER, G. (1972), "Fairness and Utility in Tort Theory," 85 *Harvard Law Review* 537–73.

FOOT, P. (1967), "The Problem of Abortion and the Doctrine of the Double Effect," 5 *Oxford Review* 5–15.

FRANKENA, W. (1962), "The Concept of Social Justice," in *Social Justice* (ed. R. B. Brandt), Englewood Cliffs, N.J.: Prentice-Hall.

—— (1966), "Some Beliefs About Justice," Lindley Lecture, University of Kansas.

FRANKFURT, H. (1988), *The Importance of What We Care About*, Cambridge: Cambridge University Press.

FREY, R. (1980), *Interests and Rights: The Case against Animals*, Oxford: Oxford University Press.

—— (1983), *Rights, Killing, and Suffering*, Oxford: Blackwell.

FRIED, C. (1970), *An Anatomy of Values*, Cambridge, Mass.: Harvard University Press.

—— (1978), *Right and Wrong*, Cambridge, Mass.: Harvard University Press.

—— (1982), "Is Liberty Possible?" in *The Tanner Lectures on Human Values III* (ed. S. McMurrin), Salt Lake City: University of Utah Press.

—— (1983), "Distributive Justice," 1 *Social Philosophy and Policy* 45–59.

FUCHS, V. (1974), *Who Shall Live? Health Economics and Social Choice*, New York: Basic Books.

FULLER, L. (1949), "The Case of the Speluncean Explorers," 62 *Harvard Law Review* 616–45.

GAUTHIER, D. (1986), *Morals By Agreement*, Oxford: Oxford University Press.

GEDDES, L. (1973), "On the Intrinsic Wrongness of Killing Innocent People," 33 *Analysis* 93–7.

GLOVER, J. (1975), "It Makes No Difference Whether or Not I Do It," 49 *Aristotelian Society Supp. Vol.* 171–90.

—— (1977), *Causing Death and Saving Lives*, Harmondsworth: Penguin.

—— (1978), "Assessing the Value of Saving Lives," in *Royal Institute of Philosophy Lectures 1976/77: Human Values* (ed. G. Vesey), Sussex: Harvester Press.

—— (1983), "Self-Creation," 69 *Proceedings of the British Academy* 445–71.

—— (1984), *What Sort of People Should There Be?* Harmondsworth: Penguin.

GRAETZ, M. (1977), "Legal Transitions: The Case of Retroactivity in Income Tax Revision," 126 *University of Pennsylvania Law Review* 47–87.

—— (1985), "Retroactivity Revisited," 98 *Harvard Law Review* 1820–41.

GRIFFIN, D. (1984), *Animal Thinking*, Cambridge, Mass.: Harvard University Press.

HAKSAR, V. (1979), *Equality, Liberty, and Perfectionism*, Oxford: Oxford University Press.

HANINK, J. (1975), "Some Light on Double Effect," 35 *Analysis* 147–51.

HANSER, M. (1990), "Harming Future People," 19 *Philosophy and Public Affairs* 47–70.

HANSMANN, H. (1989), "The Economics and Ethics of Markets for Human Organs," 14 *Journal of Health Politics, Policy and Law* 57–85.

HARDIN, R. (1988), *Morality within the Limits of Reason*, Chicago: University of Chicago Press.

HARE, R. M. (1963), *Freedom and Reason*, Oxford: Oxford University Press.

—— (1971), "The Argument from Received Opinion," in *Essays on Philosophical Method*, London: Macmillan.

—— (1974), "Rawls' Theory of Justice," in Daniels (1974).

—— (1978), "Justice and Equality," in *Justice and Economic Distribution* (ed. J. Arthur and W. Shaw), Englewood Cliffs, N.J.: Prentice-Hall.

—— (1981), *Moral Thinking*, Oxford: Oxford University Press.

HARMAN, G. (1977), *The Nature of Morality*, New York: Oxford University Press.

HARRIS, J. (1975), "The Survival Lottery," 50 *Philosophy* 81–7.

—— (1980), *Violence and Responsibility*, London: Routledge & Kegan Paul.

—— (1983), "*In Vitro* Fertilization: The Ethical Issues," 33 *Philosophical Quarterly* 217–37.

HARSANYI, J. (1953), "Cardinal Utility in Welfare Economics and the Theory of Risk Taking," 61 *Journal of Political Economy* 434–5.

—— (1955), "Cardinal Welfare, Individualistic Ethics, and Interpersonal Comparisons of Utility," 63 *Journal of Political Economy* 309–21.

—— (1982), "Morality and the Theory of Rational Behavior," in Sen and Williams (1982).

HART, H. L. A. (1955), "Are There Any Natural Rights?" 64 *Philosophical Review* 175–91.

—— (1961), *The Concept of Law*, Oxford: Oxford University Press.

—— (1979), "Between Utility and Rights," 79 *Columbia Law Review* 828–46.

—— and HONORÉ, T. (1985), *Causation in the Law* (2d edn.), Oxford: Oxford University Press.

JONES, G. (1983), "The Right to Health Care and the State," 33 *Philosophical Quarterly* 279–87.

JONES-LEE, M. (1976), *The Value of Life: An Economic Analysis*, London: Martin Robertson.

KADISH, S. (1976), "Respect for Life and Regard for Rights in the Criminal Law," 64 *California Law Review* 871–901.

KAMM, F. (1985), "Equal Treatment and Equal Chances," 14 *Philosophy and Public Affairs* 177–94.

KAPLOW, L. (1986), "An Economic Analysis of Legal Transitions," 99 *Harvard Law Review* 509–617.

KATZ, A. (1973), "Process Design for Selection of Hemodialysis and Organ Transplant Recipients," 22 *Buffalo Law Review* 373–418.

KATZ, J., and CAPRON, A. (1975), *Catastrophic Diseases: Who Decides What?* New York: Russell Sage Foundation.

KAVKA, G. (1979), "The Numbers Should Count," 36 *Philosophical Studies* 285–94.

—— (1985), "The Reconciliation Project," in *Morality, Reason and Truth* (ed. D. Copp and D. Zimmermann), Totowa, N.J.: Rowman & Allanheld.

KIKER, B. (ed.) (1971), *Investment in Human Capital*, Columbia, S.C.: University of South Carolina Press.

KILNER, J. (1990), *Who Lives? Who Dies?* New Haven: Yale University Press.

KORSGAARD, C. (1989), "Personal Identity and the Unity of Agency: A Kantian Response to Parfit," 18 *Philosophy and Public Affairs* 101–32.

KRONMAN, A. (1980), "Wealth Maximization as a Normative Principle," 9 *Journal of Legal Studies* 227–42.

LAFOLLETTE, H. (1980), "Licensing Parents," 9 *Philosophy and Public Affairs* 182–97.

LANDES, R., and POSNER, R. (1981), "The Positive Economic Theory of Tort Law," 15 *Georgia Law Review* 851–924.

LEE, P. (1986), "The Organ Supply Dilemma: Acute Responses to a Chronic Shortage," 20 *Columbia Journal of Law and Social Problems* 363–407.

LEWIN, L. (1972), *Triage*, London: Macdonald.

LOCKE, D. (1968), "The Trivializability of Universalizability," 78 *Philosophical Review* 25–44.

LOCKWOOD, M. (1979), "Singer on Killing and the Preference for Life," 22 *Inquiry* 157–70.

LUCAS, J. (1980), *On Justice*, Oxford: Oxford University Press.

LYONS, D. (1974), "Nature and Soundness of the Contract and Coherence Arguments," in Daniels (1974).

McCLOSKEY, H. J. (1957), "An Examination of Restricted Utilitarianism," 66 *Philosophical Review* 466–85.

MACKIE, J. (1977), *Ethics: Inventing Right and Wrong*, Harmondsworth: Penguin.

MANNINEN, D., and EVANS, R. (1985), "Public Attitudes and Behavior Regarding Organ Donation," 253 *Journal of the American Medical Association* 3111–15.

MARNEFFE, P. (1990), "Liberalism, Liberty, and Neutrality," 19 *Philosophy and Public Affairs* 253–74.

MASON, J., and SINGER, P. (1980), *Animal Factories*, New York: Crown Publishing.

MICHELMAN, F. (1968), "Property, Utility, and Fairness: Comments on the Ethical Foundations of Just Compensation Law," 80 *Harvard Law Review* 1165–1258.

MILLER, H., and WILLIAMS, W. (eds.) (1983), *Ethics and Animals*, Clifton, N.J.: Humana Press.

MIRLEES, J. (1982), "The Economic Uses of Utilitarianism," in Sen and Williams (1982).

MONTAGUE, P. (1981), "Self-Defense and Choosing Between Lives," 40 *Philosophical Studies* 207–19.

—— (1983), "Punishment and Societal Defense," 2 *Criminal Justice Ethics* 30–6.

—— (1989), "The Morality of Self-Defense: A Reply to Wasserman," 18 *Philosophy and Public Affairs* 81–9.

MORILLO, C. (1977), "Doing, Refraining, and the Strenuousness of Morality," 14 *American Philosophical Quarterly* 29–39.

MUYSKENS, J. (1978), "An Alternative Policy for Obtaining Cadaver Organs for Transplantation," 8 *Philosophy and Public Affairs* 88–99.

NAGEL, T. (1975), "Libertarianism without Foundations," 85 *Yale Law Journal* 136–49.

—— (1979), *Mortal Questions*, Cambridge: Cambridge University Press.

—— (1980), "The Limits of Objectivity," in *The Tanner Lectures on Human Values I* (ed. S. McMurrin), Salt Lake City: University of Utah Press.

NARVESON, J. (1977), "Animal Rights," 7 *Canadian Journal of Philosophy* 161–78.

—— (1983), "On Dworkinian Equality" and "Reply to Dworkin," 1 *Social Philosophy and Policy* 1–23, 41–4.

NATIONAL RESEARCH COUNCIL (1988), *Use of Laboratory Animals in Biomedical and Behavioral Research*, Washington, D.C.: National Academy Press.

NOTE (1969a), "Patient Selection for Artificial and Transplanted Organs," 82 *Harvard Law Review* 1322–42.

NOTE (1969b), "Scarce Medical Resources," 69 *Columbia Law Review* 620–92.

NOTE (1988), "Death Unto Life: Anencephalic Infants as Organ Donors," 74 *Virginia Law Review* 1527–66.

NOZICK, R. (1974), *Anarchy, State, and Utopia*, New York: Basic Books.

—— (1981), *Philosophical Explanations*, Oxford: Oxford University Press.

O'NEILL, O. (1981), "Nozick's Entitlements," in Paul (1981).

PARFIT, D. (1978), "Innumerate Ethics," 7 *Philosophy and Public Affairs* 285–301.

—— (1982), "Future Generations: Further Problems," 11 *Philosophy and Public Affairs* 113–72.

—— (1984), *Reasons and Persons*, Oxford: Oxford University Press.

—— (1986), "Comments," 96 *Ethics* 832–72.

PAUL, J. (ed.) (1981), *Reading Nozick*, Oxford: Blackwell.

PERRY, T. (1976), *Moral Reasoning and Truth*, Oxford: Oxford University Press.

POLINSKY, A. M. (1983), *An Introduction to Law and Economics*, Boston: Little, Brown.

POSNER, R. (1977), *Economic Analysis of Law* (2d edn.), Boston: Little, Brown.

—— (1979), "Epstein's Tort Theory: A Critique," 8 *Journal of Legal Studies* 457–75.

—— (1981), *The Economics of Justice*, Cambridge, Mass.: Harvard University Press.

—— (1985), "Wealth Maximization Revisited," 2 *Notre Dame Journal of Law, Ethics & Public Policy* 85–105.

—— (1990), *The Problems of Jurisprudence*, Cambridge, Mass.: Harvard University Press.

PRATT, D. (1976), *Painful Experiments on Animals*, New York: Argus Archives.

—— (1980), *Alternatives to Pain in Experiments on Animals*, New York: Argus Archives.

PROSSER, W., and KEETON, W. P. (1984), *The Law of Torts* (5th edn.), Saint Paul, Minn.: West Publishing.

RAE, D. (1981), *Equalities*, Cambridge, Mass.: Harvard University Press.

RAILTON, P. (1984), "Alienation, Consequentialism, and the Demands of Morality," 13 *Philosophy and Public Affairs* 134–71.

RAMSEYER, J., and NAKAZATO, M. (1989), "Tax Transitions and the Protection Racket: A Reply to Professors Graetz and Kaplow," 75 *Virginia Law Review* 1155–75.

RAPHAEL, D. (1980), *Justice and Liberty*, London: Athlone Press.

RAWLS, J. (1971), *A Theory of Justice*, Cambridge, Mass.: Harvard University Press.

RAWLS, J. (1974*a*), "The Independence of Moral Theory," 47 *Proceedings of the American Philosophical Association* 5–22.

—— (1974*b*), "Some Reasons for the Maximin Criterion," 64 *American Economic Review, Papers and Proceedings* 141–6.

—— (1980), "Kantian Constructivism in Moral Theory," 77 *Journal of Philosophy* 515–72.

—— (1982), "The Basic Liberties and their Priority," in *The Tanner Lectures on Human Values III* (ed. S. McMurrin), Salt Lake City: University of Utah Press.

—— (1985), "Justice as Fairness: Political Not Metaphysical," 14 *Philosophy and Public Affairs* 223–51.

RAZ, J. (1982), "The Claims of Reflective Equilibrium," 25 *Inquiry* 307–30.

REGAN, T. (1983), *The Case for Animal Rights*, Berkeley: University of California Press.

RESCHER, N. (1969), "The Allocation of Exotic Medical Lifesaving Therapy," 79 *Ethics* 173–86.

RETTIG, R. (1976), "The Policy Debate on Patient Care Financing for Victims of End-Stage Renal Disease," 40 *Law and Contemporary Problems* no. 4, 196–230.

ROBINSON, P. (1985), "Causing the Conditions of One's Own Defense: A Study in the Limits of Theory in Criminal Law Doctrine," 71 *Virginia Law Review* 1–63.

ROEMER, J. (1985), "Equality of Talent," 1 *Economics and Philosophy* 151–87.

ROLSTON, H. (1983), "Values Gone Wild," 26 *Inquiry* 181–207.

ROSE, C. (1987), " 'Enough, and as Good' of What?" 81 *Northwestern University Law Review* 417–42.

ROSE-ACKERMAN, S. (1989), "Dikes, Dams, and Vicious Hogs: Entitlement and Efficiency in Tort Law," 18 *Journal of Legal Studies* 25–50.

ROUTLEY, R., and ROUTLEY, V. (1978), "Nuclear Energy and Obligations to the Future," 21 *Inquiry* 133–79.

RYAN, C. (1983), "Self-Defense, Pacifism, and the Possibility of Killing," 93 *Ethics* 508–24.

RYDER, R. (1975), *Victims of Science: The Use of Animals in Research*, London: Davis-Poynter.

SANDEL, M. (1982), *Liberalism and the Limits of Justice*, Cambridge: Cambridge University Press.

SANDERS, J. (1988), "Why the Numbers Should Sometimes Count," 17 *Philosophy and Public Affairs* 3–14.

SARTORIUS, R. (ed.) (1983), *Paternalism*, Minneapolis: University of Minnesota Press.

SCANLON, T. (1975), "Preference and Urgency," 72 *Journal of Philosophy* 655–69.

—— (1978), "Rights, Goals, and Fairness," in *Public and Private Morality* (ed. S. Hampshire), Cambridge: Cambridge University Press.

—— (1981), "Nozick on Rights, Liberty, and Property," in Paul (1981).

—— (1982), "Contractualism and Utilitarianism," in Sen and Williams (1982).

—— (1986), "Equality of Resources and Equality of Welfare: A Forced Marriage?" 97 *Ethics* 111–18.

SCHEFFLER, S. (1979), "Moral Skepticism and Ideals of the Person," 62 *Monist* 288–303.

—— (1981), "Natural Rights, Equality, and the Minimal State," in Paul (1981).

—— (1982*a*), *The Rejection of Consequentialism*, Oxford: Oxford University Press.

—— (1982*b*), "Ethics, Personal Identity, and Ideals of the Person," 12 *Canadian Journal of Philosophy* 229–46.

SCHELLING, T. (1968), "The Life You Save May Be Your Own," in *Problems in Public Expenditure Analysis* (ed. S. Chase), Washington, D.C.: Brookings Institute.

SCHWARTZ, A. (1988), "Proposals for Products Liability Reform: A Theoretical Synthesis," 97 *Yale Law Journal* 353–419.

SCHWARTZ, G. (1983), "New Products, Old Products, Evolving Law, Retroactive Law," 58 *New York University Law Review* 796–852.

SCHWINDT, R., and VINING, A. (1986), "Proposal for a Future Delivery Market for Transplant Organs," 11 *Journal of Health Politics, Policy and Law* 483–500.

SEN, A. (1973), *On Economic Equality*, New York: Norton.

—— and WILLIAMS, B. (eds.) (1982), *Utilitarianism and Beyond*, Cambridge: Cambridge University Press.

SHAVELL, S. (1980), "Strict Liability Versus Negligence," 9 *Journal of Legal Studies* 1–25.

SHER, G. (1987), *Desert*, Princeton: Princeton University Press.

SIDGWICK, H. (1907), *The Methods of Ethics* (7th edn.), London: Macmillan.

SIMMONS, A. J. (1979), *Moral Principles and Political Obligations*, Princeton: Princeton University Press.

SINGER, P. (1974), "Sidgwick and Reflective Equilibrium," 58 *Monist* 490–517.

—— (1977*a*), *Animal Liberation*, London: Jonathan Cape.

—— (1977*b*), "Utility and the Survival Lottery," 52 *Philosophy* 218–22.

—— (1979*a*), *Practical Ethics*, Cambridge: Cambridge University Press.

—— (1979*b*), "Killing Humans and Killing Animals," 22 *Inquiry* 145–56.

—— (1979*c*), "Rights and the Market," in *Ethical Theory and Business* (ed. T. Beauchamp and N. Bowie), Englewood Cliffs, N.J.: Prentice-Hall.

SMART, B. (1981), "General Desires as Grounds for the Wrongness of Killing," 24 *Inquiry* 242–51.

SMART, J. J. C., and WILLIAMS, B. (1973), *Utilitarianism: For and Against*, Cambridge: Cambridge University Press.

SOPER, P. (1984), *A Theory of Law*, Cambridge, Mass.: Harvard University Press.

SPENCE, A.M. (1977), "Consumer Misperceptions, Product Failure and Product Liability," 44 *Review of Economic Studies* 561.

STEINBOCK, B. (ed.) (1980), *Killing and Letting Die*, Englewood Cliffs, N.J.: Prentice-Hall.

STERBA, J. (1986), "Recent Work on Alternative Conceptions of Justice," 23 *American Philosophical Quarterly* 1–22.

STICK, J. (1987*a*), "Turning Rawls into Nozick and Back Again," 81 *Northwestern University Law Review* 363–416.

—— (1987*b*), "Renegotiating a RUM Deal," 81 *Northwestern University Law Review* 443–51.

STRAWSON, P. (1962), "Freedom and Resentment," reprinted in *Studies in the Philosophy of Thought and Action* (ed. P. Strawson), Oxford: Oxford University Press, 1968.

Szaz, T. (1969), "The Right to Health," 57 *Georgetown Law Review* 734–51.

Taurek, J. (1977), "Should the Numbers Count?" 6 *Philosophy and Public Affairs* 293–316.

Taylor, C. (1986), "The Nature and Scope of Distributive Justice," in *Justice and Equality Here and Now* (ed. F. Lucash), Ithaca: Cornell University Press.

Thomson, J. (1984), "Remarks on Causation and Liability," 13 *Philosophy and Public Affairs* 101–33.

—— (1985), "The Trolley Problem," 94 *Yale Law Journal* 1395–1415.

Thurow, L. (1976), "Government Expenditures: Cash or In-Kind Aid?" 5 *Philosophy and Public Affairs* 361–81.

Tooley, M. (1983), *Abortion and Infanticide*, Oxford: Oxford University Press.

Trammell, R. (1975), "Saving and Taking Life," 72 *Journal of Philosophy* 131–7.

—— and Wren, T. (1977), "Fairness, Utility, and Survival," 52 *Philosophy* 331–37.

VanDeVeer, D. (1986), *Paternalistic Intervention*, Princeton: Princeton University Press.

Varian, H. (1975), "Distributive Justice, Welfare Economics, and the Theory of Fairness," 4 *Philosophy and Public Affairs* 223–47.

Vaupel, J. (1976), "Early Death: An American Tragedy," 40 *Law and Contemporary Problems* no. 4, 73–121.

Warren, A. (1975), "Fairness and a Consumption-Type or Cash Flow Personal Income Tax," 88 *Harvard Law Review* 931–46.

Wasserman, D. (1987), "Justifying Self-Defense," 16 *Philosophy and Public Affairs* 356–78.

Weinrib, E. (1983), "Toward a Moral Theory of Negligence Law," 2 *Law and Philosophy* 37–62.

Williams, B. (1972), *Morality*, Cambridge: Cambridge University Press.

—— (1973), *Problems of the Self*, Cambridge: Cambridge University Press.

—— (1985), *Ethics and the Limits of Philosophy*, Cambridge, Mass.: Harvard University Press.

Wolf, S. (1981), "The Importance of Free Will," 90 *Mind* 386–405.

Wolff, R. (1977), *Understanding Rawls*, Princeton: Princeton University Press.

Woodward, J. (1986), "The Non-Identity Problem," 96 *Ethics* 804–31.

—— (1987), "Reply to Parfit," 97 *Ethics* 800–16.

Zeckhauser, R. (1975), "Procedures for Valuing Lives," 23 *Public Policy* 419–34.

—— and Shepherd, D. (1976), "Where Now for Saving Lives?" 40 *Law and Contemporary Problems* no. 4, 5–45.

INDEX